SURVIVAL OF THE FREE

The Last Strongholds of Wild Animal Life

Eugen Schuhmacher

A herd of bison in a North American National Park

SURVIVAL OF THE FREE

The Last Strongholds of Wild Animal Life

EDITED BY
DR. WOLFGANG ENGELHARDT

TRANSLATED FROM THE GERMAN BY
JOHN COOMBS

G. P. PUTNAM'S SONS
NEW YORK

LEE COUNTY LIBRARY
SANFORD, N. C.

First American Edition 1962

First published in German by Pinguin Verlag 1956

This translation, made from the revised and enlarged German edition, 1961, is copyright ©
1962 by Hamish Hamilton Ltd and G. P. Putnam's Sons
All Rights Reserved

Library of Congress Catalog Card Number: 62 - 149 20

Printed in Great Britain
by Ebenezer Baylis and Son, Ltd
The Trinity Press, Worcester, and London

Foreword

BY

SIR JULIAN HUXLEY

THE world has at last become aware of the fact that wild life is one of its most precious resources, and yet is threatened with extinction. This book is both a symptom and an expression of that awareness. It deals primarily with the function of National Parks and Game Reserves in conserving an adequate sample of the riches of wild life for the benefit and enjoyment of the world's people, now and in future generations.

It contains a number of contributions on the problems of Wild Life Conservation in general and National Parks in particular, a list of National Parks and equivalent Reserves and Sanctuaries all over the world, and a splendid series of 150 photographs, some in colour, of the most interesting mammals, birds and reptiles in need of protection in every part of the globe.

I am sure that the book will be read with interest and enjoyment by thousands of readers, young and old, and that it will result in a great increase of support for the World Wildlife Fund and all agencies concerned with Wild Life Conservation.

Contents

	page
Foreword by Sir Julian Huxley	ix
Dr. W. Engelhardt: *Meeting the Challenge*	1
H. Heck: *The Future of Animals*	4

PHOTOGRAPHIC RECORDS OF ANIMAL LIFE

K. L. Koch-Isenburg: *Notes on the Illustrations*	17

EXPERIENCES IN NATIONAL PARKS AND NATURE PROTECTION AREAS

O. König: *A Day in the Life of a Game Warden in the Ngoro-Ngoro Crater*	51
B. J. Bridge: *Lions Hunting*	57
M. H. Cowie: *The Old Poacher*	59
W. Schack: *Kalahari—a Day in the Life of a Camera Hunter*	63
W. Schack: *The Elephants in the Addo Bush*	69
R. Hoier: *Encounters with Gorillas*	71
Dr. P. Eipper: *Adventures with Bears in the Canadian Rockies*	76
E. Waldhoer-Haehnle: *Experiences in the Camargue*	80

NATIONAL PARKS, GAME PROTECTION, HUNTING AND THEIR PROBLEMS

T. V. Bulpin: *The Animals' Kingdom—Kruger National Park*	89
V. H. Cahalane: *Africa's Game Protection Areas—Seen Through American Eyes*	95
Dr. B. Grzimek: *African National Parks—the Position Today*	101
Dr. I. Eibl von Eibesfeldt: *Galápagos, the Islands of Tame Animals*	114
F. M. Packard: *'Dangerous' Animals in American National Parks*	126
Dr. H. Krieg: *South America, the Land of Maned Wolves and Ant-eaters*	129
L. Koch-Isenburg: *Madagascar, the Living Museum*	135
Dr. W. Lorch: *The National Parks of the Philippines*	141
Dr. K. Immelmann: *Nature Protection in Australia*	148
Dr. G. N. Zimmerli: *The Swiss National Park*	152

	page
Dr. O. Kraus: *The Example of America*	156
Dr. E. Mohr: *The Last of the European Bison*	159
Dr. E. P. Tratz: *Nature Protection Parks in the Soviet Union*	165
A. Pedersen: *Animal Life in the Arctic*	168
Dr. A. Lindgens: *From Hunter to Guardian*	173

THE WORLD'S NATIONAL PARKS AND OTHER IMPORTANT NATURE PROTECTION AREAS   179

We wish to thank the numerous nature enthusiasts, huntsmen and wild-life photographers who have assisted us in the preparation of this book. We are especially indebted to:

DR. A. W. F. BANFIELD, CHIEF ZOOLOGIST, BANFF, ALBERTA

HON. M. H. COWIE, DIRECTOR OF THE KENYA NATIONAL PARKS, NAIROBI

DR. LEOPOLD FIGL, VIENNA

DR. HELMUT GAMS, INNSBRUCK

STEFAN A. GROHS, JOHANNESBURG

OSKAR KÖNIG, JOHANNESBURG

DR. OTTO KRAUS, MUNICH

DR. ARTHUR LINDGENS, GSTADT

DR. WALTER T. LORCH, MANILA

DR. LOTHAR MACHURA, VIENNA

A. MALINOVSKY, MINISTRY OF AGRICULTURE OF THE U.S.S.R., MOSCOW

FRED. M. PACKARD, EXECUTIVE SECRETARY, NATIONAL PARK ASSOCIATION, WASHINGTON

LUCIE A. PLUYGERS, SOUTH DUXBURY

WILHELM SCHACK, PRETORIA

L. K. SHAPOSHNIKOV, NATURE PROTECTION COMMISSION OF THE RUSSIAN ACADEMY OF SCIENCE, MOSCOW

DR. EDUARD PAUL TRATZ, SALZBURG

DR. GUSTAV WENDELBERGER, VIENNA

DR. G. N. ZIMMERLI, BERN

BIRD PROTECTION LEAGUE, STUTTGART

CANADIAN GOVERNMENT TRAVEL BUREAU, OTTAWA

GERMAN NATURE PROTECTION CIRCLE, WOLFRATSHAUSEN-WALDRAM

FISH AND WILDLIFE SERVICE, WASHINGTON

INSTITUT DES PARCS NATIONAUX DU CONGO BELGE, BRUSSELS

INSTITUTE FOR NATURE PROTECTION, VIENNA

NATIONAL PARKS ASSOCIATION, WASHINGTON

SATOUR, PRETORIA

SVENSKA NATURSKYDDSFÖRENINGEN, STOCKHOLM

UNITED STATES NATIONAL PARKS SERVICE, WASHINGTON

UNITED NATIONS, RESEARCH AND PUBLICATIONS SECTION, NEW YORK

WILDLIFE PROTECTION SOCIETY OF SOUTH AFRICA, JOHANNESBURG

CENTRAL ADMINISTRATION OF NATURE PROTECTION AREAS OF THE U.S.S.R., MOSCOW

THE ADMINISTRATORS OF THE NATIONAL PARKS AND WILD GAME RESERVES IN MANY COUNTRIES

Meeting the Challenge

BY

DR. WOLFGANG ENGELHARDT

NO less important a body than the Economic and Social Council of the United Nations has recently concerned itself with the subject of national parks. At its twenty-seventh sitting the council decided, at the request of the Secretary-General, to ask all states to provide information concerning their national parks and nature protection areas of comparable importance. At the thirty-first sitting of the council, on the 15th February, 1961, the result of this inquiry was made known: fifty-two countries had given information, much of it very detailed, concerning their large nature reserves, and from this information the first 'List of the world's national parks and similar areas' was compiled. An additional list containing details received too late for inclusion into the original document is now being prepared. In the discussion which took place on the occasion of the distribution of this list the representatives of all shades of political opinion, in an almost unprecedented state of unanimity, stressed the great cultural, social, economic and scientific value of these wild-life protection areas. A resolution, which was approved unanimously, called upon all member states to strive for the safeguarding of the existing parks and the foundation of new ones.

Sir Julian Huxley, the internationally renowned biologist and first Director-General of UNESCO (the United Nations Educational, Scientific and Cultural Organization), spent several months during 1960 travelling in Africa so as to gather first-hand experience of the state of affairs existing in the African wild-life conservation areas at that time, thereby acquiring the necessary knowledge to be able to recommend appropriate measures to UNESCO.

The first world conference on national parks will take place at Seattle in the State of Washington, U.S.A., in July 1962.

The general public of many countries have, therefore, at a late hour but fortunately before it is too late, recognized the incalculable value of national parks. The fact that attendance figures have risen year by year may have contributed to this fact.

The Kruger National Park of South Africa was visited in 1927, the year after its opening in its present form, by the occupants of three cars. In 1960 there were more than 140,000 visitors.

Judging by their experiences in recent years, the authorities administering the national parks in the U.S.A. reckon that they will receive some 80 million visitors during 1966, and a special programme of measures to meet this mass invasion is already being planned. During recent years, on average, every third American has visited a national park at least once a year!

Thus the national park idea, conceived by far-sighted men but long regarded generally as an object of amusement, a survival from an age of sentimentality, is now, in the era of technology, receiving triumphant proof of its value and its living strength.

Nevertheless all is far from well as regards the spread of the national park movement. As a glance at our maps will show, numerous countries still possess no protected areas of this kind, and in some it is probably already too late. Furthermore, in some of the states in which national parks have been established these 'oases of the animal world' are in danger of being destroyed as a result of the lack of foresight or of the necessary material resources.

Short-sighted economic greed declares that the water power, the mineral wealth, the forests or the soil of a wild-life protection area are needed 'for the good of the community'—and the animals are evicted.

Political turmoil and warfare endanger what has already been done to preserve nature, and animals pay the cost of human conflict with their lives.

Mankind assumes complete superiority over the works of the Creator, and no protest is made when whole species of living beings are exterminated.

At long last responsible people have begun to devote earnest thought to the question of the future of mankind. In view of the apparently limitless increase of the human race which is now in progress it is said that the national parks can be preserved for only a short time to come. This argument can only be answered by asking a question: which is better, to have a numerically limited world population leading happy lives free from privation, or to have the human race increasing to an unlimited extent, with the resulting poverty, hunger, and finally chaos? Those in authority will soon have to find the only possible answer to this question. A bright future demands the continued existence of the national parks with their wild life which, if it is once destroyed, can never be replaced. Such riches as we now possess are, when we consider the opposition which has had to be overcome, splendid fruits of the tenacious and often self-sacrificing efforts made by many lovers of nature and of animal life from all parts of the world. Among them are hunters who, recognizing that protection is the principal task of the present-day hunter, have made an abiding, immeasurable contribution to the saving of the free-living animal world. We have no right to sacrifice this heritage on the altar of temporary confusion during a period of transition.

The general public in most countries still know far too little about the nature and importance of national parks.

Numerous colleagues have assisted me with advice and work. The publishers have been most ready to comply with all our wishes. My esteemed colleague Dr. Egon Popp carried out most conscientiously the exacting task of drawing the maps.

My warmest thanks go out to all of them. We launch this revised edition with three wishes:

May it win new, wholehearted supporters for the national park idea!

May it give pleasure and impart knowledge to all lovers of nature and animals, and may it prove a reliable guide to those fortunate enough to be able to visit one or more parks, both before and during their journeys.

The Future of Animals

BY

HEINZ HECK

Director of the Hellabrunn Zoological Gardens, Munich

At the time when man first entered the theatre of life as a thinking being, with the coming of the Ice Age, animals were already on stage. Free creatures responded to the forces in the world around, threatening their existence, by such means as lay within their power: by moving to more favourable areas, by increasing their numbers rapidly, or by tenacious resistance. If circumstances favoured an unnaturally great increase in the numbers of particular classes of animals which formed the prey of carnivorous species, those species would themselves increase by rearing more young, and the growth of the number of hunters would reduce the herds of their prey to the normal level.

The numbers of polar hares and Arctic foxes shot in the polar areas scarcely touched by man still bear witness to the validity of this law which once held good all over the world. In Africa, too, an increase in the numbers of such beasts of prey as the lion and hyena is to be observed during periods when climatic conditions favour the growth of the antelope herds.

It was only at a very late stage in the world's development that man, one of the youngest branches of creation, intervened in a dominating manner in the biological life of our planet. Life has existed on earth for hundreds of millions of years, and flourishing animal species which had once spread all over the world became extinct even without man's intervention, while others emerged without ever coming into contact with the master of the earth.

Everything that lives has originated from the minutest beginnings, from a single cell. Cells, individual building stones, make up the living organism, whether it is a mighty oak tree, a mouse or a man. As far as life is concerned there are no really fundamental differences between the various forms it takes. We all originated in the primeval ocean. Should the mere fact that the same link connects us with all living creatures of the earth not give civilized man good reason to respect all forms of life, and prevent him from destroying it unnecessarily?

The survival of living beings demands a constant process of formal change.

Progress is the sign of life, and the climatic and geological variations which have taken place in all areas of the world during its long history have demanded corresponding changes in all living beings. At the beginning of the cretaceous period, during which climatic zones began to be differentiated, the vast saurians that had once dominated the earth were forced to make their exit from the stage of life. Their anatomical structure, suited to high temperatures, could not adapt itself to the gradual cooling process which had set in. Nature discarded them in favour of newer, better-equipped forms of being, derived from them, but so constructed as to retain constant bodily warmth. The way was open for the appearance on earth of the noble family of mammals.

However, not only climatic changes but also the inherent tendency of certain species towards the development of unnecessary ornamental features led to their becoming extinct. Thus the disappearance of the gigantic elk of the Ice Age was probably due solely to the over-development of its huge palmed antlers—it was certainly not caused by the hunting prowess of primitive man. The great antlers, whose width on a fully-grown male was about twelve feet, attained such a prodigious weight that the animal was undoubtedly hampered by sinking into swampy ground. Even if it was able to reach firmer land, it could easily suffer a fatal accident on account of the mass of horn on its head. In consequence of the unnaturally high mortality rate in males caused by this disability, the giant elk eventually became extinct. Highly complicated activities of other creatures, such as elaborate ritual during the mating and breeding seasons, which are a hindrance in the struggle for existence, can only continue in places where that struggle is less severe than is usually the case—places where the creature has very few or no natural enemies, as is often the case on islands, or in Australasia.

The remarkable babyroussa, the stag-hog whose upper tusks grow upward and backward so as to form what look like the horns of ruminants, lives only on the island of Celebes. The birds of paradise, with their lovely tail feathers which greatly impede their flight, inhabit islands in the New Guinea area on which there are no cats or martens to hunt them, while birds of prey cannot reach them in the shelter of the thick foliage of trees. Species of fowl which do not hatch their eggs but build a pile of leaves and rotting plants round them so that the warmth of the sun and of the fermentation of the vegetable matter will do the job for them, the chicks therefore growing up without maternal protection, can only survive in outlying parts of Australia and South America.

Primitive man took his place in the natural order. His crude weapons enabled him to slay sufficient animals to keep him alive, but never seriously to endanger the continued existence of the vast herds living in freedom. Originally man hunted only to satisfy his need for food: he took no more than he and his family required. The desire to adorn himself which, as we know, soon manifested itself, was not by any means to lead to the extermination of such creatures as gaily-coloured birds. What did it matter if a Stone Age beauty wore the plumage of a single kingfisher as a decoration in her head-band?

For long ages man, together with so many other creatures, was a victim of the great beasts of prey. Admittedly the big cats, the bears and wolves did not spare him. However, the attitude of the human race towards nature soon became marked by a delight in wanton destruction. Man's ravages grew with his increasing intelligence; they spread all over the world wherever he set foot. Eventually side by side with the simple hunter who was content when he had eaten his fill there appeared the speculator, the businessman. The gaps which human greed and 'sport', that is to say mass-slaughter which served no useful purpose, tore in the animal world during the ages which followed soon became too wide to be closed by the natural means of the propagation of species.

The world's population figures have leapt upward during the past three hundred years. In the year 1650 the world was inhabited by some 470 million people. In 1750 the number was 694 millions, by 1850 it was 1,094 millions, in 1900 1,430 millions. Within the past fifty years, despite two world wars, this number has been almost doubled. The statistics for 1951 indicate a world population of 2,430 millions. By 1960 it was 2,800 millions. The annual increase of the human race amounts at present to some 48 millions; every day it increases by about 130,000—the population of a large town. It is estimated that in 1965 the population of the world will number some 3,000 million souls. In 1970 it will be 3,500 millions, and by the year 2,000—only 38 years from now—mankind will have more than doubled, numbering 6,200 or even 6,900 millions.

It should also be borne in mind that only a comparatively small part of the earth's surface is habitable by man. Even technical advances which have made possible the cultivation of large areas of hitherto unused land will not greatly alter the situation, for almost two-thirds of the face of the earth is covered by water. Also uninhabitable are the icy wastes of the Arctic and Antarctic, the upper reaches of high mountains, and the deserts of both the Old and New Worlds. At one time far more than a third of the land surface of the earth was covered by forests; today only 15 million square miles, that is to say about thirty per cent, are more or less densely wooded. Only 26 per cent of the area of Europe is wooded, although according to its geographical position Europe clearly belongs to the wooded belt of the northern temperate zone.

There is no doubt that the world's population will continue to increase at a similar rate, for civilization is ever achieving greater longevity and a reduction of infant mortality.

At the present moment food can be provided for the world's population only by intensive use of the soil's resources, and in the near future it will be impossible to provide sufficient nourishment unless vast new areas, hitherto untouched, are converted into arable land. Therefore man will not be able to avoid still further restricting the areas in which animals can live in their free state—simply because he has to live. Nevertheless the methods which man employed in the past in his clash with the animal world must not be repeated. Campaigns of extermination are unworthy of mankind.

Mass destruction of animal life commenced with the age of discovery. Many lovely species of birds, including several varieties of the bird of paradise, have vanished for ever. European speculators instructed the natives of the Arau Islands to creep up on the male birds of paradise during their pairing dances, when their feathers were at their brightest, and to capture them by means of forked arrows, which would hold the birds fast without damaging their bodies— since no blood was to be allowed to spoil the wonderful plumage. When Paris, which then dictated the world's fashions, decreed that it was no longer the mode for ladies to wear feathers, tens of thousands of precious, irreplaceable bird of paradise skins were left to rot in the ports of those islands far from civilization. As in the case of the African ostrich, it is several years before the male bird of paradise achieves his full glory of plumage, so it was the finest mature males that had been slaughtered—a deadly blow to the survival of the species in any considerable numbers.

In Africa the ostriches, fleeing on foot as they are unable to fly, were pursued by hunters on horseback until they dropped exhausted; the males were then slain with clubs so that the white tail and wing feathers should not be spattered with blood.

The flocks of egrets, which bear the lovely white 'osprey' feathers during the mating season, dwindled to a small proportion of what they had been. Thousands of these birds were slain ruthlessly in their breeding areas, and their young were left to starve to death.

Almost as soon as the New World became known to Europeans a hoard of gold-greedy adventurers descended upon it. It took them less than a century to bring the bison, which had roamed the vast prairies in herds totalling some sixty million before the coming of the white man, to the verge of extinction. For many centuries whole nations of Indians had lived by these herds, from which they obtained their food and clothing, without seriously reducing their numbers. Then, as the railway pushed its way across to the Pacific coast during the sixties, cutting across the prairies, thousands upon thousands of the majestic beasts were shot merely for the pleasure of killing. The fact that in the early days of the massacre the tongues were taken from the bodies was no more than an excuse for what was really primitive blood-lust. The bison of the plains were completely annihilated, only a few of the forest bison remaining.

The passenger pigeons, the flocks of which once darkened the sun, and whose weight would sometimes break the branches of trees on which great numbers alighted, have been so thoroughly eliminated from the roll of living creatures that not a single pair remained in the vast expanses of their American homeland. Businessmen formed 'hunting associations', and scores of them descended upon the birds in the places where they slept. Canning factories were set up in the woods. The birds were dazzled by powerful lamps suddenly directed on them at night, and a single shotgun cartridge would bring down dozens. In the morning pigs were driven to the scene of the slaughter, there to be fattened on the flesh of the stricken birds which had been free creatures of the woodland and sky.

Since the beginnings of 'Christian navigation' in the Mediterranean the seafarers had seized for food the animals of isolated islands; in many cases, owing to the lack of an inborn instinct to flee, they allowed themselves to be slaughtered without attempting to escape.

Visits by ships became more and more frequent, and the advent of modern times found only a few scattered survivors of such classes of wild creature as Steller's sea-cow of the Bering Sea or the strange dodo, that flightless bird larger than a turkey formerly found on the island of Mauritius, the last specimen of which ended up as an exhibit on show in London. The harmless, grass-eating giant tortoises of the Pacific islands, too, almost all ended their days salted down in the holds of ships. Whales were almost completely exterminated in the Arctic Ocean, so that the world's whaling fleets now have to operate in Antarctic waters. After the numbers of the vast aquatic mammals had begun to diminish rapidly there, too—until recently, 50,000 blue whales were slain each year—an international commission sitting in 1953–54 fixed the quota of 15,500 blue whales which it was permissible to kill annually. Some 25 million tons of edible fish are caught by man every year. Experts consider that this figure could be increased to 50 million without the survival of the various classes of fish being endangered. However, if the population of the world doubles itself, as seems likely to happen within a relatively few years, this source of food will become appreciably less abundant.

In order to help stamp out cannibalism among the natives of certain Australasian islands pigs were introduced there, since one of the basic causes of cannibalism was the islanders' need for meat. The pigs, once they had run wild, proved a grave menace to the endemic animals, which were powerless to withstand the onslaughts of the new enemy. Thus the New Zealand bridge lizard, the last true saurian left on earth, managed to survive in only a few remote rocky areas. Sparrows and finches which had been imported from Europe so hampered native birds in their quest for food and places in which to breed that many species died out—for it is a law of nature that primitive forms must yield to those that are more fully developed. The European rabbit made several types of kangaroo rare in Australia. House dogs run wild destroyed the Tasmanian wolf, a pouched animal, while domestic cats, similarly gone wild, decimated the marsupial badgers and the banded ant-eaters, and European foxes destroyed hundreds of times more wild creatures in Australia than the native beasts of prey had slain in thousands of years prior to the arrival of the foxes.

The Kea-Nestor, a remarkable land parrot of New Zealand, changed its way of life after flocks of European sheep had been introduced into the country. Previously it had lived on roots and fruit, but it suddenly began to attack living sheep. The white settlers had the habit of hanging the skins of slaughtered sheep on their huts to dry, with the flesh side facing outward. The Nestor parrots soon discovered that the white fat which still adhered to the skins tasted very good, and they made their way daily to this convenient source of nourishment. These intelligent birds thus conceived the idea of sheep as booty, and eventually began to tear holes in the skins of living animals. That was naturally the signal for a campaign to wipe the birds out.

Even in comparatively recent times Alexander von Humboldt saw tens of thousands of chinchillas, beautiful little rodents, on the slopes of the Andes in South America. However, as soon as ridiculously high prices began to be offered for their pelts in the New York fur markets, the Indians and white men commenced a wholesale slaughter of the harmless creatures—with the result that they are now no longer to be found in freedom.

The South African quagga, a zebra less pronouncedly striped than others of the family, suffered the same fate on account of its fine leather. The mountain zebra of the Cape was saved from annihilation at the eleventh hour, being granted asylum in two parks. The animals of South Africa have suffered terribly from the coming of civilization. The blue horse antelope has vanished for ever. The white-tailed gnu, the bontebok, and the South African elephant, once roaming in great herds—all these survive only in very small numbers.

Under the eyes of civilized communities the aurochs, ancestor of our present-day domestic cattle, perished. The last of this ancient breed, a cow, died during the year 1627 in a wood near Warsaw. These beasts, which preferred open country to thick woods, were more exposed to the ravages of man than the European bison, which lived in forest land. The same was true of the mouse-grey wild horse or tarpan, the last survivors of which ancient stock lived on into recent times in the mountainous Vosges area. However, the habit of wild stallions of descending by night on the enclosures where villagers kept their horses, to break the fences down with their hooves and release the tame mares so as to take them away to freedom, was the undoing of the tarpan. This breed was completely annihilated, and it is only in very recent years, by crossing country horses which still contained tarpan blood, that the strain has been bred back into existence.

The wild horse of the steppes, or Przevalsky horse, was also long considered to have become extinct in its free state. Recently, however, Soviet zoologists have made the surprising discovery that a few families of these horses still exist in the vicinity of the Tahin-Shara-Nur Mountains. Some 60 of these creatures at present live in zoological gardens, principally at Munich-Hellabrunn and Prague.

The last bear on German soil was killed near Ruhpolding in 1836. The 'lammergeier' vulture is now extremely rare; examples are seen from time to time in the Alps, but no breeding pairs are ever seen today.

The fate of the European bison seemed to be sealed at the end of the First World War. Then a few breeders and enthusiasts got together, and in 1923 they founded in Berlin the International Society for the Preservation of the Bison. A detailed list was made of the animals of this class still living in various European zoos. Altogether there were 56 of them: 27 bulls and 29 cows, including 10 calves, and 2 cows which were already too old to breed. The European bison generally gives birth to its first calf at the age of 4, and remains capable of breeding until about the age of 24. Thanks to the endurance and fecundity of this ancient breed—some cows bear as many as 20 calves in all—the survival of the European bison can now be regarded as certain. There are today at least 500 pure-blooded specimens in zoos and protected areas in the northern hemisphere.

The situation regarding the aurochs was seemingly hopeless, for not a single specimen was still in existence to use for breeding purposes. We knew from old sculptures and paintings exactly what the aurochs looked like, and we knew its colouring (black in the case of the bull, while the cow had a reddish tinge, both sexes having a light border round the mouth). Since all present-day breeds of cattle derive from the aurochs, it was thought possible to 'reconstruct' the ancient strain by careful crossing of animals still bearing certain of its characteristics. Strains which had retained primitive features, such as the Spanish fighting bull, the cattle of Corsica, the Hungarian plains and the Scottish Highlands, provided material from which, in a fairly short space of time, we were able to breed an animal which gives us a good idea of what the ancient aurochs looked like. It is a striking and highly interesting fact that since aurochs have been bred back into existence their offspring have continued to bear all the marks of the ancient race—there has been no slipping back into those of modern cattle. The habits of our 'artificial products', too, are in all respects those of beasts which had never departed from the wild state. Set at liberty in nature reserves, they behave exactly like their ancestors countless centuries ago.

However, all the ruthless, ill-considered and short-sighted methods of wild-life destruction adopted by man have not between them struck such deep wounds in nature as those caused by the rapid expansion of urban civilization since the beginning of the twentieth century. The extensive changes in the landscape, the home of wild animals, have attacked the roots of all living creatures. Compelled by the massive and constant increase in the population to provide more and more places for human habitation, man is changing the face of whole continents. The draining of swamps means that every creature for which water is a prime necessity of life, from the salamander and frog to the bird and mammal, is robbed of one of the basic elements on which its survival depends. The forests are reduced by felling, and that means the disappearance of all woodland life, for the small wooded areas still remaining lack the 'forest atmosphere', made up of many elements, which is vitally necessary to many of the wild creatures native to wooded areas. There is no place for large mammals and birds in the countryside of highly civilized lands. Furthermore the disappearance of forests alters the supply of water over great expanses of land. Rainfall becomes meagre and increasingly irregular, and the saplings of woodland trees can often find insufficient nourishment in ground which is excellent except for being dry. Once the *Circulus vitiosus* has been set in motion it begins slowly but inexorably to transform into a barren desert land which was once extremely fruitful.

In North America sandstorms now rage in areas where luxuriant woods once flourished, or where a covering of grass held the surface of the prairie together. In Madagascar the dry plains of the south are extending further and further north every year, gradually wiping out an animal world which is unparalleled anywhere else on earth.

When it was already almost too late, thinking people in all civilized nations began to raise their voices in protest, and the call 'Save what can still be saved!' rang out too loudly to be ignored.

Thus in many parts of the world reserves of various sizes and kinds were created; areas which will not be ruined by human exploitation, in which there is no hunting, and where the landscape will not be forcibly transformed. These reserves will give later generations a glimpse of the riches which once existed everywhere. Unfortunately no very rapid change can be brought about in the development towards taking over land where animals formerly lived. Already we can see far fewer of the works of nature than our fathers saw, and despite all the efforts now being made our grandchildren will only be able to enjoy pitifully small remnants of the free life of the world as we know it. Nevertheless all those who realize what is at stake must fight for the idea of nature conservation, and make their views known again and again to governments and people in authority. Unrestricted despoliation of open country such as the last few decades have seen must not continue. If we achieve a state of affairs in which, whenever large-scale inroads into the countryside and the life of nature are planned, an expert ecologist is consulted, that will be a major point gained.

It is, of course, evident that all habitable parts of the earth will eventually have to be developed for the use of the human race. Even on the boundaries of nature reserves which are as yet remote from the world of man there will eventually be the pressing demand of civilization to seize the land for its own growth. Even though the times when such questions become acute may still be far away, it is certainly not too early for us to accustom ourselves to the idea that one day the animals will dwell among us. The inviolacy of a nature protection area is basically only relative, and the use made of any such area will always have to be determined by man.

Backwaters of rivers, a paradise for water and swamp birds, become unusable unless someone clears away excessive growth of rushes and banks of reeds from time to time. It has been known for wild animals to leave game reserves on the African plains because of the fact that the custom practised by men for hundreds —perhaps even thousands—of years of burning off the dry grass was suddenly discontinued as part of the nature protection campaign. The dry stalks lay on the ground, became matted, and hampered the growth of new grass. The result was that the pasture became insufficient to support animals living on grass. Man, too, has an important place in even the natural world around him, and an area which has long been influenced by human activity changes its character when the hand of man is suddenly removed.

It is not sufficient to turn districts which are unfruitful and which do not come into consideration for the building of towns over to wild animals, and to leave them there to fend for themselves. Without human intervention such animals, accustomed to better grazing land, will diminish in size during the course of a few generations, and their descendants will be mere weak shadows of the creatures we know today. In places where the supply of natural feeding-stuff does not suffice, additional food must be provided by man. Where nourishment is hard to come by in game reserves of restricted acreage it is sometimes found that the equal numerical balance of male and female animals cannot be upheld; too many males would be taking a share of the limited amount of fodder available. In most cases one male suffices for a number of females, and stocks of half-tame animals undoubtedly do better if the superfluous males are removed. Consideration should also be given to the possibility of ensuring that the stock remains pure and healthy by the means which have long been practised in the case of the red deer, the American bison and several other species: only the strongest males are kept for breeding purposes. All that do not come up to the highest standards of the species in strength, health and appearance are done away with, in order that the herd as a whole should not suffer a decline in standards. The former natural consequences of the law of the survival of the fittest must now be carried out by man. Here is an important task for the genuine, experienced huntsman.

The different continents and nations are being brought ever closer by improvements in methods of transport. Only in a few areas is it still correct to speak of natural features as belonging solely to a particular district. Animals, plants and human beings have been, and will continue to be, so intermingled that it can no longer be our task to speak of rigidly 'national' nature protection. For example Germans frequently refer to the 'German' woods. But are they really still purely German? Canadian fir trees and American pines, poplars and willows from other lands are now at home everywhere in the temperate zone. The fallow deer and rabbit were not originally creatures of central Europe, and neither is the pheasant. Nevertheless we have become accustomed to these creatures living in our midst.

The animal world is the common heritage of all mankind, and protective measures can only be effective if put into force on a broad basis. The desire to preserve animals in their natural surroundings is fine and laudable, and several future generations can strive to see it fulfilled. Eventually, however, the only solution will probably be to preserve each species somewhere in the world, no matter where.

Perhaps I may be permitted at this point to mention some of the eventualities which may come to pass in the future—and some possibilities which I hope are nothing more than unfounded fears. . . .

To go straight to one of the possibilities which we may fervently hope will never materialize, what would become of the animals in the nature protection areas if a great native uprising were to take place in Africa? Would they share the fate of the last herd of Père David deer in the Imperial Park of Peking when revolutionaries stormed the palace in 1911? But for the fact that a few of these deer were living in European zoos, which made it possible to breed a new herd in the deer park at Woburn, the seat of the Duke of Bedford, this creature would have vanished from the face of the earth.

It is true that veterinary science has made great progress, and that much has been done towards stamping out epidemics among animals. Nevertheless hitherto unknown diseases can still cause terrible havoc, as was proved in recent years by the spread of myxomatosis among rabbits. How can the herds in the game reserves be protected against the possibility of a similar catastrophe?

At some time in the not too far distant future the animals living in freedom may have to be regularly provided for. Man will not only have to play a part in their everyday lives, but may also be compelled by circumstances to make drastic movements of stock. There are many parts of the world in which African antelope, for example, could live in large reserves—and why shouldn't European bison be taken to North or South America, so as to have herds of them safeguarded there at all times? The importance of zoos, too, cannot be exaggerated. They are storehouses of animal life from which breeding stock can always be supplied to form the basis of new herds in wild-life conservation areas, or to increase herds already in existence. Had it not been that a few survivors were preserved in zoos the European bison and the wild horse would have long since become extinct.

The relationships between mankind and animals are of endless diversity, for the road along which they have travelled together leads back into the grey mists of pre-history. The efforts which must be made to preserve wild creatures—as far as possible in their free state, and in cases where that is impossible in zoos—are not merely idealistic, for they have at the same time a basis of economic reality. Man, uniquely poised between heaven and earth, is more spiritual in his requirements than he himself realizes, needing many things apart from nourishment for his body. A race which treats its fellow-creatures, 'dumb animals' though they may be, without consideration and in a spirit of hostility is unable, in the long run, to uphold its civilization. It loses its vigour, its spiritual possessions melt away, and its creative strength ebbs more and more the wider the gap becomes which separates it from its fellow beings.

Ever since the earliest times Nature has provided mankind with a rich source of nourishment from the quickening spring of life, to which we are all indebted for what we are. Circumstances now compel us to channel the current of nature in such a way that its benefits flow where they are of most use to mankind. However, we must not disturb the source itself, if future generations are to find living water in their days. We have a great responsibility here and now. Something vital is at stake, something which can never be restored if it is once destroyed. There is still time—all is not yet lost!

Part One

PHOTOGRAPHIC RECORDS OF ANIMAL LIFE

Notes on the Illustrations

BY

KARL LUDWIG KOCH-ISENBURG

These notes, like the photographs to which they refer, are intended to awaken a desire for further knowledge by opening up a small part of some of the rooms in the vast building of many departments which we call nature. It goes almost without saying that neither the photographs themselves nor the notes which follow make any claim to be systematic, comprehensive, or in the strict sense scientific. Their purpose is to arouse interest, to give pleasure, and to create sympathetic understanding.

Elephants

These animals of the order of proboscidea are members of an ancient family of mammals found all over the world in prehistoric times. Having their origin in creatures the size of pigmy hippopotami, trunked animals developed over the course of millions of years into members of six groups divided into 113 known species. One of these forms was the enormous mammoth, which attained a shoulder height of nine feet, and whose tusks were sometimes twelve feet long. It was a contemporary of Ice Age man.

Today only three species still exist: the African elephant of the plains and of the forests (considered by many experts to be variations of one type), and the Indian elephant.

The area inhabited by the African elephant in ancient times extended from North Africa, where the Carthaginians are known to have tamed many of them, right down to the Cape. Nowadays they are to be found only south of the Sahara; in the Union of South Africa they live only in protected areas. During historical times Indian elephant inhabited a vast area stretching from Asia Minor across Syria, Iraq and the whole of southern Asia as far as southern China. Today they remain only in the tropical forests of India and Further India, Ceylon, Malaya, Sumatra and northern Borneo.

The Indian and the two classes of African elephant are easily distinguished even by those without expert knowledge, since the Indian elephant has a domed forehead almost vertical at the front, comparatively small ears, and a convex back.

The forehead of the African elephant recedes from a point in front of the eyes, its ears are enormous, and its back is slightly concave.

The African elephant of the plains, with a shoulder height of more than nine feet and a weight of up to about 8,800 lb., is the largest land-dwelling mammal on the earth today.

The most remarkable feature of the elephant is its trunk—in fact there is probably no other organ in the entire animal world capable of being used in so many different ways. Firstly, as a greatly elongated nose it is the elephant's respiratory organ, and the creature is able, by holding it high over its head, to detect scents in the air. The tip of the trunk is highly sensitive to touch; like a hand it is able to grasp and hold firmly a wide range of objects ranging from isolated roots and leaves to thick tree-trunks, though in the latter case the whole trunk has to be brought into service. The elephant can also deal powerful blows with its trunk. He uses it to suck up water, which he then sprays into his mouth, or—in order to keep cool and cleanse his skin—over his back and flanks. Finally the trunk also serves as a musical instrument: by forcing a considerable pressure of air through it the elephant makes its loud trumpeting noise.

The elephant's tusks, on account of whose ivory these beasts have long been hunted, are not eye-teeth but elongated incisors. Here again the African elephant of the plains holds the record as regards weight: the two tusks of a bull together weighed 495 lb.

Despite its massive appearance the elephant moves with surprising agility. In mountainous areas it ascends by narrow paths to far above the timber line, and it is less subject to cold than was formerly believed. Like all large animals it will test the ground carefully if there is any danger that the surface is not sufficiently firm, before venturing into new territory. The huge feet, which leave an oval impression in the case of a female elephant and a round one in that of a male, possess a fine sense of touch through the soles, which are rich in blood vessels and well upholstered.

Everyone acquainted with elephants knows that a sizeable herd standing in woodland quite close to him can steal away so noiselessly that he is quite unaware of the fact. The great grey forms glide through the twilight like cats. They avoid every dry branch whose cracking might betray their presence. It is only when they feel absolutely secure that they will make plenty of noise, tearing branches from trees in order to eat the bark off them. Small trees, up to the thickness of a man's arm, are devoured root and branch. As soon as elephants detect the slightest suspicious noise, however, they immediately relapse into complete silence, while they ascertain the extent of the danger. If a watcher has managed to get close enough undetected he is often able to locate the herd by the sound of rumbling in their digestive organs.

Elephants are slow breeders. Not until they are twelve to fifteen years old do they reach the age of puberty. They are fully mature at about the age of twenty-five. Their life-span is 50 to 70 years. Stories of elephants 200 years old are mere phantasy. As the period of gestation is between twenty and twenty-two months, and as the calf is unable to look after itself for a considerable time, cows give birth to a calf only once in about eight years.

The colossus naturally needs a vast amount of nourishment, and a large herd has to roam across an enormous tract of land, even in tropical districts where luxuriant vegetation abounds, if all its members are to have their fill. In captivity a fully-grown elephant consumes daily about a hundredweight of hay and up to 45 lb. of root crops, oats, bread, etc. On a hot day it will drink up to 44 gallons of water. The elephant cannot gallop, but a greatly alarmed or wounded elephant can thunder along at about 25 miles per hour in an ungainly trot.

Many of the geographical variants of the three classes of elephant have already become extinct. Before the establishment of national parks and large game reserves the African elephant was being decimated even in the places where numbers are now again increasing. Thanks to the protective measures which have been put in force, the herds have risen to an estimated total of 300,000 head.

Lion, Leopard, Cheetah

Not the lion, but the bloodstained hyena, hunting in packs and bringing down the quarry at the end of an exhausting chase, is the most dreaded beast of prey on the African plains. One often sees in Africa how lions that have had their fill and are not hungry will move among grazing herds of antelope without in the least alarming the herds, since they are clearly aware of the fact that the lions are not hunting. If, however, a hyena appears on the horizon, the grass-eaters at once flee. The 'regal' lion enjoys comfort before everything else. He spends the daytime in his lair or, if he feels secure, lying in the shade of some trees.

It is only with the coming of night that he begins hunting—if he is hungry. It is uncommon for a lion to hunt alone; generally he is accompanied by his wives and their older children. Large prides of thirty and more lions such as hunting writers referred to in the past are, however, very rarely to be seen nowadays. One or more males generally lead the hunt, and drive the quarry towards the spot where the lionesses are lying in wait. The area in which a family of lions operates covers some ten to twenty square miles.

In ancient times the yellow-brown big cat was to be found in large areas of southern Asia, Africa and Europe. They were common in a few parts of Ancient Greece. Today the Asiatic lion is only to be found in India, in fact only in the 'Forest' of Gir, a nature protection park in the Kathiawar Peninsula. Lions still exist in fairly large numbers only in certain parts of Africa.

Far more widely to be found than the lion, in Asia as well as in Africa, are the leopard and the other closely related form of big cat, the panther. They exist over astonishingly large expanses of the earth, although they avoid open savannas as a rule, preferring as their hunting grounds flat forest areas or the dense jungle. In the northern parts of its Asiatic territory the leopard even approaches the southern border of Siberia in the vicinity of the Amur River. Leopards are also to be found on the Pacific islands as far south as Java. In the black continent this spotted freebooter is a native of many areas extending right down to the Cape. He lives on the plains and in mountainous districts—anywhere, provided that sufficient cover is available. A leopard skeleton was found on Mount Kilimanjaro at a height of 15,000 feet above sea-level. There is scarcely another carnivorous animal as adaptable as the leopard regarding terrain, altitude and climate. Unlike the lion he prefers to hunt alone, and soon separates from his wife.

His prey consists for the most part of medium-sized animals, principally monkeys, since he is as much at home among the branches of trees as on rocks or flat ground. He will often lie in wait on a branch, to pounce on the neck of any animal which passes underneath. His spotted coat, in which the patches of light and shade in the foliage of trees seem to be reflected, completely conceals him from view among the leaves and twigs. He takes the remains of his meal up into the tree where it will be safe from hyenas and jackals; he returns to the spot whenever he wants another meal, until the carcass has been stripped of meat. In places where he feels safe the leopard will sometimes behave with incredible impudence, and will often seize domestic dogs, apparently a favourite meal of his, sometimes in full view of their masters. He comes and goes like a swift shadow, leaping with a grace and ease probably unparalleled among animals. He is the very acme of feline perfection.

The cheetah, or hunting leopard, is a big cat with a great turn of speed. His long, dog-like legs with only partially retractable claws have a bearing on his method of hunting rather than indicating a relationship with dogs. Over short distances he is the fastest runner in the whole world of mammals. He can reach a speed of 60 miles per hour, but his endurance is very limited. The Asiatic cheetah was formerly used as a hunting animal, but has now become rare. He favours broad plains, where he pursues antelope by day.

Vultures

Vultures are to be found in all countries with hot climates, and one form, the 'lammergeier', formerly bred in the Alps. All vultures are true carrion birds, whose amazingly keen eyesight enables them to spot fallen animals from almost unbelievable distances. However, it is only their eyesight which leads them to food: if a carcass is covered with a light cloth they will not notice it.

Hyenas

The hyena proper and the strange aardwolf or earth wolf form a group of their own among beasts of prey. There are three classes of hyena. The striped hyena ranges from the Transcaspian area, across Afghanistan down to southern India, from the southern part of Asia Minor and southern Arabia down to Ethiopia and northern Tanganyika. The brown hyena, sometimes known as the beach wolf, was formerly to be found in coastal territories of Africa from Somaliland down to the Cape and up the west coast as far as southern Angola, but has become extinct in many of these areas. The spotted hyena, the largest of the three varieties, inhabits Africa south of the Sahara.

All hyenas are primarily carrion-eaters, but sometimes, when they are hungry, they will attack small and medium-sized animals. They generally hunt in small packs, except that the brown hyena prefers to hunt alone. The long-drawn-out howling of hyenas and a characteristic barking sound they make, reminiscent of mocking laughter, are among the most frequently heard nocturnal noises in the African bush.

Rhinoceroses

The rhinoceros family, which is one of great antiquity, today comprises five sub-species. Among these, however, the three native to Asia have become almost extinct, while the two found in Africa have been saved from a similar fate, at least for the time being, by strict protective measures. The principal reason for the ruthless pursuit of these creatures has been the belief, which still persists in many Asiatic races, that the powder produced by crushing the horn which the rhinoceros bears on its nose or on its nose and forehead has wonderful aphrodisiac properties! All rhinoceros are vegetarian: the black variety has a pointed, extensile upper lip enabling it to grasp leaves and twigs, while the square-lipped rhinoceros grazes on grass. They remain in the same places, the boundaries of the area occupied by each being clearly marked by its droppings. This characteristic, which seems strange to the uninitiated, is also to be observed in zoos. The female, after being gravid for eighteen months, gives birth to an infant which is capable of walking, and which she suckles for two years. In many books on hunting and exploration the rhinoceros is described as an 'evil-tempered, treacherous' beast. This is quite incorrect. The truth is that the creature is very short-sighted, and very nervous. It will therefore rush blindly at a foe, real or imaginary, trusting in the power of its charge as its means of protection.

The tough hide of the Indian rhinoceros looks like armour plating, the 'plates' joined by deep creases. Only about 700 of these animals still survive in the mountain forests of Assam, Bhutan and Nepal. They have been bred successfully in the Basle Zoo.

The smaller, but otherwise very similar, Java rhinoceros was formerly to be found not only on that island but also in Sumatra and Further India. All but a few dozen of these creatures have now been exterminated.

The situation is even worse concerning the Asiatic double-horned rhinoceros, the smallest variety with a height of only 3 ft. 6 in. Its hide is covered with hair, which is fairly long in places. Some 15 of these creatures are said to survive in Sumatra. There may also be a few in the jungles of Borneo, Burma, Cambodia, Laos and Viet Nam. One lives in the Basle Zoo.

The African double-horned, square-lipped rhinoceros (also known incorrectly as the 'white' rhinoceros) is the largest member of the family; his height can be six feet, his length more than twelve feet, and his weight over two tons. This breed was almost wiped out a few years ago, but fortunately rigorous protection measures have enabled it to increase to some 1,600 head, principally in national parks and game reserves of the Union of South Africa (Umfolozi and Hluhluwe protected areas), the Congo (Garamba National Park), Sudan and Uganda. Only the 'black' rhinoceros (which, too, has a smaller horn above the principal one) is still so common in the savannas of East, Central and South Africa (11,000 to 13,000 head) that there is no appreciable danger of its becoming extinct.

Hippopotamus

The vast hippopotamus herds seen by the early white settlers in Africa are a thing of the past. However, these bulky creatures (whose feet, bearing an even number of toes, indicate their kinship with pigs rather than the horses referred to in their name) are still to be met with in many lakes and sizeable rivers in the interior of Africa, sometimes in quite large numbers. The hippopotamus lives for a far greater part of the time in the water than on land; its young are even born in the water, and suckled on the river bed. Their food consists of grass and weeds which can be eaten, principally by night, on ground close to the water. The hippopotamus always makes for water if pursued. A wounded specimen is a dangerous opponent. An old bull hippopotamus can attain really massive proportions: he may be 14 ft. long, with a shoulder height of 4 ft. 10 in. and a weight of more than 4 tons. The tusks of the lower jaw, which project forward, can be as long as $27\frac{1}{2}$ inches, with a weight of nearly nine pounds. They supply ivory which is softer than that of the elephant, and less valuable.

Cape Buffaloes and White Herons

There is only one breed of cattle native to Africa, the Cape buffalo, of which a number of varieties exist, distinguished by their size and colouring.

The massive, black Cape buffalo once lived in great herds on the plains of East and South Africa. The powerful horns of an old bull would often cover its entire forehead. The red buffalo is less heavily built; it prefers to live in lightly wooded country.

Herds of buffalo (like those of elephant) are generally accompanied by flocks of white herons, which alight on the animals' backs and walk about on them as if they were rocks, picking ticks and insects from the folds in their hides. The sight of these birds in the air often indicates to hunters the whereabouts of a herd of wild game.

Antelopes

Africa is really the continent of the antelope. It is true that members of this family of ruminants are also to be found in Asia and America, but nowhere else is there the variety of antelope native to Africa. In the Dark Continent they inhabit forests, reed thickets, deserts and swamps, but the largest herds live on the grassy plains or lightly wooded savannas. From the large eland by way of the elegant kudu, the deer-like impala and the sabre-horned oryx down to the madoqua, a dwarf antelope the size of a hare, the basic form of this cloven-hoofed quadruped is varied in countless ways. The days are past when antelope herds numbered in thousands filled the vast expanses of the African plains. It is now only in nature protection areas, where hunting is prohibited, that large herds, together with zebras and ostriches, can be seen moving across pastureland. Most of the antelope of the plains are very gregarious; only species dwelling in wooded country and the splendidly coloured bongo, which is the size of a red deer, live in small groups or in pairs. The gnu, with its cow-like head, deserves a special mention. This temperamental runner gives the impression of having been put together from component parts of several different animals. In the opinion of the native inhabitants it possesses the body of a cow, the legs of a gazelle, the mane and tail of a horse. Its character seems most akin to that of fiery breeds of horses; biting and lashing out at one another in their impetuosity, herds of gnu gallop across the plains. One of the two varieties, the white-tailed gnu or 'wildebeest' of the Boers has been wiped out as a free-living species. The other, the black-tailed or brindled gnu, is still common in protected areas. An antelope of particularly attractive colouring is the bontebok. The clear white of the face, belly, tail portion and legs stands out in sharp contrast to the lilac-tinted brown of the remainder of the body. Vast herds of these creatures were formerly to be found on the South African plains. All that remain today are some 200 in the Bontebok National Park and about the same number on various farms.

Zebras

The brightly coloured tiger-horses of Africa attracted the attention of mankind even in ancient times. The zebra, donkey, ass and horse are members of the family of *equus*, horses. They are so closely related that cross-breeds are common, the best-known example being the mule (the result of the mating of a horse and an ass). For experimental purposes comparable half-bred zebras have often been produced in zoos, the father generally being a zebra stallion. The offspring bears faint zebra stripes against a dark background, with more pronounced stripes on the legs. All such bastards of members of the horse family are, however, generally incapable of breeding—the surest sign of the fact that the once similar blood of these animals has long taken on clearly distinguishing characteristics. The zebra is wrongly considered to be untameable. Zebras, trained carefully from an early enough age, can be harnessed to draw a cart; nevertheless large-scale attempts to turn the zebra into a new draught animal, accustomed to tropical conditions, have been given up. Nowadays three classes of zebra are distinguished in Africa; the mountain zebra of Cape Province (almost exterminated) and of mountainous areas of South-West Africa (now rare there too), the common zebra of the plains, with four sub-species found in areas ranging from Ethiopia to the Cape, and the large Grévy zebra, whose stripes are particularly narrow, native to the plains of north-east Africa (Kenya, Ethiopia and Somaliland). The quagga and Burchell's zebra, varieties of the zebra of the plains, became virtually extinct in 1883 and 1910 respectively.

Giraffes

The giraffe and okapi together form a family in the zoological world. The okapi, which is about the size of a zebra, has—by comparison with the giraffe—an only moderately elongated neck. It is a creature of the forest, to be found only in the densest jungles of the Congo area. It was not discovered until 1901, the first live specimen reaching the Antwerp Zoo in 1919. It is strictly protected.

On the other hand the giraffe, several varieties of which are to be found scattered all over Africa south of the Sahara, favours lightly-wooded savannas. This creature, which appears so grotesque in captivity, can be appreciated only in its natural surroundings. The enormously long neck and the long legs indicate an eater of leaves on tall trees. Acacia foliage forms the staple diet of this ruminant. It is drawn into the animal's mouth by its long tongue.

Curious though the colouring appears at close quarters, it is most apt. The spots and lines break up the outlines of the giraffe's body, and a herd can apparently disappear even at a short distance, when they stand in the shade of a mimosa grove.

The giraffe is the tallest and, in relation to its height, shortest of all mammals. A mature male, whose trunk is only about 7 ft. long, has a height to the top of its head of 16 ft., the shoulder height being only 10 ft. Despite its length, the giraffe's neck, like that of other mammals, has only seven cervical vertebrae.

After a period of gestation of 14 months the giraffe generally gives birth to only one calf; nevertheless this species has shown how rapidly its numbers can again increase if it is safe from hunters.

Long-Tailed Monkeys

Long-tailed monkeys are the universal apes of Africa. Many varieties are common all over the continent south of the Sahara. Together with the baboon they sometimes cause considerable damage to human property, especially plantations. However, their agility and cunning has enabled them to survive all attempts to get rid of them. They go in troops consisting of several families. Like all higher apes, they generally bear only one infant at a time.

Anthropoid Apes

Anthropoid, or man-like apes of the Old World have narrower noses than their cousins of the New. The orang-utan and gibbon belong to Asia, the chimpanzee and gorilla to Africa. The most thoroughgoing tree-dwellers among them are the orang-utan and the gibbon, while the chimpanzee is often, and the gorilla generally, to be seen on the ground. Full-grown male gorillas are far too heavy to ascend far up into trees. Strict protection measures are required, especially on behalf of the gorilla and orang-utan, if these remarkable and highly developed creatures are to be preserved for future generations.

Anthropoid apes have few enemies in their natural surroundings. For one thing they are so intelligent—their brains have the same basic form as those of human beings—that they are fully capable of recognizing danger far enough in advance to take appropriate action, and for another the mature males, especially gorillas, orang-utans and chimpanzees, are extraordinarily powerful. No beast of prey would dare tackle a fully grown male gorilla in single combat.

Only the leopard lies in wait high up among the branches of trees to catch unwary chimpanzees; his victims are the occasional female and young apes which are unprepared for the danger. Among all mammals which have been studied so far the chimpanzee has most in common with man as regards the constitution of its blood. Nevertheless modern analytical methods can differentiate between the blood serum of chimpanzees and that of man. The shape of the chimpanzee's skull, with the brain cavity very similar to that of man, is another reason why science has rightly classed this creature as a close relation of ours. It would, however, be foolish to regard the chimpanzee as man's distant ancestor. While there are surprising parallels there are also essential differences. Nevertheless it can hardly be doubted that the chimpanzee and man have developed from the same primeval form.

Crocodile

Although in the days of the Pharaohs it was to be found down to the lower reaches of the Nile, the African crocodile has now been restricted to some parts of Central Africa, and exists in any large numbers only in the remotest areas. It can attain a length of up to 30 ft. Its food consists for the most part of fish, but it will not hesitate to seize even large animals which come to the water to drink, dragging them under.

Chameleon

Some 90 varieties of the chameleon, that strange tree lizard, are to be found in Africa and Madagascar, a few varieties also living in Arabia, India and Ceylon. They are admirably suited to their natural habitat, in the crowns of trees. Their toes, in groups of twos and threes, have developed into powerful pincers, while the tail serves as a fifth hand. The large eyes have circular lids, which leave only the pupils exposed, and the two eyes function independently. The amazingly long tongue can dart out of the chameleon's mouth with the speed of lightning, directed unerringly at any insect in the vicinity, which is then drawn back into its mouth. The proverbial changes of the chameleon's colour are far more dependent on its feelings (hunger, fear, etc.) and on the conditions regarding light and temperature than on the colour of its surroundings. Most chameleons lay eggs, but in a few cases the young are born alive like those of a mammal.

Hyrax

These creatures are members of a large family of rodents native to all parts of the world except for the Australian region and Madagascar. Related forms include the weasel, marmot and prairie dog. They live in earth burrows like the rabbit. Many hibernate during the winter. All are gregarious.

Maki, Loris

These are members of the lemuroid family, an unusual group of animals combining characteristics of insect-eaters with those of monkeys. Recent research has shown that the loris and several species of lemur, including the aye-aye, are largely independent, equally valid forms. The island of Madagascar, which became separated from the African and Asian continents as early as the tertiary period, is the habitat of most of these creatures, including the largest of them, the indri, which can grow to about two feet long.

In Africa and Asia these primitive, nocturnal creatures proved less hardy than monkeys, which may be regarded as a higher form springing from a similar original. Only a few forms about the size of a cat survive, notably the galagos or bushbabies of Africa.

Scaly Ant-Eater

The scaly ant-eaters or pangolins are mammals in a class of their own. They have a certain outward resemblance to reptiles, as the sides of their bodies are covered with hard scales, overlapping like tiles on a roof and constantly growing.

During the daytime these creatures rest in burrows in the ground. At night they go in search of food: ants and white ants, whose hills they tear open with their powerful claws, then extracting the insects by means of their long, sticky tongues. Scaly ant-eaters—seven varieties—live only in the Old World.

Komodo Dragon

The Malays of the innumerable islands lying between south-east Asia and Australasia told early seafarers spine-chilling tales of huge, dragon-like creatures that charged across dry land like a tornado, supposedly attacking all living things they encountered. The small islands of Komodo and Rintja, in the Lesser Sunda group towards the eastern end of the island chain, were especially dreaded in this respect, and no one would venture to land on their coasts. Finally in the year 1912 a Dutchman named Aldegon became the first white man to set eyes on the fabulous 'Komodo dragon', *varanus komodoensis*, a huge form of monitor. Over the slopes of hills crowned with woodland, their lower reaches littered with jagged rocks and impenetrable vegetation, these monstrous lizards up to 9 ft. long were moving about like the dragons of prehistoric ages. Aldegon and his companions saw them seize and devour young wild pigs, and even fawns of the elegant island deer.

In the meantime a few creatures of the same kind have been discovered in remote parts of the island of Flores. However, wherever they still exist they are rare. This is not surprising in view of the huge amount of food needed by these vast carnivorous lizards, a fully-grown male sometimes weighing more than two hundredweights. The number still living has been estimated at around a thousand. They are strictly protected. These Komodo monitors are found only in the Old World; they can live only in hot, tropical regions. Skeletons of creatures of this class, dating from the tertiary period, have been found in southern Europe. Apart from this largest of all lizards its immediate family also includes dwarf forms barely the size of a green lizard. All, though, are characterized by a lust to kill and consume all creatures that come within their power. The Komodo monitor lays eggs whose shells resemble parchment.

Lyre-Bird

Australasia, so rich in zoological rarities, is the home of the remarkable lyre-bird, which exists in two varieties. Judging by its size, bodily form and splendid tail, it might be thought to be a member of the pheasant family. However, ornithologists, who go by inner construction and not outward appearance, number the lyre-bird among the songbirds. This bird inhabits the densest and most inaccessible expanses of woodland, and is one of the shyest creatures on earth. Only the male possesses the lovely tail plumage. During the mating period he unfolds it to its full extent and it moves forward over his back, the outside pair of the sixteen tail feathers together forming the shape of a lyre. The lyre-bird is renowned as an imitator. He gives vocal impressions not only of sounds in nature but also of such noises as those of motor hooters, locomotive whistles, etc. In addition he has a song of his own. The female is far smaller, her plumage of no distinction. She lays only one egg each season.

Bird of Paradise

When skins of birds of paradise first reached Europe the legs had been removed by the natives of the Arau islands who had caught the birds. A belief therefore grew up that this species of bird had no feet; creatures of fairy-like beauty, they were supposed to hover over the woods all their lives, living on dew and blossom. The birds of paradise, several varieties of which are now practically extinct, are songbirds, allied to crows, occurring in many different forms and colours. The lovely decorative feathers of the mature male can be found on his head, neck, wings or tail.

Birds of paradise live on fruit and insects. Most of the 43 varieties live in New Guinea, a few in Australia and the Molucca islands.

Pouched Animals

Australia and its neighbouring islands are the principal homeland of pouched animals, or marsupials, of which some 300 kinds still exist. The young of these creatures are born, after a short period of gestation, by no means fully formed. They continue their development, until ready to stand on their own feet, in the mother's 'pouch', a fold of skin intended for this purpose. In the pouch the young suckle from the mother; until they are old enough to suck, the milk is sprayed into their mouths.

The giant kangaroo is the largest of the pouched animals. Sitting on its back legs and tail, it reaches a height of nearly 6 ft. The red variety have become rare, but grey kangaroos still abound.

However, civilization is pushing inland in Australia to an ever greater extent, and the primitive marsupials, which have little adaptability, are also losing a great deal of their natural food to higher mammals whose ancestors were taken to Australia by settlers and which have run wild.

Kiwi

The smallest bird of the ostrich family is the kiwi or apteryx of New Zealand, which is about the size of a domestic cock. Its stunted, useless wings, which are about 2 inches long, are completely hidden within the covering of greyish-brown or light grey feathers, whose barbs hang loose and disconnected. The kiwi's nostrils are placed far forward, almost at the tip of its long, slender bill, and (unlike most birds) it has a good sense of smell. By night this bird prowls around, feeling and smelling the ground in its search for food, which consists of worms and insects that it can dig up from below the surface of the soil with its bill. The female lays only one egg, in a hollow—it often weighs nearly a pound. Three varieties of the kiwi still exist, and they deserve a place among the living monuments of nature. Thousands upon thousands were slain in former years, largely because their feathers were considered to provide excellent artificial flies for anglers. The kiwi is now strictly protected.

Duck-Billed Platypus

The Australian duck-billed platypus has a remarkable attribute in common with the porcupine ant-eater (which also exists only in the Australian region) which distinguishes these two species from all other mammals and puts them in a class by themselves: they lay eggs, which they hatch out (the porcupine ant-eater in its pouch, the platypus in a nest on the ground). However, the young are fed on the mother's milk! These creatures have no nipples, so the infants lick the milk from a fold in the mother's skin, which point it has reached by way of long hairs from milk ducts on the surface of the mammary glands. These creatures are slow breeders, producing only one or two offspring each year.

Tiger

Despite the fact that its appearance is quite unlike that of the lion, the two are so closely related that it has often been possible in zoos to produce cross-bred cubs. However, the two big cats differ greatly in their way of life. While lions roam across the open landscapes of lightly-wooded savannas in groups, the tiger generally hunts alone in the dense jungle. His principal prey is the wild pig, but he will slay any wild game which he is able to tackle. When larger booty is scarce he will eat a wide range of small creatures, right down to locusts. Two or three cubs are generally born in each litter. The habitat of the tiger stretched at one time from the Amur River to the eastern Caucasus, from Java to Siberia. Eleven sub-species exist in different regions, some of them differing considerably in size and colouring. The most powerful forms are the Bengal tiger of India and the Siberian tiger, while the Bali tiger is the smallest. The westerly limits of the areas in which tigers are still to be found are in eastern Persia; the Siberian tiger was practically extinct before the Second World War, but under strict Soviet protection it again seems to be flourishing.

Muntjak

Several varieties of the muntjak, which possesses close points of resemblance to the musk-deer, are found in India, Further India, southern China and Formosa, from Borneo, Bali and Lombok to the southern slopes of the Himalayas. This creature's sleek body, rising rather high at the rear, indicates its ability to 'glide' between closely-growing trees in the forests which it inhabits. The antlers are fairly small, but the upper canine teeth of the male project out of his mouth like tusks, and these are used as weapons when the animal is brought to bay.

Gaur

Small herds of gaur inhabit the high-lying forests of India, Burma, Indo-China and Malaya. They are splendidly-coloured wild cattle: the powerful bull (shoulder height up to 6 ft.) is glossy black, the cow a reddish brown, both having white legs. The more thickset, domesticated gayal (*bibos frontalis*) was bred from the gaur (*bibos gaurus*).

Condor

Among the 8,500 species of birds at present existing in the world the condor of the South American Andes can claim the distinction of being the largest bird capable of flight. This huge vulture weighs some 22 lb., and his wingspan is some 10 ft. Like all very large birds the condor has become a rarity.

Colibri

Among the 300 or so varieties of the American humming-bird is the 'bumble-bee *Colibri*', the world's smallest bird, which is in fact scarcely larger than a bee, and weighs only about 2 grams. Humming-birds hover above blossoms, their wings moving at such a speed (50 to 200 strokes per second) that they are invisible to the human eye, this motion of their wings making a humming sound like that of a swarm of insects. These little birds are described, justly, as flying jewels. They eat pollen and small insects, also drinking nectar from flowers. For many years they were slaughtered in great numbers owing to a whim of fashion, as their feathers were used to decorate ladies' hats.

Penguins

Penguins (the name derives from *pinguis*—fat) are birds of the Antarctic corresponding to the auks of the Arctic. However, while the auks (apart from the great auk, which is now extinct) are still capable of flight, the scaly wings of the penguin are only of use when swimming.

The homelands of penguins—which exist in 16 varieties—are in Antarctica. However, following cold sea currents, they have long settled, too, in areas far to the north, breeding on the shores of land masses and on islands in subtropical and even tropical latitudes. Thus some specimens found their way with the Humboldt Current to Peru and the Galápagos Islands, others with the Falkland Current as far as Rio Grande do Sul on the east coast of South America, others again with the Benguela Current to South-West Africa. Colonies are also to be found on the coasts of Southern Australia, Tasmania and New Zealand.

All types of penguin are extremely gregarious, living together in large numbers, and everything they do is done by all of them at the same time, often with almost the precision of soldiers on parade. Even the young are brought up in 'kindergartens', and while their parents are away taking part in mass fishing operations they are looked after by a 'governess' to whose care they have been entrusted.

Sloth

Sloths—six forms are known, all native to Central and South America—belong to the edentate group of mammals, a primitive class lacking incisor teeth. Sloths have only ten teeth in the upper jaw and eight in the lower. They spend almost all their time in trees, hanging with their backs towards the ground. It is in this position that they sleep, mate, and give birth to their young. Only to leave their droppings do they descend to the ground. Their food consists of leaves and blossom.

Their bodily structure bears witness in several interesting ways to the fact that they spend their lives hanging from the branches of trees: their fur is parted at the belly; their stomach, liver, spleen and pancreas are shifted out of their normal positions, in some cases about 135 degrees.

The hairs of the fur contain curious layers of cells permanently inhabited by various classes of tiny plants. In addition the sloth's fur harbours the grubs of many small varieties of butterfly.

The young sloth—almost invariably only one—is born very small but able to see. For several weeks it is carried about by its mother.

Ant-Eater

Ant-eaters are classed among the edentate mammals, and rightly so, as they have no teeth at all. Our picture shows the great ant-eater, or ant-bear, which lives in the wooded savannas of South America. A fully-grown male of this species measures, from the tip of its snout to the end of its tail, some 6 ft. With the claws of its powerful forelegs it breaks open the stone-hard ant hills. Then its long tongue darts out and the insects stick to it in great numbers. Termites, or white ants, are the ant-eater's principal source of nourishment. It also frequently eats black ants, and appears to be particularly fond of fat beetle larvae, which it extracts from rotten tree stumps. Sitting up on its hind legs it can deal such fierce blows with its forelegs, armed with their sharp claws, that even the jaguar is afraid to attack. Only one child is born at a time; during its first months of life it is carried about on its mother's back.

In addition to the great ant-eater there exist the smaller tamandua or three-toed ant-eater, and the dwarf, two-toed ant-eater.

The Sea-Elephant

The sea-elephant, also known as the elephant seal, substantially exceeds even the walrus in both length and weight. A mature bull has a total length of 20 ft. and a weight of more than 6,600 lb. The sea-elephant is therefore the largest of all species of seal. Its principal distinguishing feature is the proboscis-like nose of the male, which is about 15 inches long when the creature is in repose, and can become twice the size when he is excited. In their breeding areas, the seas of the southern hemisphere and the northern Pacific, sea-elephants travel great distances, only going ashore during the mating season. Once on land these indolent creatures lie about, completely docile. They allow other seals and even human beings to move among them. They are of a peaceful disposition. The sea-elephant appears to be as inquisitive as other kinds of seal.

The mating period is during the months between September and February. Only then do the ungainly monsters show signs of animation. At that time fierce battles take place among the males.

Llama

The llamas, really camels without humps, are among the most characteristic animals of South America, as they are to be found only in the New World. The vicuña, which is about as large as a fallow deer, is a creature of mountainous districts—living at altitudes of up to about 17,000 ft.—while the larger guanaco is also to be found on the plains. Herds of guanaco, each generally consisting of one male with some thirty females and young, find their way south, sometimes right down to the Tierra del Fuego.

From the vicuña there has been developed a domesticated variety known as the alpaca, while the llama proper, with its woolly fur coloured chestnut-brown with light patches, is a later derivation of the guanaco. Llamas and alpacas were the most important domestic animals of the old Indian civilizations. They served as beasts of burden, also providing wool, meat and milk.

Iguanas

Iguanas—there are more than 500 varieties—are a branch of the lizard family. Dr. Eibl von Eibesfeldt writes fully about the two species of iguana found in the Galápagos Islands in his chapter on Galápagos animal life.

Galápagos Buzzard

Buzzards form a family—whose members differ widely—among the diurnal birds of prey. A hooked bill, sharp claws, and splendid prowess in flight characterize this extremely able aerial robber. They seize most of their prey on the ground, but in some cases they will catch small birds on the wing, or on the branches of trees. There are 29 species of buzzard, with many sub-species. See the chapter by Dr. Eibl von Eibesfeldt for details of the Galápagos buzzard.

Tortoises

Tortoises are members of a sub-order of reptiles. Their principal distinguishing feature is the bony box, covered with leathery skin or horn plates, forming an armoured shell protecting the body, and into which the head, legs and tail can all be drawn to a greater or lesser extent when danger threatens. There are more than 250 varieties, most of them native to tropical and sub-tropical regions, including the related family of turtles dwelling in fresh water and in the sea. All varieties lay circular or elliptical eggs with chalky or parchment-like shells, but do not hatch the eggs out. Tortoises are vegetarians, while fresh-water turtles live principally on water creatures of many kinds, and most sea-going turtles are wholly carnivorous. Numerous varieties of both tortoise and turtle have long been hunted so relentlessly on account of their flesh or eggs that they are in serious danger of being wiped out altogether.

For an account of the giant Galápagos tortoises see the chapter by Dr. Eibl von Eibesfeldt.

Cormorant

The cormorant family comprises 30 varieties. They live solely on fish, being excellent divers and swimmers. They generally breed in colonies of varying sizes, on rocks or in trees according to the characteristics of the different sub-species. Several varieties found on the coasts of Peru, Chile and South Africa are among the most important sources of guano (a valuable fertilizer obtained from their droppings). In eastern Asia cormorants are used in fishing; a ring of hempen twine fastened round the bird's neck prevents it from swallowing the fish it has caught. For details of the flightless cormorants of the Galápagos Islands see the chapter by Dr. Eibl von Eibesfeldt.

Armadillo

Armadillos, which are divided into 20 classes, are found in many areas from the southern states of the U.S.A. southward to Patagonia. The upper part of the body and the tail are protected by armour plates rather like a coat of mail, consisting of bone with a horn covering. All varieties live in underground burrows, and prefer open country to densely wooded areas. Only a few varieties enter forests. They live on ants, termites, and a great many other insects, together with small animals such as mice, and they will eat carrion. They are able to burrow with surprising rapidity, even in hard ground, many varieties constructing large tunnels as much as 15 ft. below the surface.

Alligator

Apart from a few exceptions such as the Chinese alligator, which is, however, almost extinct, the alligator family are to be found only on the American continent. Alligators are differentiated from crocodiles by the fact that the long fourth tooth of the lower jaw disappears into a cavity of the upper jaw when the mouth is closed, instead of remaining visible as in the case of the crocodile. The armoured lizards do not differ greatly from class to class in their way of life or their method of reproduction.

Puma

The American silver lion or mountain lion once abounded in every part of the immense double continent from Alaska in the north to Patagonia in the south. Nowadays it is extinct in inhabited regions, surviving mainly in mountain areas. As it is native to so large an area, it is natural that this elegant feline beast varies regionally in colour and build. In some cases the puma is silver-grey, in others it is nearly the yellowish-brown of a lion. In hot, tropical areas it is smaller than in the cooler north or south. Pumas prey mainly on birds, and small to medium-sized animals. Their tracks have been found up to an altitude of 17,000 ft. in the Andes. The puma will attack human beings only in self-defence.

Prairie Wolf and Grey Wolf

The prairie wolf or coyote is the most characteristic beast of prey of the American prairies. Pairs generally remain together for several years, and bring up their offspring together. The prairie wolf digs holes in the ground, or appropriates those dug by others. Its menu consists of every kind of animal which it can overcome: from the prairie dog by way of birds of all kinds to fish, frogs and shellfish.

The grey wolf, until recent years inhabiting many northern lands, is now practically extinct in the United States. Only in the far north, in the Arctic taiga, is it still common. From there it makes its way to the mossy plain, the tundra.

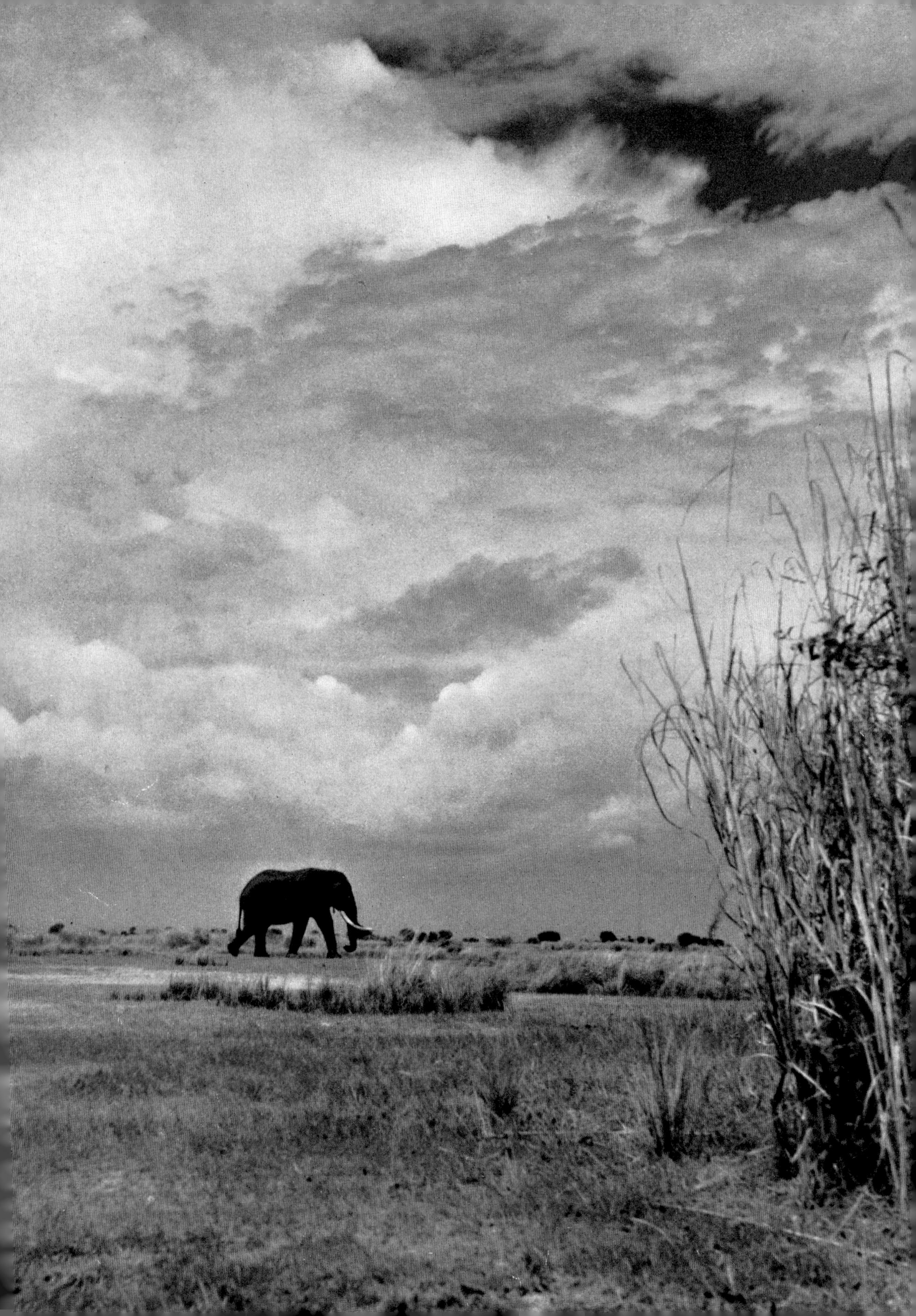

Dr. Arthur Lindgens

Above: Elephants live in herds – some on the plains, some in the forests. Elephants of the plains are often accompanied by antelope (in this case a waterbuck, near Lake George in Uganda). *Below:* Elephants cannot exist for long without water. They know how to probe for it below the surface of dried-up river beds. *Right-hand page:* The principal distinguishing features of the African elephant are its enormous ears and receding forehead.

Wilhelm Schack

Wilhelm Sch

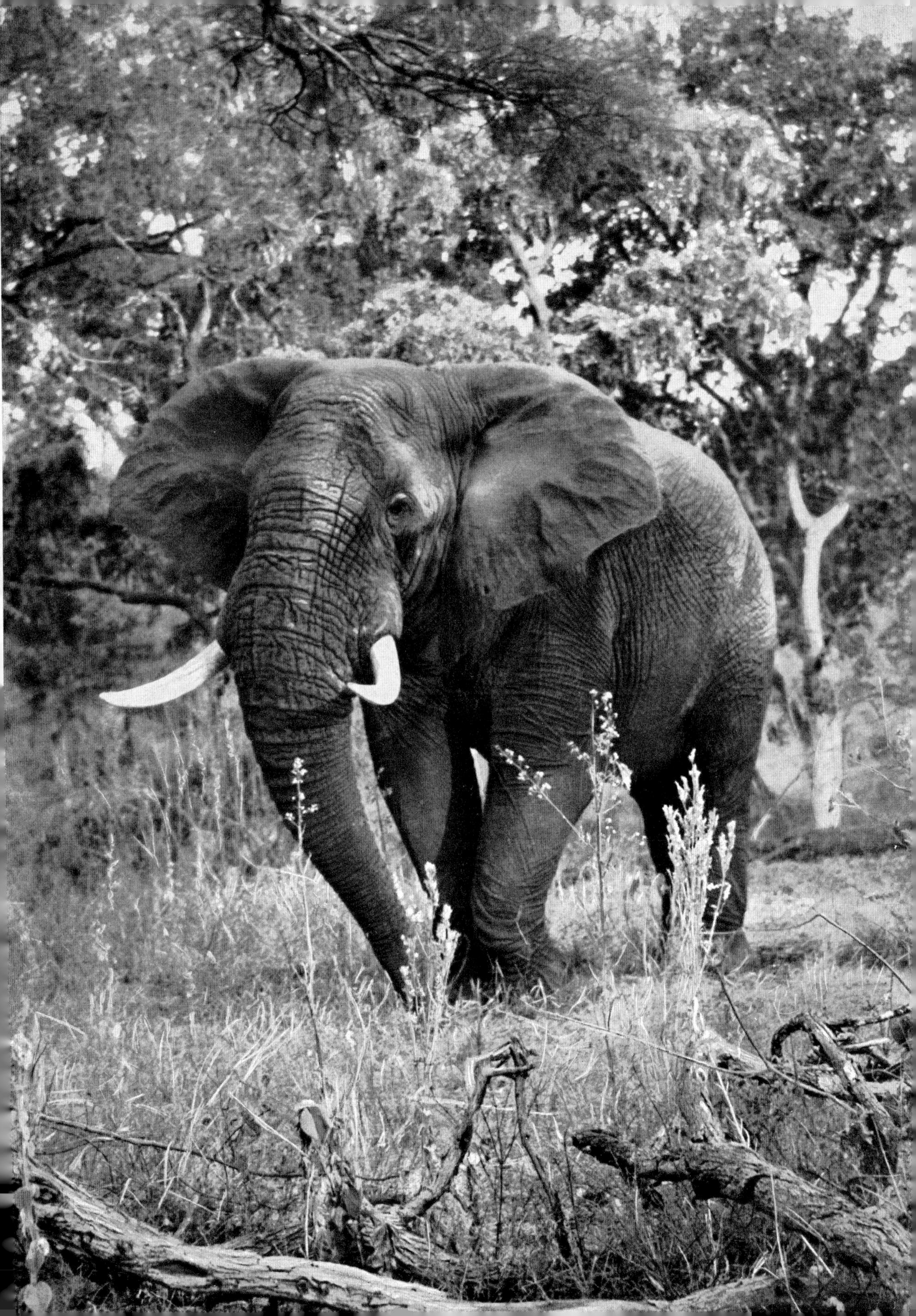

Helen Fischer-Wehr

Snow-white herons are always to be found accompanying herds of the larger animals in Africa. They are seeking out ticks and insects from the rough hides of these elephants.

In the Addo bushland: Startled by the cameraman, a cow elephant charges blindly toward the cause of her alarm.

Wilhelm Schack

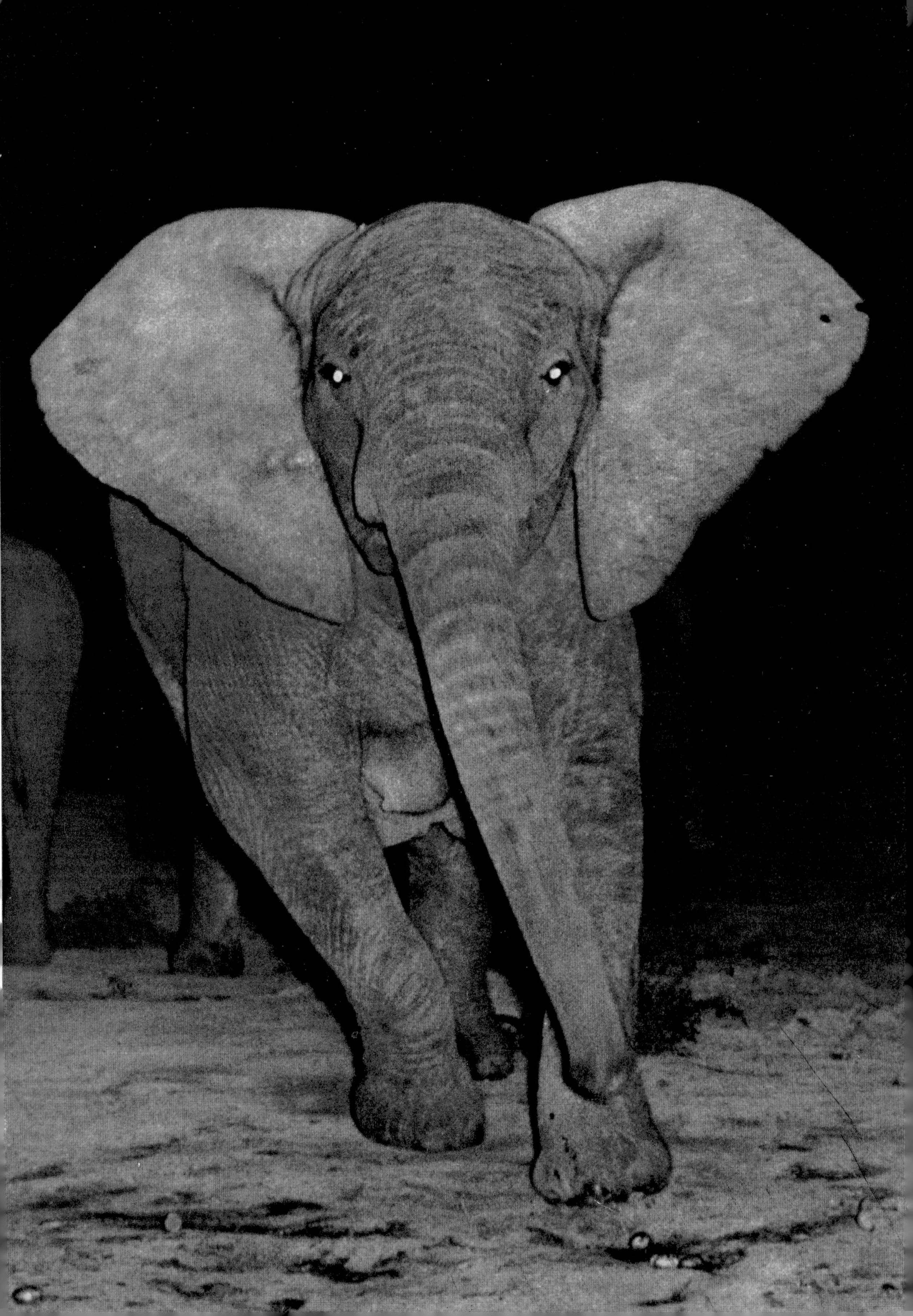

Dr. Arthur Lindgens

Lions are sociable creatures, and hunt their prey in groups. The powerful male lions eat first, keeping the remainder of the group away from their victim until they have finished.

Hawkins, N. Rhod. Inf. Dept.

Right, above:
Unless he is provoked, even the king of beasts keeps clear of human beings. (Shown here with a guinea-fowl he has caught.)

Right, below: The lion is reputed to be the laziest of the big cats. He is roused to action only when he has no alternative.

Wilhelm Schack

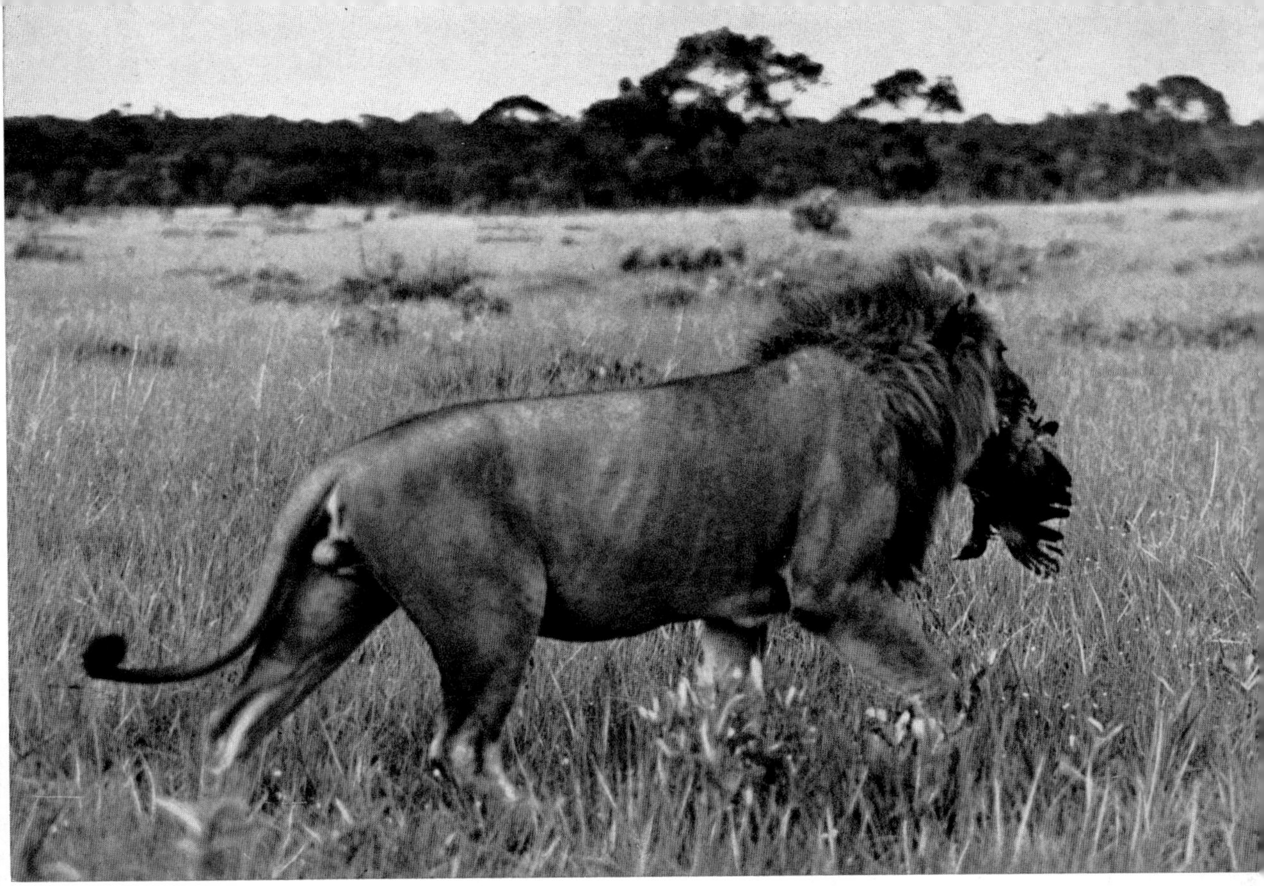

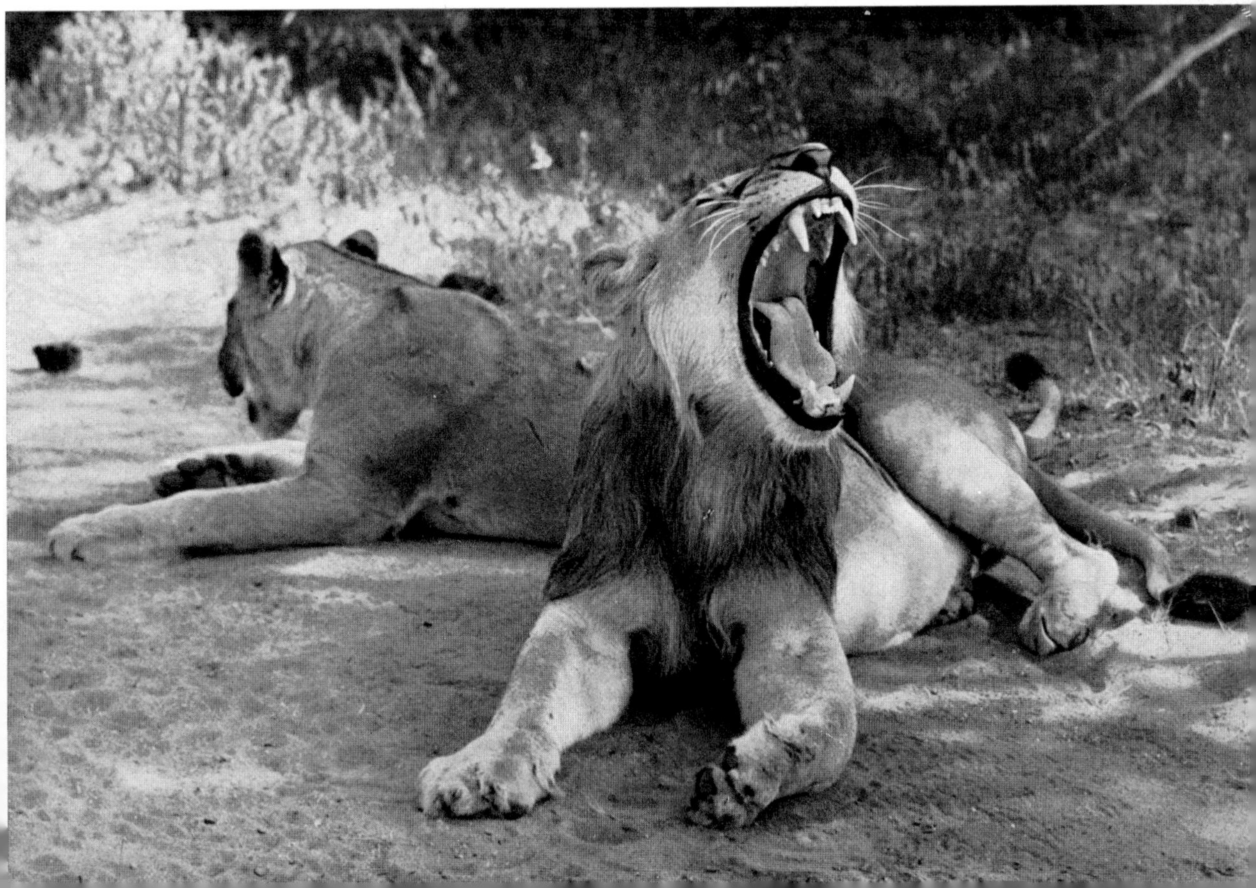

Vultures are the public health authority of the African bush. This skeleton is all that remains of a gnu, slain by a lion.
Wilhelm Schack

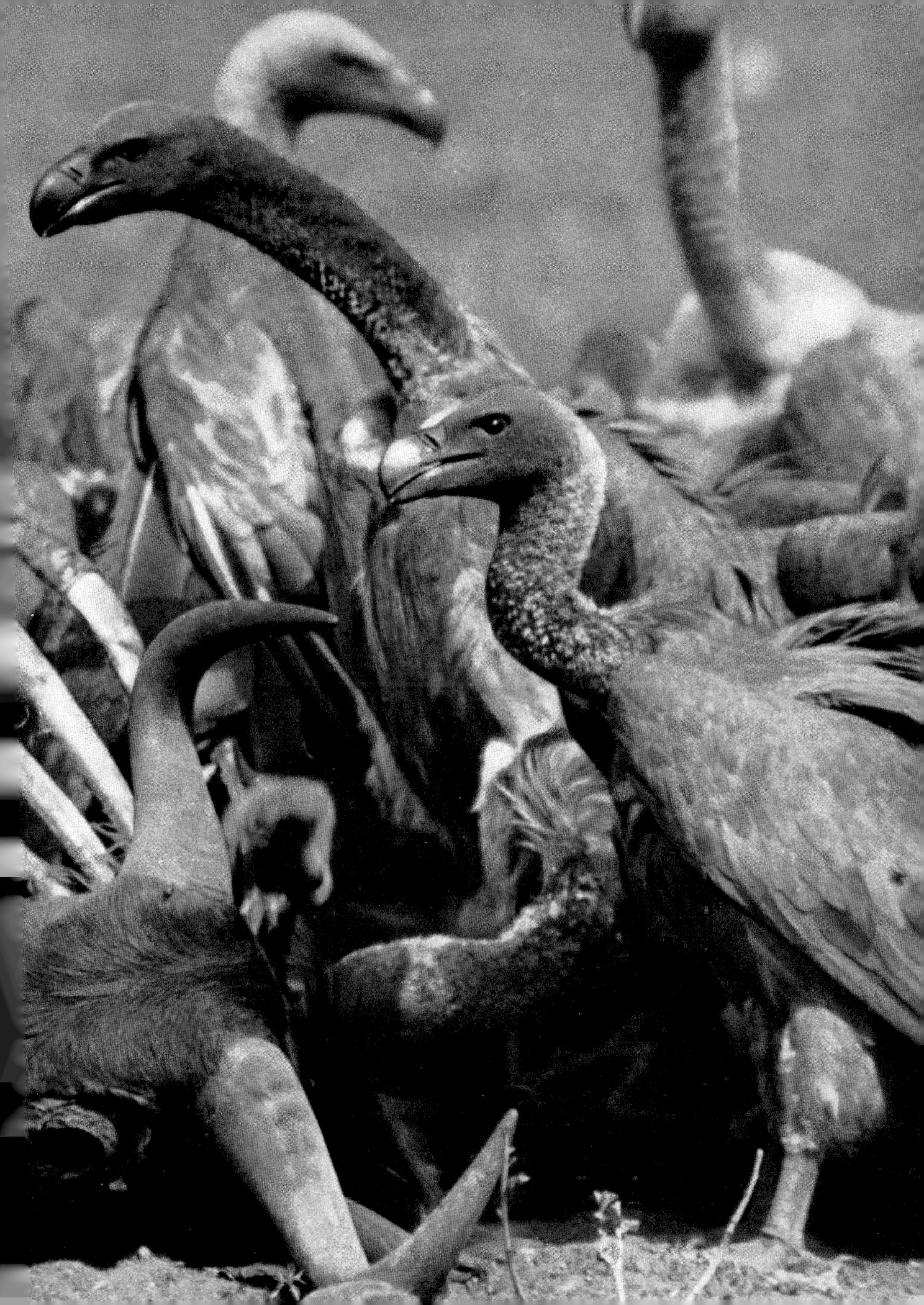

Ylla-Wehr

The lion's favourite food is the flesh of equine animals – that of the zebra when he is at liberty, and horsemeat when in captivity. (A lion with a particularly fine mane, and an old scar on his back, in the Masai Reserve.)

The feelings and intentions of lions are often indicated quite clearly by their facial expressions. (Lioness in the Kalahari National Park, South Africa.)

Wilhelm Schack

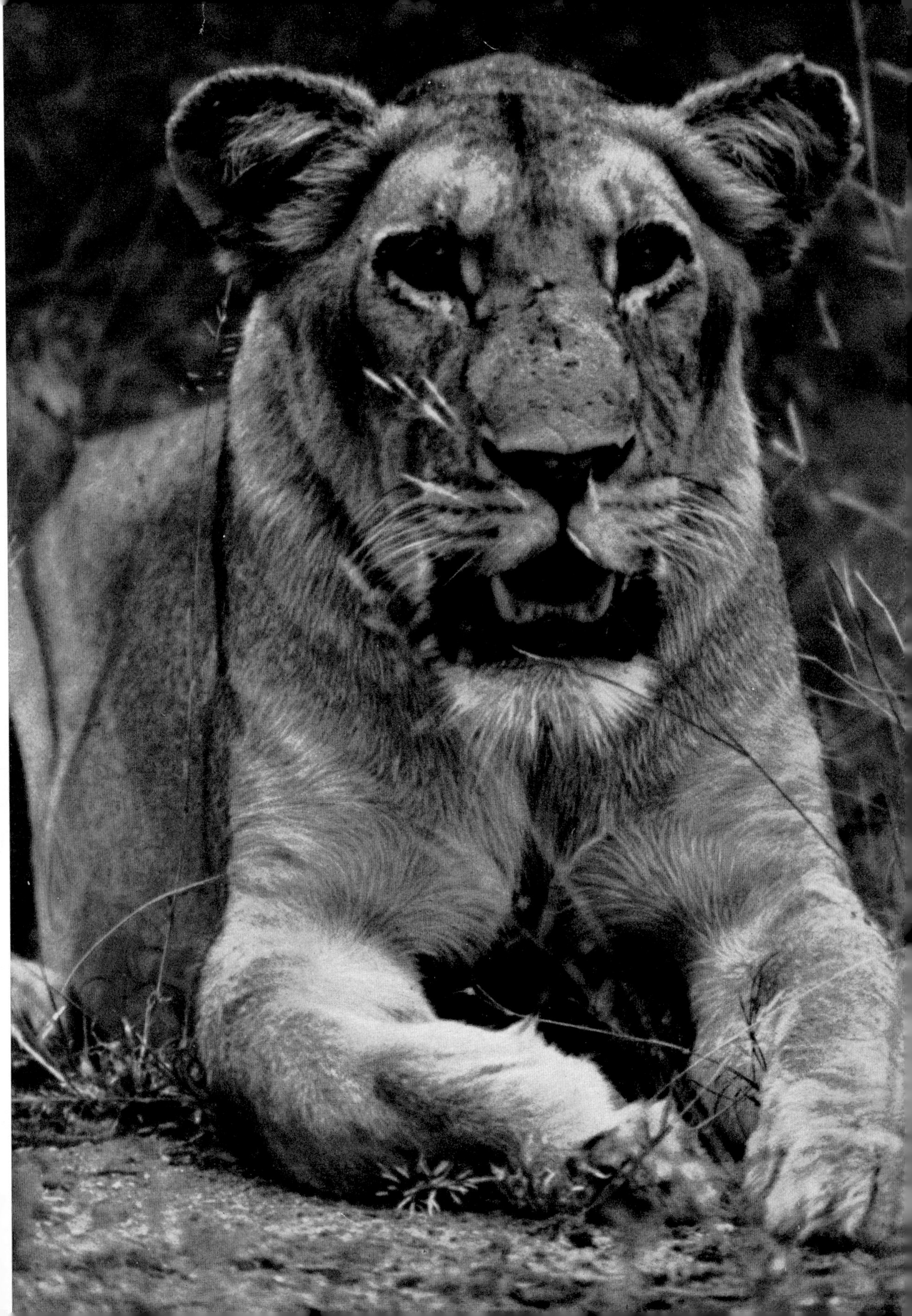

South African Railways

Cheetahs, or hunting leopards, are swiftly-moving feline beasts, unique in their bodily form.

The leopard, a large member of the cat family found in many parts of Asia and Africa, is still fairly common, thanks to its (by comparison with the lion) small size, and its skill in concealment.

Dick Wolff

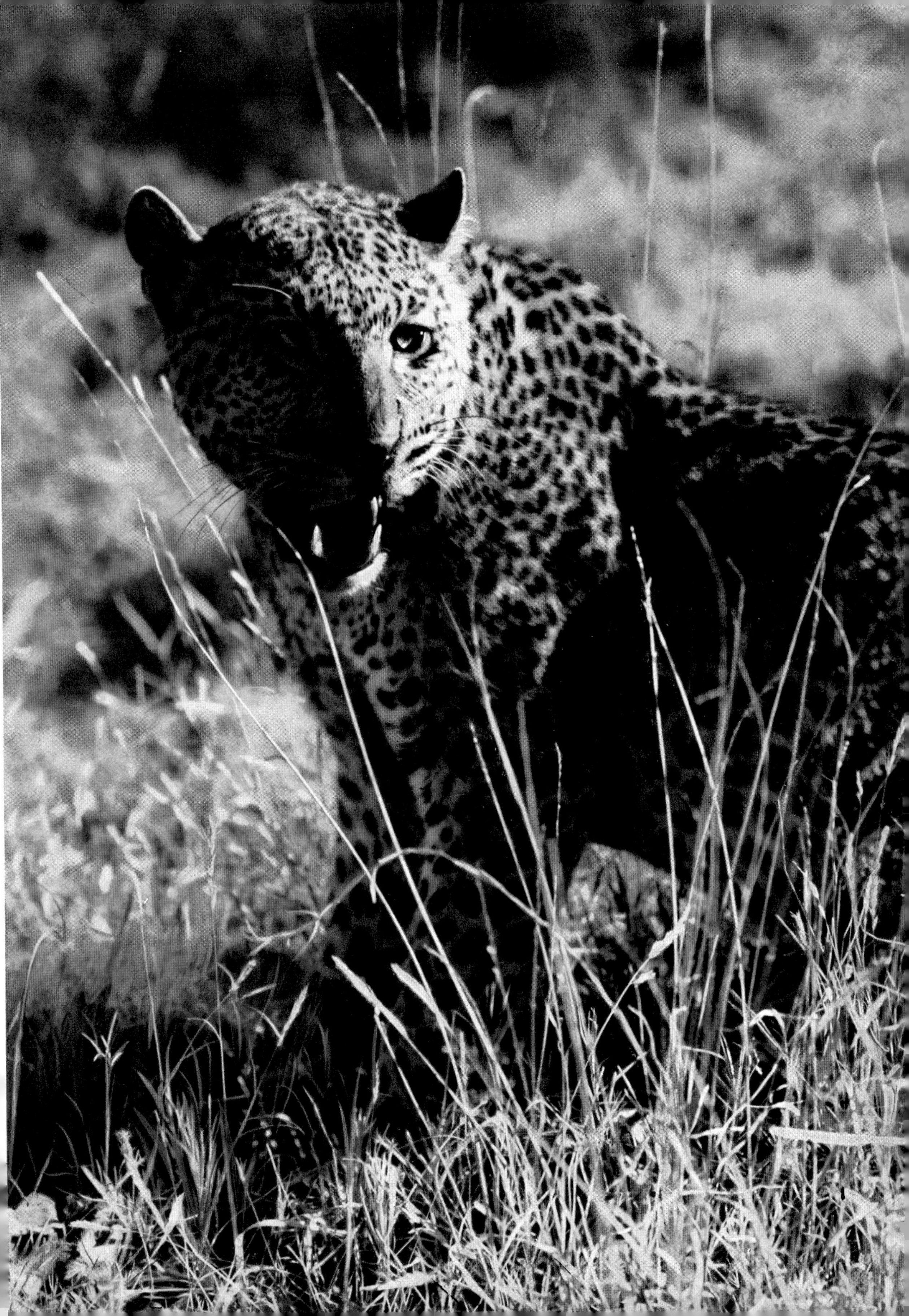

Dick Wolff

Defenceless game and carrion are the principal food of the spotted hyena, but these animals have often proved a menace to sleeping or exhausted human beings.

Young hyenas are as tame and faithful as dogs, but as they grow up it is necessary to guard against a bite from their powerful jaws, which can crush the largest bones.

Herbert Kaufmann

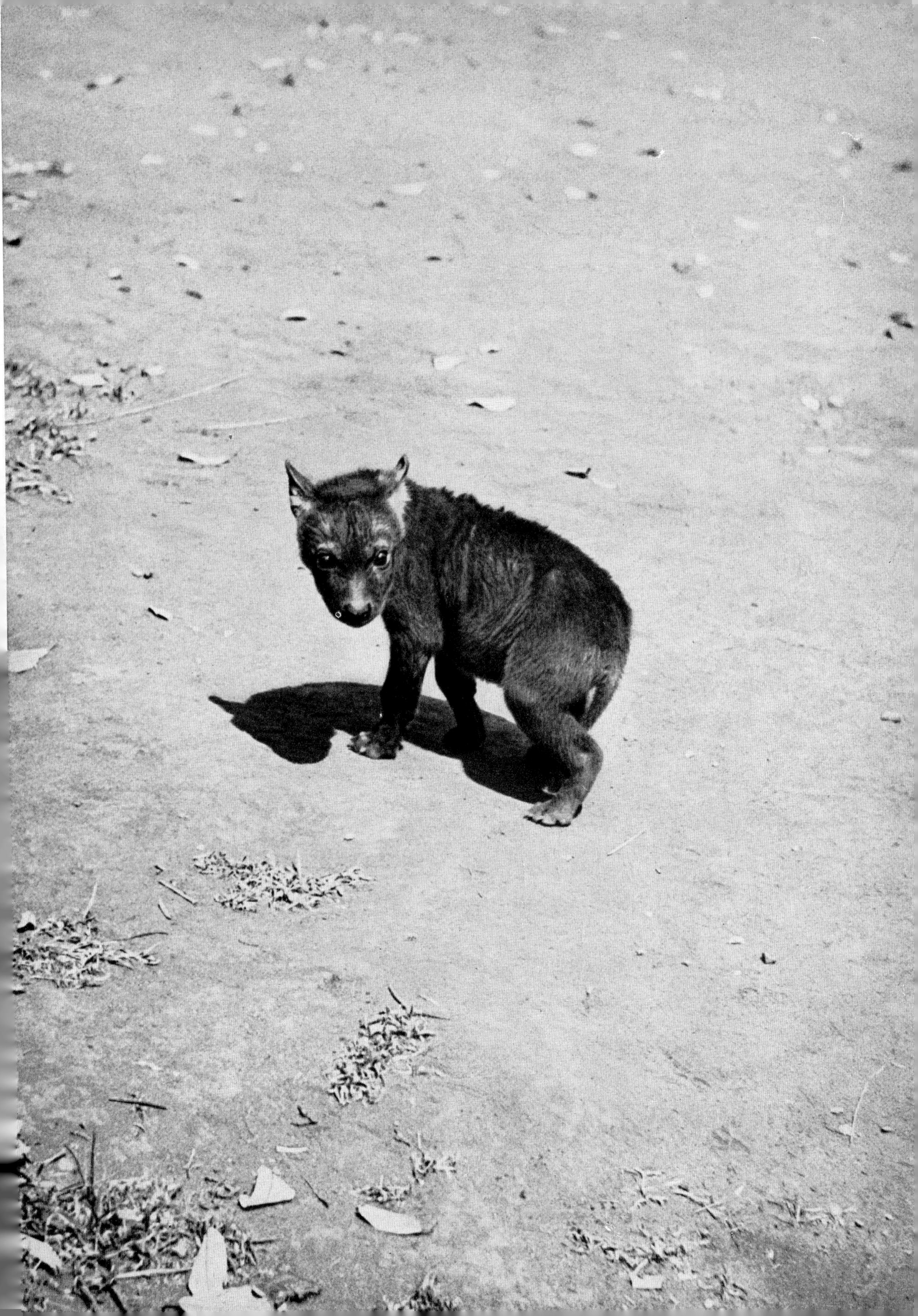

Wilhelm Schack

The poor eyesight of the black rhinoceros seems to be the principal cause of his irritability. To him attack is the best means of defence. (Above and on P. 43: Black rhinos photographed in South African National Parks.)

Prof. Dr. A. Heim

A maned lion by the carcass of a Cape buffalo.

Eugen Schuhmacher

Square-lipped rhinoceroses in the Umfolozi Game Reserve (Union of South Africa).

A black rhinoceros in the South African National Park.

Wilhelm Schack

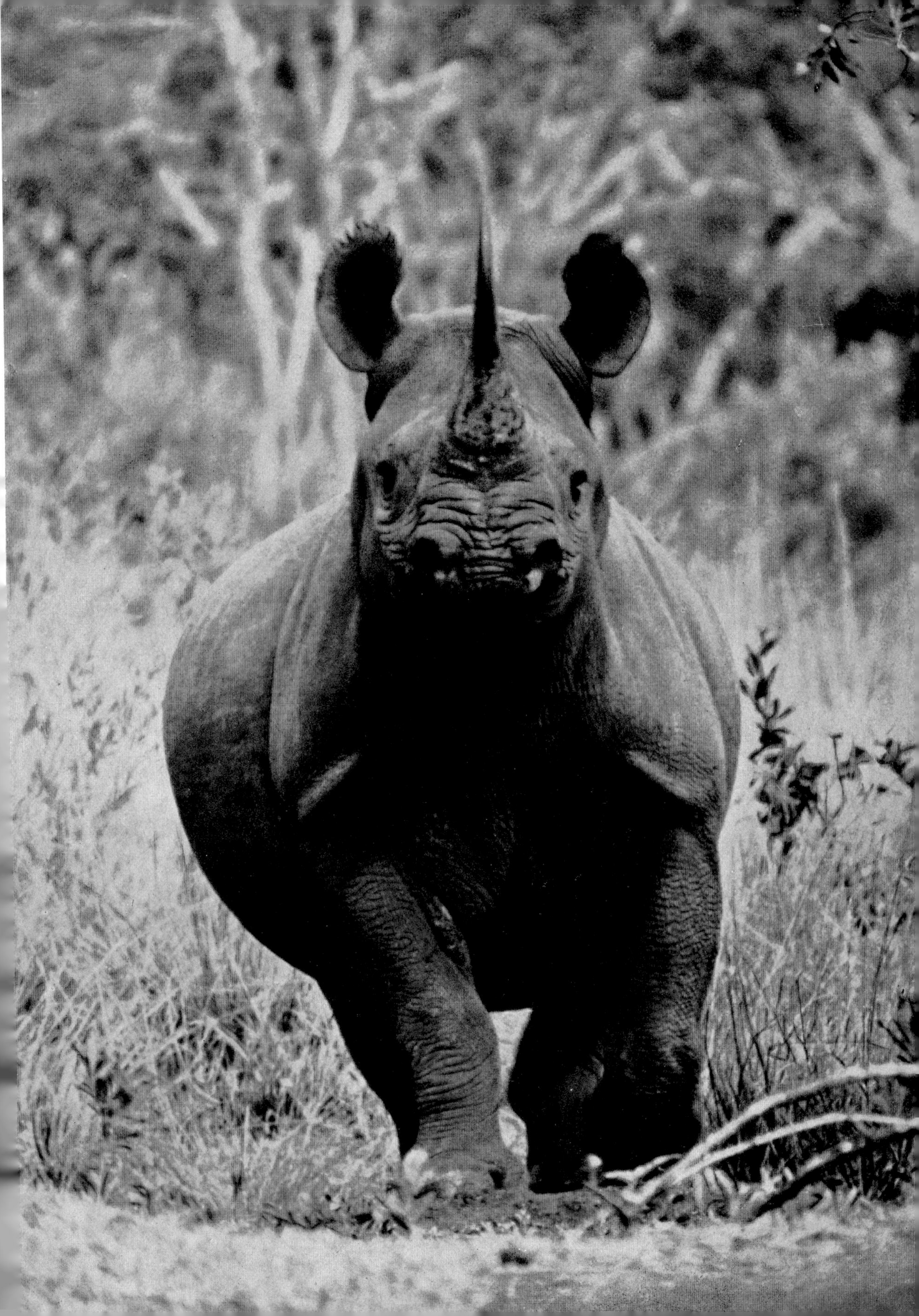

Hippopotami are still to be found in all the major rivers and lakes of Africa, but it is now only in protected areas that they remain in large numbers.

Popper-Wehner

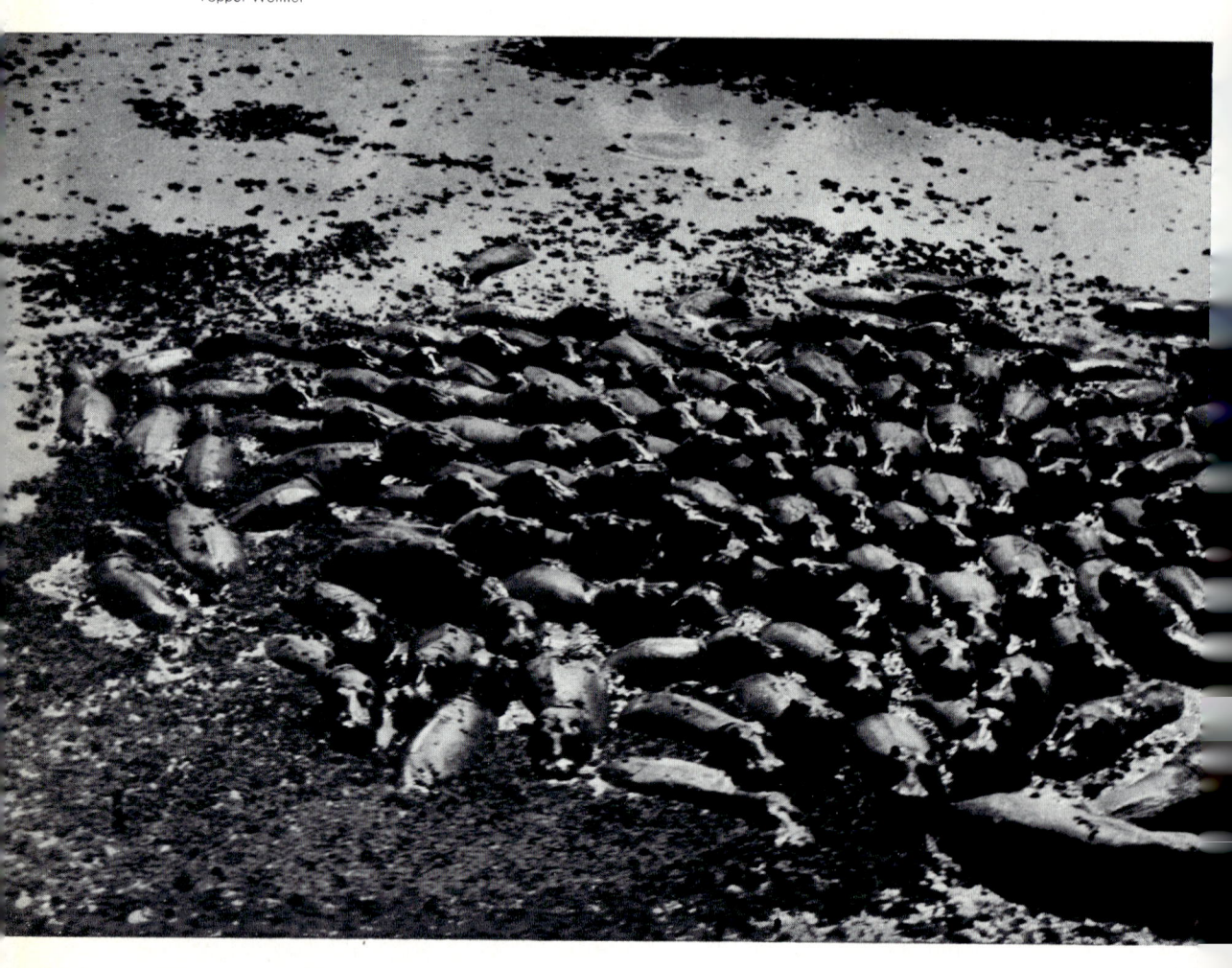

Feuerstein-Scuol

The hippopotamus is not, as its name implies, an aquatic member of the horse family, but rather a gigantic river pig. However, the more zoologically appropriate name potamochoerus already belongs to a class of pig.

Baumann-Bildpost

Unless it believes itself to be in imminent danger, the Cape buffalo will flee from human beings, despite its formidable horns.

When enraged, a mature bull Cape buffalo is more dangerous than a lion or tiger. His charge is sudden and unexpected.

Wilhelm Schack

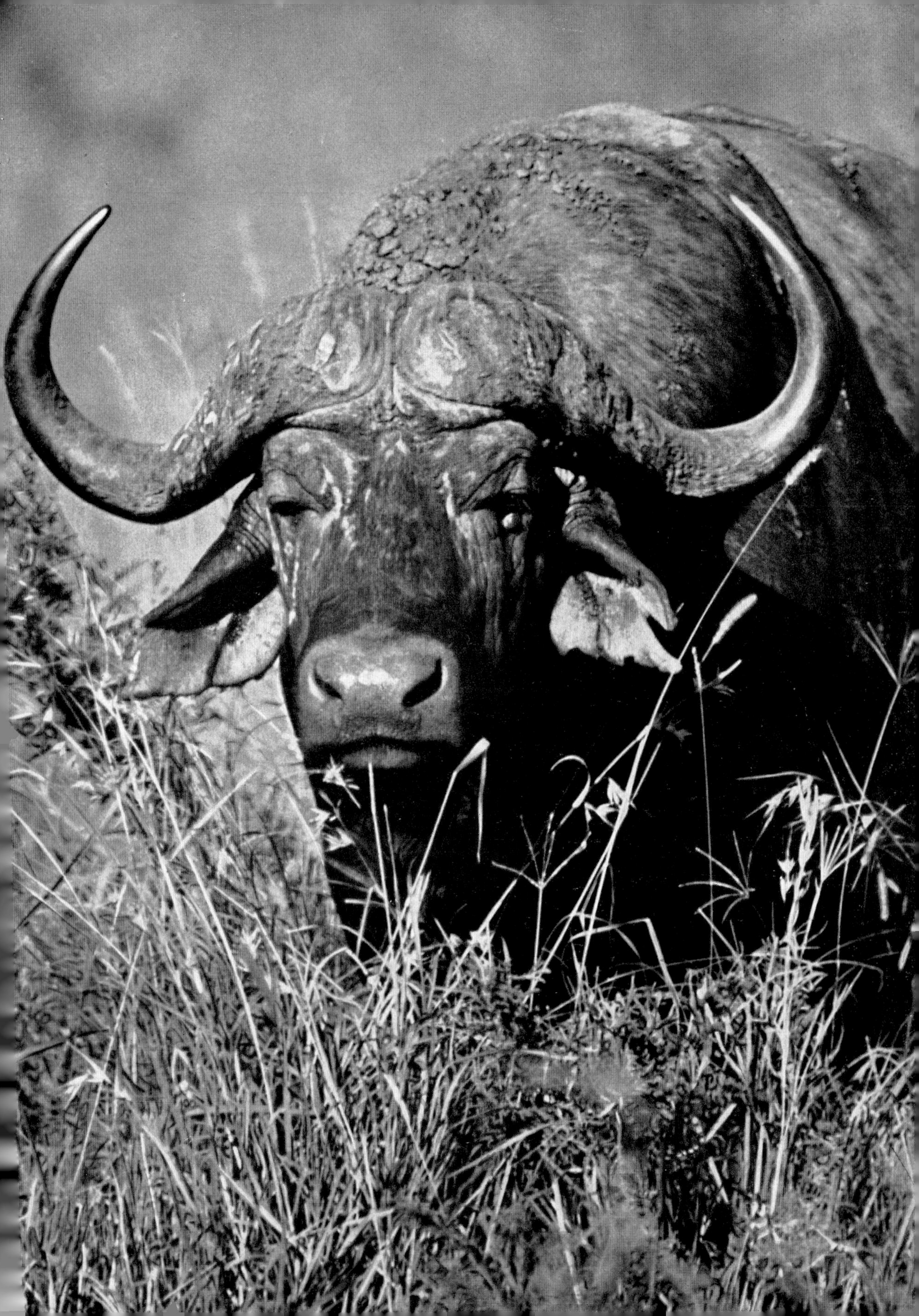

The impala, or black-heeled antelope, which is about the size of a fallow deer, is still to be found in large herds on the African plains.

Ylla-Wehr

Wilhelm Schack

Brindled gnus and impalas at a water-hole.

The fount of all life in the dry season: the water-hole. This photograph shows zebras and gnus in the Kruger National Park.

South African Railways

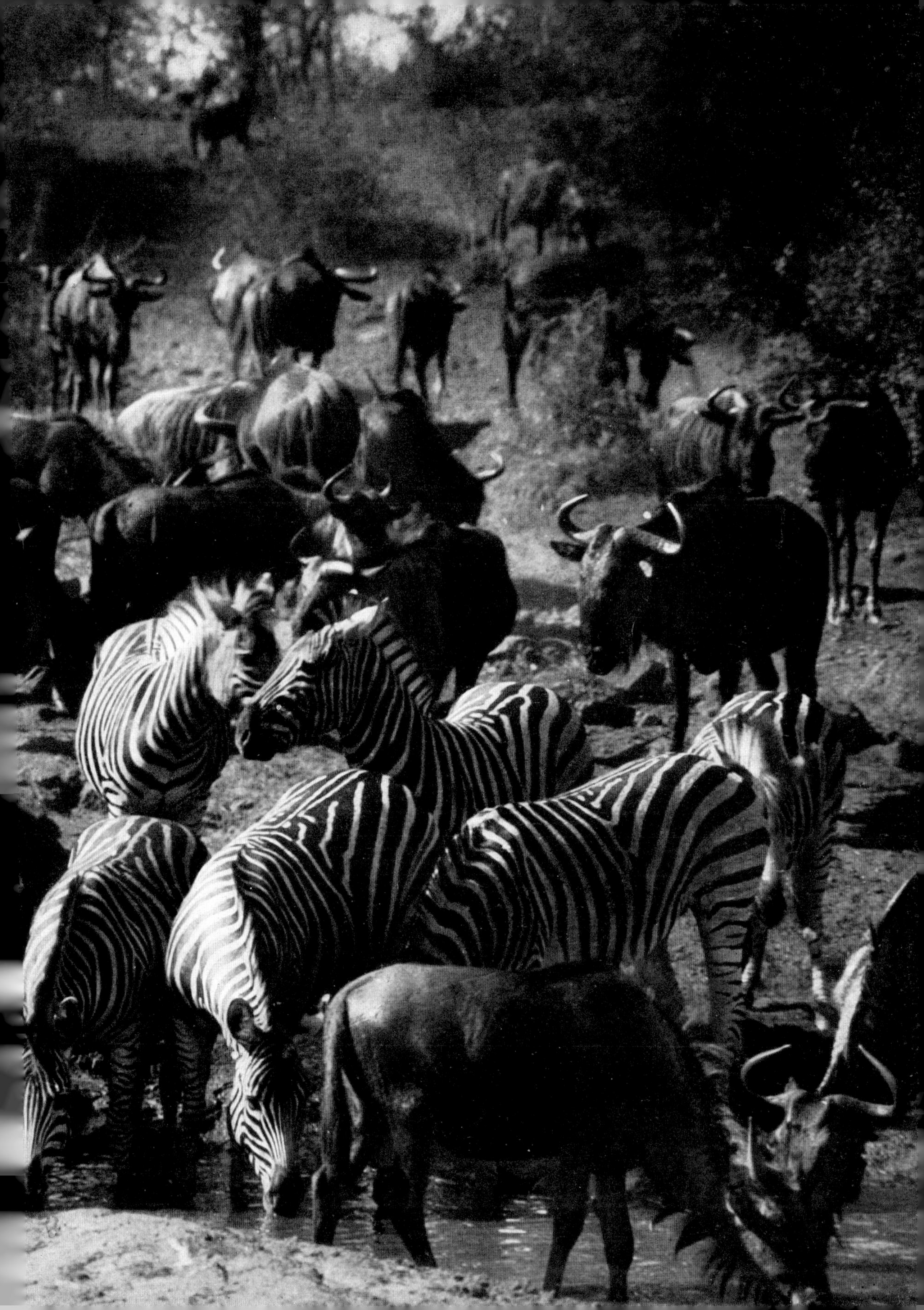

Wilhelm Schack

The once innumerable herds of the great beisa antelope have now greatly diminished in size. Relying on its yard-long horns, which are spiralled at the base, this large antelope will even venture to fight a lion.

The head of a bull kudu. This powerful breed of antelope is one of the noblest of the whole species.

Wilhelm Schack

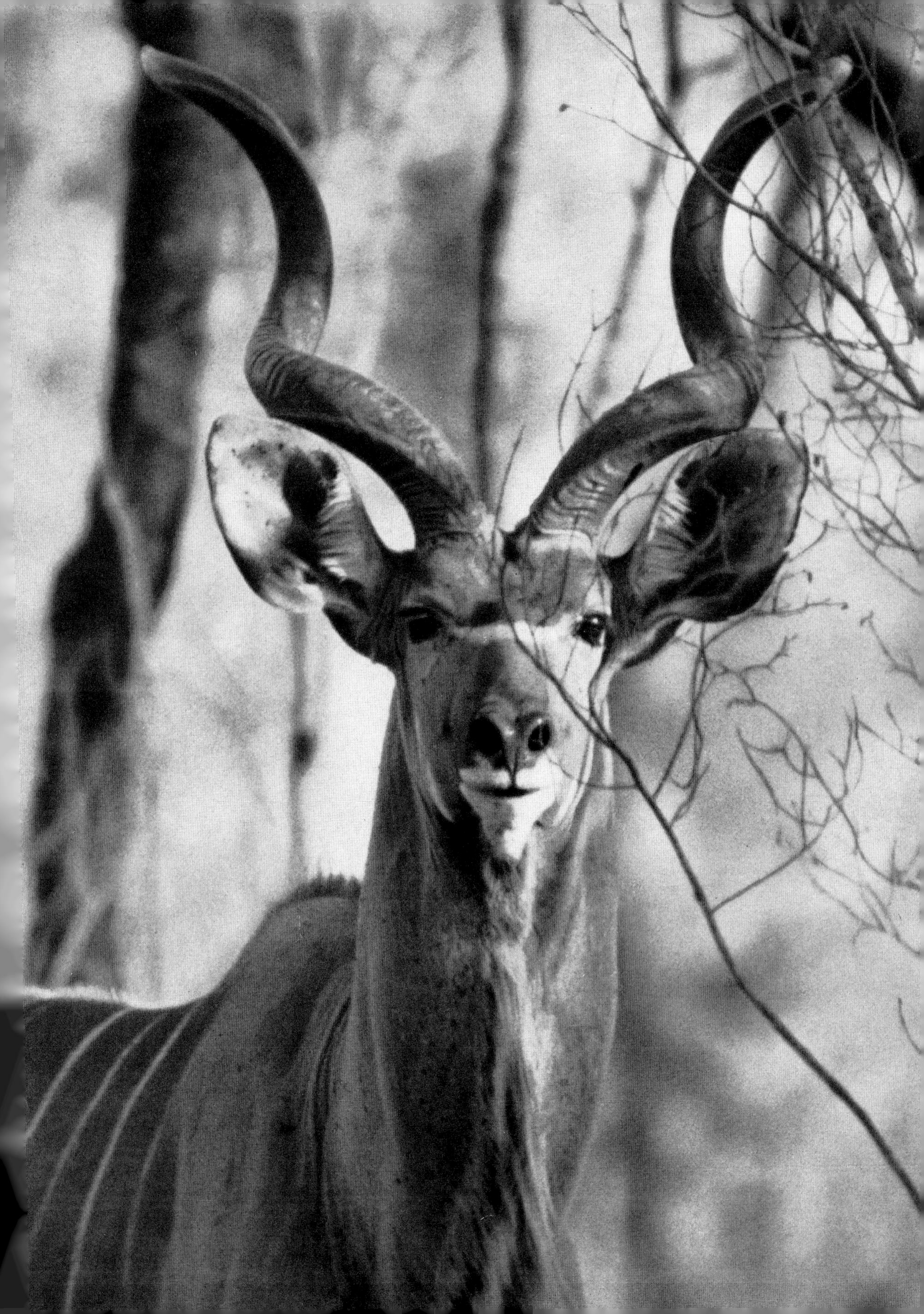

South African Tourist Corporation

Such encounters are not uncommon in the Kruger National Park.

13 varieties of the giraffe inhabit lightly-wooded African savannas south of the Sahara.

Ylla-Wehr

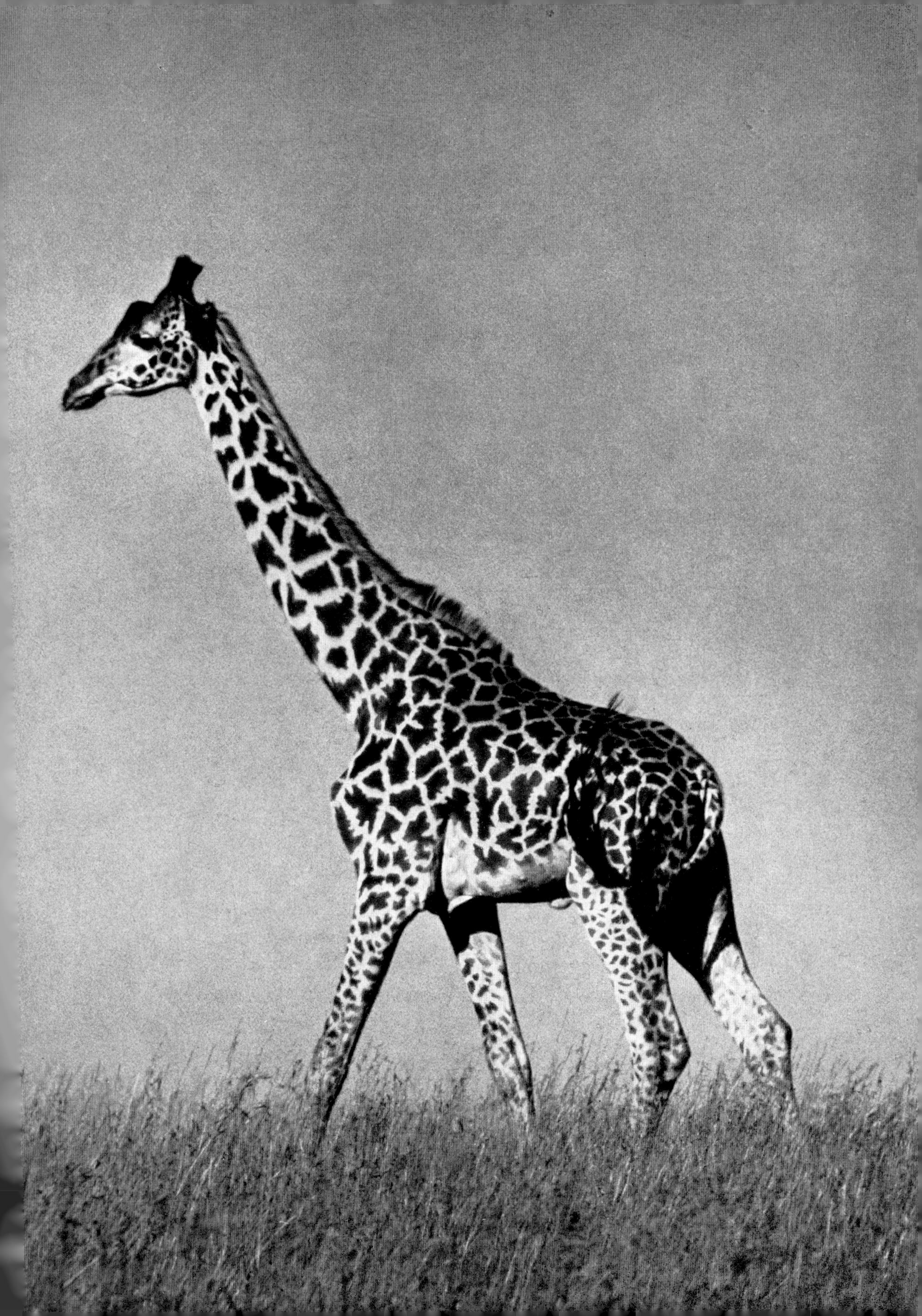

Page 57, above: The white-faced bontebok, one of the finest of the antelope family, was near to extinction. Today, however, a few hundred again live in the Union of South Africa.

Eugen Schuhmacher

Page 57, below: A mountain zebra galloping in the Mountain Zebra National Park, South Africa. The horizontal stripes on the hind quarters, a distinguishing feature of this breed, can be seen clearly.

Eugen Schuhmacher

Startled by the photographer's aeroplane, a herd of sable antelope prove themselves powerful runners as they gallop across open country.

Popper-Wehner

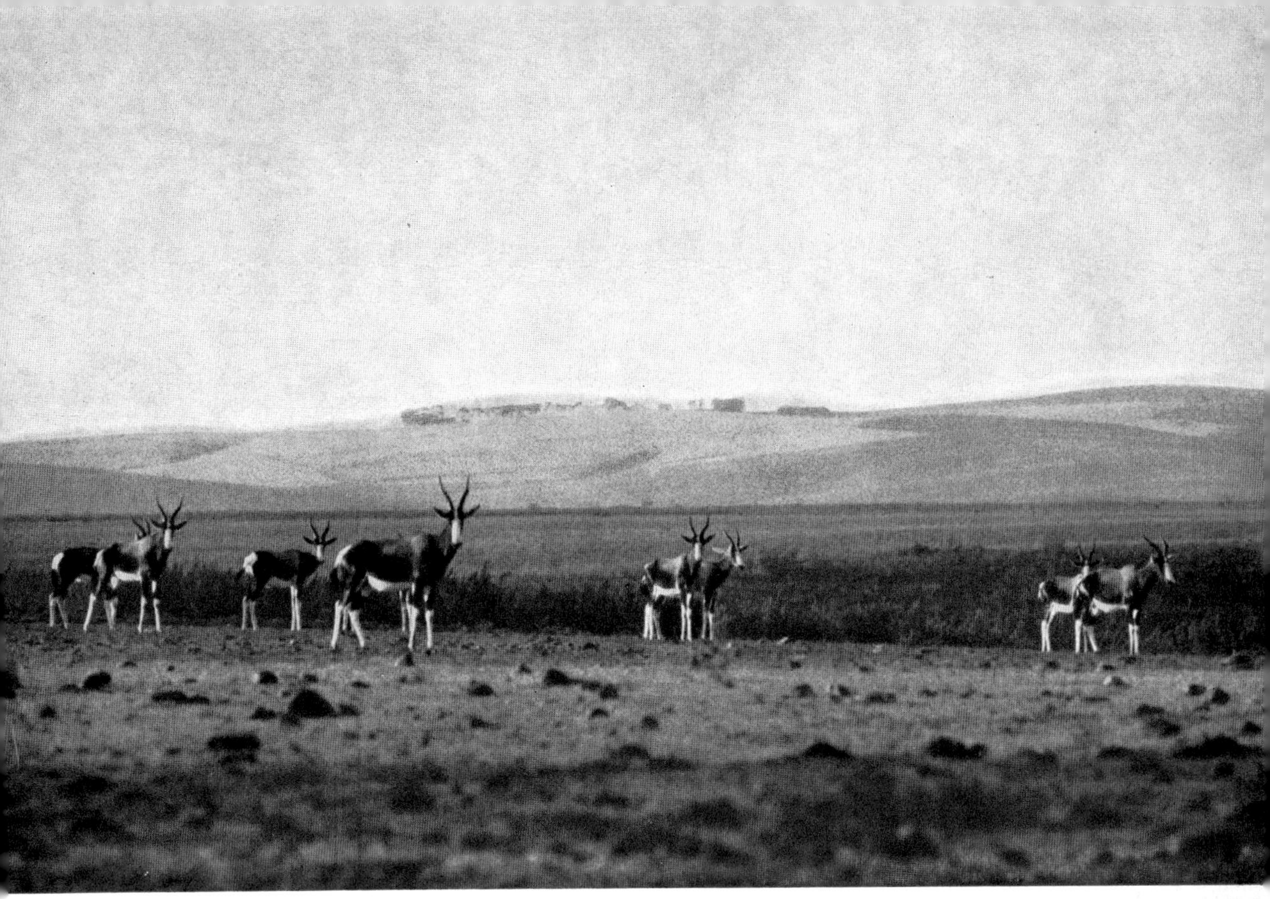

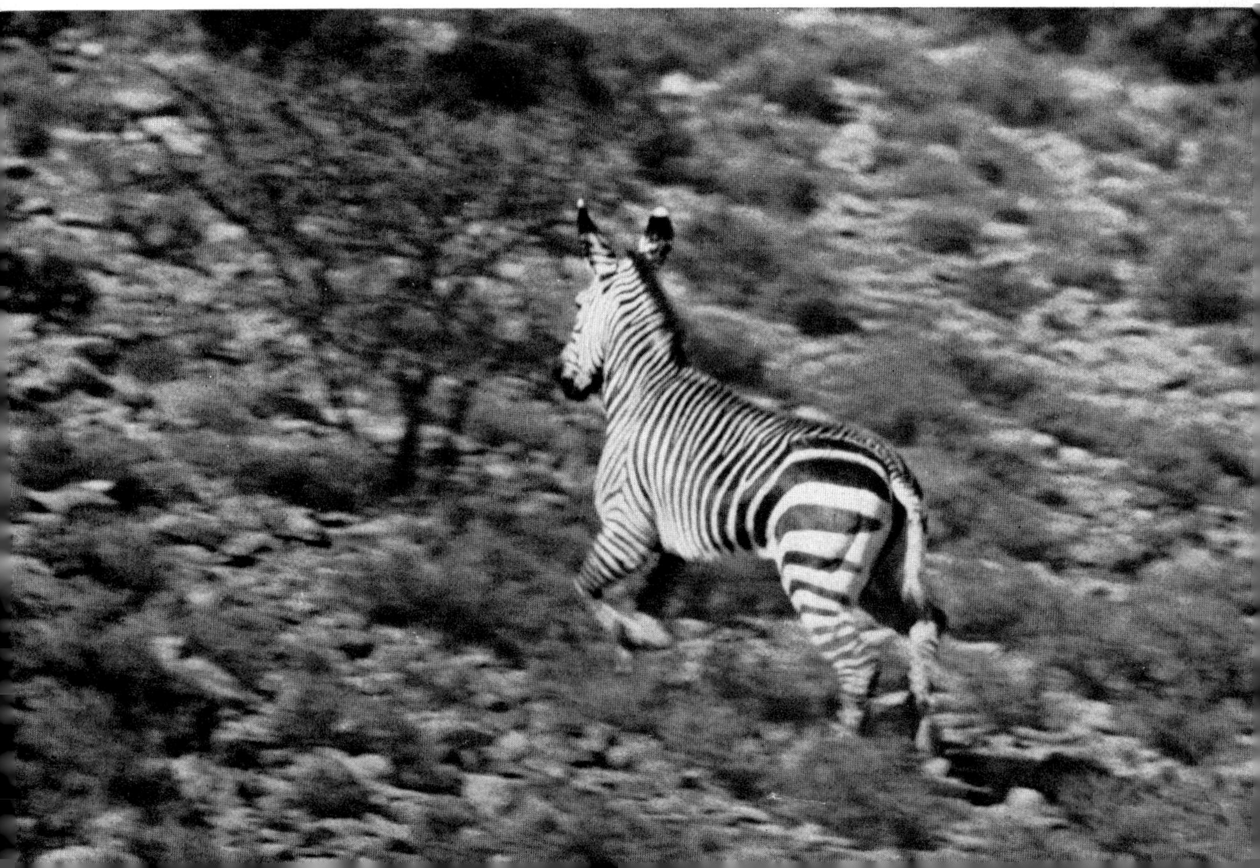

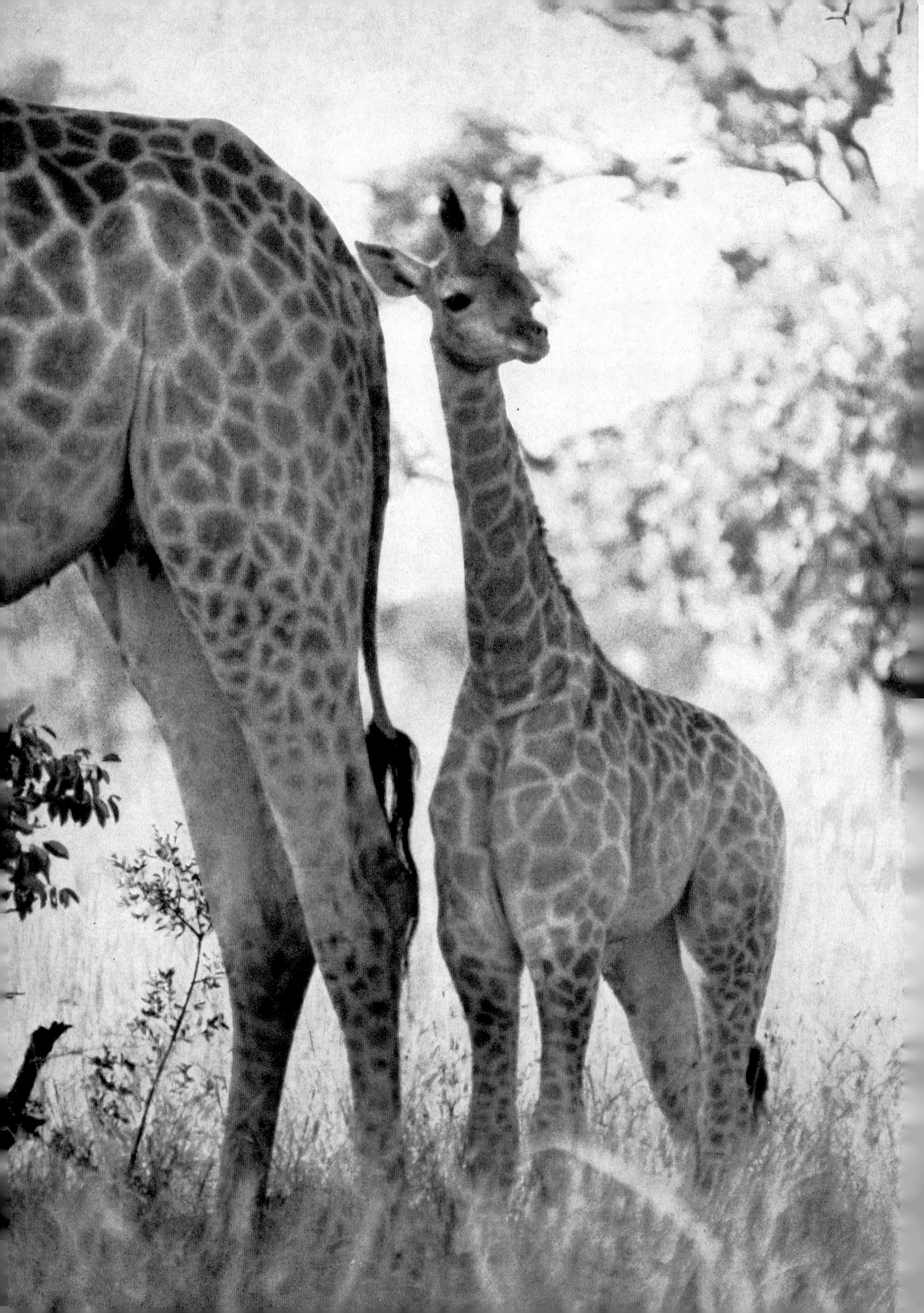

Satour-Johannesburg

Giraffes in the Kruger National Park.

*ft-hand page: The giraffe calf enjoys careful maternal
tection. A blow of the mother's steel-hard hoof has been known
smash a lion's skull.*

Right, above: When two giraffes engage in combat, the struggle often resolves itself into a unique trial of strength of their necks.
Right, below: In order to drink water at ground level, the giraffe has to spread its forelegs wide apart and bend them at the knees.

Photos: Wilhelm Schack

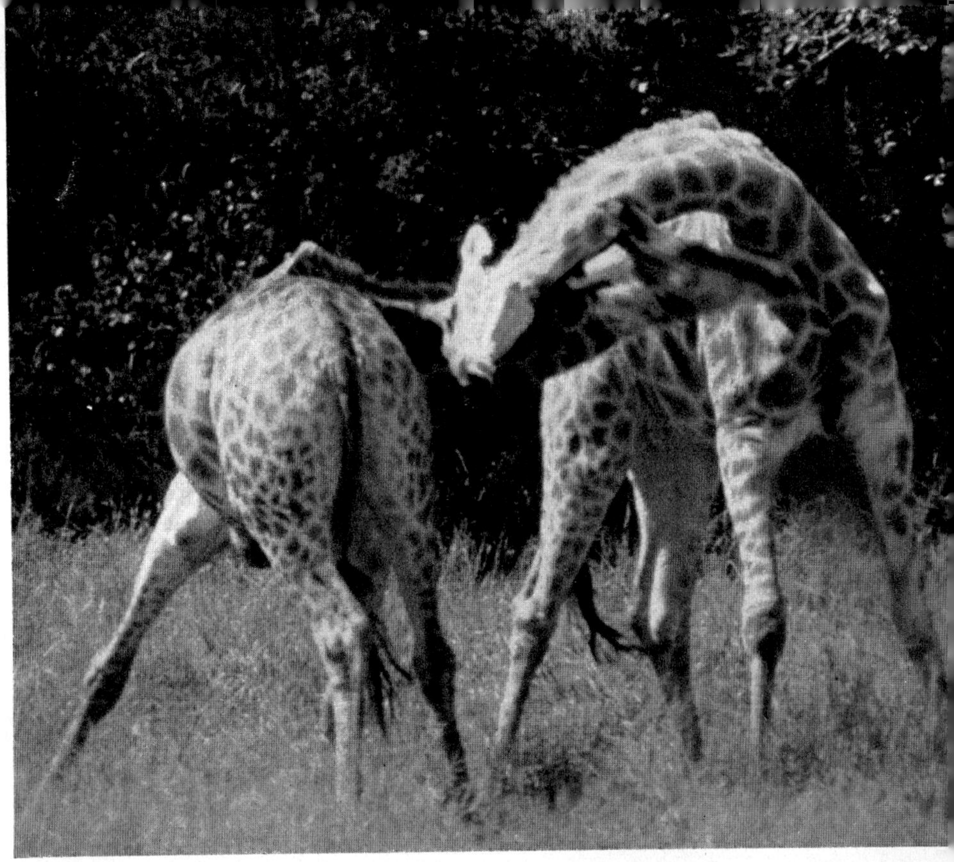

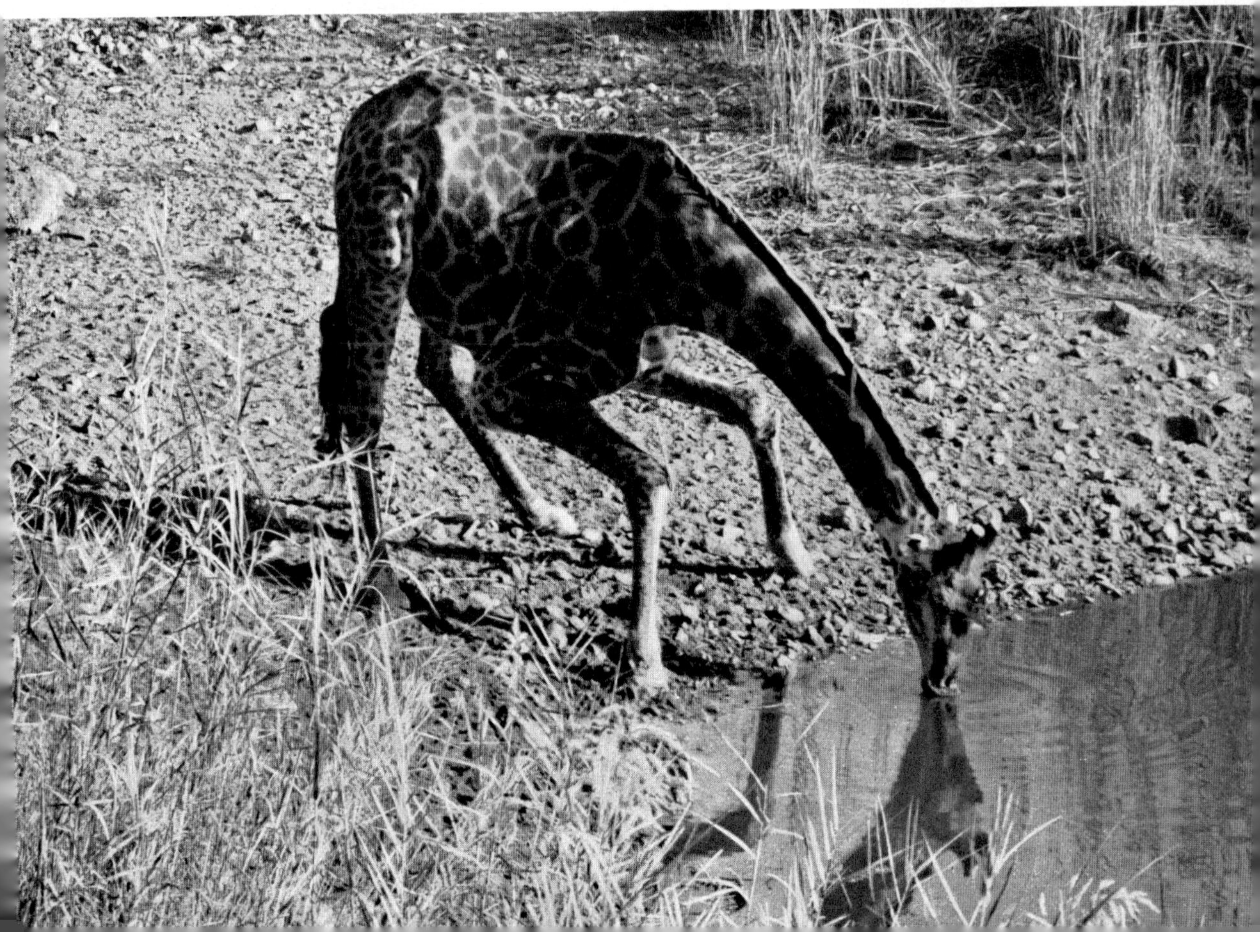

Popper-Wehner

A treasure to be cherished! A herd of lechwe antelope near the River Zambezi.

Right-hand page, above: The life and work of a game warden in a National Park are hard and exacting. A cup of tea first thing in the morning – then out for the whole day, travelling across scrubland in the fierce heat of the sun. Right-hand page, below: Then in the evening, paper-work! Each observation has to be entered in a diary. Only in this way can the authorities ascertain the numbers and categories of the animals, and thus put into force adequate measures for their conservation. (Photographs from Ngoma, Northern Rhodesia.)

British Official

Ylla-Wehr

The green long-tailed monkey is the "universal ape" of East Africa. Whether in the jungle, on the savannas, or in fruit plantations, troops of them are everywhere to be seen.

Ylla-Wehr

Like all the anthropoid apes, the chimpanzee is in great need of protection. All-too often the rarer and therefore more precious an animal becomes, the quicker that species dies out.

The Nile crocodile formerly abounded in all the lakes and rivers of Africa. Since men have taken to using its skin for making expensive leather goods, numbers have greatly diminished.

Popper-Wehner

Photographs of gorillas in their natural habitat are extremely rare. These pictures of the mountain gorilla were taken in the Albert National Park in the Congo.

Noxwell

Noirot

Feuerstein-Scuol

The three-horned chameleon looks like the outcome of an eccentric fancy in creation. These strange tree lizards are native to Africa and Madagascar.

Wilhelm Schack

The charming African hyrax is a cousin of the squirrel. He lives in burrows in dry, warm areas.

Above: An orang-utan. In youth the skull of this anthropoid ape of the islands of south-east Asia is rounded, and therefore more like that of a human being than it becomes in a full-grown animal.

Below: The days of the lovely silver-coated maki living in the thorn woods of Madagascar are numbered. It belongs to the lemur family, curious creatures half-way between insect-eaters and monkeys.

Koch-Isenburg

Popper-Wehner

Popper-Wehner

The loris is an Indian relation of the lemuroids. He is a creature of the night, with great owl-like eyes, and hunts insects high up in the branches of trees. Unlike the Madagascan lemurs, the loris always produces two offspring.

The five-toed scaly ant-eater is one of the most primitive of mammals. (Pictured: an Indian pangolin.) This species has survived almost unaltered for hundreds of millions of years.

Popper-Wehner

Popper-Wehner

The Komodo Dragon lives on the island of Komodo in the Sunda Archipelago. Up to 10 feet long, he looks like a successor of the legendary monsters of old, a chance survival in the present-day world ...

Riedel

The lyre-bird is a rare creature of Australia. Despite his resemblance to a pheasant, he belongs among the singing birds. He builds his nest on the ground.

In the coastal districts of New Guinea, the vast island to the north of Australia, the lovely birds of paradise have been practically exterminated. However, several varieties still flourish in the high-lying tropical forests of the interior. (Pictured here: a Greater bird of paradise.)

Wissenbach

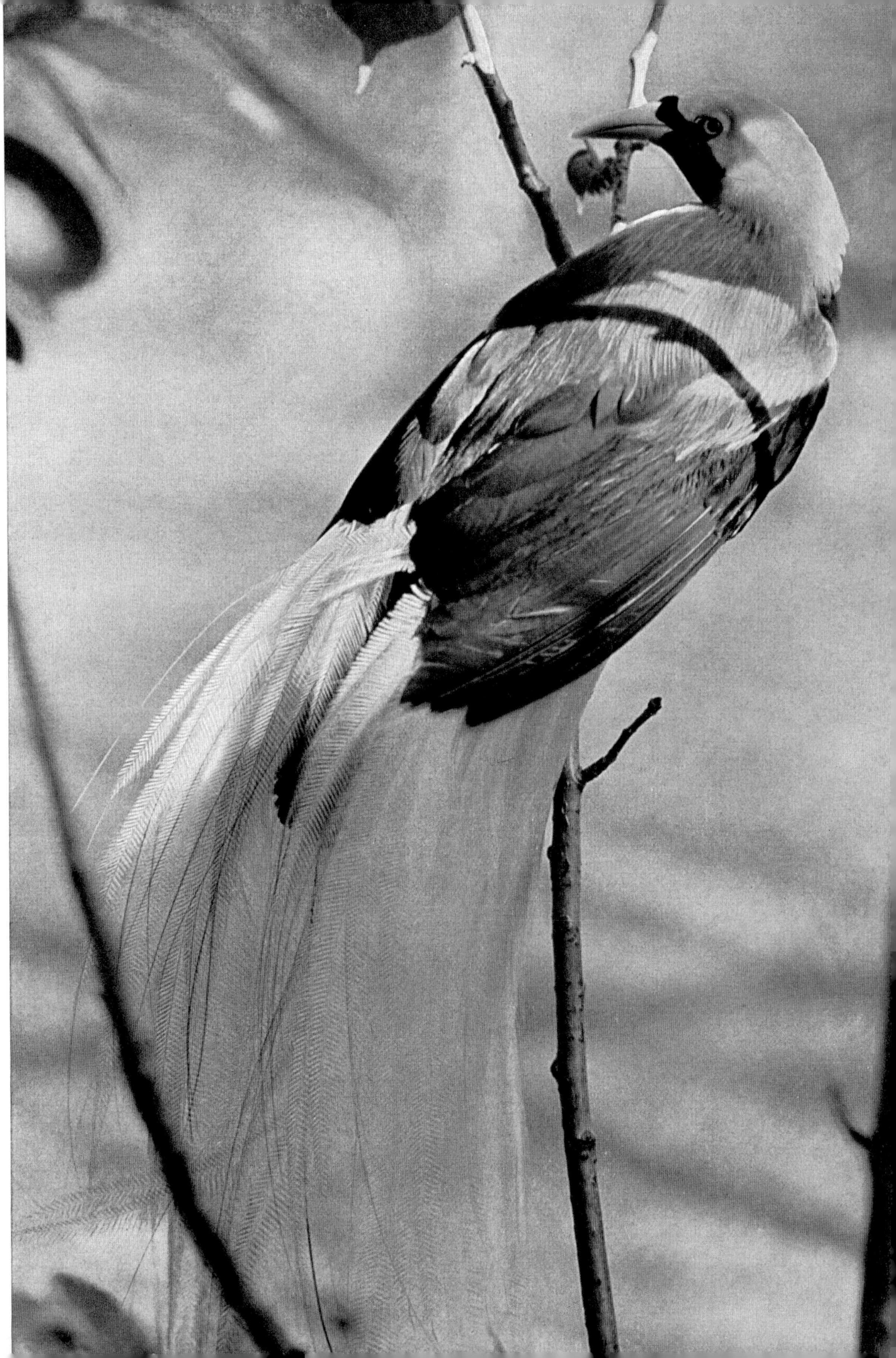

Australian Information Bureau

The herbivorous kangaroo is the only native representative in Australia of the smaller ruminants, since no "modern" mammals were to be found in that continent until imported from elsewhere. Pictured: grey Great kangaroos.

The young of these pouched animals are born after surprisingly short period of gestation, by no means fully formed. Not until several months have elapsed do they leave the mother's pouch.

Australian Information Bureau

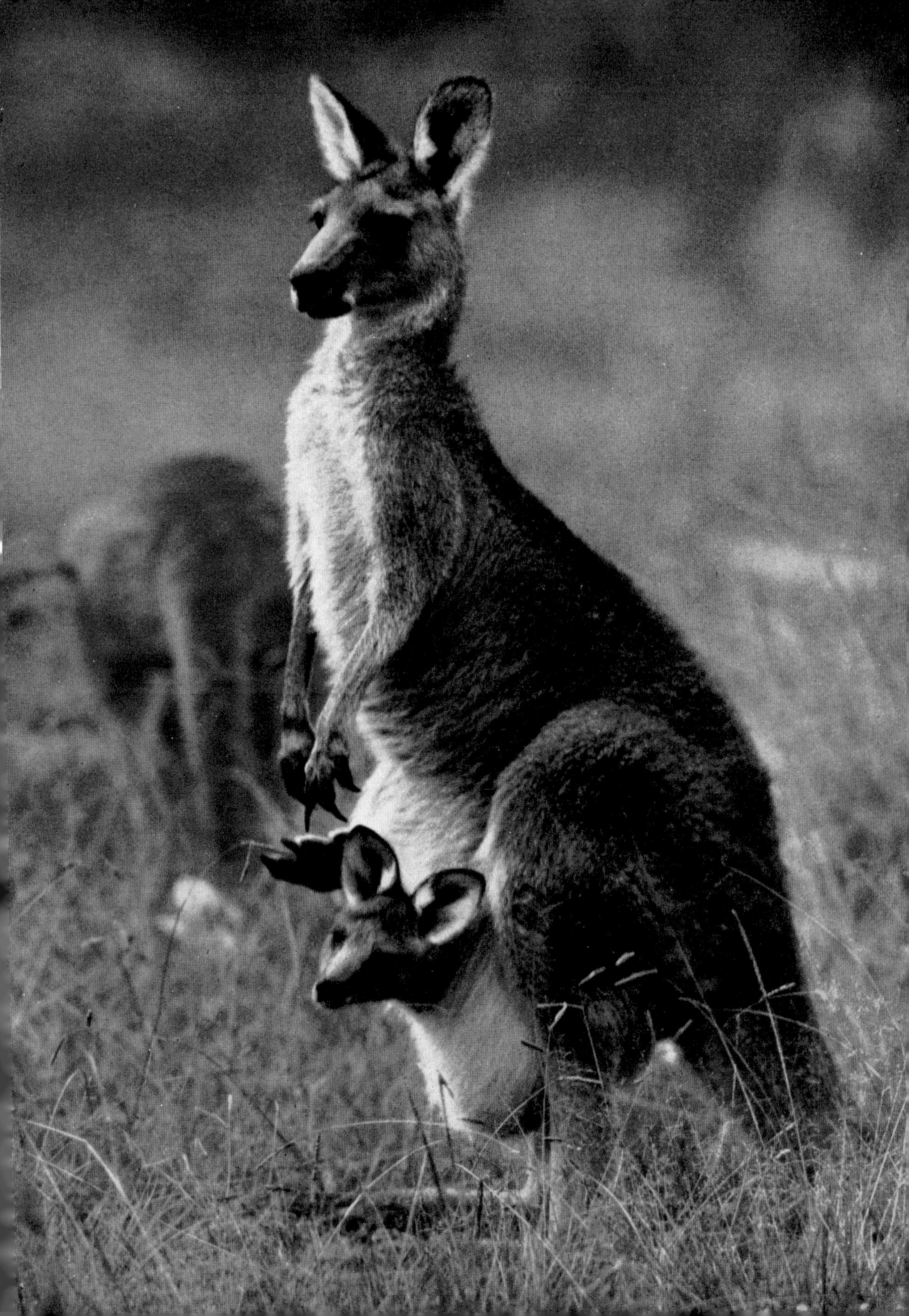

Left: Like so many other ancient species, the strange wingless kiwi of New Zealand, a member of the ostrich family, is in danger of dying out.

Below: Among creatures still extant in the world the "living fossil" of Australia, the duck-billed platypus, has a place all of its own. The female lays eggs, but then feeds her young with milk.

Right-hand page, above: The favourite habitat of the tiger is the jungle.

Right-hand page, below: The Indian rhinoceros, with the folds of its thick hide giving it the appearance of armour plating, was formerly to be found in all the valleys of north-eastern India. By the end of the 19th century it was practically extinct, and only about a dozen survivors were living in what is now the Kaziranga Reserve. Today, thanks to strict protective measures, the stock has increased to some two hundred and fifty.

Australian Inforation Bureau

Popper-Wehner

Photos: E. P. Gee

*Left: A muntjak (Asiatic deer) in an Indian game reserve.
Below: A herd of gaur in a mountain forest clearing.*

E. P. Gee

E. P.

Eugen Schuhmacher

Above: The largest bird capable of flying is the mighty condor, a vulture of the South-American Andes. *Right:* The red-billed colibri in this picture is one of the "larger" of the enchanting South American humming birds, although he is smaller than a gold-crested wren. His relation the "bumble-bee colibri" is the smallest of all birds.

Wissenbach

Photos: Popper-Wehner

Above: Penguins are admirably suited to life in the water. Their feathers are like the scales of a fish, and their wings serve as fins. It is still possible to see colonies of thousands on the Falkland Islands near the southern-most tip of the American continent (shown in this picture). *Below:* The two-toed sloth or unau is a woodland animal found in the tropical forests of South America. He seldom descends to the ground. A creature of very little intelligence, he nevertheless moves with stealth and care.

Right above: The great ant-eater is undoubtedly one of the most remarkable of animals. *Right, below:* Sea-elephants like to lie on beaches. Their diet consists of fish, shell-fish, cuttle-fish and seaweed.

photos: Eugen Schuhmacher

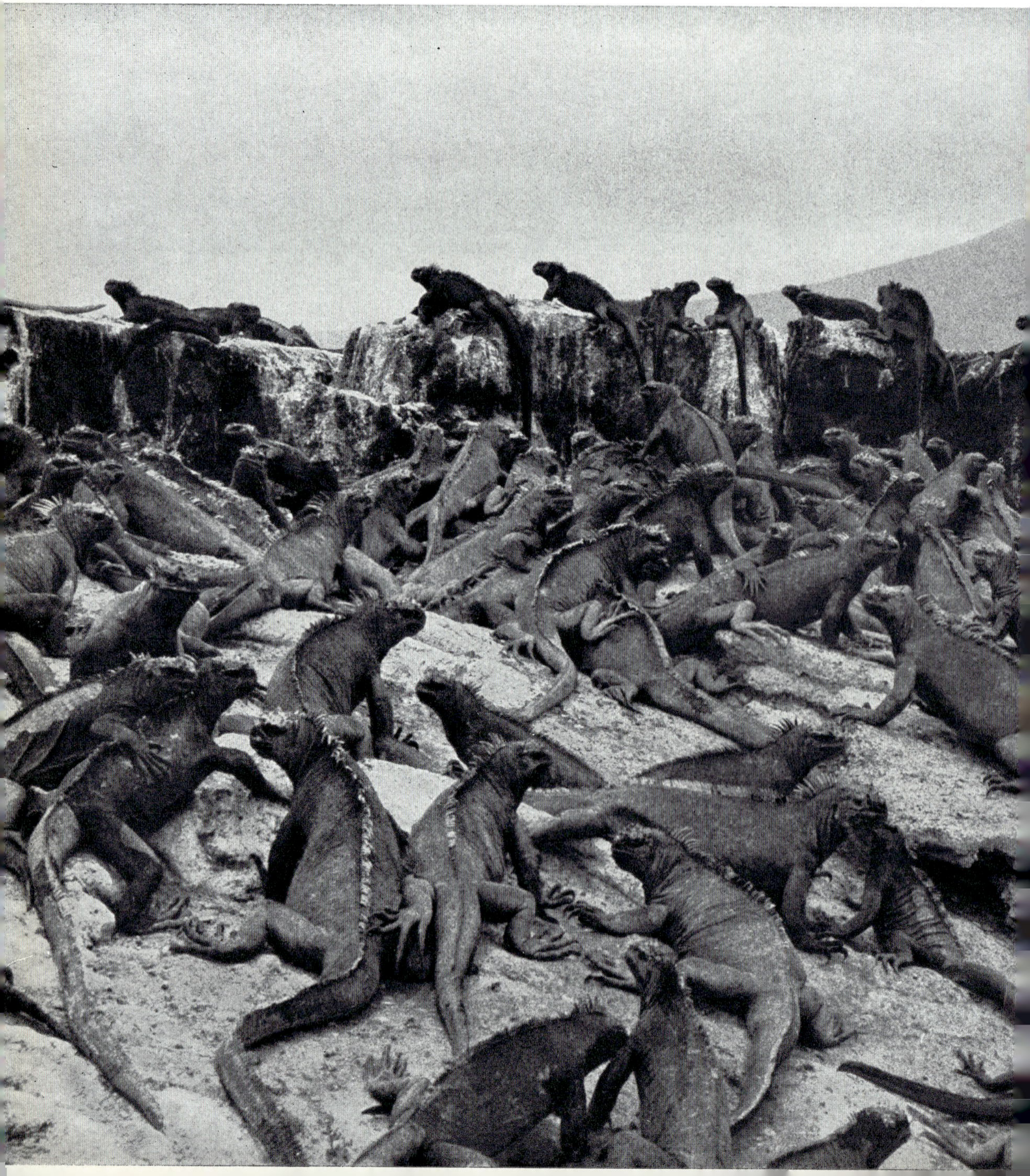

Photos: Dr. J. Eibl v. Eibesfeldt

Above: The volcanic islands of the Galapagos Archipelago have very little vegetation over large areas.

Left: This assembly of Galapagos marine iguanas looks like a scene at the dawn of history!

Pampaluchi-Bavaria

The most graceful of the llama family, the Vicuña, inhabits the grasslands of the Peruvian and Bolivian Andes. As these creatures, related to the sheep and the camel, are already rare, it is forbidden to export them. The young Vicuña can run faster than a man as soon as it is two days old.

Dr. J. Eibl von Eibesfeldt

Male Galapagos marine iguanas.

The Galapa[gos]
buzzard kn[ows]
nothing of [man]
as the wors[t]
enemy of w[ild]
creatures, s[o it]
can almost [be]
touched, an[d]
even fed by
hand, like a
tame bird.

The giant Galapagos tortoise is almost extinct.

Photos: Dr. J. Eibl v. Eibesfeldt

Dr. J. Eibl v. Eibesfeldt

The Galapagos cormorant has lost its ability to fly.

U. S. I. S.

The American armadillo is the tortoise among mammals. He can roll himself into a defensive ball, and is then well protected by his armour plating. (Picture from Texas.)

The American alligator has been hunted so extensively for his hide that many of the surviving specimens are now protected in farms. The pike alligator (pictured in Florida) lives mainly on fish.

American J. S. B.

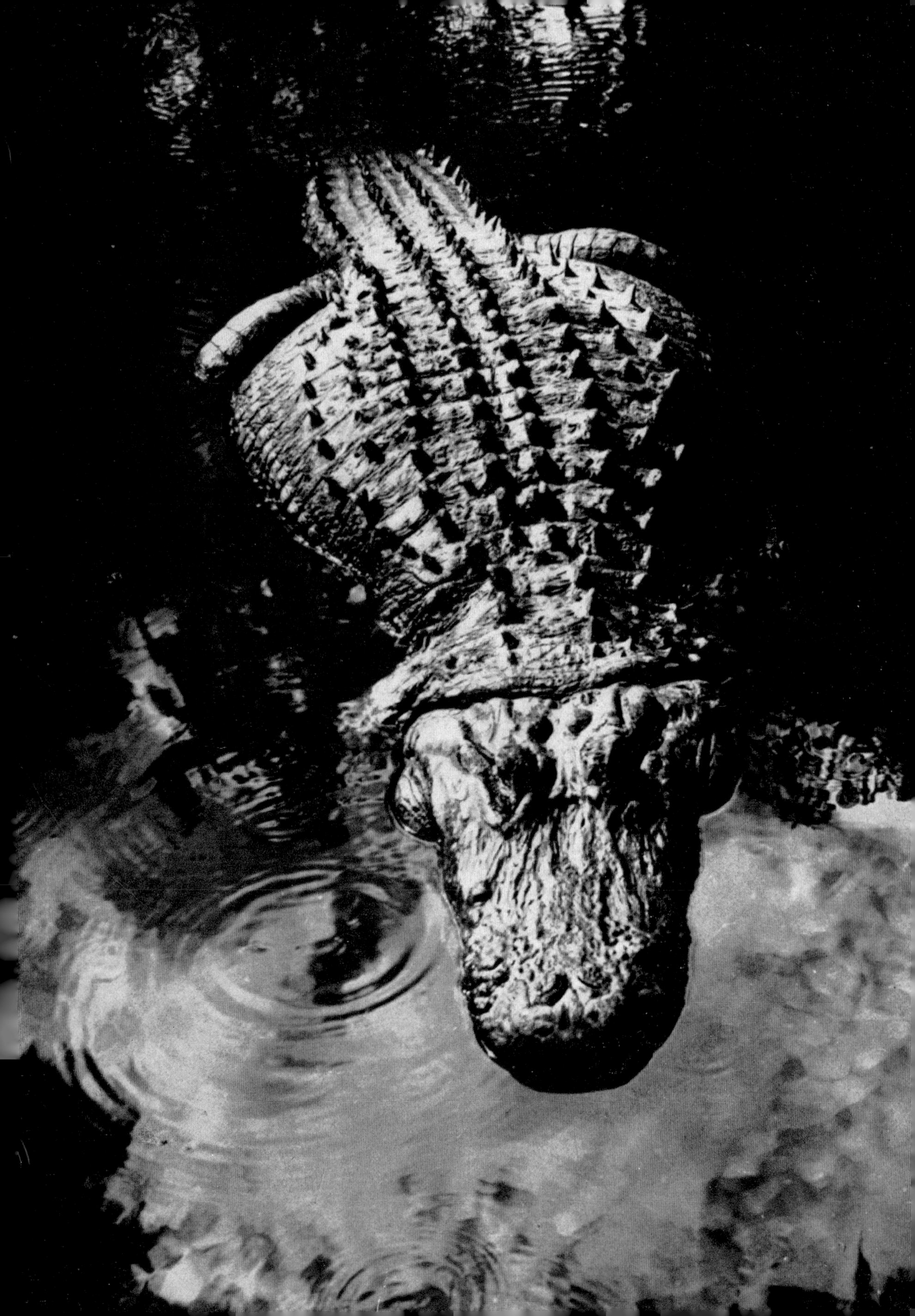

E. P. Haddon, U. S. Fish and Wildlife Service

The puma, or silver lion, was formerly to be found in both Americas to as far south as Patagonia. He is now practically extinct, even in areas where he once abounded.

E. P. Haddon. U.S. Fish and Wildlife Service

The prairie wolf of the new world corresponds to the jackal of the old. From time immemorial the coyote has followed herds of larger animals, seizing for food those that lag behind on account of age or sickness. (Picture from Colorado.)

Photos: L. M. Chace

Action pictures of the American great horned owl. In the north and in high-lying forests this breed still flourishes, while in Europe the great horned owl is no more than a memory in the annals of natural history. This bird requires large expanses of quiet woods, and is an enemy of civilization. Above: Taking off. Right-hand page: In flight (above) and alighting (below).

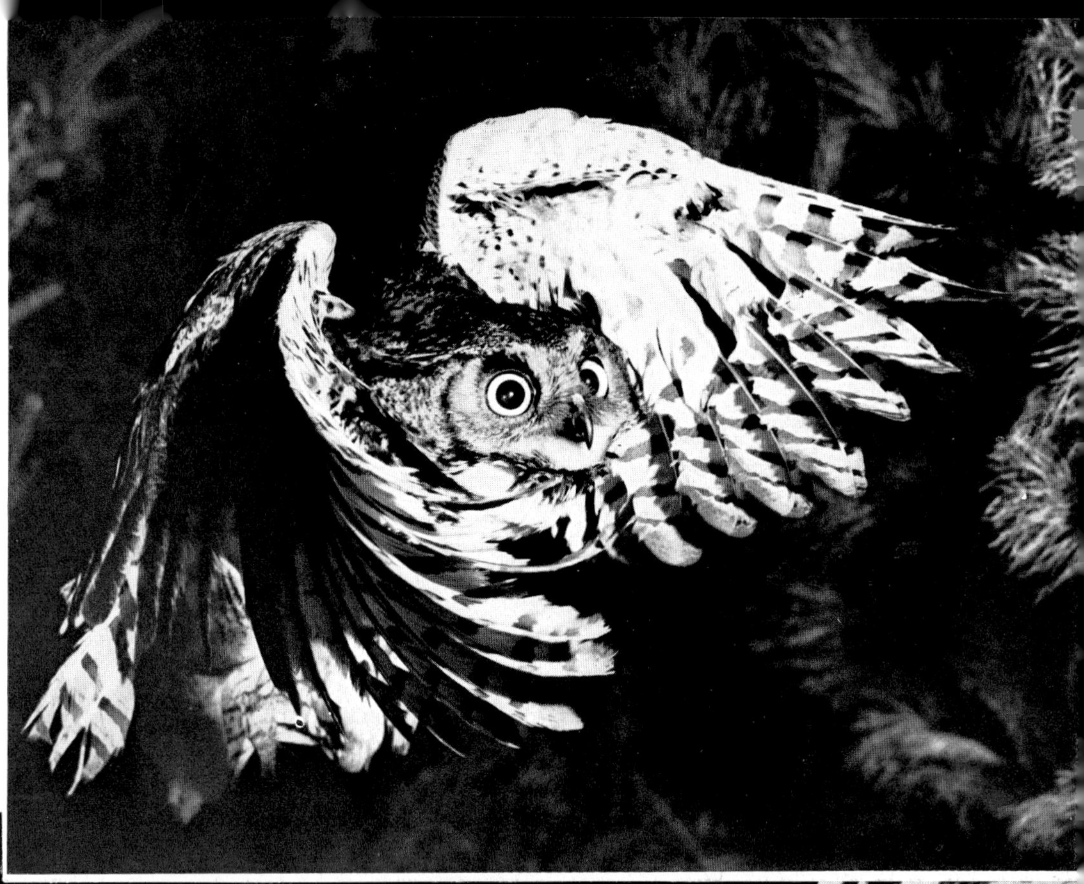

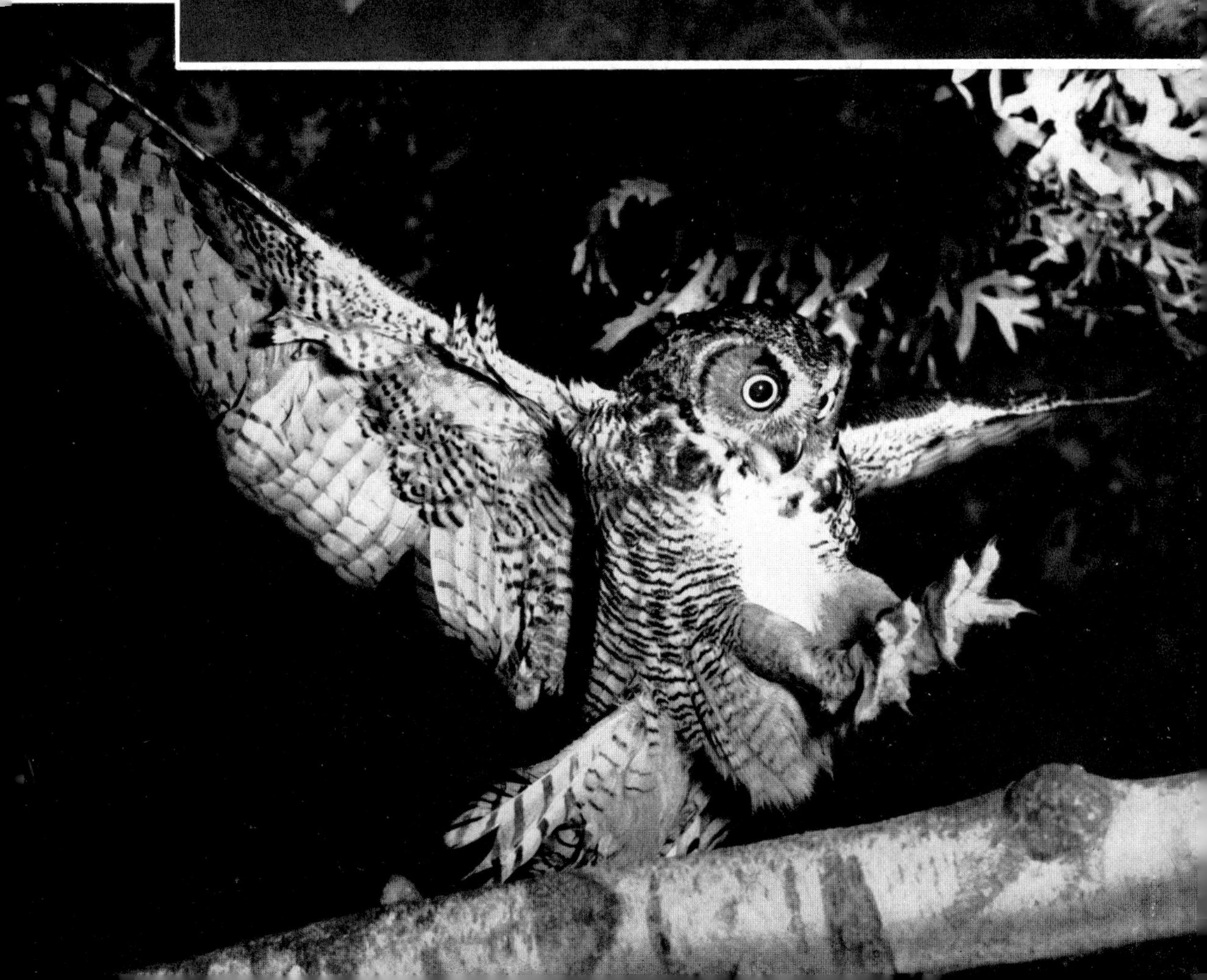

E. P. Haddon, U.S. Fish and Wildlife Service

The mightiest member of the deer family is the American wapiti. (Photo: National Elk Range, Jackson, Wyoming.) Vast herds of wapiti are a thing of the past, but thanks to effective conservation, together with the creature's natural adaptability, there is no danger that this noble beast will become extinct.

Ancient Douglas firs of enormous height in the Olympia National Park (State of Washington, USA). This tree from the American Pacific coastal area is also valuable to Europe, owing to its ability to grow to vast proportions.

U.S. Nat. Park Service

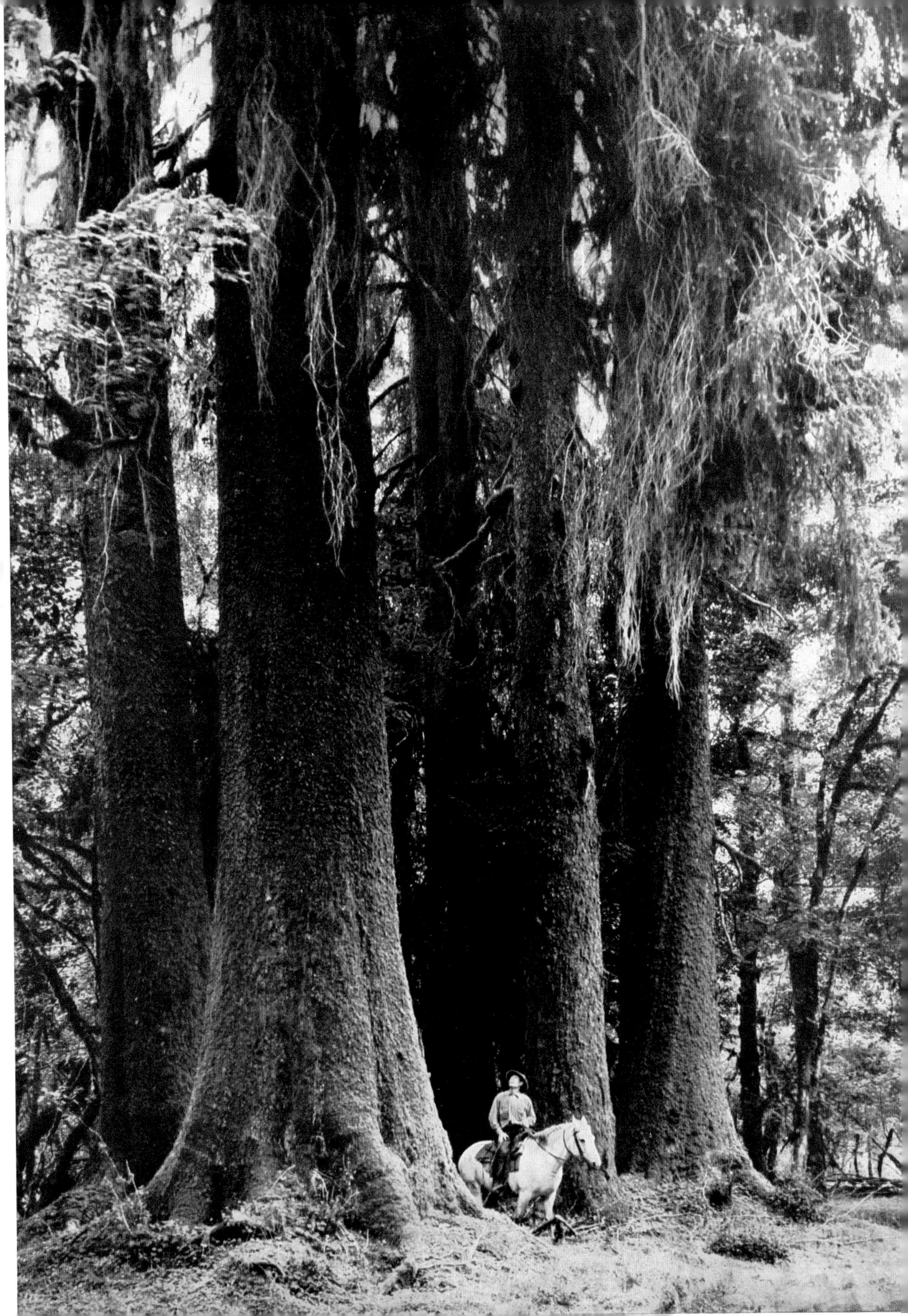

E. P. Haddon, U.S. Fish and Wildlife Service

At the last moment the American bison was saved from complete annihilation. Today the protected herds contain an occasional white specimen, an indication that they are becoming domesticated. (Mission Valley, Montana.)

The herds of bison, the mighty North American buffalo, were once numbered in millions, ranging over the rich grazing lands of the prairies, and providing the means of life for all the Indian tribes.

U. S. I. S.

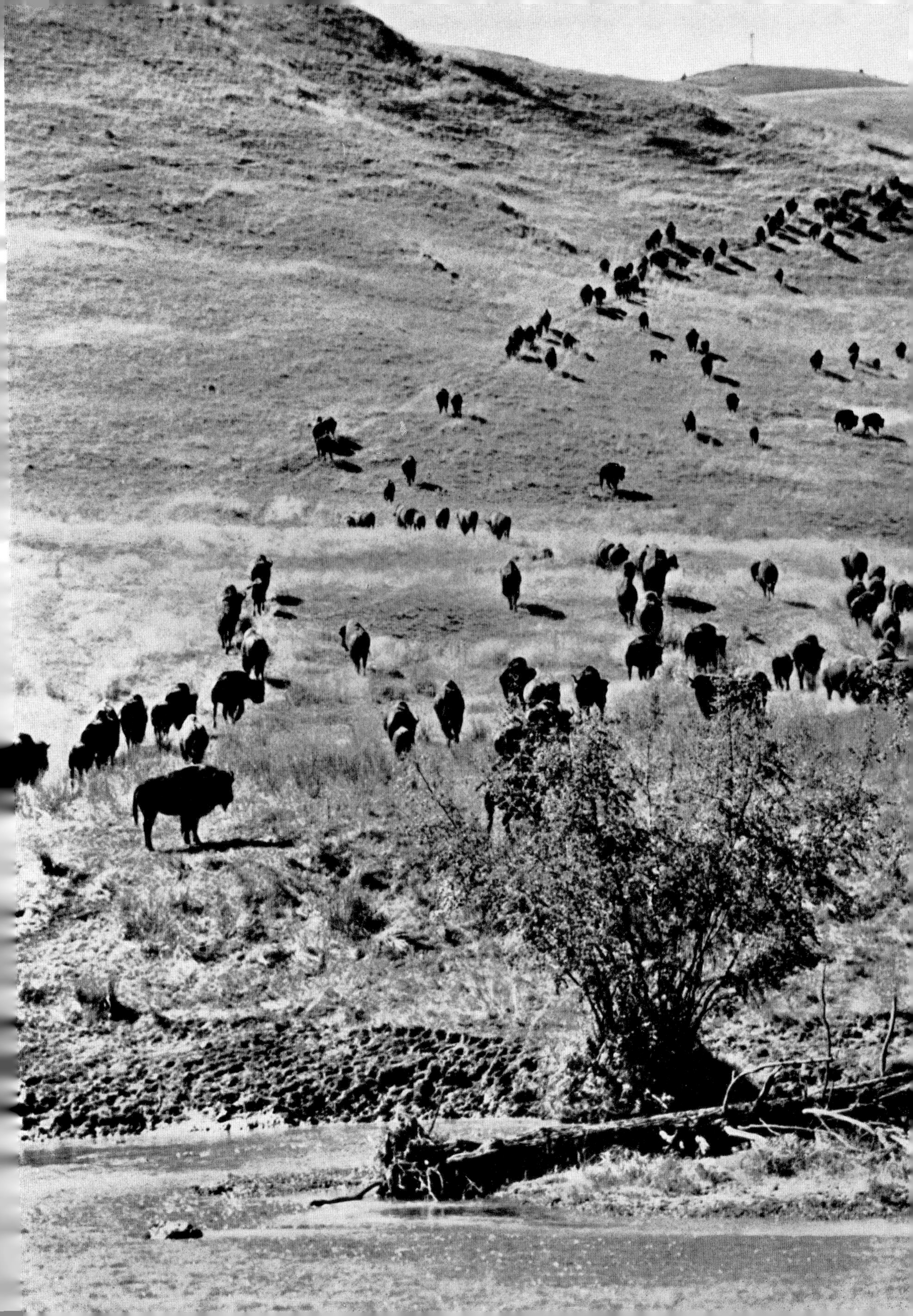

Tenn. Cons. Dept.-Ullstein

The little black bear or baribal is only about 4½ ft. long, and is one of the most harmless of the bear family. In the American National Parks he has lost all his shyness in the presence of human beings.

A mother black bear with her children at play.

National Film Board, Canada

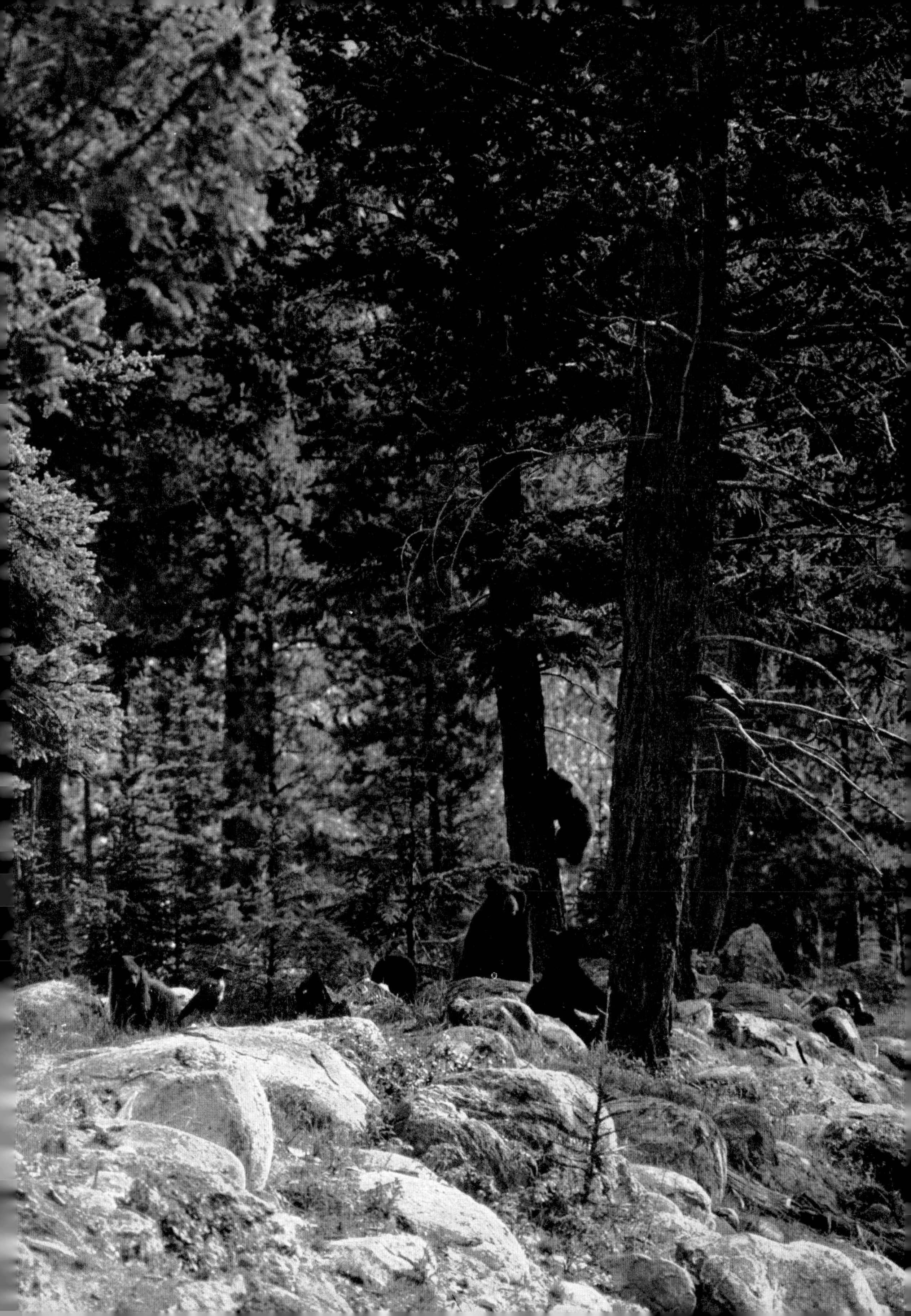

Popper-Wehner

Until the middle ages the beaver was common everywhere in the northern hemisphere. Today numbers have been greatly diminished even in North America, where beaver pelts once formed the basis of the Canadian fur trade.

The Alaskan bear, the world's largest beast of prey, fishing for salmon.

Dr. Arthur Lindgens

Right: The massive grizzly bear of the western parts of America is far larger and stronger than the black bear, also proving far more dangerous. (Pictured in Yellowstone National Park.)

Nat. Park Service - Ullstein

The elk, once common in Europe and America, has almost disappeared in its free state in Europe, but is still to be found in large numbers in the USA, and to an even greater extent in Canada and Alaska.

Helen Fischer

Helen Fischer

The most powerful of the stag family, the elk is a creature of almost primeval majesty. Old bull elks can attain a weight of more than 1,000 lbs. (Both photos from Banff National Park, Canada.)

Canad. Govt. Travel Bureau

There still flourish among the scarcely accessible mountain crags of North America several breeds of bighorn sheep. (Shown here in Jasper National Park, Canada.) The ram can weigh as much as 385 lbs., his massive horns alone tipping the scales at more than 55 lbs.

The snowy goat shares the habitat and the lot of the bighorn sheep. However, this creature, native to the remotest areas of the Rocky Mountains, receives a greater measure of protection.

Eugen Schuhmacher

The impressive, shaggy musk-ox is accustomed to near-arctic conditions. When danger threatens, these beasts cluster together to form a defensive wall or a "porcupine" with the calves in the middle.

Vitalis Pantenburg

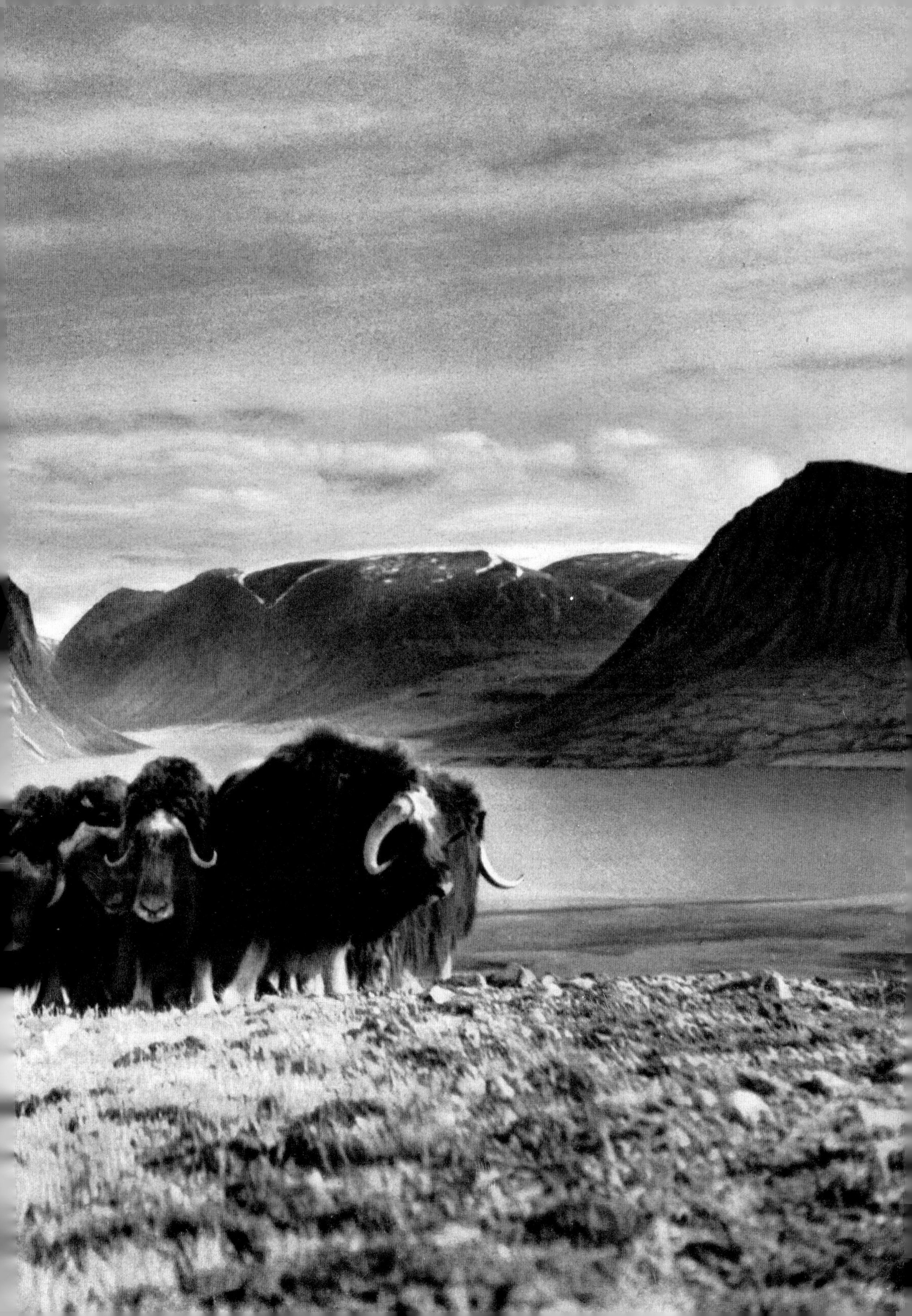

Alwin Pedersen

The cumbersome walrus, one of the largest members of the seal family, attains a weight of up to 2,200 lbs. and a length of 14 ft. Nowadays he is found only in the extreme north, although until the late middle ages he was frequently to be seen on the Scottish coast. Seal hunters of former times took a fearful toll of these great creatures.

The polar bear of the far north seldom comes into contact with man. He is still to be found over vast areas of land, but nowhere in large numbers. He lives mainly on seals of all kinds, together with fish. He is at home both on land and in the water.

Vitalis Pantenburg

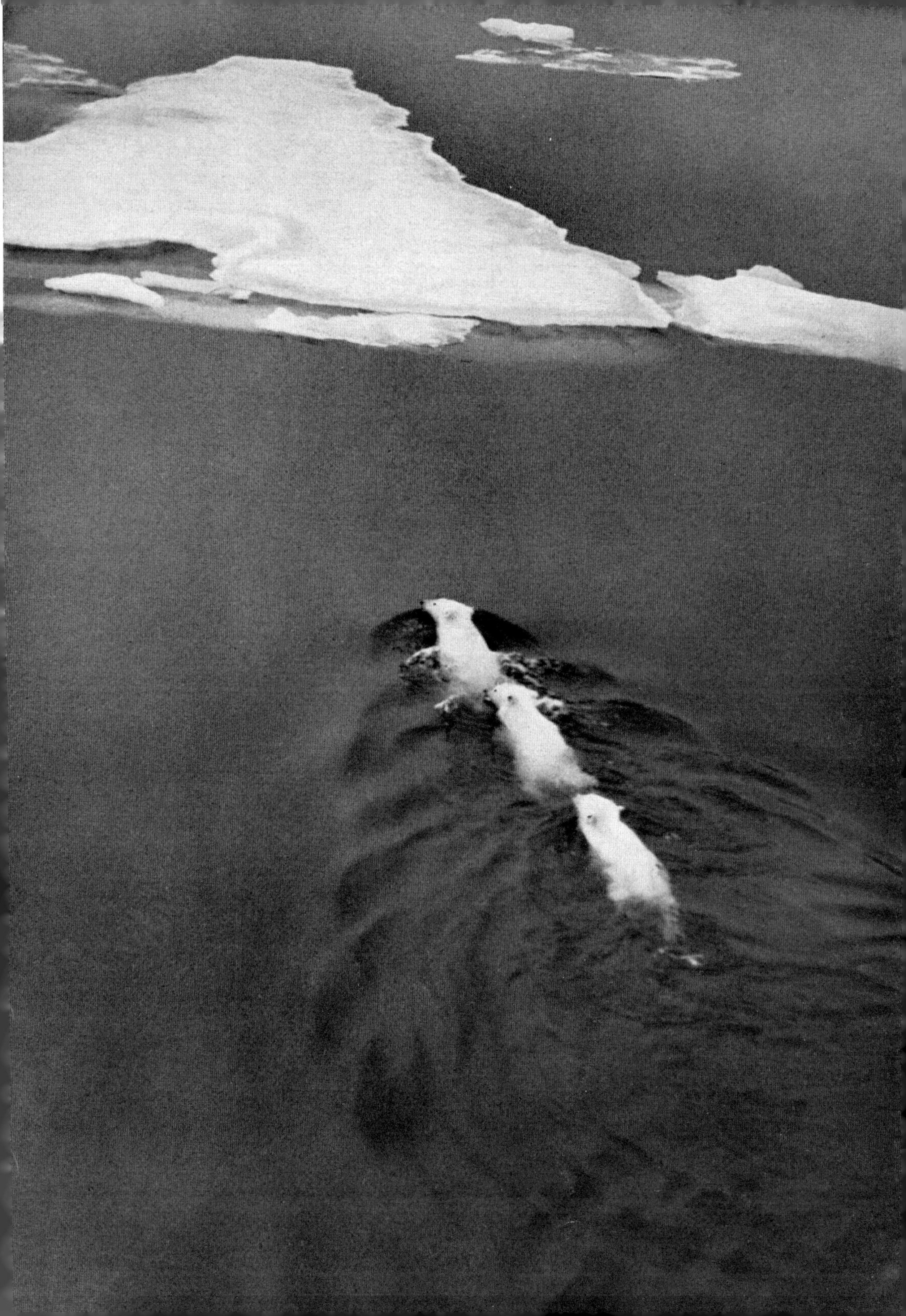

Popper-Web

Above: It was only comparatively recently that the Wedd seal, which lives in the wastes Antarctica, came to the not of Europeans. However, o discovered, large numbers these creatures were s slaughtered. *Below*: The seal or sea dog has, in its ea years, a white or light-colou coat.

Alwin Pedersen

Right: Arctic ursine seals, male and female.
Below: During the mating season great numbers of fur-seals come ashore on the lonely Pribilov Islands off the coast of Alaska, then each bull collects a harem of cows around him. When a fight breaks out between bulls they frequently inflict dangerous wounds.

Photos: Popper-Wehner

Contax-Foto: Walter Hege

A herd of red-deer stags swimming across a bay in the Scottish Highlands.

Right-hand page: Aerial photographs of a herd of wild reindeer, which are still to be seen in thousands on the Dovre-Fjell Plateau in Norway, and which sometimes entice tame reindeer back to the wilds.

Billed-Wehr

Gillsäter

The wolverine, or "glutton", a creature of the far north, is not related to the wolf as its name suggests, but to the marten. It lives mainly on berries, lemmings, birds it can catch on the ground, and a wide variety of small creatures.

During the middle ages the lynx lived in many mountainous areas of central Europe, the Harz Mountains, the Bohemian Forests, the Vosges and Switzerland.

Gillsäter

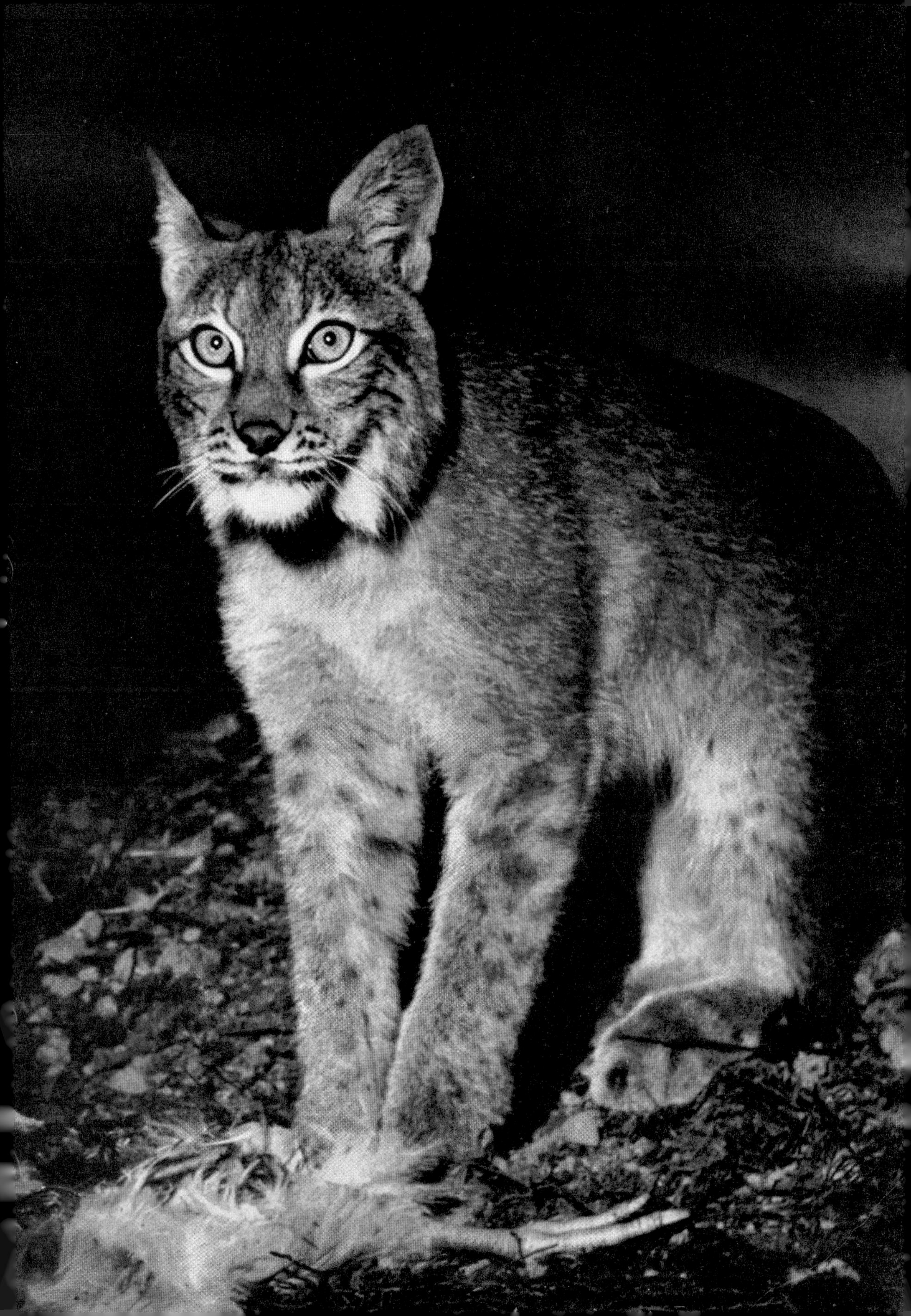

U.S.S.R. Nature Conservation Authority

In the endless wastes of Russia grey wolves still abound. During hard winters a few of these animals travel westward, sometimes even as far as central Germany, where wolves were common until the middle ages. (Photo from a Russian wild-life conservation area.)

U.S.S.R. Nature Conservation Authority

Until recent times the mounds and dams of the beaver were features of the landscape in the river valleys of Europe. Today the European beaver is only to be found in any large numbers in Norway and Russia. (Photo from a Russian wild-life conservation area.)

During the mating season the male fighting snipe wears a ruffle of feathers round his neck. This serves as a shield during his harmless mock-battles. (Picture from the Polish nature conservation district, Bialowiez.)

Puchalski

Puchalski

The badger is one of the world's few beasts of prey to rest in the winter. This rather plodding walker is a cousin to the agile marten. (Picture from the nature conservation area of Niepolomice, Poland.)

Above: A herd of stags passing by on a misty morning. *Below:* Thanks to the devoted efforts of European zoologists the European bison, Europe's largest animal of the cattle class, was saved from extinction at the last moment. The survival of this splendid beast now seems assured.

Photos: Dr. Arthur Lindgens

Dr. Arthur Lindgens

During the summer period of intensive feeding, stags – male deer – keep company in bachelor herds ("stag parties"). Only at the beginning of the mating season, early in September, do they part company. The stag is the proudest member of the deer family.

Among the larger wild animals the stag has been the most successful in coming to terms with civilization, thanks to his foresight, and the prolificacy of the breed.

Dr. Arthur Lindgens

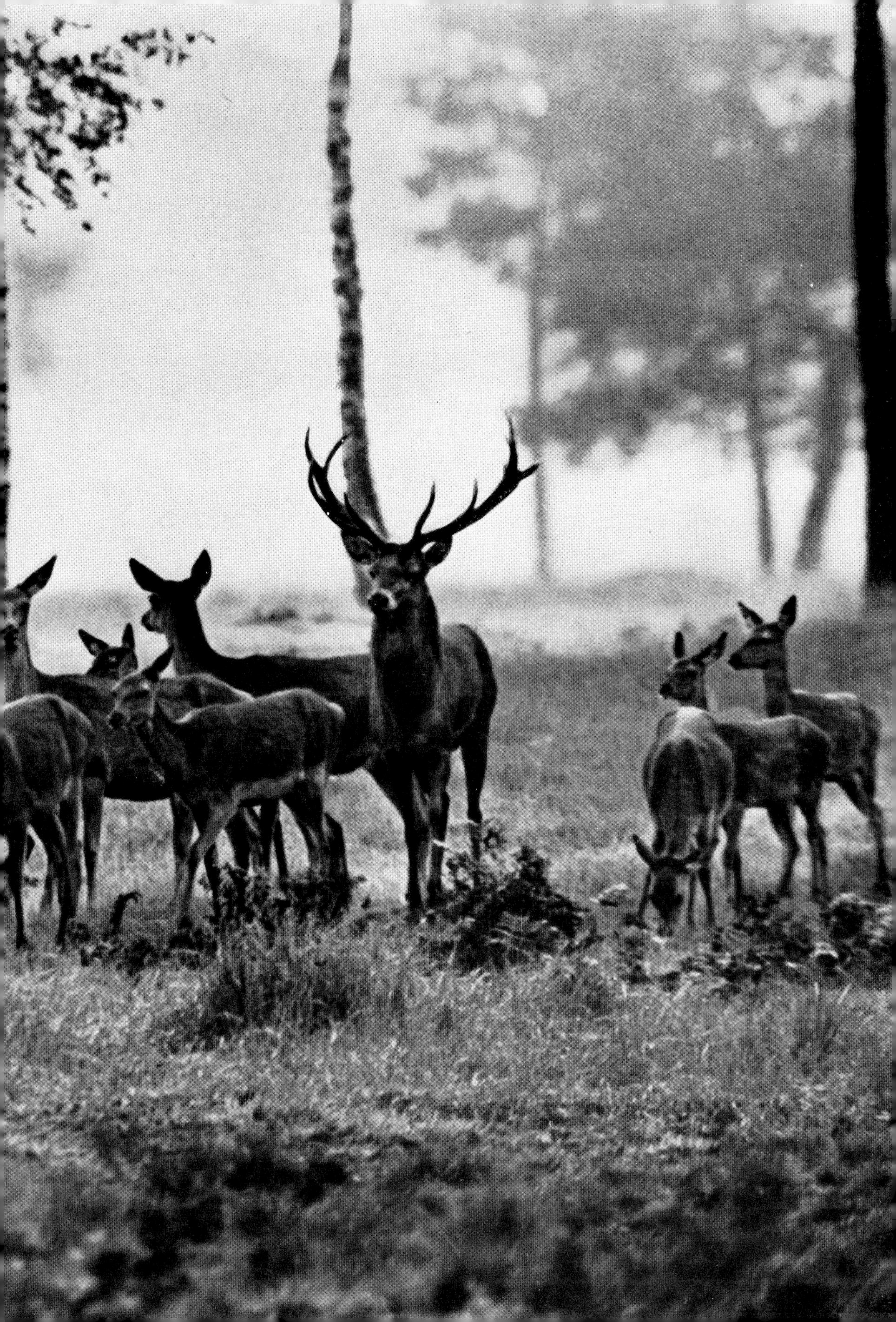

Dr. Arthur Lindgens

Playful so-called mock battles between males during their summer period as bachelors precede the real duels of the rutting season. When they fight in earnest the weaker combatant is torn to pieces by his opponent's antlers, unless he escapes in time.

Day and night during the mating season the male jealously watches the coming and going of the rest of the herd. He prowls tirelessly round the females, emitting his battle cry.

Leica Photo: J. Rödle

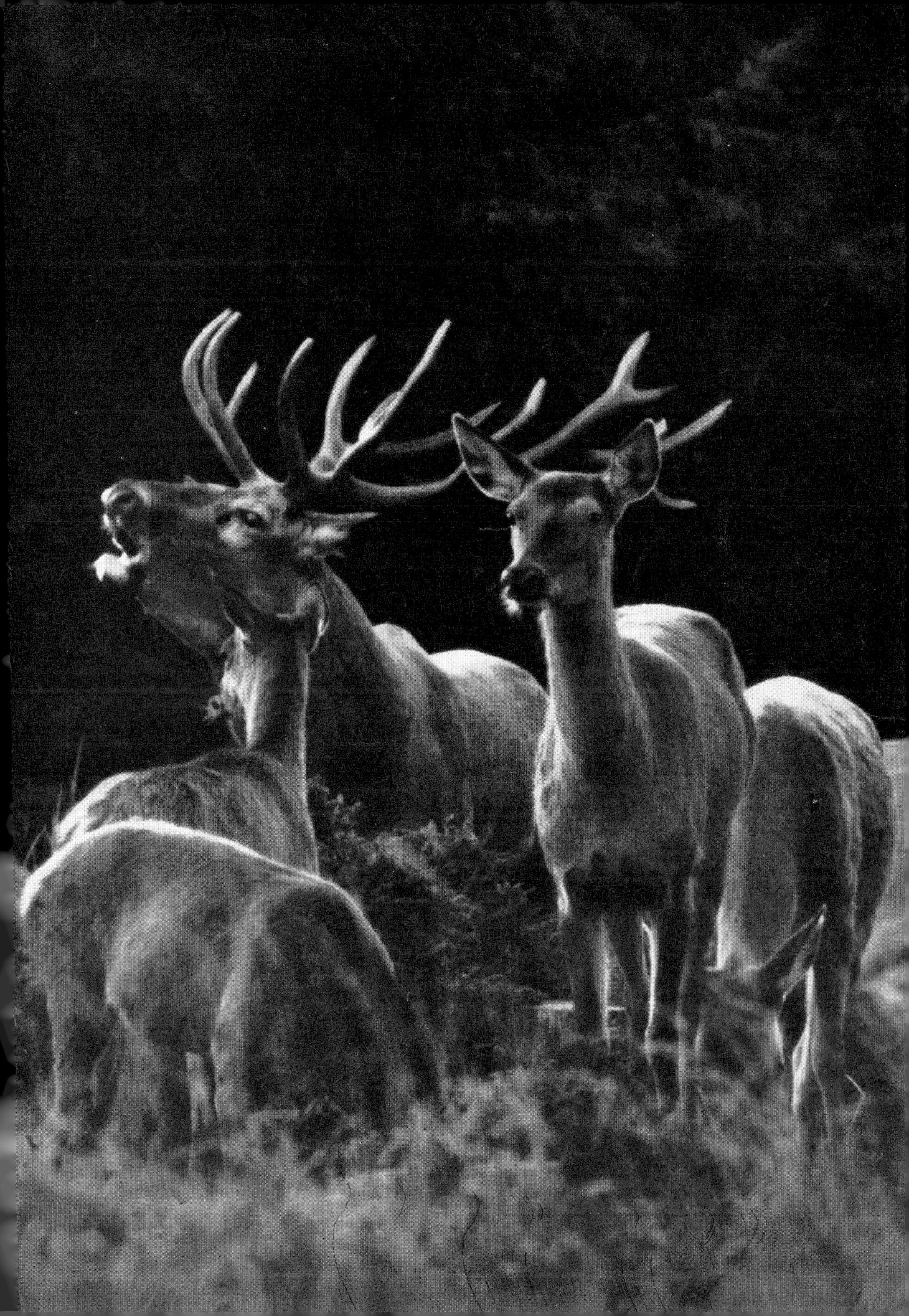

Feuerstein-Scuol

Above: This fawn bears the white markings of most young deer. The patches correspond to the light and shade of the undergrowth in which it shelters. *Right-hand page:* The "sixfold antler" is the most elaborate generally to be found on European roe-deer.

J. Rö

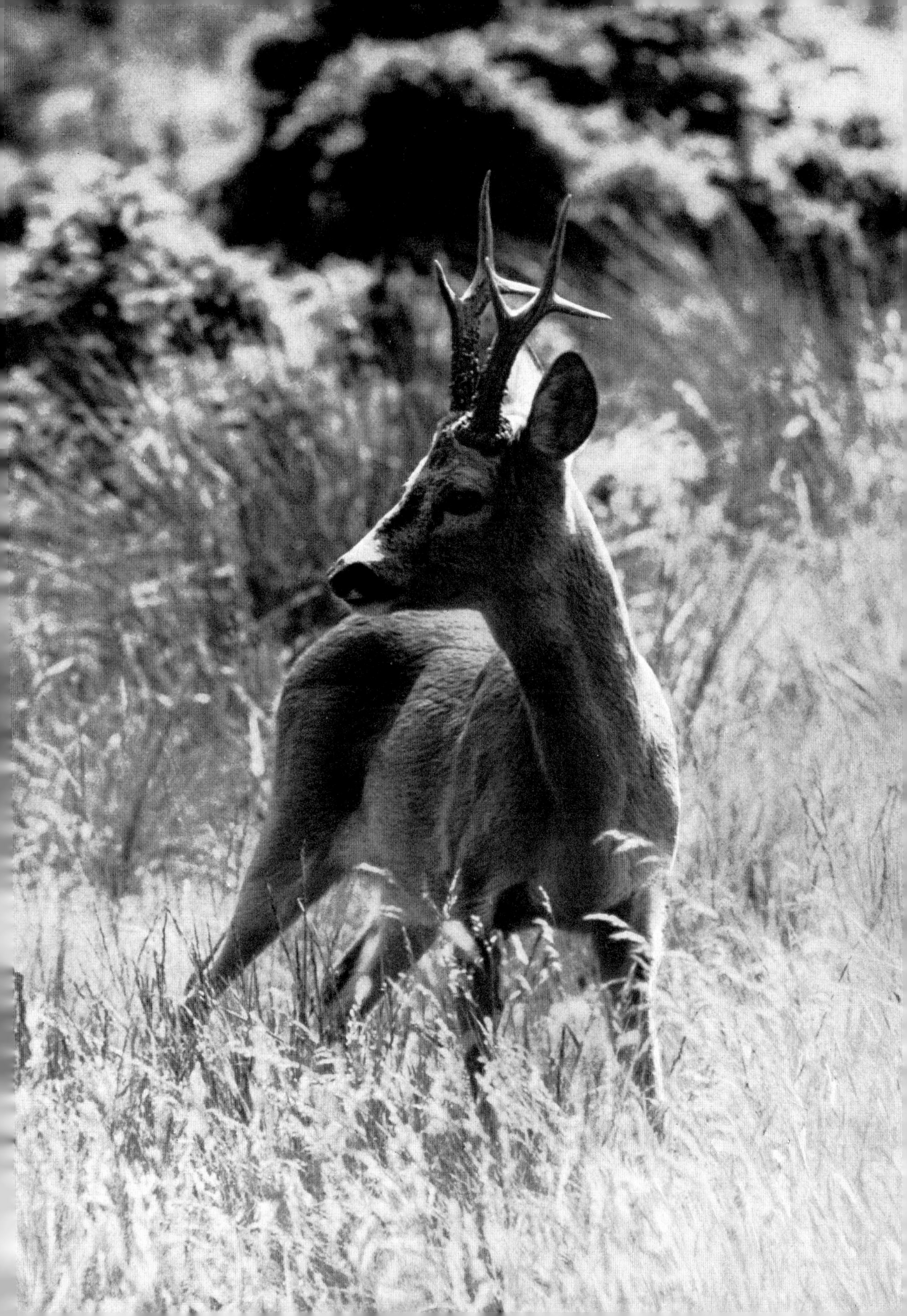

Feuerstein-Scuol

The Swiss National Park encompasses an enchantingly lovely part of the Lower Engadin. Nature among high peaks is there preserved unspoilt by man.

Plattner-Pedrett

The bouquetin, or Alpine ibex, a bold mountaineer, came near to extinction. However, timely protective measures and the skilful movement of stock to the most suitable areas have ensured the survival of this proud Alpine beast.

Pictures on this page: The Alpine marmot hibernates during the winter. At high altitudes this rodent often has to remain in his burrow for more than half the year. At one time he was hunted for his flesh and fat, but today he enjoys protection in certain areas of the Alps.

Photos: Otto Färber

In June and July the Alaska bear, the world's largest beast of prey, fishes with amazing dexterity for salmon which have left the ocean and are swimming up the rivers to spawn.

Dr. Arthur Lindgens

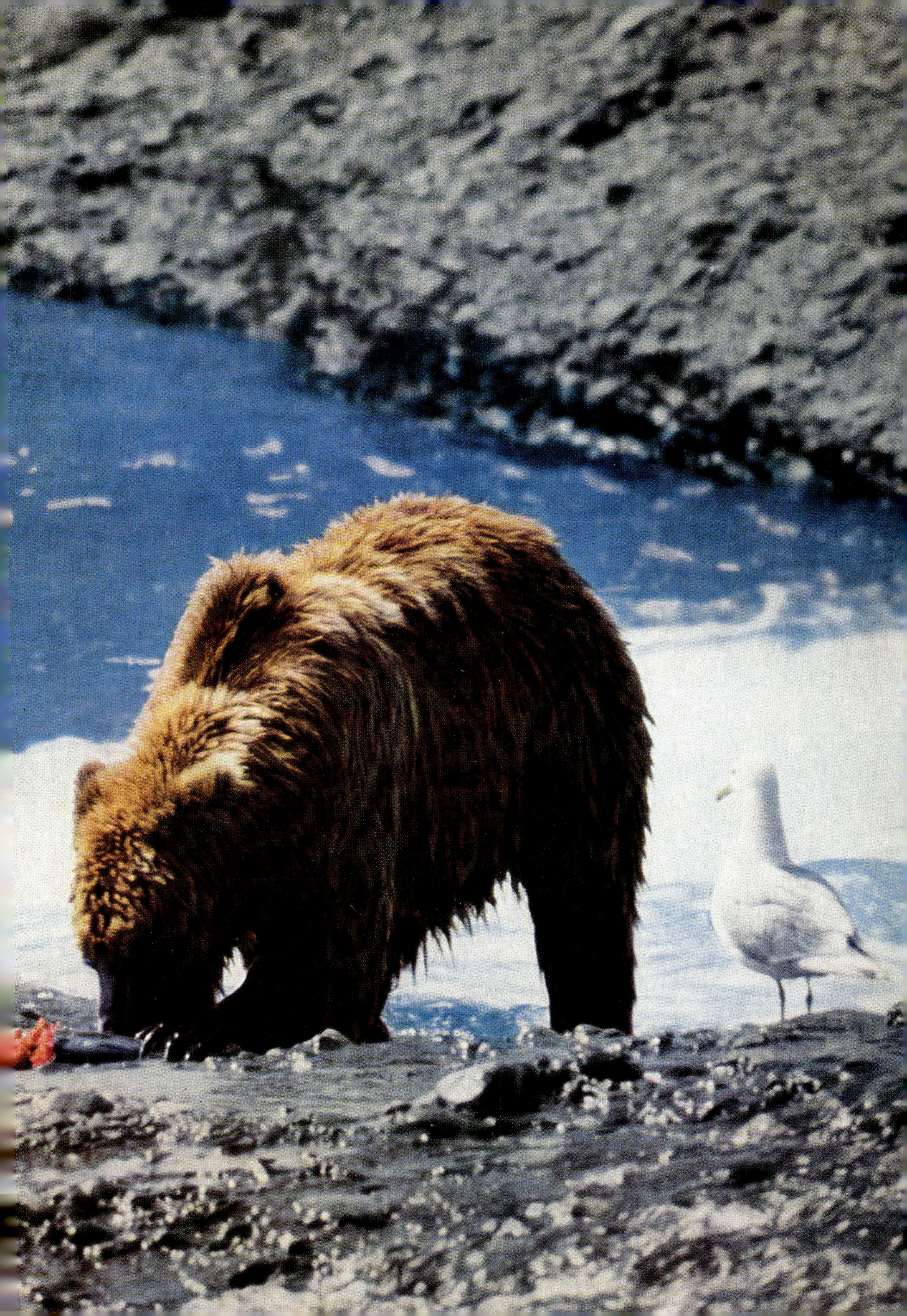

A bou
in t
Alp

Otto

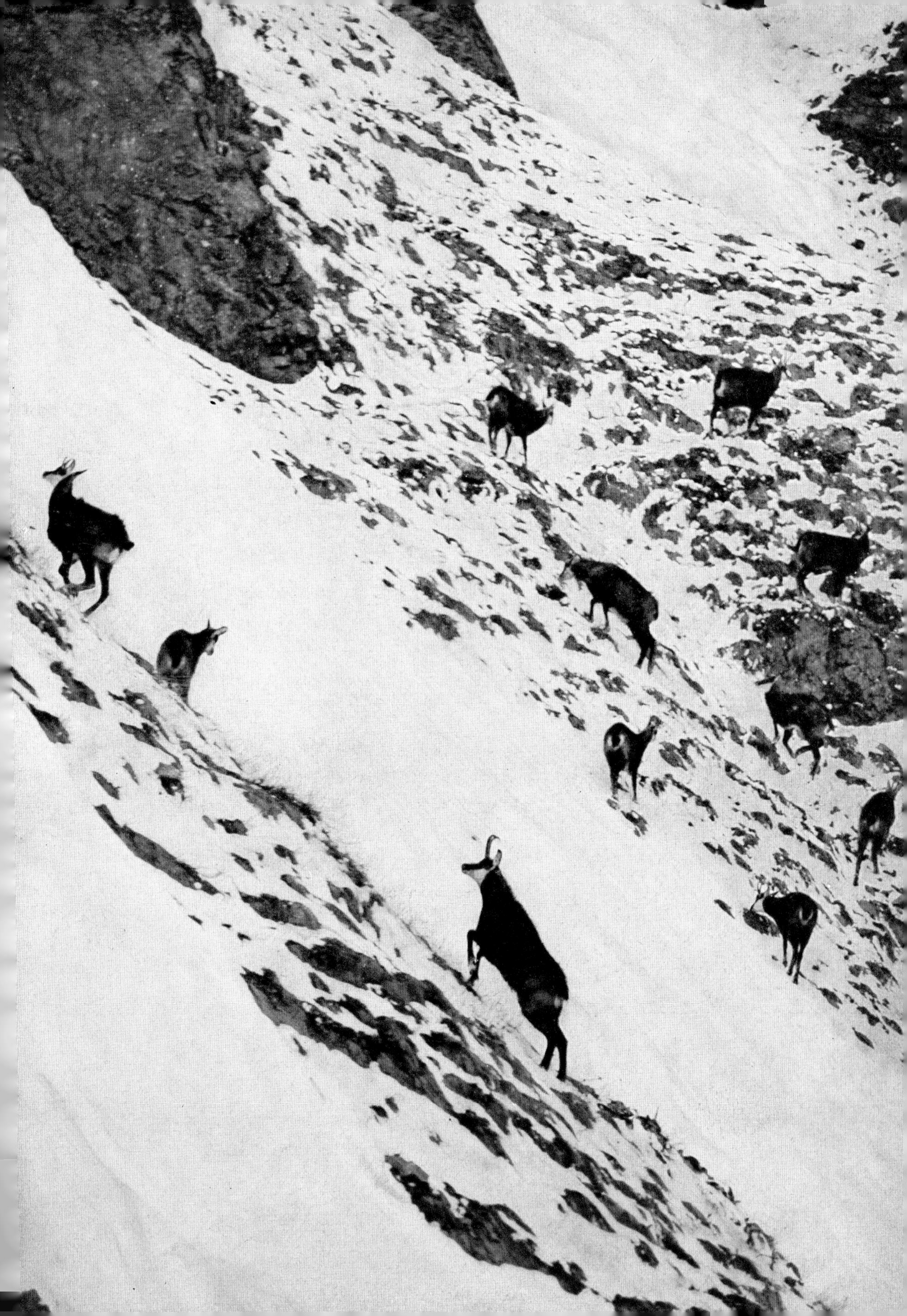

Feuerstein-Scuol

Among all carnivorous animals the cunning fox has been the most successful in surviving the impact of civilization. Inborn mistrust, and fecundity, have probably assured him of a permanent place in the wild life of Europe.

On page 133:
The chamois, a thoroughgoing mountaineer, is to be found only on high peaks, except that some have recently been re-introduced into the Black Forest. Sensible conservation measures have resulted in the fact that fairly large numbers now flourish in the Alps.

Feuerstein-Scuol

J. Rödle

The fox has been unjustly suspected of robbery on an intolerable scale. The male fox lives mainly on mice, only the vixen, who has to provide for a large number of offspring, also carrying off farm poultry. But for foxes the prey of the hunter would be left to rot, for they are the sanitary police of the woods.

All photos: Dr. Arthur Lindgens

Above: Bustards, long-legged birds the size of turkeys, avoid woodland. Their real homeland is on the plains of eastern Europe, but they are also to be found on large expanses of arable land in central Europe. Vast numbers once lived near Berlin and in the area around Erfurt. Almost extinct since the war, strict protection measures have ensured that they have again increased in numbers. *Below:* The capercailzie, moorhen, black cock and white grouse are four species of fowl once common in Europe, but now restricted to a few areas. Only the moorhen is still sometimes to be seen on moors and heaths. There, in the early spring, they perform their fascinating pairing dances. *Right-hand page:* When this heath cock begins his antics winter and spring are still vying for supremacy. At daybreak the cock sings his love song on the branch of a tree; when the sun has risen higher he begins his dance on the ground.

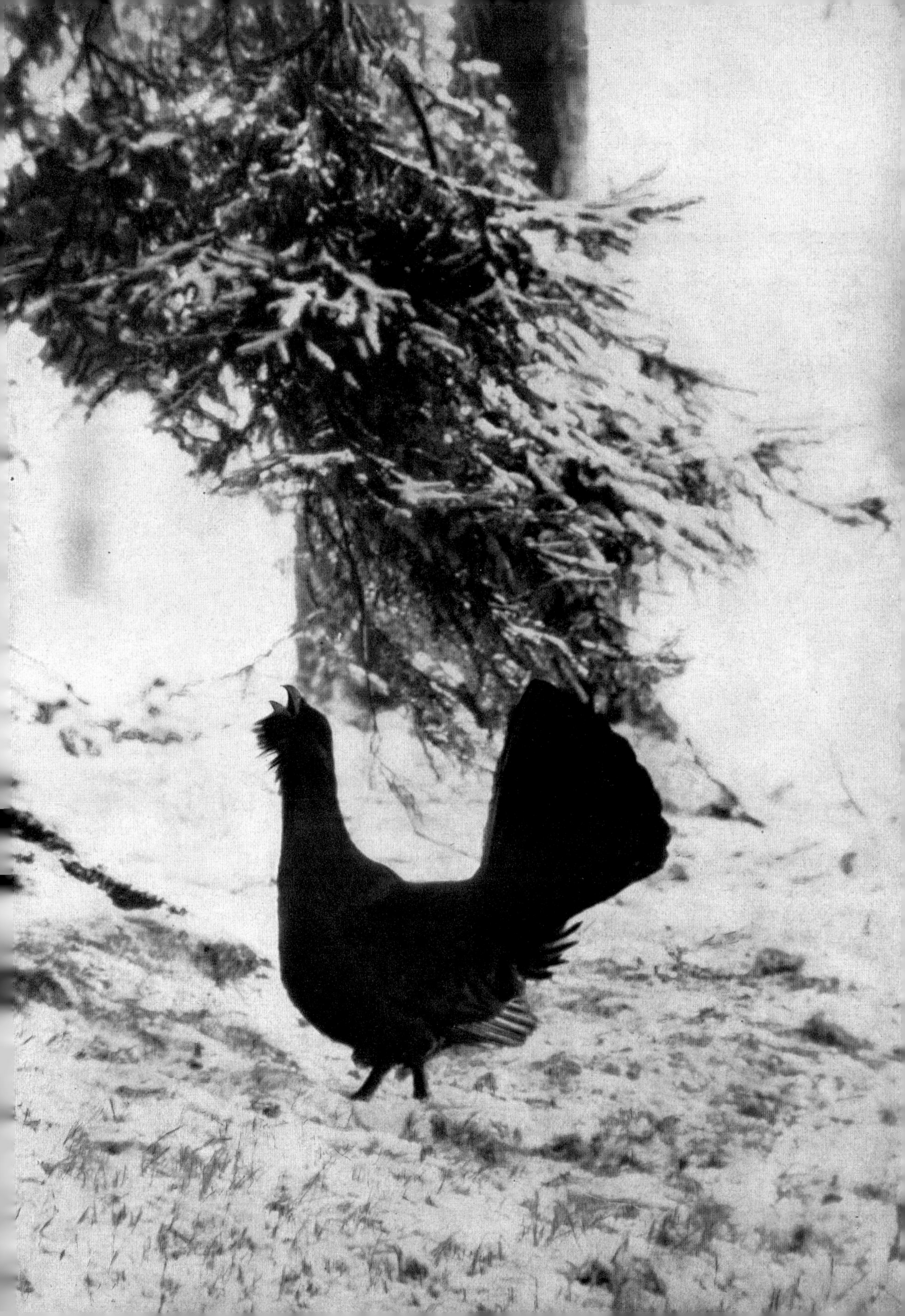

Pictures on this page: As intensive forestry work involves the felling of hollow trees, their larger inhabitants such as the wood owl become increasingly rare. However, this wise-looking bird is adaptable enough to make use of such things as disused crows' eyries when seeking a home.

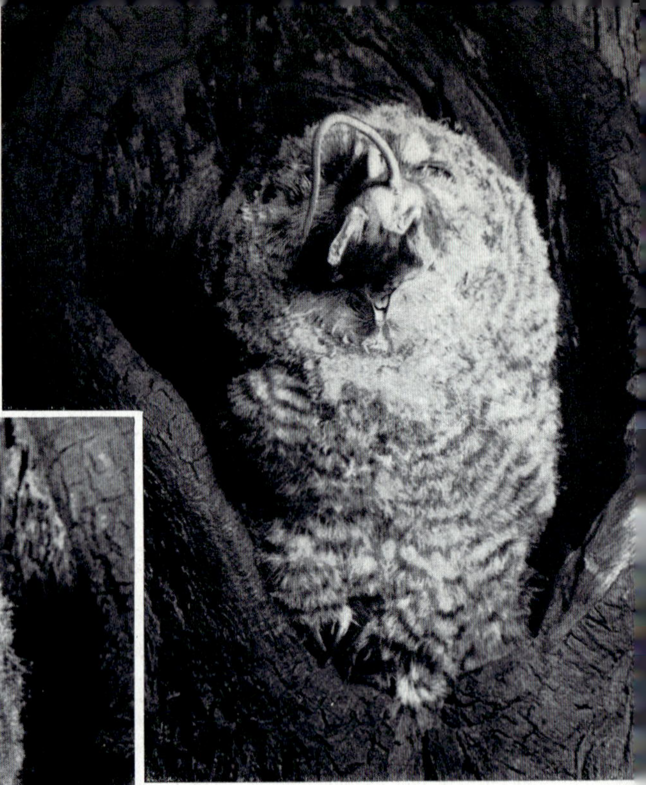

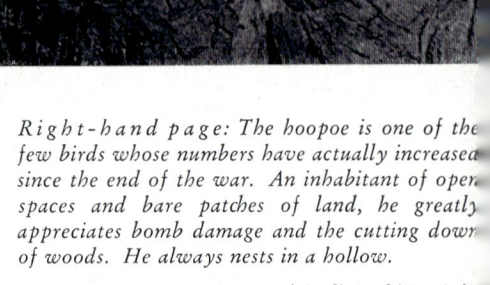

Right-hand page: The hoopoe is one of the few birds whose numbers have actually increased since the end of the war. An inhabitant of open spaces and bare patches of land, he greatly appreciates bomb damage and the cutting down of woods. He always nests in a hollow.

Leica-Photo: Schützenhofer

Photos by Robot-Photos: Dischner

Above: This photo is the first of a little series depicting an everyday event in the life of the woods, finishing with the picture at the bottom of the page . . .

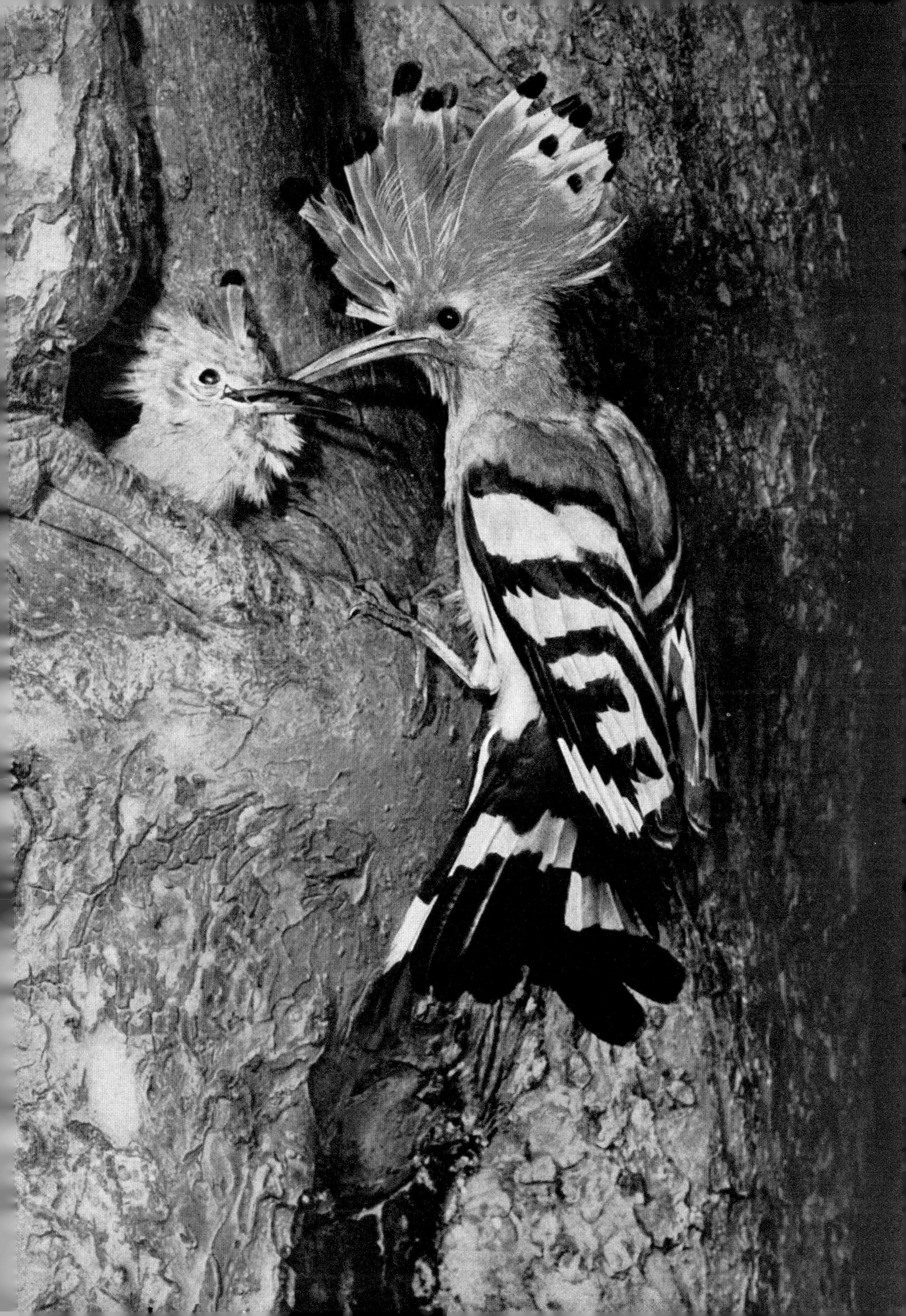

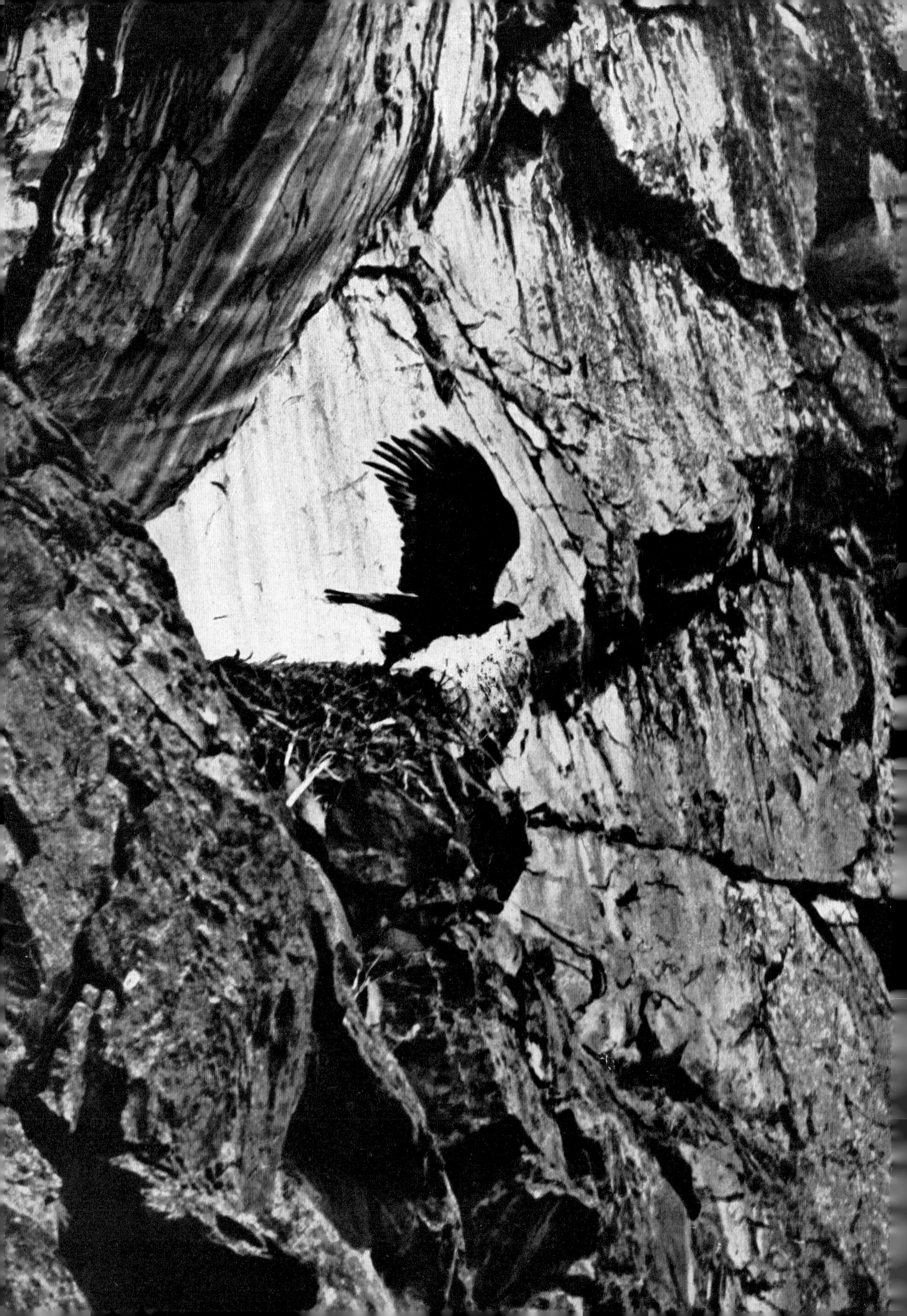

Löbl

The head of a young eagle (40 days old). – The golden eagle produces no more than two or three offspring in a year, and often only one of them survives to reach maturity. The low rate of reproduction, coupled with the fact that the great bird cannot breed until its fifth year, limits the extent to which the race can increase.

←
An eagle flying from its eyrie. Pairs of golden eagles are now rare in central Europe, although at the turn of the century these regal creatures of the air still lorded it in mountainous areas of Europe.

Plattner-Pedrett

Harrandt

The vast wilderness of reeds by the low-lying Neusiedler See in Austria shelters water-fowl almost completely untroubled by man. Splendid white spoonbills, too, still breed there in colonies. Despite its resemblance to the heron, this bird is a member of the ibis family.

It is an undeniable fact that the grey heron consumes large quantities of valuable fish. However, what a magnificent spectacle this fisher makes as it skims through the air, and what a wealth of interest a breeding colony of these birds affords! They once belonged to the landscape as much as do rivers and woods, but the few breeding colonies still existing now require planned protection.

Arthur Christiansen

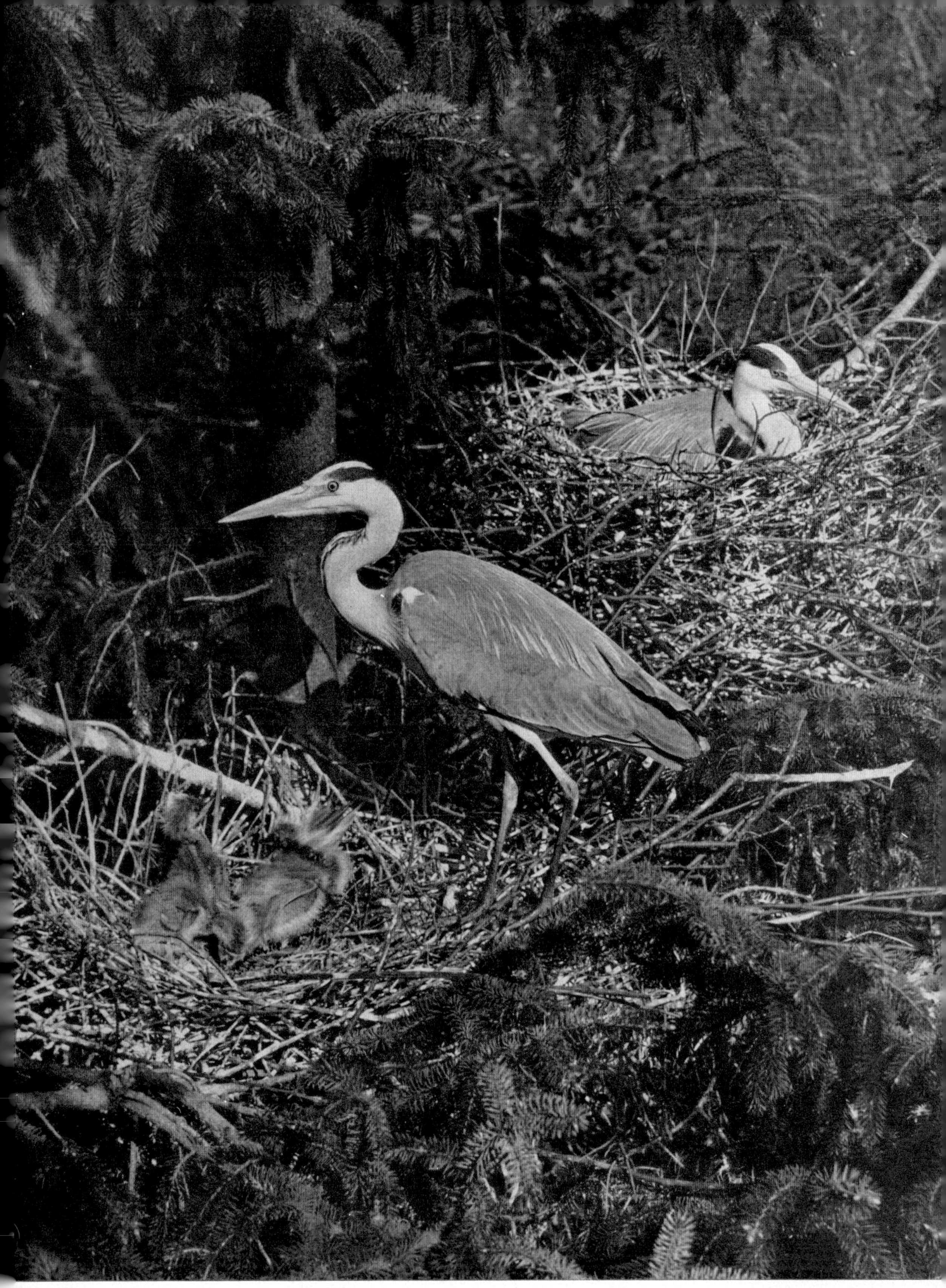

Arthur Christiansen

Wild geese share the destiny of all large birds. They are steadily becoming rarer, as they need broad, inaccessible expanses of marshland for their breeding grounds. During the migration period ringed geese visit the island of Jordsand off the coast of Jutland (pictured). It is only in northern countries that they still breed in large numbers.

Arthur Christiansen

The seabird conservation area of Hirsholmene in the northern Kattegat still gives an impression of former conditions on many islands and tongues of land. This photograph shows herring gulls (seated), with laughing gulls and some sea-swallows in the background.

Photos from "Die Flamingos der Camargue" by E. Gallet, published by W. Krebser, Thun

The fabulous pink-backed flamingo is a creature of hot southern climates. Only occasionally does one penetrate, by accident, as far into Europe as Lake Constance. Flamingos have an area to themselves in the Camargue (Rhone Delta). Their offspring, very awkward at first, are autophagous.

The shallow mud nests of the flamingos are built close together near the water's edge. Each female lays only one egg in the nest. Many young birds are brought up together, since flamingos are very sociable, and never nest alone.

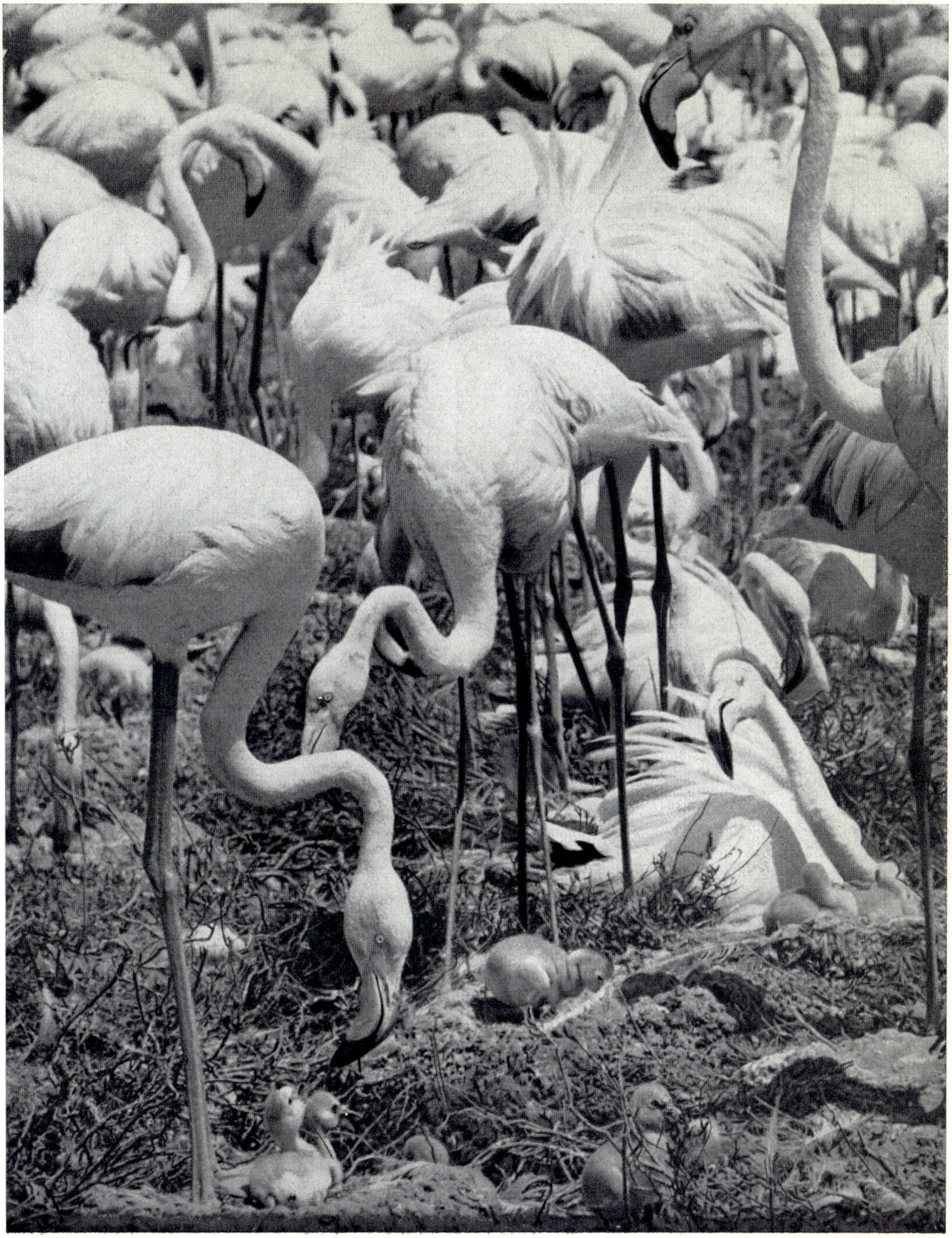

Black bears fighting.

Eugen Schuhmacher

Owls

Owls are not related to the birds of prey active in the daytime, as was once believed. They are essentially creatures of the twilight and night. The large eyes, directed forward along parallel lines, give the owl's face a certain similarity to that of man. The head can be swivelled backwards some 250 degrees. All owls are very keen of hearing. Their diet consists very largely of mice of all kinds, and they are therefore man's most valuable allies in his fight against these pests. Undigested food is rejected—unlike other birds of prey the owl similarly rejects the bones of its prey.

The king of the species, the great horned owl, which is almost as large as an eagle, was still to be found in almost all extensive woodland areas of Europe about the beginning of the present century.

Today, however, it shares the fate of all large animals and is becoming increasingly rare. On account of its size it needs extensive hunting grounds, and how many huntsmen would willingly allow owls to rob them of such hares as are still to be found! Nowadays the great horned owl lives mainly in mountain crevices, where the female can lay her two to five pure white eggs in an inaccessible niche among the rocks. Attempts have been made to reintroduce this majestic bird in certain areas, but not always with success.

The smaller classes of owl have been more successful in coming to terms with agriculture and civilization, except in cases where the disappearance of deep, silent woods has destroyed their breeding areas. In particular those among them that live and breed in hollow trees, such as the screech owl, suffer from a shortage of accommodation, since modern, intensive forestry methods demand that all old, hollow trees should be felled. Wood owls are using old crow or buzzard eyries as their nests to an ever-increasing extent, but not all kinds of owl are adaptable enough to be able to change their way of life in a few generations.

Wapiti

The huge wapiti, a member of the red deer family, has disappeared completely from the eastern areas of America. It is still, however, to be found in its wild state in many western districts. In the far north it is still present in small numbers up to the beginnings of the American taiga, and fairly large numbers still flourish in the Rocky Mountains. Although it is not really a creature of the high mountains by nature, it has found a refuge from man in the Rockies. Its great antlers sometimes have a length of over 5 ft.

Bison

It is estimated that at the beginning of the nineteenth century some 60 million bison roamed the American prairies. At the end of the nineteenth century only about a thousand remained of these most sociable of all hoofed animals, among which the males and females stay together in the herd throughout the whole year. All the others had been slaughtered by white pioneers within the course of a few decades. Bison herds are made up of family groups, each consisting of an adult couple with calves of various ages. Formerly the herds wandered over vast expanses of land, but the plains are now split up by railway lines, farms, etc., and the journeyings of the bison have had to cease. Larger numbers of the somewhat smaller Canadian forest bison have survived the coming of the white man. The two species have now become generally blended into a composite form, since numerous bison from the American plains have been taken to the woodlands of the north where there is more chance for them to live and breed.

Following upon the introduction of strict protective measures, stocks have increased considerably within a comparatively short space of time. The total number of bison at present living in nature protection areas and national parks of the United States and Canada is estimated at some 20,000. The idea of wildlife preservation is firmly established in Canada and the United States; the New World is striving generously to make good the wrongs done to the animal world of America during the early days of exuberant pioneering.

Grizzly, Baribal, Polar Bears

The pine forests of the far north of America are today the last places giving refuge over large areas to the grizzly and the smaller black bears. It is only in the forests and gorges of the Rockies that these bears find their way further south, black bears also surviving in high-lying wooded areas on the east coast down to Florida. It is becoming clear that there can be no place for such large beasts of prey in a land dominated by man, even though all land bears live as vegetarians during the period of the autumn when berries are ripe, sometimes for weeks on end, and although the ferocity of certain types, particularly the great grey bear, is often exaggerated. The large land bears, both those of America and the brown bear of Europe and Asia, are lone hunters, and each individual needs an area of some 6 to 8 square miles if it is to find sufficient food to live. The cubs are born in the bear's winter lair. They are helpless, blind, and no larger than a rat, often remaining in the mother's care for as long as two years.

The polar bear of the far north is distinguished by its white fur, its small head with a flat forehead, and the hairy soles of its feet—all these features differentiate it clearly from the brown bear. Nevertheless these two species can be inter-bred and the offspring are capable of propagation, a proof of their very close relationship. The polar bear lives mainly on seals, fish, sea birds, and—during the polar summer—berries and other vegetable matter. He will often lie in wait for seals at their air holes in the ice during winter. The female polar bear gives birth to her cubs, generally two, in a well-dug hole in the snow during the bleak Arctic night.

Beaver

Just as the stag is dependent on the virgin forest, so the beaver can exist only along the banks of undisturbed rivers. When rivers are canalized, their banks straightened and walled, this large rodent can no longer survive there. He once abounded in many parts of Europe, and the names of many districts and towns still bear witness to the former existence of the beaver in those places. Today, however, the only areas where beavers still live in Europe are in the south of Norway, Sweden, near the mouth of the Elbe trough, in the Rhône delta, at Rybaki in Poland, and in many parts of the Soviet Union. The North American beaver is very similar to its European cousin. In the New World, too, numbers have fallen dangerously. The reason for this is not far to seek: in the year 1875, for example, the Hudson Bay Fur Trading Company exported 270,903 beaver skins.

The constructive energy of the beaver is proverbial. Families and even whole colonies working together construct their dwellings, strong huts of branches, brushwood and mud several feet high, with entrances below the surface of the water. The building of these dry sleeping quarters involves the erection of dams sometimes more than 100 yards long and an involved system of haulage to get tree-trunks and branches into position. For use in these activities, and for their food, which consists mainly of the bark and foliage of living trees, beavers will fell trees, generally of soft wood, with a diameter of up to 2 ft., by gnawing through the trunks with their sharp, powerful teeth. For some years now beavers have been employed by man on a considerable scale in Canada. In areas where it is desirable to retain water by the construction of numerous dams beavers have been set to work—arriving there by aeroplane. The animals are dropped in crates each provided with a parachute, the crates opening automatically when they reach the ground.

Elk

The elk, a creature dwelling from the earliest times in the Arctic regions, survives in the far north of Europe, Asia and America. Its way of life in the Old and New Worlds is the same. In general the American elk is rather larger and heavier. Elks flourish in water and on swampy ground. They swim with ease across broad arms of the sea, and feed for preference on water plants in shallow stretches of rivers and lakes. Otherwise their diet consists of the leaves and young shoots of softwood trees (willow, alder and hazel) rather than grass. They are solitary creatures: it is only during the mating season that the stags go with the hinds. In northern districts where troublesome insects abound elks often spend hours standing up to their nostrils in water.

The only European countries in which elk still exist are Poland, Russia, and the Scandinavian lands.

Snowy Goat, Bighorn Sheep

Both creatures live among rocky peaks, where, as thoroughgoing mountaineers, they are in their element. The snowy goat, in particular, is a creature of great heights, and even in the hardest winter it will seldom descend to the regions of Alpine pastureland. The scanty supply of food to be gleaned from the bare rocks suffices for these undemanding animals. During winter they assemble at spots on the mountain slopes which blizzards have swept clear of snow.

The bighorn sheep exists in very different colourings in different areas, dark brown in Alberta and British Columbia, and a pale yellowish grey in the mountainous deserts of northern Mexico. Only the females and the young live together in groups. The males are lone wanderers that seek feminine company only during the weeks of the mating season.

Musk-Ox

Among hoofed animals the musk-ox is the best suited to life under Arctic conditions. His thick coat with its abundant under-wool protects him against even the icy snowstorms of his native lands. The description 'sheep-ox' has more connection with his Latin name (*Ovibos*) and his moderate size than with any relationship to the sheep. The small herds of musk-oxen are made up of polygamous families, and are always led by a bull. These beasts are now only to be found in Greenland, in a few protected areas of Canada, in Spitzbergen (small select herds), in Norway between Tromsö and Narvik, and on the island of Nunivak off the coast of Alaska.

Seals

Seals of one kind or another are to be found in all major seas with the exception of the Indian Ocean. The great majority, however, live in areas approaching the North or South poles. Science differentiates three families: the eared-seals, which have small external ears and hind limbs powerful enough to enable them to walk on land, the phocidae or ordinary seals, whose hind limbs are permanently stretched out behind the body, and walruses. After a period of gestation lasting between ten and twelve months they generally produce only one infant; that of the fur-seal is born with a white or light-coloured coat. Pairing takes place soon after the female has given birth; that is the only time when these creatures stay on land. The fur-seals, or sea bears, are a group of eared-seals which have wool of silky softness under their coarse outer coat. It is the soft undercoat which is supplied to the garment manufacturers as 'sealskin'. This undercoat is lacking in the other sub-group, the sea-lions.

Like all other seals, the eared-seals have decreased enormously in numbers. As recently as the beginning of the present century 140,000 skins of eared-seals were supplied to the trade every year. In one year 30,000 young seals, whose mothers had been slaughtered, starved to death on Pribilov Island. While the number of sea bears on that island in 1870 was some 4½ million, it had decreased by 1914 to about 200,000. Thanks to the fact that at long last protective measures were put in force, the stock has again risen to more than three million.

Common seals are divided into four sub-species: the harp seal of northern waters, a number of kindred classes living in antarctic, tropical and sub-tropical seas (among these is the Wedell seal, the monk seal, and finally the cystophora, including the saddle-backed seal and the sea-elephant or bottle-nosed seal. In these creatures every feature is suited solely to life in the water; they have no external ears, and their hind limbs are usable only as floats. Seals can dive to great depths, but they are certainly unable to stay under water for hours, as has often been claimed. A period of eight minutes under water is probably the longest of which these air-breathing creatures are capable. They can cut through the water like a torpedo, and overtake the swiftest fish. The majority of seals can move only awkwardly and slowly on land.

Walrus

One of the largest and heaviest of all seals is the walrus of the far north. Males, which attain a length of about 14 ft., weigh more than 2,000 lb. They have no external ears. The tusks which protrude from their mouths are incisors of the upper jaw, which continue to grow all the animal's lifetime. These tusks exist in both sexes, and are used to prise crustaceans from the sea bed. This food is swept into a pile on the rocks by the water's edge by means of the walrus's hard, brushlike 'moustache', and so into its mouth. The tusks also serve to lever the heavy creatures up on to drifting ice-floes. In former times the walrus abounded along coasts north of the Arctic Circle. Brehm writes that over two hundred years ago more than a thousand walruses were often slain by seal hunters during a single day. The walrus long seemed to be in danger of complete extermination, but thanks to protection measures numbers seem to have risen slightly during the past few years. The walrus gives birth only once every second year.

Red Deer

In contrast to the roe deer, the red deer (whose male is the noble stag) flees from civilization. If forests are too greatly reduced, and the red deer is thereby robbed of its solitude, it will go to the remotest place possible, and finally vanish altogether. A further hindrance stands in the way of the red deer when woodlands come under the supervision of man. The lack of undergrowth such as berry-bearing bushes drives the deer to strip the bark off trees for food. Thus regulated forestry and a large stock of red deer are scarcely compatible.

Reindeer

The reindeer or caribou is the only member of the deer family native to the northern polar regions, and is hardly to be found south of the Arctic Circle. During the Ice Age, however, reindeer were to be found throughout Europe, right down to the Pyrenees. The reindeer's feet are large, and spread in walking, a help when travelling over frozen ground. This is the only class of deer in which the females bear antlers. Wild reindeer live in large herds, which move southward during winter and northward during summer. They are extremely shy and difficult to chase.

Glutton

The glutton is a carnivorous animal of the far north. It occurs over an area ranging from Scandinavia across southern Siberia to North America and Greenland. In summer it travels long distances across the treeless plains of the north in pursuit of polar hares, moor-hens and lemmings. During winter it withdraws to the coniferous forests of the polar regions, where it finds more shelter. There it will lie in wait on a branch and leap on to the neck of any animal which passes underneath. Like other members of the marten family the glutton leads a solitary life. The female generally keeps her offspring in the shelter of fallen timber in the remotest parts of the territory over which these animals roam.

Lynx

The lynx is the largest feline animal of the northern taiga areas, although Siberian tigers also penetrate into the coniferous forests of those parts. Lynx still abound in the almost uninhabited wastes of the Asiatic and American territories approaching the polar regions. Very few specimens still live freely in central Europe. Like other wild cats the lynx lives alone, attacking every creature which it is able to overcome from young deer down to wild poultry and lemmings. If the lynx fails to seize a prospective victim in its first spring it will not pursue the fleeing creature for more than a few steps.

In southern Europe, the Caucasus, Asia Minor and Persia there can be found the pardel lynx, distinguished by its particularly clear spots and long ear tufts, while in North America, a little to the south of the line dividing Canada from the United States, there lives the red lynx.

Fighting Snipe

This long-legged snipe breeds in northern Europe and Asia, spending the winter in southern Asia and South Africa. The female is about the size of a thrush, the male that of a turtle dove. This bird was formerly common in central Europe, but as almost all marshes and swampy land have been drained for cultivation wading birds such as this are found principally beside large expanses of water. The interesting thing about this bird is that one hardly ever sees two males whose bright feathers, displayed at pairing time, are identical. Anyone unaware of this fact would scarcely believe a number of males, in their gaily-coloured wedding garments of such different patterns as white patches over yellow, reddish, dark brown and black spotted, speckled or striped, to be members of the same breed. At pairing time the male will challenge a rival to combat, ruffling up his neck feathers and going into battle like a fighting cock. They seem brimming over with aggressive exuberance—but it is seldom that either combatant loses so much as a feather in the course of what are in fact only mock fights. With the change from the wedding garments to summer plumage the show is at an end; the males live peaceably from then on, and their grey-brown dress looks as unassuming as that of the females.

Badger

Badgers are carnivorous animals found in many parts of the northern hemisphere, somewhat similar to martens. They lack, however, the agility of their relations the marten proper and the weasel. On the contrary, the earth-dwelling badger, particularly when amply nourished towards the end of the summer, looks more like a small pig. When it is pursued, however, the badger can demonstrate dexterity, and will put up a brave fight against such foes as the dachshund (whose name means 'badger dog', this breed being used to attack badgers in their holes), its powerful, needle-sharp teeth being inferior only to those of the otter among comparable animals. The badger lives on mice, birds which nest on the ground, insects, snails and worms, as well as fruit, berries and roots. His dwelling consists of a chamber, with a lining of soft material, having a number of entrance tunnels and ventilation shafts. Some distance away from this living accommodation there is a hole used as a lavatory. The mating season is between April and August, but there is sometimes a secondary mating period in the late autumn. Normally the eggs begin to develop soon after they have been fertilized, but then they develop no more for several months, activity re-commencing only about 35 days before the young are to be born. The period of gestation lasts for so long a time only if fertilization has taken place during the secondary mating period. The mother suckles her 3 to 5 offspring for about 8 weeks.

European Bison

The European bison belongs to the same family as the bison (commonly but incorrectly known as the buffalo) of the American prairies. Bison were found in the Vosges until the seventh century and in Switzerland until the eleventh. In the year 1921 the last bison living in freedom in Europe, at the spot where the remnants of former herds had found refuge in the Polish forest of Bialowiez, was shot by a poacher—a former forest-keeper. An article elsewhere in this book tells of recent developments concerning the European bison. This beast is not to be confused with the aurochs, which became extinct. The aurochs was common in the Vosges until the Merovingian period. The last specimen, a cow, was killed by a poacher in Poland during the year 1627.

Roe Deer

Among the classes of deer found in Europe the roe deer appears to have a good stretch of free life still ahead of it, while the red deer, whose male is the stag, can hold its place in the world of free animals only as long as large expanses of fairly dense woodland remain in Europe. The roe deer, a creature of open parkland, fits in well with the life of the countryside in civilized lands, with fields of grain, meadows, and cattle enclosures. So long as cereal crops are growing high this slender, graceful creature has no need of woodland to provide cover. During the remainder of the year a few clumps of trees or even bushes suffice for his needs by day. He fits in easily with man and with human activities. It is an astonishing fact that so common and ubiquitous a creature still posed a baffling problem until very recently. It has long been known that the mating period of roe deer is in July and August, but it was not thought possible that so small an animal could have so long a period of gestation as from then until the following May, when the young are born. That seemed contrary to all natural laws. It was therefore assumed that a second rut must occur in the autumn, and that conception must take place then. It has now been discovered, however, that after the egg has been fertilized in the uterus of the female it develops only over the first stages, then lies inactive until midwinter. Not until the approach of spring does the foetus begin to grow. It has since been found that this characteristic is shared with most animals of the marten family and with the badger.

Bouquetin

The bouquetin, or Alpine ibex, the proudest European member of the goat family, became totally extinct in the German and Austrian Alps. However, small numbers were taken from areas where the species still survives, particularly from what is now the Gran-Paradiso National Park in the Italian Alps, and they have again established themselves in more northerly Alpine areas. On the other hand the Nubian ibex, formerly found on the coastal mountain ranges by the Red Sea, appears to have become extinct, and only a few small, threatened colonies of the Iberian or Pyrenees ibex still survive. Except during the mating season the male and female ibex go their ways separately. They are creatures of the highest, most exposed pinnacles of rock even more than the chamois. Surprisingly enough pairing takes place in January, during the depths of the Alpine winter. Only in the very worst winter weather do these creatures descend to seek shelter in the mountain forests.

Our domestic goats are not descended from the ibex, although crossing is possible, but from the bezoar goat, still to be found in Crete, the Cyclades, Montecristo, and in a few districts of Asia Minor and Persia.

Alpine Marmot

The Alpine marmot is found not only in the Alps but also, in diminishing numbers, in the Black Forest, the Pyrenees and the Carpathian Mountains. Another species, the bobac, inhabits the steppes of Asiatic Russia.

The Alpine marmot, purely a creature of the daytime that enjoys sunning itself, lives in large or small colonies. While searching for food it keeps stopping to look around in case there is any danger of attack by enemies, the principal foe being the eagle. While scouting the marmot sits up on its haunches. If attacked it lets out a shrill cry and flees into its subterranean burrow, the entrances to which are often camouflaged with grass and leaves. There it sleeps throughout the winter. The marmot was formerly very common in the Alps. However, great numbers were shot by country people towards the end of the summer, and were dug up by them in winter, on account of their flesh, and the extraordinary healing properties attributed to their fat. As the result of this persecution they became practically or completely extinct in many Alpine districts. The marmot is now generally protected, except that in some parts of the Alps it is permissible to shoot them during a few weeks of the year.

Chamois

Chamois exist in most high mountain ranges of central and southern Europe, and eastwards as far as Asia Minor; they have even been introduced successfully into the Alpine area of New Zealand. The chamois is better equipped for life above the timber line than almost any other hoofed animal. Rock ledges no wider than a man's hand are wide enough for these nimble-footed creatures to ascend the face of a mountain, and they are unperturbed by great chasms below them. The small chamois herds consists only of females with their young. The bucks join them only during the mating season in November and December. The warning signal of the chamois is a shrill whistle. The 'gams-beard' which often decorates the hats of huntsmen in Alpine areas consists of long hairs from the mane which runs along the back of the chamois.

Fox

Hardly another beast of prey in the whole animal kingdom has the adaptability of the red fox. He knows all the secrets necessary to lead the life of a freebooter, and still manages to exist even in some heavily populated industrial areas. During the Second World War foxes even made themselves at home amid the ruins of buildings in large towns of central Europe, bringing up their young (there are generally 3 to 8 in a litter) in ruined passages and cellars amid houses and streets. In view of this ability to make the most of any surroundings it is probably safe to say that of all wild animals the fox has the most certain expectation of survival as a species.

Great Bustard

Bustards became common in Europe only after the primeval forests had largely been cleared, and great expanses of land put under the plough, since these birds, some originally native to Asia and some to Africa, are creatures of open land, avoiding areas of woodland and dense bushes. The great bustard now lives in small numbers, as a protected species, in central Europe. The male can weigh up to 32 lb. No 'marriage' takes place, the males going to every female that approaches them during the mating period. At that time the male puts up a remarkable display, blowing out the sac at his throat, while his tail goes forward over his back in the shape of a fan, and the feathers of his wings and neck are puffed up.

Moor Fowl, Capercailzie

There is no room for rough-legged fowl in the countryside of today. They require large expanses of undisturbed territory, and retreat further and further as civilization advances. The moor-hen, previously abounding in many parts of Europe, has now become rare, particularly since many stretches of flat open country have been used for cultivation or building. There are few places where the sounds and dancing antics of the heath cocks are still a feature of the spring mornings, when they assemble from all sides to display themselves in all their glory before the admiring hens. The wild leaps, beak-clapping and wing-fluttering of the amorous heath cocks are said to have given the Bavarian peasants the idea for their characteristic folk dances. The capercailzie, a large member of the grouse family, has become even more of a rarity. Unlike heath cocks the males do not congregate together for their pairing dances. Each cock dances alone on a horizontal branch of a tree. He begins his unusual mating song in that position in the early morning, often continuing it on the ground as the day progresses. After this song has run its course the cock consorts with the hens that have been attracted by it.

Hoopoe

This unusual bird with a crest like the headdress of an Indian chief favours pastureland and clearings in the woods as areas in which to live. Shortly before the outbreak of the Second World War it had become rare in central Europe. However, thanks to the cutting down of woods during wartime, numbers have increased to a surprising extent. This bird will nevertheless never be as common in northern Europe as it is in the south. In the villages nestling among the vineyards of southern France the monotonous 'hoop—hoop' call to which this bird owes its name can be heard from morning to evening, even in the village streets, and in the Berber townships of North Africa these colourful birds are everywhere to be seen, searching for insects in the alleyways and perching on the rooftops in numbers as great as those of the sparrows in Europe.

Golden Eagle

The breeding area of the golden eagle in Europe is now restricted to the Alps, although these great birds formerly also nested in trees on level ground. Thanks to years of effort by nature protection enthusiasts the golden eagle is now protected in Germany, Austria and Switzerland.

The eggs are generally 2 or 3 in number, but almost invariably only one young bird is reared to maturity; it does not become capable of propagation until it is five or six years old.

Spoonbill

Although often described as a form of heron, this bird is more nearly related to the ibis. The only spoonbills still nesting in western Europe are some 300 pairs in Holland. They still abound, however, in the swamps near the mouth of the Danube. They always breed in groups, often in company with herons, terns and skimmers. Their food consists of fish, molluscs, shellfish, etc. They are migrants, spending the winter in Africa.

Herons

The grey common heron is to be found in all parts of the world from the far north down to Africa and Madagascar. At one time it was a common sight in Europe, and whole colonies would build their nests of twigs in trees near the banks of rivers. There these large birds would stand in long rows by the waterside, fishing. At that time, when the rivers were still pure and unpolluted, they contained enough fish to feed this host of fish-eaters, and still to leave plenty for human anglers. The primary reason why fish are now in short supply in many rivers is not that birds such as the heron have consumed an undue number, but that canalization and other artificial alterations of river banks and beds, together with pollution by industrial waste and the contents of sewers, have greatly reduced the numbers of fish. Sensible nature protection demands that herons should be encouraged and assisted, for the sight of this indolent-looking bird with its neck bent gracefully back belongs to the landscape. This characteristic bending of the neck distinguishes the heron in flight from the stork, which flies with its neck stretched straight out.

Wild Geese

The grey goose, the ancestor of the domestic goose, is the most common of the wild geese native to Europe, although this shy, cautious bird has been driven from many areas where it once flourished by the spread of civilization. The grey, or grey-lag geese nest in a community on islands or swampy ground to which access is difficult. If the nesting area is disturbed by human beings during the breeding period the pairs of geese will move elsewhere rather than have their offspring endangered by possibly hostile visitors. Geese have good memories, and there is no justification in the use of the term 'silly goose'. Their attitude and actions in connection with unusual experiences have been found to show intelligence and an ability to profit by such experiences in later occasions. Wild geese are far more creatures of the land and far less at home in the water than ducks. When the young are old enough to fly the families frequently move to stubble fields, there to glean such corn as remains on the ground. However, they always sleep in remote marshy spots. If they have been shot at in a particular haunt of theirs they will avoid it, or fly so high that they are out of range of any sportsmen who may be in the vicinity. The closely related bean goose breeds mainly in the far north of the Old World, coming south only during migration. This species is often wrongly described as the snow goose, probably because it sometimes happens that the first light snowfalls of winter are accompanied, at night, by the desolate cries of flocks of these geese high in the air. The real snow goose is snow-white all over except for the first ten wing feathers. These birds nest in northern Siberia, in the far north of America and in Greenland, seldom being seen in Europe. Bernacle geese nest between the 60th and 80th degrees of latitude—the polar regions. Their principal breeding grounds are situated in Greenland. They are true coastal birds, migrating for the winter to the British Isles and western Europe. Male and female geese cannot be distinguished by their plumage. A pair remain together all their lives. Geese are invariably conscientious parents; while the female is sitting on the eggs her husband keeps watch nearby. During the period when they are moulting geese are unable to fly, and can therefore easily be captured in large numbers. It is an astonishing fact that man has so far domesticated only three classes of goose out of the many useful and attractive wild forms that exist. These domesticated classes are the grey-lag, the Asiatic hump-backed or swan goose, and in recent years the Canada goose.

Gulls

Seagulls are related to skuas and terns. One of the forms most frequently to be seen inland is the laughing gull. Large colonies of these birds nest along coasts, and near the banks of large expanses of land-locked water. Like crows they will often follow the plough in search of cockchafer grubs and mice, for they are birds of prey, and do not live wholly on fish as do some of the ocean-going gulls. They are always to be seen in groups, since communal living is a characteristic of this group of birds. Deserted cliffs in northern waters are often covered by breeding pairs of gulls in uncountable numbers. Apart from the shooting of gulls, which was formerly a popular pastime, the factor which did most to reduce the numbers of many classes of gulls was the taking of their eggs during the spring. Today gull shooting is forbidden, and the collecting of their eggs is restricted by law. The kittiwake, one of the smaller gulls, has a scene of action extending over the whole north Atlantic area. It owes its zoological name, *rissa tridactyla*, to the fact that it lacks the fourth toe of other gulls. In winter it comes south to coastal areas of central Europe, often following rivers far inland. The most accomplished flier and diver of the family is the sea-swallow or tern. They owe the former name to their prowess as aeronauts, and to the fact that their tails are forked like those of swallows. While gulls have a slightly hooked bill, that of the tern is straight, coming to a sharp point. There are some 80 known classes of gulls and terns, inhabiting most parts of the world where there is water. They are primarily fish-eaters, generally finding their way to cliffs, islands and rocky coasts, seldom to shores or river banks overgrown by vegetation.

Flamingo

The large, deep-pink flamingo lives in Spain, the Camargue of southern France, in Africa and various countries of Asia. With its peculiarly hooked bill it rakes in the water for all kinds of molluscs and shellfish. Like most swamp and water birds the flamingo is companionable, lines of these stately pink creatures providing a fine decoration of the landscape. At times other than the breeding period flamingos fly far afield, often being seen in regions thousands of miles from the areas in which they normally live. Their breeding grounds are on islands or on the loneliest stretches of beaches. The flamingo's nest is one of the oddest structures in the world of birds. It is nothing more than a simple, knee-high hillock of mud, with a depression at the top, often rising out of shallow water. The female generally lays only one egg, which has a white shell and weighs about 5 oz. The parents take it in turns to sit on it. The young birds soon leave the nest, going to the water about four days after being hatched out.

Part Two

EXPERIENCES IN NATIONAL PARKS AND NATURE PROTECTION AREAS

A Day in the Life of a Game Warden in the Ngoro-Ngoro Crater

BY

OSKAR KÖNIG

THE mist lies like a thick eiderdown over the camp high up on the rim of the crater. The chimneys of the log huts make a determined effort to push fingers of smoke up through the blanket of mist. A native boy, shivering in the frosty air, runs with the morning tea to the game warden's hut, and hurries inside to escape from the cold.

While Bwana, the game warden, drinks his hot tea, he opens the window. An icy east wind blows across the mountains bordering on the Rift Valley. From the crater some 300 ft. below comes the last threatening hunting call of a lion, and a hyena, sated with food he has gorged during the night, lurches past the camp on his way to hide at the approach of day.

Up here, almost 6,500 ft. above sea-level, it is bitterly cold in the early morning. Everyone longs for the hot tropical sun, but it is often a very long time before its rays can penetrate the low-lying clouds. In a quarter of an hour the game warden is ready to leave. Sheltered from the wind behind the hut stands his robust shooting brake, and he is soon driving at a moderate speed along the forest road, with its tortuous bends, until at the end of a strenuous journey uphill and downhill he finally reaches a picturesque clearing, behind which begin bamboo woods and the dense primeval jungle.

Long-held trumpet notes sound from a high-lying part of the forest still shrouded by a blanket of mist. Evidently the elephants are amusing themselves at a water-hole. The car moves slowly forward. Below, on the plain, a bushbuck stands grazing, dark brown with white patches, and bearing a noble pair of horns. Great shaggy grey waterbucks block the track at the next bend—stag-antelopes which are so similar to the Carpathian stag, crossed with the wapiti, that one's thoughts turn, unwittingly, to far-distant woodlands. . . . Everything is astir in the early morning. Less than 300 yards further on a whole herd of buffalo have evidently decided to make use of the track in order to avoid the long grass, which is wet with dew. The herd probably passed along half an hour ago.

The car slowly follows the trail of dung, with its smell of cow stalls. When he has reached the top of a hill, the game warden leaves the car, slings his rifle over his shoulder, and climbs out to inspect the salt licks in the valley. Only his old gunbearer and guide is with him.

Within a few seconds both men are wet with the icy dew soaking the three-foot-high grass. Their teeth chattering with cold, they push onwards down the slope towards the valley. There they come to a series of water-holes which have been strengthened by means of small dams in order to raise the level of the water. These are the bathing pools of all wild animals. . . .

A rhinoceros wallowing in the water suddenly makes for land, snorting loudly, for all the world like an over-heated locomotive. On the bank stand a herd of waterbuck, hopeful, interested and dignified. A bushbuck is startled by the noise of the rhino, and rushes away from the scene. Bau . . . Bauuhh . . . Bauuuhhh, he cries out in alarm.

The game warden is glad to see that the salt licks are proving popular. With the exception of the elephants, all the 'regular customers' have already been there. After stalking cautiously forward for a few hundred yards, the two men reach a large clearing beyond the water-holes, surrounded on all sides by tall forest trees. This spot enjoys the deep peace of untouched woods; the earth breathes the pure, primitive air of creation.

Soon, however, nature presents a new and imposing picture. On the slopes above the track there appear buffalo in dark, massive formations, five, ten . . . , twenty-five, forty . . . , perhaps sixty of the massive beasts. First goes an old bull, the leader of the herd, shambling along in his shaggy mantle of hair, his shoulders held high, his head almost horizontal, so that the heavy horns rest on his withers. Behind the bulls come the cows, with their calves in a confused flurry as they press forward. The old bulls know full well that they are the masters up here.

The game warden goes slowly back to the path; everything here is in perfect order. A few of the bull buffaloes stop to glare at him mistrustfully, but he is now on his way back to the elephants, hoping that they will emerge now the sun has at last succeeded in breaking through the mist, its first rays bathing the landscape in a magnificent early golden glow. That should bring the big fellows out of the forest. On the opposite slope, grazing peacefully, is the rhino which left its bath so precipitately, and not far away stands the bushbuck, recovering from its recent fright. A slight misunderstanding in paradise. . . .

The game warden hurries towards the other large clearing from where, first thing in the morning, he heard the trumpeting of elephants. As soon as the two men have crossed a steep ridge they can see the great grey beasts at the edge of the forest. Winding trunks, gleaming white ivory, mothers watchfully guarding their noisy calves.

Leading the herd is a medium-sized bull elephant—no weakling, but where is their master, the old, ill-tempered giant with long tusks, who has made himself generally unpopular? Not long ago he even demolished a native hut.

Ah, there he comes, crashing through the undergrowth. He is obviously in a bad mood, apparently looking for a fight.

'The day will come when I have to get rid of you, old chap,' thinks the game warden. 'Do me the favour of behaving yourself.'

On the way back to camp he soon meets a group of African tree-fellers going to work in the forest.

'Jambo, Bwana,' they exclaim. 'That old elephant over there give us plenty of trouble. He's real angry, only thinks about vita' (fighting).

'That's just too bad,' laughs the game warden, 'but listen to me: when you boys start sawing today, watch your marking lines carefully. When I say an inch I don't mean one-and-a-half above and three-quarters below!'

The natives go on their way grinning—the Bwana has sharp eyes!

The early sun is now streaming down on the camp, which lies on a ridge of rock a thousand feet above the world's largest extinct volcanic crater: Ngoro-Ngoro! Seen from above, the crater presents a panorama of indescribable grandeur.

A salt lake lies in the centre of this magnificent landscape, which looks like a giant's golf course, flanked by great forests, and farther away are the silver threads of little rivers and streams.

Wherever one looks across the vast expanse below, thousands upon thousands of black specks are to be seen . . . , animals . . . , animals everywhere. Although the game warden sees this breathtaking spectacle every day, he always finds it difficult to tear his eyes away from the majestic scene.

However, it is now time for breakfast. He quickly helps himself to three fried eggs with plenty of bacon; six pieces of toast and several cups of coffee follow—this meal has to suffice until evening. He does not want to waste valuable time having a full-scale picnic lunch down in the crater. He also changes out of the clothes which have had a soaking in the damp grass.

After three-quarters of an hour everything is ready: vacuum flasks full of tea, and a light rifle with enough cartridges, because down there among the animals of the plain a bullet is sometimes needed in order to put some suffering creature out of its misery. Four boys climb into the car; perhaps there will be work for them.

The descent is steep; the way down to the valley is a roughly-hewn zigzag track. Although the car is kept in bottom gear, the brakes have to help keep it in check. Half-way down the slope the first zebras come into view; a reedbuck rushes away from them, crying out shrilly. The black specks visible on all sides are becoming larger every minute—black specks whose vast numbers bear out the statistical fact that more than 40,000 wild animals live in this crater.

Over there can be seen herds of gnu two miles long and nearly a mile wide. These enormous herds, with the bulls that lead them well to the fore, are so densely packed that it would be impossible to estimate their numbers. Zebras probably hold the second place, numerically, the zebra herds often consisting of 500 to 1,000 head.

Once down on the crater floor, driving over the wide expanse of short grass is far easier, and the car runs smoothly along at about 18 m.p.h. The route to be taken today runs to the Lion kopjes (small hills), from there to the great Leitokitok swamp, where water birds twitter, and then back to the south side. A round tour of the crater floor covering almost 50 miles!

Rocks look like lions, and lions like rocks—and there are enough of both here. Over there a whole family are on view; the old maned lion is lying on a rock as though he were a bronze statue—hmmm, that's the old fellow with the dark brown mane; when he stands up he looks almost like a poodle. His wife is behind him, surrounded by her offspring, which are playing like frisky puppies in the sand. Yellow, cat-like eyes glance towards the car without interest. . . .

A few miles further on, and they are among the zebras. Four hundred on the left, three hundred on the right, six hundred straight ahead—striped bodies everywhere. They leave only just enough room for the car to get by, and some rush past, rear up on their hind legs, come to a halt, then gallop off again, their hooves flying. It's a grand game, showing a modern automobile what speed really means! At length the car is through the herd. What's that? Hyenas—more than a dozen of them—in a semicircle, noses down, stalking something in their rapid, ungainly manner. What are they after?

Suddenly their prey comes into view: from the bush there emerges a zebra, severely injured by lions. Blood is streaming down its flanks and quarters. The beast's belly has been torn open and its entrails are hanging out, but it staggers on in a desperate attempt to escape from its pursuers. This is an occasion on which man may take a hand in the workings of nature. The situation calls for a bullet to put an end to unnecessary suffering. A shot rings out; the zebra stallion rears up for the last time, then collapses.

The hyenas start back in alarm, a group of silver-grey Grant gazelles trot hurriedly away, gnus turn in astonishment towards the unusual noise, but then go on with their grazing. The crack of the rifle is soon forgotten; its sound, re-echoing many times from the crater walls, is attributed to natural forces.

The game warden glares after the hyenas—how he would enjoy sending a shot after those carrion-eaters! He hates the cowardly robbers, but here in a national park even hyenas have the right to live.

At Leitokitok begins the swampland, and a detour has to be made through a stretch of country lightly wooded with acacia trees. There—over there is a magnificent herd of eland, 200 strong—200 of the world's largest antelope, which can attain a weight of 2,000 lb. They pass at a steady trot; sometimes one will spring playfully over another, then with amazing agility one of these huge creatures will rear up on its hind legs.

On the marshland below are waterbuck and elegant, reddish impala, while on the upper slopes are zebras, gnus, kongonis, Thompson and Grant gazelles. Further away there is a large herd of splendid oryx antelope, well protected by their needle-sharp horns.

In the crater there are probably more than thirty different kinds of animal (figures cannot be exact), including even the rhinoceros, while in the marshes there live hippopotami whose ancestors were here in prehistoric times—no one knows how many thousands of years ago. Today the nearest large lake is 56 miles from the crater—a long walk for a hippopotamus!

Only the elephants and buffaloes are unwilling to leave their leafy paradise in the depths of the forest.

40,000 wild animals live in the crater. Including the Serengeti plains, which extend over thousands of square miles, this area probably harbours almost 400,000 animals.

The game warden gets out of his car and sits down beside a little woodland lake. How many years ago was it?—yes, more than twenty-seven, since he *walked* to Ngoro-Ngoro that first time—a distance of over 185 miles!

Near that streamlet he shot his first lion, and here by the lake the delicious plump becassins. What tasty morsels! How many shots, on average, did each one cost him? There—two are making off now, in their characteristic zigzag flight. Today no one shoots at them. Human beings, who can never keep peace among themselves, have made here a paradise on earth for the creatures of the wilds.

A plaintive cry brings him back to reality. It sounds as though there is a baby animal somewhere in the vicinity, yes—there in the thicket. He hurries over to the spot and finds a young impala, probably born yesterday. The little creature stands there on stiff, unsteady legs, its eyes almost unnaturally large. Its mother is nowhere to be seen.

The game warden picks it up carefully. The little thing at once tries to suck from him, as young animals so often will when they feel the warmth of a human being. He carries it into the clearing, puts it down, and hurries away, in the hope that its mournful crying will bring its mother to the spot.

However, there is still no impala to be seen, and without its mother the little creature would become the prey of jackals and hyenas during the coming night. The game warden quickly makes up his mind what to do, carries the little bundle to his car, and puts it in the lap of Saidi, who is used to this kind of rescue work. He keeps it warm during the drive back past the water-courses, which shine with a silvery glitter in the afternoon sunlight. Wild duck and geese rise into the air, filling it with their harsh cries, while on the other bank stately cranes survey the scene disdainfully.

At length the car winds its way up the tortuous track towards the camp, the engine roaring angrily and the radiator giving off clouds of steam. Thus the little expedition arrives back at the log huts.

'Ali—quick, warm milk, warm water, and the baby's bottle!' This last is always kept handy for use on such occasions, and for calming baby animals found abandoned in the bush. The impala kid starts sucking from the bottle at once, almost violently, it is so tired and thirsty. In a few weeks' time it will be leaping gaily round the camp, and perhaps one day return to the plain, if it feels so disposed. Here it is free.

The first drink of the evening is the best, taken sitting in a canvas chair after a long, hot and dusty journey. The game warden gazes out with something akin to awe and wonder as night falls slowly over Africa. The last pink rays of sunlight die out on the steep walls of the crater; the broad expanse below is seemingly bathed in a gentle violet twilight. After a while the colour has changed to dark lilac, and soon the crater is lost to sight in the dark blue expanse all around.

The evening breeze brings the first patches of mist overhead, and a goatsucker swoops past in happy flight. Listen—down there, far away, a deep sound reverberates through the night: the first lion. . . .

Lions Hunting

BY

B. J. BRIDGE

AS a keen observer of animal life in Africa I have had opportunities, over a period of many years, to watch instances of practical collaboration between animals of the same class. Numerous species of animals undoubtedly possess an effective method of communicating with one another which we are unable to comprehend. The instinctive mating call, the various expressions of warning, fear, rage and pain—all these are familiar, everyday utterances of animals of all kinds.

However, there are also occasions when there occurs a kind of thought transference, something lying beyond the boundary of pure instinct, and almost within the realm of the communication of definite ideas. During a trip which I recently made with my family in the Kruger National Park we witnessed an extraordinary example of collective endeavour undertaken by a pride of 16 lions hunting for food.

The lions emerged from the bush in twos and threes until the whole pride was clustered close to our car. After a while we noticed—as did the lions—that some buffalo were grazing about 150 yards away. It looked as though some of the lions were discussing the situation, because they began to stare intently in the direction of the buffalo. After a few minutes the pride split up into three hunting parties—let us call them the 'attack group', the 'support group' and the 'ambush group'. The attack group, consisting of three large lionesses, moved forward in a wide semicircle to the right of the road, in the general direction of the buffalo herd. The support group, three large and three smaller lions, struck out in a more restricted arc to the left, towards a spot likely to be in the path of the quarry when fleeing from the attack group.

The ambush group, consisting of nine young lions all told, lay down in a straight line, one behind another, in the middle of the road, so that they were hidden by the tall grass on either side unless they rose to their feet. The attack and support groups soon vanished from our sight. The ambush group remained in hiding blocking the most probable escape route of the buffalo herd, each of the lions quite clearly avoiding making any noticeable movement. From time to time the leading lion of this group got up and peered towards their prey. The third time he did this he waved his tail, whereupon the others all immediately rose and looked in the same direction as their leader. After a minute or two they all lay down again. We noticed that the leading lion looked around him on both sides for a while, and that those lying behind him at once followed suit.

It was quite clear, although we could not see the other two groups, that their lines of attack would be chosen in such a way as to drive the quarry towards the ambush group. During this period we could see the buffalo grazing peacefully, apparently quite unaware of the approaching danger. Suddenly, however, four of them took fright. They ran at top speed to the left, obviously alarmed by the attack group, which had skirted round them and had come in from their right flank. It looked as though the buffalo would be driven straight into the jaws of the support group, whose position had been chosen so skilfully that the buffalo were heading straight for the spot where they were lurking. At the last moment the buffalo saw the danger. They veered round, and the support group now drove them towards our car. Meanwhile the original attack group had stopped and crouched down, with their heads almost touching the ground. These lions seemed to know perfectly well that they had nothing more to do except to await developments. The buffalo thundered towards the final ambush, but after a few hectic yards they realized they were running into a deadly trap, and made instead for the verge of our road. Four of the ambush group of lions leapt up and pursued them for a few yards—but without success. The buffalo changed direction again, and rushed right across the road, only to have at least another four lions spring at them. Nevertheless the prey again escaped—and again only by a hair's breadth!

Within a few seconds the buffalo had vanished into the thick bush, and their pursuers gave up the chase. This negative result of the hunt must be reported here in the interests of credibility!

However, the method of attack demonstrated an almost human intelligence; the planning of the operation could hardly have been bettered. The failure of its final stage was no doubt to be attributed solely to the youth and inexperience of the ambush group, the last to go into action. We, having witnessed all that had occurred, were full of incredulous admiration for the perfect co-operation displayed by the lions. Each of the 16 lions knew every detail of the plan and acted accordingly. We could not tell whether the leader had explained the strategy and tactics to each individual or only to a few of the others, those leading the various groups taking part in the combined operation. The fact remains that each single animal was fully aware of the part assigned to it in the campaign plan—at the same time also knowing in advance what the intentions of each of its colleagues would be. . . .

The Old Poacher

BY

M. H. COWIE

The seriousness of the problem summarized in this experience of the Director of the Kenya National Parks can be judged by the fact that while every year in Tanganyika alone some 14,000 *wild animals are shot legally,* 150,000 *fall victim to poachers.*

RIVERS, which offer water and cool shade, thereby attracting animals in large numbers, are also the favourite haunts of native poachers. During the course of our journeys we had seen signs of their activities: rotting carcasses, bee-hives, and platforms in trees. All the time, more or less instinctively, we were on the look-out for further traces of these pitiless killers. For hundreds of years they have taken a heavy toll of elephants and rhinoceros—on account of their ivory. Poaching is easy enough if it is merely a matter of lying in wait at a vantage point where animals must pass, or near a water-hole, in order to strike down the first suitable victim with a poisoned arrow. The ivory is smuggled by devious routes to the coast, and is then transported by Arab sailing ships to the Orient.

The midday sun was already beating down fiercely when Warden Sheldrick's sharp eyes suddenly detected fresh footprints in the sand. I sent my men out scouting around, while our native assistants followed the tracks. Just as we were examining the sandbanks by the river, a shot rang out ahead of us. We hurried in the direction from which the shot had come, but were only in time to see three dark shapes disappear into the undergrowth beyond a cluster of palm trees. Warden Marshall drove his car across the bushland bordering on the river in an attempt to catch the marauders. One of them, suddenly aware of the car close behind him, was so terrified that he at once gave himself up. He had probably never been near a motor vehicle in his life. We brought him back to the sandbank in triumph.

Warden Sheldrick had frightened a herd of buffalo in his efforts to cut off the poachers. This meant that he lost valuable time, as he was forced to stand motionless on an anthill for several minutes while the herd thundered by, in constant danger of being trampled on. After that an exciting chase began, but the other two poachers managed to escape. It was perhaps fortunate for us that they did, because when we exchanged details of our experiences afterwards, as is customary on such occasions, it transpired that at the beginning of the pursuit one of the poachers had let off a poisoned arrow, missing our leading man by inches. Nevertheless the game warden had demonstrated great self-control, merely firing a shot in the air, although the law of the wilds would certainly have given him the right to draw a bead on the fugitive. He described the whole incident, as the African always will, in great detail, and showed us the poisoned arrow still sticking in the sand.

As it was clear that we had no chance of capturing the other two poachers, we continued our journey downstream with the prisoner. He was a little, dried-up man, dressed only in a dirty, shabby lion skin. We began the usual interrogation concerning his activities in the bush, wild game in general, and many points which we hoped he would elucidate for us. His replies to our questions were extraordinarily interesting—in fact he proved himself to be a real mine of information.

Natives of his kind lead adventurous lives. They are enabled to exist by the experience of past generations in their struggle against nature in the raw. They have learned how to find food and water in barren places, and to defend themselves against attack by lion, buffalo and rhinceros. They know how to tap plants for liquid in dry regions, and how to discover traces of hidden sources of water. They are especially adept at finding and gathering honey, a commodity in which they also trade. Each of them has his own area of trees, in which he leaves his bee-hives. It appears to be an unwritten law that no one may help himself to another's honey.

Further along the river we found a honey container which had fallen from a tree. Bees were swarming around the newly exposed honeycombs. The old man's eyes lit up when we told him to collect the honey. He looked around for the materials he needed in order to make a fire in the manner to which he was accustomed: a stick of hard wood and a hollowed-out piece of soft wood. In order to save time we gave him a box of matches, but he had no idea what to do with it. One of our game wardens had to demonstrate to him this piece of white man's magic. Then the old poacher picked up a dry lump of elephant dung, and set light to it. When it was burning well and giving off thick smoke he covered his head and neck with his old, grimy loin-cloth. Stark naked except for this cloth, he walked calmly towards the enraged bees. Evidently he had learned from past experience that the only place where he was vulnerable was on the neck; he seemed quite unconcerned by the danger of being stung on any other part of his body.

In one hand he held the smoking, stinking elephant dung, and with the other he carefully picked up the honeycombs, brushing aside the bees, which had been rendered almost insensible by the smoke. From time to time he would pause for a few moments to enjoy a mouthful of honey. All that the old man had done was quite simple, but the skill with which he had carried out every movement, without receiving a single sting, filled us with astonishment. With the natural courtesy of the African he offered each of us a piece of honeycomb. After we had stowed the rest of the honey away in the car, we continued our journey. On arriving at the furthest point along the strip of sand which was usable by cars, our goal for that day, we looked around for a suitable spot to camp. The old man was given some food, then we showed him where he was to sleep, between two African game wardens.

The chirping of the grasshoppers died away, and we soon sank, pleasantly weary, into that deep sleep which the cool, clear African night provides after the exertions of the day.

Early next morning, as the outlines of the rocks and trees were beginning to take shape, I discovered that the space between the two game wardens was empty. The old man's sandals, bow and arrows were still there, but he had slipped away in the silent night, taking with him only his bush knife and gourd-bottle. Evidently he was sure he would be able to make his way back alone, and rejoin his comrades.

Although I did not say so to the others, I could not repress a certain feeling of relief at the thought that the old man had regained his freedom. He was an unprepossessing, shrivelled-up creature, a mortal foe to our projects for the conservation of wild life, and a pitiless killer of animals—nevertheless he himself was a creature of the wilds. . . .

Today, as for so long in the past, the remoter areas of many national parks are a paradise for poachers, whose activities have to be kept in check, as far as possible, by the authorities responsible for the protection of game, using all the skill and knowledge at their disposal. The native poachers work in gangs of up to 50 men. They have many advantages in their cruel campaigns against animals. They shoot their poisoned arrows from cover—from high up in a tree overlooking a water-hole, for example, or from a rock which herds must pass. It is thus an easy matter for them to choose their victim and bring it down, without being in any danger themselves. If the poison does not act quickly enough, they have only to wait until the vultures circling in the air show them where the carcass is to be found. Then they can make off with the tusks of an elephant or the horn of a rhinoceros. They bury this booty until an opportune moment when it can be spirited away, or it may be sold at once, for a considerable sum of money, through a widespread illegal smuggling organization whose ramifications extend to the other side of the Indian Ocean. The poacher can earn as much on a single hunting foray as he would for two years' work on a sisal farm.

Native hunters, too, have the advantage over our game wardens in that they know the location of all the water-holes, and they can travel light through the bush, at high speed, leaving no trace behind them. It isn't easy to deal with them, particularly in view of the fact that they will sometimes even shoot at our men—fortunately without fatal consequences so far. One of our game wardens had a poisoned arrow shot at him. It pierced one side of his water-bottle, but the other side saved him from the fate of the elephants for which such arrows are normally intended—there is as yet no known antidote to the deadly poison on these arrows. . . .

Kalahari—a Day in the Life of a Camera Hunter

BY

WILHELM SCHACK
Pretoria

THE fiery glow of the morning sun begins to spread in the eastern sky. I become aware of this first sign of a new day through half-closed eyes— I am barely awake. . . . From minute to minute the play of colours just above the horizon becomes more and more intensive, as ever-new tints are reflected on the delicate cloud formations high overhead. The air can be as clear as this only in the Kalahari—an enchanted land of hard, impressive grandeur, so unflatteringly described as a desert. . . .

Have I been asleep? Not really. The Kalahari night is bitterly cold. Bitterly cold, and full of the noises which send pleasant shivers up the spines of the audience at a film whose scene is set in Africa. However, these noises are not so pleasant for a camera hunter spending the night lying on a hard mattress in the open air, guarded by a camp-fire near a water-hole; they follow him in his restless dreams: the screeching of night birds coming from everywhere and nowhere, the mournful wailing of jackals, the evil laughter of hyenas. They form a choir whose sound no one in such a spot can avoid, until from far and near, and coming steadily closer the bass part of the chorus begins to predominate: the rumbling growl of the king of the Kalahari, beginning his hunting forays under cover of darkness. The lions, which I am here to hunt, armed with nothing but a camera, have announced their arrival.

Still half asleep, I recall the distant roaring during the night which has just ended. The lions were holding conversations—or at least the males were; they keep in constant touch with each other during the hours of darkness. Do they exchange details of their hunting plans? Nothing is heard from the lionesses, but they must be there too, as I know full well, because they are the real hunters. Their task is to seize and slaughter the prey which the males have driven towards them.

I've wasted too much of the morning dreaming. . . . I get up and stretch my arms. I must make use of the cool morning hours, the only period of the day when it is possible to move about without becoming bathed in sweat. They are, in addition, the only hours when lions are to be seen lying in the open, digesting their night's meal, before escaping from the fierce heat of the midday sun into the protective shade of the thick undergrowth.

Two hours later we catch sight of the first lions.

I am already sitting at the wheel of my car when, for some reason or other, it occurs to me to have a look before starting off, at the water-hole which lies only a stone's throw from our camp, partly hidden by grass and bushes. After all, we haven't spent the night near that spot purely for our own comfort. A Kalahari water-hole is a meeting place for animals of every kind, as they all have to come there from far and wide when they want a drink.

I hang the Leica camera round my neck, get out of the car, and begin to stroll in the direction of the water-hole, hands in pockets. . . . Suddenly I see two lionesses in front of me! Their destination is the same as mine, and they come to a halt, as surprised to see me as I am to see them. Only the tips of their tails swing slightly to and fro. Needless to say, I stand stock-still. It occurs to me that the two of them have undoubtedly spent the whole night roaming about near our camp. Lions are not great travellers; they generally live near their water-hole, and never go far away from it. Moreover lions, like all the other members of the cat family, are notoriously inquisitive. And as for lionesses . . . I wouldn't be surprised if they had prowled round my bed during the night. . . . They are both splendid-looking specimens, well nourished, their coats perfectly smooth and sleek.

The question of whether lions kill through lust for blood—that is to say when they have already eaten their fill—has often been discussed in the comfort of arm-chairs round the fire at home. It is often said, and I believe quite correctly, that the only lions really dangerous to human beings—apart from those which have been shot at—are a few abandoned by their families, and some old, sick beasts.

That is the opinion generally held before a cosy fire at home. It is a totally different matter when one is suddenly confronted by two fully-grown lionesses, who possibly do not know whether they are 'dangerous' or not. The only thing they know for certain is that they want to get to the water, and that I am in their way. I, a creature that, oddly enough, spent the night by the fire over there.

Quite understandably they don't regard my presence in a very favourable light. (I can still see that fact quite clearly shown in the photos which, needless to say, I hasten to take.) The whole episode lasts for perhaps a quarter of an hour. One of the most tense quarter-hours of my life. . . .

A lioness comes nearer, looking at me questioningly, with the tip of her tail twitching. She attempts to summon up enough determination to break through to the water-hole, but fails. She lies down in the grass, then gets up again and goes back to join her companion, who makes a similar attempt—with the same negative result. All this takes place, if the distance-finder of my camera is telling the truth, some fifteen or twenty yards from where I am standing. However often the manœuvre is repeated it doesn't bore me. Finally it is the two lionesses who lose patience, and they withdraw into the bush with what I can only describe as a look of part-astonishment, part-disappointment, on their faces, leaving me alone with the water-hole, and a roll of film full of pictures of lionesses.

In the evening Willem, my coloured assistant, and I will have reason to regret the fact that the lionesses have not gone far . . . but more of that later.

As soon as they are out of sight I go back to the car. Willem has watched the whole scene from there, his eyes wide open in alarm.

Following a trail overgrown by grass, we make our way with difficulty across a long, monotonous chain of dunes, until we reach a dried-up river bed. It must have been from here that we heard the roaring of lions during the night.

'There, Baas!' Willem points excitedly up into the sky. A tiny black speck is plunging earthward out of the steel-blue infinity above, growing larger every moment. Then, I too, realize what it is: a vulture! And where there is a vulture plunging downward there must be food for it. I start the car, and drive towards the spot to which the flying public health police of the Kalahari have directed our attention. A whole squad of them, summoned by mysterious signals, are now close behind their leader. One speck after another plunges down from the heights.

I drive on for a few hundred yards, then we notice a yellow shadow moving through the tall grass. It vanishes behind a low bush. A stone's throw further on we come to the savaged carcass of an oryx antelope in a small clearing. The lovely eyes torn, the splendid horns in the dust, it lies in a pool of its blood—here, where yellow death lay in wait for it during the early hours of the morning as it went its way, peacefully grazing among the herd. Now, under cover of the same bush which concealed the killer, jackals and hyenas wait for us men—who are powerful and dangerous enough to drive even the king of beasts from his meal—to leave the field clear for them. Their curved beaks lowered, wings puffed up and bare necks bent in blissful anticipation, the vultures perch on dead branches of nearby trees, awaiting the meal which falls to them from the table of the four-legged robbers.

Our arrival has disturbed the 'natural' course of events, the course they have followed for thousands of years. I climb out of the car and walk the few steps to the dead antelope. Numerous tracks lead to it. At least three lions have been feeding here! When they heard the approaching car they must have made off through the long grass. From where I am standing I can see jackals watching from among the trees all around. Now I can also clearly see the lions, lying in the grass some distance from the jackals; they raise their heads from their front paws half inquiringly, half angrily, as I bend over to examine the horns of their victim.

I know that the beasts of prey, which must have almost eaten their fill already, will not attack me. This is not the first time I have driven a lion away from its prey, on foot, and armed only with a camera, in order to get some good photos.

Barely a hundred yards away from me there still stand the herd of antelope from among which the lion seized its victim. They gaze at me inquiringly, with their heads raised high: a man, one of the killers they fear far more than the king of beasts, who only slays when hunger compels him to.

I manœuvre the car out of the wind into position so that I have a clear field of vision for taking photographs, and stay seated at the wheel with my camera at the ready. Nothing happens. Nothing at all! Not even a vulture swoops down from one of the trees on to the carcass. For almost two hours I wait in the growing heat—then I decide to take the body in tow. There can't be any doubt that numerous animals will follow the powerful scent. How wrong I am! Not even the jackals consider it worth the trouble, not, at least, while the sun is still in the sky.

As it nears the horizon I give up waiting. Almost the whole day has been wasted—more than enough time.

To the east banks of delicate pink cloud hover in the light blue expanse above the buff-coloured sand dunes, and behind them the glowing ball of the sun sinks down between the silhouettes of dead acacia trees. I simply must photograph that!

Behind Willem, who is carrying the camera tripod, I walk slowly towards the dunes, but the further we go, the more impossible it appears to be to get the picture I want. Either the tree silhouettes are not right, or the crests of the dunes seem to cut into the clouds, and spoil the effect. In short, nothing doing. Annoyed, I call out to Willem to turn right and make for the water-hole, where there stands an old wind pump which I decided earlier would make a good vantage point. It rises from the top of a low dune barely a hundred yards away. I do not yet know that those hundred yards are to be the most dangerous of my life as a photographer. As Willem turns towards me he lets out a piercing yell, drops the tripod, and runs like a man possessed....

A glance over my shoulder, and I am petrified with horror. A huge lioness is following me at a steady trot—in a few seconds she would have reached me! I am glad, and even a little proud, to be able to say that I don't drop the camera —I place it on the ground, if rather hastily, before rushing off after Willem.... The lioness, now pursuing me in long, graceful bounds, is only a few yards away as I reach the wind pump tower, and streak like lightning up its oily ladder.

The normally talkative and ever-smiling Willem is staring down from the highest point of the tower at the lioness, who, in turn, is glaring up at us. She gives no indication at all that she is thinking of going away....

It is often stated that lions, however harmless they may be at other times, will wait with patient tenacity when their first attack has merely resulted in their prey being driven up a tree. In fact they really haven't anything better to do.

Some time elapses before this aspect of the situation occurs to me. At first my principal sensation is one of relief at having escaped from the deadly peril which suddenly threatened me. Then, however, as the lioness shows not the slightest sign of giving up her vigil, I try to visualize a cold night spent without a bed or blanket, hanging on to the filthy struts of a wind pump. I am quite unable to visualize it.... The longest half hour of my life crawls by.... Then the lioness's attention is attracted by something more interesting.... She pricks up her ears and moves off on an east-north-east course, not without giving us a parting look, as if regretting what might have been. A second lioness emerges from the bush to meet her, and the pair of them are soon lost to sight.

Meanwhile, at the appearance of the second beast, a thought occurs to me: aren't they the same two lionesses who wanted to drink at the water-hole early this morning? Didn't they then disappear in the same direction as that from which they appeared this time? No doubt about it, it was the same pair!

It is rapidly becoming darker. We must make haste if we are to reach the car while there is still some light. While Willem stays at the top of the tower to warn me, if necessary, I quickly clamber down to the ground. The car is about two hundred yards away, two hundred yards which I cover with very mixed feelings, running cautiously from tree to tree.

I have almost reached the car when I see the silhouette of a lion rise from the dunes.

I drive to the pump tower to pick up Willem, my camera and its tripod. Not until we are on the way to our nearby camp does Willem find his voice again, and then tries to make up for lost time by talking far faster and louder than usual —but I'm not listening. I'm thinking what a fool I've been. How could I so quickly forget my experience in the morning! Of all idiotic things to do, blindly walking into the territory of the lions I'd met and annoyed during the morning!

Not far from our camp a large thorn tree stretches its dead branches, split by lightning many years ago, up into the quickly darkening sky. We move the camp nearer to the tree, and set fire to it. We are sure its thick trunk will burn so brightly all night that no lion, however inquisitive, will venture to approach us. We eat a supper out of tins, and lie down on our hard mattresses.

For a long time I remain awake, gazing up at the black sky with its multitude of stars. I think about the fortunate outcome of my encounters with the lioness, and my bad luck in being unable to photograph her at our second meeting.... About midnight I wake up for a short time. Far away in the distance lions are roaring. The fire is still blazing with unabated vigour....

By the time the first pale beams of the morning sun are beginning to light up the dunes, we are already up and dressed. I go the few steps to the place where we left the dead antelope after towing it there yesterday evening. Nothing to be seen. At first I think I've made a mistake. Was this really the spot? No doubt about it; Willem bears out what I say. We can't imagine what has become of the carcass. Then, as we stand there, we notice on the bare patch of earth the prints of many feet, showing all too clearly what has been going on during the night. In the silent hours hyenas, jackals—and possibly even our pair of lionesses—have polished off the meal.

On closer examination I find a trail of something which has been dragged, leading into long grass. I follow it—to the spot where the head of the oryx antelope lies alone among the stalks of grass.

The Elephants in the Addo Bush

BY

WILHELM SCHACK
Pretoria

FORTY miles from Port Elizabeth lies a unique animal protection area—the Addo bush, in which a small herd of elephant have now at last found shelter. They are the last survivors of the multitudes which once possessed a measureless empire of their own in this part of the world. Twenty-one of the giant beasts still live in the Addo bush. They have found peace and security now that the 8,000 acres of their refuge have been surrounded by an eleven-mile-long fence (too modest a word, surely, for a construction of steel tresses and railway lines!)

The last Addo elephant had already been sentenced to death. Frequent complaints by farmers, who had long ago cultivated the land all around, had forced the government to take this step. The idea was to make a clean sweep. A sharpshooter was engaged, and shot more than a hundred elephants. Then the tables were turned, and the hunter became the hunted. The few elephants which had escaped the slaughter became so shrewd and so violent that they gained precious time, and—a rare occurrence in the history of the animal world—the death sentence was repealed.

In the meantime the world had become aware of what was happening, and protests against so drastic a measure were received from many countries. The same administration which had ordered the massacre of the elephants ordered a cease-fire. Fifteen of the intended victims were left. . . .

Poor creatures! These elephants, driven by their ever-present fear of violent death to hide by day in the almost impenetrable Addo bush, had no easy time of it. Ever since the days of the shooting, the survivors have broken off all contact with the outside world. They live in the densest and darkest patches of the Addo bush; it is only at night that they venture out, and they are then foes of all living things.

Man, their former enemy, is naturally well known to them—they hate him with an irreconcilable hatred which still remains undiminished. Woe to anyone who crosses their path. No mercy will be shown! These Addo elephants have become the most dangerous in Africa—and no wonder, for they have good reason to hate mankind. . . .

It is said that time heals all wounds. This is not, however, true of the relationship between the Addo elephant and human beings, even though man now does everything in his power to help the animals. The Addo bush was declared a national park, which means that elephants and other wild animals are to be spared there—in all circumstances. The provision of water for the animals was increased, and a strong fence was built to protect them from human marauders—all by the government which had previously sentenced the elephants to death. What a blessing it is for all living creatures that the idea of animal protection has now become so powerful a force.

Nevertheless, without being a pessimist, one is bound to ask oneself the question: for how long? How many more generations will have the chance to see these last survivors of their race alive? How large a community can be built up on the basis of a dozen elephants? At present all is well, and calves are being born every year, but will signs of serious degeneration not manifest themselves sooner or later? Then there is the question of increased living space for these animals. More land is constantly being required for cultivation, leaving less and less territory free for wild animals. Let us hope that when another crisis occurs fate will again take a hand on behalf of animal life.

I took my camera to the Addo elephants. They presented me with new problems of animal photography, because during the day they remain hidden away in the bush, so that I was only able to photograph them at certain places by night, using a flashlamp. Not without danger, because telescopic photo-equipment is no help at night—one has to get close to the elephants!

Only the blinding light of my flashlamp saved me from furious charges. It was thus that I obtained my night photographs of Addo elephant, one of which is reproduced in the pictorial section of this book. They again place my grey friends in the centre-point of interest, this time, however, with the sole purpose of creating friendship and understanding for them—as a small act of reparation for what once happened to them and their kind. . . .

Encounters with Gorillas

BY

R. HOIER

Formerly Game Protection Official in the Congo

BEFORE I write of some encounters with the 'gorilla of the volcano area' (*Gorilla gorilla beringei*) I will give a brief description of the Albert National Park, where this creature is to be found. (His near relation is the 'mountain gorilla', *Gorilla gorilla rex pygmaeorum*.)

The Albert National Park lies in the 'great African trough' on either side of the equator. Within its bounds are a chain of eight great volcanoes, the two at the western end of the chain being still active, the others extinct. (This chain forms the watershed between the river systems of the Congo and the Nile.)

In the western section of the National Park rise the Mitumba Mountains; there, on the highest reaches, between 7,000 and 10,000 ft., the mountain gorilla is to be found. To the east of the trough is the area of the volcano gorilla (*Beringei*), within the limits of the National Park, as well as in the Kanyonza forest, which also lies in a volcanic area, to the south-west of Uganda.

In the Albert National Park the habitat of the volcano gorilla is dependent on the vegetation. He is to be found in the high-lying bamboo forests (*Bambusa alpina*), which grow at altitudes of between 7,000 and 9,000 ft. in the Hagenia region (isolated specimens occurring from 7,800 ft., while larger numbers live between 8,800 and 10,500 ft.), and in adjacent areas of wooded heathland. Beyond lie regions covered by low vegetation.

These mountainous areas are extremely cold and damp. The Hagenia district seems best suited to the gorilla. Although he descends to the bamboo forests only when, following a dry period, rain promises fresh bamboo shoots, of which he is very fond, in the district which he principally inhabits he lives on wild celery. This flourishes in the undergrowth, together with wild blackberries, which are plentiful up to about 11,200 ft. For additional nourishment, I believe he enjoys a rich booty of insects, eggs and young birds. In any event, it is only very rarely that he descends to the lower-lying districts where there are native settlements.

Gorillas live in families and larger groups of up to 20, or sometimes even more. A strange custom, unique to gorillas, is that of making a primitive nest in a forked tree or among bamboo, some nine to twelve feet above the ground—solely for their young. Their elders sleep on the ground, often on a pile of leaves. The curious point about this nest-building is that it does not occur regularly, but only on occasion. A gorilla will never use the same sleeping place twice. Pigmies explain that this is because he leaves it in such a filthy condition. . . .

But why a nest at all? No one knows for certain. I believe that the mother gorilla is concerned with protecting the young animals from the dampness underfoot, and therefore provides them with a crude shelter raised above the ground. It is also possible that the older and stronger beasts, sleeping on the ground, believe they are thus in a better position to protect their young from leopards prowling in the night. (I have sometimes seen lion, too, in this district at a height of 8,500, even 10,800 ft.)

In the year 1935 I accompanied the Rector of the Free University of Brussels, Monsieur G. Smets, on an ascent of Karisimbi. We did not follow the example of most parties by using the only path, which runs between the Mikeno saddle and the Rukumi plateau, but hacked our way through the bush in order to reach a ravine to the west of the plateau. We had almost reached it when I heard a noise coming from the other side of a dense clump of blackberries and other bushes—it sounded as though someone was coming towards us. I asked my native assistant, a pigmy named Maguru, whether it could be one of his fellow-tribesmen, because the guttural noise which I had heard sounded similar to those by which pigmies communicate with one another when hunting at night. Maguru made a gesture to signify a reply in the negative, then he whispered to me the word 'Ngagi!' meaning 'gorilla'. We paused for a moment, then went round the bushes, and at once found the track which the great beast had made through the undergrowth on its way down the mountainside. It was evidently a mature male, on its own, and it could not have heard us. This was fortunate, for none of us had any great desire to be suddenly confronted face to face by a gorilla, particularly as we had no weapons with us.

Whenever I recall this near-meeting I hear again in my imagination the deep, rough voice of the animal, which was holding a conversation with itself, and therefore failed to hear us. Often in later years I have heard young gorillas screeching when they are squabbling among themselves, but this sound bears no resemblance at all to that made by the old male talking to himself.

At about the time when I first went to the Albert National Park, in 1931, Colonel Maxwell arrived there from Nairobi. He is deservedly famous for his photographs of big game, and had received permission to visit the gorilla territory in order to take a series of photographs of this rare creature. (The results were rather meagre, on account of the extreme difficulties involved.)

After someone had reported the whereabouts of a family of gorillas, the Colonel made for the spot led by two native assistants—one of them was Maguru—and followed by his white hunter. The family was found to consist of a powerful male, several females, and their young. They all retreated when they first saw the men—but a little while later the male gorilla suddenly charged out of the undergrowth towards the little group, knocked Tshabo, the second native assistant, over with an almost casual sweep of his hand, and made straight for the Colonel. . . . The white hunter, bringing up the rear, had just time to bring the beast down with a shot before it could seize the Colonel.

From then onward I have made it a rule never to carry weapons, being careful instead not to disturb the great apes when I am in their territory. Above all I never try to follow them in an attempt to keep them under observation because every instance in which a man has had to resort to the use of a firearm against a gorilla has originated with the same situation: the male gorilla has gone over to the attack when it knew the females and young were on their way to safety. Then it has turned on the pursuers, covering the family's retreat with its own body. This action is in accordance with the instinct of almost all animals living in families or larger groups: the male places itself between its fleeing family and what it believes to be the attackers, and is at once ready to make the supreme sacrifice for the others.

In order to illustrate this admirable characteristic of the gorilla it seems fitting to quote from the book *Gorillas* by Ben Burbridge, who, in 1922, received permission to catch some young gorillas on the volcanoes Mikeno and Karisimbi. He was descending one of the mountains with his booty—several young gorillas secured in primitive cages—when he passed near the spot where he had captured them (page 237 of his book):

'Suddenly a face, fringed with long hair, emerged from the undergrowth in front of us. The pigmies and cage-bearers started back in alarm. I took my gun from my bearer. We stood there for a moment, our eyes trying to penetrate the green wall of the primeval forest. No one said a word. Suddenly we heard a cry from about 30 yards away. A gorilla broke through the thicket which surrounded us—rushing forward, then going back again. The movement of the foliage showed us which way he had gone; his cries rent the silence of the forest. The camera was set up. . . . I had long hoped for such an encounter, and it seemed that my dream was at last to become reality. I had often tried to film a gorilla, but always without success. My gun-bearer got into position behind the camera, with his hand on the handle. Two bearers, who were standing in front of me with a caged gorilla, now approached the steaming undergrowth where the gorilla family were hiding. The young prisoners suddenly shrieked loudly in reply to the calls of their parents. That was the signal. The two men began to move with their dangerous load. Like lightning, without any warning, a huge gorilla charged forward out of the shadows of the jungle, running unsteadily on his short legs. Out of the corner of my eye I could see Joe turning the camera handle. I looked round just in time—to see the gorilla almost on top of me. He was so near that I was compelled to pull the trigger of the gun which was levelled at him, in legitimate defence. This was the only shot of the encounter. The beast dropped, and a howling of many voices from the gorillas behind him answered the shot. They immediately fell silent, however, struck as if by lightning at the sight of what had happened. With a last glance at the lifeless body of their leader they vanished, one after another, into the jungle. I was sorry, very sorry, for I did not want to destroy this magnificent creature who had fought for his young.'

This, then, is an example of the 'evil nature' and belligerent intentions shown by the gorilla. What did he do? He attacked the man who had robbed him of one of his children, and had goaded him to the point of desperation by having the young carried, shrieking, past the spot where he and the others were hiding. Such a case of 'legitimate defence' has far more of a challenge about it. . . .

On each of his two expeditions Ben Burbridge captured four young gorillas. Only one among the first four arrived in Belgium; the other three were dead by the time the party reached Dar-es-Salaam. The fourth died soon after its arrival in the Antwerp Zoo.

Almost all the expeditions which visited the Kivu volcanoes were involved in similar cases of killing in 'legitimate defence', and the number of slain gorilla grew so rapidly that the danger of this species becoming extinct was soon acute. In consequence the three volcanoes Mikeno, Karisimbi and Bishoke were declared a national park, that is to say an area in which wild life receives unqualified protection, with the result that the continued existence of the gorilla was at last assured.

By comparison with the events already described, my own encounters with the great anthropoid apes may seem insignificant. Nevertheless I will say something about them, as they concern the gorilla seen in peaceful circumstances and—perhaps!—already to some extent accustomed to meeting human beings.

In February 1937 I was on my way to the peak of Karisimbi, where the meteorological service of the colony had placed a rainfall-gauge, whose findings I wanted to read. I spent some time at a rest hut known as the Kabara, waiting for the bearers who had dropped a little way behind. Suddenly, after we had been there some ten minutes, Maguru exclaimed, 'Ngagi!' There they were for all to see: behind the hut, the first about twenty yards away, the other two a little further off, were three gorillas, old males with the fur on their backs silver-grey. The first, somewhat perturbed by our presence, made his way slowly on up the thickly overgrown slope, while the other two did not move. Then all three sat where they were while our bearer walked past them at a distance of some forty yards. We then continued on our way with the bearers. The gorillas neither made the slightest sound nor showed any alarm, let alone hostility.

I have never myself seen a gorilla beating its chest with its fists in a rage, as Du. Chaillu described in his book. However, Alex T. Barns and other explorers have witnessed this drumming, which is said to be terrifying in its effect. I believe the gorilla only gives vent to his feelings in this way on occasions when he is furiously angry.

While descending from Karisimbi in 1938 I had an opportunity to watch a family of 16 gorilla, who were divided from my party by the Kanyamagufa ravine. I had twelve bearers with me, and we were about fifty yards from the animals, who could see us clearly. For about ten minutes I watched them through a telescope, but could not estimate the size of individuals with any accuracy as the difference of level—I was considerably higher than they were—made judgement difficult, even though the ground was covered only with low ferns and wild celery plants. Divided from us by the ravine, they felt completely out of danger. Native bearers who passed by next day saw them still in the same place.

On another occasion we came almost face to face with a gorilla. Travelling towards the Bishoke volcano we were following the pigmy Kagimba through a trackless forest. He was walking a few steps ahead of the rest of the party, occasionally striking off a few blackberry shoots with his bush knife. Suddenly we saw him start back, then we heard the sound of a large animal breaking through the undergrowth. We had stumbled on a lone gorilla who was slaking his thirst from a little stream, and immediately made off when the pigmy suddenly appeared scarcely six feet away from him.

Our negro game wardens often come across gorillas during their tours of inspection, but the animals have never shown the least signs of hostility. As our men are unarmed, they naturally cannot risk any provocation. . . .

West of the line Mikeno–Karisimbi I have never found traces of the gorilla below the 7,500- or 7,800-ft. level. The reason for this is not far to seek: the lower-lying areas abound with chimpanzee, and these two classes of anthropoid ape do not get on at all well together.

In this article I have tried to rectify, to some extent, the opinion generally held of the volcano gorilla—that he is a dangerous and naturally hostile beast. On the other hand, how can we blame an animal which knows it is being hunted, if it tries to defend itself and its family?

Adventures with Bears in the Canadian Rockies

BY

DR. PAUL EIPPER

THE black bears or baribals of the mountain parks are not vicious, menacing beasts of prey, but neither are they harmless domestic animals. When a car comes to a halt at a vantage point along one of the park roads, at one of the spots where fires are allowed to be lit, or at a camp, at least one blacky will at once come ambling along to get whatever may be going. He frolics about so delightfully and is so photogenic that pieces of chocolate, sandwiches and oranges are showered on him. However, if the supply of tit-bits is meagre, or is cut off too soon for his liking, the amiable beggar becomes suddenly transformed into a snapping, importunate highway robber. The park authorities have therefore erected large notices forbidding the feeding of bears on pain of a 500-dollar fine, and even imprisonment.

I am not exaggerating when I say that we, Eugen Schuhmacher, my wife Veronika and I, saw a good 200 blackies during the months we spent in the Rocky Mountains, and some of them had not yet learned to beg. We had been granted permission by the authorities to make use of the narrow 'fire roads', bumpy earthen tracks designed to enable fire-fighters to reach the scene of forest fires, and normally closed to private vehicles. These tracks took us in our sturdy car into vast tracts of wooded and mountainous wilderness devoid of human habitation. We were thus enabled greatly to increase our knowledge of bears. I now know that the blacky mothers demonstrate a remarkable degree of patience in the face of bad and even violent behaviour on the part of their offspring. If driven too far, though, the mothers will sometimes box their insubordinate children's ears and drive them up to the tops of tall fir trees. There the youngsters amuse themselves vastly, shinning up the trunks and from branch to branch, making a great deal of noise. Meanwhile the mothers rest at the foot of the trees, apparently relaxed but ever alert, ready to protect their offspring if danger threatens.

Veronika once unintentionally roused a large black bear from its winter sleep. One night at the beginning of October a fierce snowstorm roared through the crags of the Rockies. On the following morning the slope where we had spent the night was knee-deep in snow, and when the midday sun began to touch the cold splendour all round with a magical glitter of silver we set forth uphill, eager for adventure. There wasn't a bear to be seen anywhere, or indeed any living creatures apart from a couple of Whisky Jack jays. It wasn't easy to get up the steep slope with its tangle of low bushes, camera at the ready. Veronika stumbled, and as she struggled to her feet the ground in front of her came to life. There was a rustling and a flurry of snow, then in the hollow between some bushes and a clump of old pine trees something dark appeared: a blacky sitting up on his haunches. Obviously he had allowed the snow to cover him during the night, and was so startled by his rude awakening that it was some time before he could get his muscles and tendons to begin working. Veronika immediately took a photograph, which remains as a permanent proof of how bad tempered the bear looked as he glared at the unexpected brightness all around. His left eye was still half closed. Higher up on the slopes during the next hour we came across seven blackies, all thawing out and drying their fur in the sun. They would scurry to and fro, turning somersaults, and sometimes slide down the hillside on their ice-encrusted hindquarters. Two youngsters were apparently wrestling, in an upright position. They would hold each other fast by the shoulders and neck, growling and crying out in what seemed to be a raging fury, though they were probably doing no more than playing like rowdy boys. Black bear mothers sometimes give birth to a litter of cubs of various colours, for example one black and one reddish-brown. We saw one cinnamon-coloured baby and its black mother playing with a large snowball which they had made. They had a fine game with it, until at length the white sphere disintegrated. A few weeks earlier we had seen a badly deformed adult blacky with his snout askew, a hairless patch on his left shoulder, and scars on his cheek. One ear was missing. We imagined that these injuries were the results of fighting, but a game warden told us that the damage had been caused by frost-bite. In the previous, particularly cold winter the poor creature had evidently been unable to find a sufficiently warm shelter.

Privation still exists in the world of bears. One frosty morning I saw two blackies knock over the heavy dustbins in front of the houses of Banff in an attempt to appease their hunger. However, I would rather describe a happier experience which we had during summer by the Muleshoe Lake. Tired out by the strong wind and a long search for beavers, I lay stretched out in the midday sun beside that woodland lake far from even the outposts of civilization. In a hollow a little way away Eugen was kneeling down, repairing the wooden camera tripod. Suddenly he started to his feet: 'Hey, something black has just flown past my shoulder!' I swallowed a few times then pointed to the nearest tree. 'Yes, a blacky, it's hanging on that tree trunk recovering from its acrobatic display!'— Barely ten seconds before that I had heard a humming sound behind me, and had cautiously turned round. Above me, on the embankment beside the lake, appeared the head of a black bear. My first thought was to raise the alarm, but there wasn't time. The bear had already seen the two of us, had taken fright and started to rush down the slope. Failing to halt, it had instead made a leap which took it past me and immediately above Schuhmacher, to land in the tree. When Veronika returned from a berry-picking expedition she refused to believe our story although we swore it was true—until a few days later when, after a thunderstorm, two noble stags fled in terror out of the woods, with a ball of black fur tearing furiously after them. Yes, the clumsy blackies can certainly be extremely swift and agile on occasion!

*

Enough about baribals, about black and cinnamon-coloured specimens—let's get on to the brown bear. 'He's a gentleman, really the king of the forest,' the wardens say. 'You must be polite to him, and make yourself known at once. The best thing to do is to knock on a stone or against trees when you get on a lonely trail in his territory. Loud singing is good, too. If you disturb him at close quarters during his sleep he'll feel trapped, unable to escape, and may attack you savagely. The only thing to do then is to climb for dear life up a high tree; the grey fellow can't climb!'

My friend Eugen, whose principal objective in the Rockies was the filming of grizzly bears, came to a totally different conclusion from the generally held opinion concerning the *'ursus horribilis'*, the 'dreadful bear'. 'He's a poltroon, a coward! You only have to cough quietly or scratch a piece of wood with your fingernail, and he'll make off hell for leather.' It's a fact that most grizzlies which we heard or managed to see for a moment vanished at once, and although we got close to grizzlies eighteen times not one of them attacked us. 'You've been lucky—you might have had a nasty surprise,' replied the game wardens, who are neither given to exaggeration nor naturally nervous men. 'Ninety times the grizzly makes himself scarce; at their ninety-first meeting he attacks like a bolt of lightning, with the result that the man almost certainly bites the dust.'

Grizzlies are everywhere and nowhere in the world of the Rockies. They are said to be great travellers, covering up to 25 miles in a day. During the weeks of summer when insects abound they climb up to the high ground where berries grow in profusion, then they again descend to the valleys, often to seek out a dump, one of the deep hollows in the woods which are used for the refuse from human settlements. We spent many nights in a jeep with the game warden Frank near the huge Jasper dump, gazing intently at the pile of dully smouldering refuse. This warden has worked for 45 years in one of the best grizzly bear districts of Canada, and thanks to him we suddenly saw an enormous grizzly rise up on its hind legs amid the smoke, only about fifteen yards away from where we were sitting. The colossus didn't move, but looked inquiringly in our direction. I don't know how long it stood thus, and I can't remember being afraid—I certainly had no sense of imminent danger. The sight was so splendid and majestic that I enjoyed it for its own sake, forgetting all other considerations.

In one place we discovered a tree which grizzlies had been scratching with their claws; the deep furrows in the bark extended up to about eight feet from the ground. At the end of September the marks of a grizzly's paw could be seen clearly in the snow covering a lumberjacks' bridge; I was able to lay my hands side by side in the impression left by the paw without touching either edge of it. About $3\frac{1}{2}$ inches in front of the paw mark were the holes made by the grizzly's long, curved claws. This was at a tributary of the Spray River, amid rocky crags, where Eugen and I had constructed a look-out post in the trees on the far side of the river, and had spent many long hours in the evenings and at night keeping watch in the freezing cold. We had no success until the day before our departure. That morning a female grey bear with her two children passed across a nearby patch of open ground at a time when the light was just right for filming. Schuhmacher richly deserved this success, not only as a reward for his patience in waiting so long, but because all through the period of disappointment, when grey bears had appeared only during dark nights, he had brought tempting presents, leaving a large, smelly fish-head in the clearing, and daubing every tree trunk in the vicinity with syrup.

However, we got our clearest view of a grizzly without going to any trouble at all. We were just finishing an evening trip on the Jasper Plateau when a huge object appeared moving between some bushes and trees in the valley a little way below. 'It's a bear—no doubt about it, but it's got much longer legs than a blacky. It's got an enormous head, almost round, a ruff of fur at the neck, a ridge between the shoulders, and a straight back. From the shoulders over the flanks to its dark brown legs there's a light grey shimmer running over its fur. It's a silver grizzly, the king of the whole race!' Behind him appear two younger grizzlies. All three ambled, even walked, calmly along, confident in the knowledge of their power; we got an uninterrupted view of them as they passed along the edge of the woods. . . .

Experiences in the Camargue

BY

ELEONORE WALDHOER-HAEHNLE

'ANYONE who wants to experience Africa in Europe must go to the Camargue!' Those words made such an impression on me as a child that I never quite forgot them. They were spoken by C. G. Schillings, celebrated for his explorations in Africa, during one of his many visits to the house of my grandmother, an enthusiast for nature conservation. However, many years were to elapse before the dream of my childhood became reality. Then, on a hot day in August, I first set foot in the Camargue.

A hazy mist above the swamps reaching to the horizon, myriads of mosquitoes, tamarisk bushes rustling in the breeze, great clumps of green and vivid red salicornia rising from the yellow sands which almost burned the soles of my feet in the fierce sun, interspersed by glittering white patches of crystalline salt; dragonflies whirring through the air, the millionfold chirping of grasshoppers, gaily-coloured tropical bee-eaters, dazzlingly white herons in the deep blue of the sky, shy purple herons, and thousands of pink and white flamingos standing elegantly in the swamps. . . . Yes, this was really Africa!

At Arles the Rhône splits into two arms, the 'Grand' and 'Petit' Rhône, and the land lying between these arms, bordered on the south by the Mediterranean, is the Camargue proper. In a wider sense the term Carmargue also includes a narrow strip of land to the east of the Grand Rhône on the edge of la Crau, and to the east the Petite Camargue at Aigues-Mortes. The delta formed by the two arms of the Rhône has an area of some 187,725 acres, of which 33,350 acres enjoy nature protection—a lasting service of the *Société Nationale d'Acclimatation de France*.

Professor Tallon, the great champion of the idea of wild-life conservation in this area, is the head of the *Réserve zoologique et botanique de Camargue*, which was founded in 1928. This expanse of land, whose location makes access difficult, offers ideal possibilities for its preservation as a place where animal and plant life can flourish in their natural conditions, since there is no disturbance caused by human activity. Adjacent to the territory of the 'Réserve' lies the extensive property owned by a Swiss industrialist named Hoffmann, who is untiring in his efforts on behalf of nature protection and research. He has established there a most up-to-date laboratory for scientific study, and this is open to visitors. All researches in the field of natural science receive generous support at the Hoffmann residence in Tour de Valat.

It is only during the past ten years that the long arm of civilization has stretched out towards the hitherto almost entirely ignored Camargue, with the cultivation of rice by modern methods beginning in the area. The rice fields now extend to some 30,000 acres, which together with other areas now being developed will supply almost all the rice that France requires. Although in general animal life is gradually driven out of the areas under cultivation, there are various creatures which do not let the proximity of human activity disturb them in their search for food. It is frequently possible to see flying over the rice fields vast numbers of sea-swallows, catching insects as they sweep gracefully along, while the stilt-birds on their long red legs stalk proudly about among the bright green rice in their quest for food.

Here, among other birds of the titmouse family, we find the otherwise very rare bearded tit (*Panurus biarmicus*), and it is always fascinating to watch the young bearded tits playing among the reeds. They clamber up stalks, shaking in the wind, make seats for themselves from blades of grass, and from those vantage points stare inquisitively at the intruder who has dared to enter their domain. The colouring of the young birds is perfectly matched to that of the reeds, yellow, beige, brown and black predominating. The nest is built from stalks of the previous season's growth, and the contrasts between brilliant light and dark shadows on the ground produce exactly the same nuances of shading.

Another delightful member of the same family is at home in the Camargue: the penduline titmouse (*Remiz pendulinus*), which builds what is probably the most artistic nest known to us in Europe. Wearing Wellington boots, I have followed the soft call of 'ziih, ziih' through thickets of tamarisk and blackberry bushes, tall reeds and bulrushes, until I suddenly find myself confronted by the miracle of the penduline titmouse's nest. One asks oneself in astonishment how such a thing is possible. How can so small a bird create this amazing work of art, using only its beak? The nest hangs from fine tamarisk branches like a huge pear, built with infinite care from plant sinews and poplar wool. At the top of the nest there is an entrance hole, and inside, as it sways in the wind, the mother bird feeds her young.

Gulls and terns of many kinds flock above the swamps and lagoons in their thousands, also seeking for food in the flooded rice fields. The visitor sees a magnificent spectacle when the otherwise so shy purple heron (*Ardea purpurea*) stands on the verge of the drying swamps, motionless as a statue, then suddenly darts down to pluck a fish out of the shallow water. I was once lucky enough to see no fewer than 37 purple herons by a lake! The sight was one that can probably be seen nowhere else in Europe.

When the swamps dry up in the fierce heat of summer one can sometimes catch sight of a vulture. It is an Alpine or Egyptian vulture (*Neophron percnopterus*). These nest in the Cévenne mountains, flying to the Camargue in order to seek easy prey there. For hours, even days on end, they circle in the air, searching for victims. If one sees that an animal has come to grief somewhere on the plains or in the swamps, they all dive towards it, and very soon nothing but a skeleton remains to bear witness to the tragedy.

Now I wanted to see another treasure of the Camargue, the colourful bee-eater (*Merops apiaster*). True, I had seen a few isolated specimens by the great lake on the border between Austria and Hungary, but I hoped that I would have a chance here to set eyes on an entire breeding colony. This wish, too, was fulfilled in the Camargue, where it is a matter of no great difficulty to watch a considerable number of these brightly-plumed birds during the mating season, at the edge of the 'étang'. Even from afar off one sees the beautifully-coloured birds wheeling around in the air above the bank. Soon they have alighted, and perch alone or in groups on the tamarisk bushes growing by the waterside, then some take up their positions on the branches of old, dead trees and bushes floating in the shallow water of the lake. They push their large breeding reeds into the sandy walls of the 6- to 9-ft.-high bank, driving them in a distance of up to 6 ft. in a horizontal position. At the end of each reed there is a hole in which the eggs are laid, and where the young birds are reared. It is easy to see which reeds are in use, because they bear the marks left by the birds' feet as they go backwards and forwards along them. The adult birds often sit at the end of these reeds, and one then has an opportunity to enjoy the sight of their wonderful colouring. The underside of the bird is coloured a bright turquoise, the upper side of the wings and the back are of rust-red, the throat lemon-yellow, the eye markings black, the eyes a glowing red—truly a never-to-be-forgotten sight! A bird will often return from a food-gathering expedition with a large, colourful dragonfly in its beak, and when several, holding these spoils, sit side by side on the branches of the swaying tamarisks the picture thus created is one of impressive beauty.

Another spectacle. Turning away from the lake to gaze across the seemingly endless plain we see a cloud of dust in the distance. It draws nearer. There they are, the famous white horses of the Camargue! In the centre of the troop gallop the black foals, among them the dark grey yearlings and older colts whose coats have already turned a lighter shade of grey. On the outside are the mares, many of them over twenty years old, and the snow-white stallions. It is really breathtaking to watch them as they thunder along in unbounded freedom, the last remnant of Europe's once innumerable troops of wild horses. If one is needed, a 'guardian' will catch it and saddle the temperamental creature. Having mounted, he travels for hours on this fiery steed as it gallops across the wide expanses of the countryside, crossing the swamps and keeping watch over the great herds of black cattle and the white Camargue horses. But where are the cattle? I scan the horizon intently through my binoculars—and suddenly I see them, like tiny black dots: the 'toros', the famous black bulls of the Camargue!

They are bred here, spend their youth here, and many an old, tired fighting bull returns after brave combats in the arena to the wild freedom of the plains, and to sire new generations of sturdy cattle. The young calves, which are coloured a dark rust-red, move across the countryside day in and day out under the care of their mothers; they have no stalls, and seldom see the 'guardian' galloping by on one of the white horses.

In our search for the blue roller (*Coracias garrulus*) we wandered, one afternoon, along the road between St. Giles and Aigues-Mortes, our eyes fixed on the telephone wires running along beside the road, as rollers are often to be seen sitting on them. We noticed nothing of interest, until suddenly we saw in the distance a host of white specks in the trees of a pine wood. Could that be the breeding colony of silken herons (*Egretta garzetta*), of whose existence we had heard? Upon inquiry we discovered that the pine wood was private property, and that permission was necessary before we could enter it. After some searching we found a local man who was good enough to show us everything. The path we took led through straight rows of vines, which were in full bloom, in vineyards, across soft sand to the edge of the wood made up of great pines and fir trees.

We entered the wood cautiously, and soon found numerous large trees which had been whitened by the birds' droppings as though someone had whitewashed them. An offensive smell assaulted our nostrils, and those troublesome creatures the mosquitoes greeted us with pleasure. We utterly ignored the many painful bites, though, so fascinated were we by the sight that met our eyes. On the tall pine trees sat hundreds of snow-white silken herons, which rose into the air like a fleecy cloud each time a movement of ours disturbed them, but which immediately returned to the trees when we stood still. We had soon erected a camouflaged tent, from which we were in a position to watch the birds without alarming them. Now we could see them from close quarters: the elegant, slender, snow-white body on long, greyish-black legs, the long, fine, dark grey beak, the white neck feathers fluttering in the wind, together with the magnificent long feathers they wear during the mating season, for which they are so often hunted.

On almost every tree there were 10 to 20 nests, made of thin twigs and wedged in the forks between branches, completely hidden from above by the thick foliage, and as well camouflaged from below. Each nest contained three or four eggs, on which the mother heron sat. Many already had infants; we could see the adults coming back with a catch and feeding them. Small fishes such as we sometimes found lying below the trees were probably the birds' principal source of nourishment. These white herons are everywhere to be seen searching for their prey in the lakes and ponds of the Camargue.

Returning after one of its lengthy fishing expeditions over the étang, the adult bird lands carefully on the tip of a pine branch with an incomparable degree of elegance. Then he moves cautiously along the branch into the heart of the tree, where the nest containing his family lies concealed. As he appears, a great commotion begins, since each of the youngsters wants to be fed first. The older fledglings will leave the nest and clamber along the branches, but they remain in the vicinity so as to be able to return to the nest without delay when the parent bird returns with food.

We were also able to see some nests of the night heron (*Nycticorax nycticorax*). The same tree which houses the nests of white herons generally also contains one or two nests of the darker, greyish night heron, which is easily recognizable even in flight on account of its shorter legs and more thickset body. This bird, too, brings up its three or four young in the pine wood; it is more timid than the white heron.

However, the most enthralling experience of all those who visit the Camargue is the sight of the great bird so rare in Europe, the flamingo (*Phoenicopterus ruber*). The only places in Europe where this rarity among the larger birds has breeding grounds are here and at the mouth of the Guadalquivir in Spain.

The flamingo will only stay in a location where the water is very salt. These creatures are often to be seen, as they stand in the shallow water of the étang, stirring up the mud with their long pink legs, then filtering the dark mass through their huge bills. It is wonderful to see thousands of these magnificent white birds standing together, to rise in graceful flight like a pink cloud as soon as the watcher attempts to get nearer. It is only then that one sees the carmine-red colouring of the wings, with their black pinions, and this colour symphony in white, rose-pink and black creates an unforgettable impression against the deep blue of the sky. When I first experienced that vision I thought there could be nothing more lovely on earth . . . but during my next visit to the Camargue, which I had grown to love dearly, I was to learn better.

This time I wanted to see the flamingos at their breeding ground. Strangely enough they do not breed every year, and science as yet knows of no explanation for the fact that during some years no breeding colonies are formed at all. We were fortunate, though; after a long search we found one. My companion and I willingly accepted the exertions of the task we had set ourselves.

We knew from past experience that it would certainly not be easy to get near enough to the birds with their eggs to film them. We knew that millions of mosquitoes would be our constant unwelcome companions—that we would have to walk through the mud without rubber boots, as they would have been stuck fast by the time we had taken three steps forward—that the concentrated salt would cause us to remember painfully every scratch or graze on our legs—that the fierce heat of the sun and the horrible swamp odour would be ever present—but none of these facts could prevent us from going to seek the fabulous birds. On this occasion their breeding ground was in the salt swamps of St. Giraud, where, thanks to the strict supervision of the area by the *Compagnie*

Salinière de la Camargue, they enjoy the greatest measure of protection, although this district is not part of the *Réserve zoologique* proper. No one is allowed to set foot in this part, where sea salt is obtained from huge basins several square miles in area, without permission. This is a fact greatly to the advantage of the flamingos, which are thus able to breed there almost undisturbed.

In order to get as close as possible to the flamingo colony we made our way along a dyke several miles in length. From far away we could see a long, pale pink line on the water, and could hear the continuous cries of the birds—ear-piercing and nerve-shattering in effect. On getting nearer we were astonished to see that a small, flat island was completely covered by thousands of flamingos and their nests. We were simply overwhelmed by the sight of so vast an assembly standing and sitting in such a tight mass on the islet that neither earth nor sand could be seen at all.

When we tried to get closer still the whole colony of birds rose up as if at a command, forming so dense a cloud in the air that we could see nothing but the colours carmine-red, black and white.

When thousands of these splendid birds take wing at the same moment the spectacle they create is far more breathtaking than that which I had seen when a large number had risen into the air from the étang during the previous year. In order to avoid disturbing the brooding we at once withdrew a few steps. Immediately the birds returned and alighted carefully, with their pink and black wings still beating the air, on to their eggs. Some remained on guard, however, standing on their long legs a little way from the colony, peering out in all directions. The nests are 12 to 16 in. high, made of mud, slime and roots. In them the birds lay their eggs, only one in each nest, above the size of goose eggs. Some are still beautifully white, but many are so covered with mud that they look grey. We also saw some lying between the nests in the shallow water, an easy prey for the flamingo's worst enemy the large herring gull (*Larus argentatus*) with the red spot on its strong yellow beak. A few of these beautiful greyish-white robbers often to be seen circling round the flamingo colonies, always ready to swoop down and seize an unguarded egg or even a young bird.

The thief dives swiftly at its prey, immediately emptying any egg which it succeeds in carrying off. Time and again we were horrified to see this happen, and we asked ourselves why it was that the flamingos put up no resistance. They greatly outnumber the gulls, as well as being far larger and more powerful, yet they look on with apparent equanimity while their precious eggs are eaten nearby.

Despite these ravages by herring gulls there were hatched out, a few weeks later, hundreds of flamingo chicks—tiny, downy creatures light grey in colour, with red beaks and red feet. At first they lay in the nests, but soon they were getting about in the shallow water between the long red legs of their parents. They grew apace, so that in a few more weeks' time they formed a whole flock of grey fledglings, able to seek food for themselves, but always protected from marauders by a few adult birds standing among them like watchmen.

For the last time I stood on the edge of the great étang and allowed the grandiose spectacle to exercise its magic on me as the blood-red ball of the sun sank slowly beyond the broad plains, and in the air above us the last formations of flamingos, seen only as black silhouettes in the gathering dusk, headed for their sleeping quarters. I felt certain that deep longing for this fragment of primeval nature would draw me back here again and again, and my lips instinctively formed the parting words: *'Au revoir, Camargue!'*

Part Three

NATIONAL PARKS, GAME PROTECTION, HUNTING AND THEIR PROBLEMS

The Animals' Kingdom: Kruger National Park

BY

T. V. BULPIN
Johannesburg

THE fascinating old Africa of trading safaris, hard-bitten hunters in search of slaves and ivory, adventurers of all kinds—which still exists in a few remote, isolated areas of the continent—lives on to a far greater extent in story and memories. However, before the advance of civilization could quite destroy the magic of this vast land of adventure, some surviving fragments of its primeval majesty were saved by the wisdom of one man. We refer to the creation of the Kruger National Park. This bushland territory in the eastern Transvaal was once, in far-off days, a wild garden of the great god Pan. Here adventurers could roam in absolute freedom, desperadoes found asylum and peace, passionate hunters sought ever new sensations—and pale stars shone down on to flickering camp-fires, each a tiny point of light against the black satin mantle of the tropical night.

All this romantic enchantment would have been destroyed irrevocably but for the fact that there was created here, thanks to the foresight of President Paul Kruger, a sanctuary of unspoilt African wild life. It was in 1884 that Kruger first conceived the idea of establishing a nature protection area, and fourteen years later, in March 1898, this expanse of thorn bushes and wide plains was finally declared to be a nature protection park. It was known originally as the Sabi Game Reserve. The Reserve covered the whole area between the Crocodile and Sabi Rivers to the south and north, and the Lebombo and Drakensberg mountains to the east and west.

The Boer War halted the development of the project for a time. Nevertheless four years later, in 1902, Colonel J. Stevenson-Hamilton, an army officer who had distinguished himself by virtue of his affectionate understanding of African animal life, was appointed to be the first director of the Reserve.

At the end of an abandoned railway line which had been built years before by gold speculators, where the remains of old, rusty railway lines were the only sign of civilization for miles around, Colonel Stevenson-Hamilton established his base.

Here in the wilderness he created the headquarters of the 'land of animals'. In accordance with their tribal custom his native assistants gave their director an honorary name in their own language—*Skukuza*—and the name became attached, also, to his residence. Under this name the administrative headquarters of the Kruger National Park are today known all over the world, a constant reminder of the vigour and enthusiasm of the Park's first director.

From these headquarters Colonel Stevenson-Hamilton kept watch over his 'land of animals'. In those days it was in a sorry plight. Generations of hunters, traders, and men in search of adventure had slaughtered vast numbers of animals, so that only the strongest and most resilient had survived. In fact two species, the bad-tempered rhinoceros and the charming golden-fawn oribi antelope, had completely vanished. The other classes of animal were represented by only small herds or scattered individuals; protection was urgently needed if their numbers were to increase.

This protection they received from Colonel Stevenson-Hamilton and his assistants. He began by engaging two game rangers. One of them, a seeker after adventure named Gaza Gray, was entrusted with the charge of a post on the lower Sabi River. The second was Harry Wolhuter, a one-time farmer and hunter. He erected the game ranger post on the Pretorius-Kop, a well-known landmark of the lower part of the territory.

The old Sabi Game Reserve, the original heart of the Kruger National Park between the Crocodile and Sabi Rivers, had always contained a great diversity of wild life. In 1903 a further area was added, distinguished by its especial character and beauty, and above all by its wonderful abundance of bird life.

This new area, later to be known as the Shingwedzi Reserve, consists of an expanse of acacia bushland some 100 miles long and 50 miles wide, lying between the Letaba, the 'Sand River' and, on the north, the great Limpopo. It is radically different from the neighbouring territories. The soil has a chalk content, as opposed to the infertile granite to the south, and as this area is lower-lying it has a tropical climate, with more abundant vegetation offering ample fodder to animals and birds of all kinds. In the clumps of acacias and fine-limbed palms innumerable species of wild creatures have always found nourishment. More than three hundred different kinds of bird flutter among the branches, twittering, cackling and calling shrilly in a confusing babel of voices.

All the classes of animal to be found in the original section of the Park, the Sabi Game Reserve, were also represented in the new area to the north—with the exception of giraffes which, no doubt owing to reasons concerned with their choice of food, have seldom continued their foraging expeditions beyond the Olifants River. As if to make up for their absence, the Shingwedzi Reserve proved itself to be a favourite sports ground for elephants. In consequence large stretches of this territory looked as though they had been struck by a hurricane. Great trees lay uprooted on the ground, scattered over a wide area, because the gigantic beasts are particularly fond of tasty fresh shoots from these trees. They are also partial to the berries of the marula tree, which have quite an intoxicating effect during the season when they are ripe, and which have often sent an animal which has eaten its fill of them stumbling back to its den in a decidedly erratic manner. . . . Porcupines and warthogs are especially prone to succumb thus to the delights of these berries.

The elephant had been hunted here for years by the fiercest of all beasts of prey—man. At the time when fifty shillings and more was being paid for a pound of ivory, countless thousands of elephants were slaughtered in Africa. The pursuit of ivory was as profitable as it was exciting. Great bull elephants with a shoulder height of 11 ft. and more were chased for long distances—the hunter always hoping that he could equal the record of one who brought down an elephant whose tusks yielded 480 lb. of ivory. Each of this monster's tusks was 11 ft. long.

The footprints of an elephant tell the experienced tracker all he wants to know about the beast. A large bull leaves a print with a diameter of at least 20 inches, and the exact figure gives a clear indication of the animal's height. Double the circumference of the print shows the shoulder height. The sex is shown by the form the print takes—round in the case of a male, oval in that of a female.

An elephant about 10 ft. high consumes some 900 lb. of vegetable matter and more than 10 gallons of water in a day; it is therefore easy to imagine how deeply its feet sink into the ground. . . . Despite its weight, the elephant has the ability to move with a quietness which is as astonishing as it is alarming, and with its speed of up to 25 m.p.h. it is a formidable opponent. Fortunately it has an equable disposition, provided that it is not disturbed while indulging in one of its favourite occupations: consuming vast quantities of foliage, smothering itself with river mud to cool down, and then, with a branch clasped in its trunk, scratching those places on its rump which it cannot reach in any other way. . . .

The majority of water-holes, however peaceful they may appear on the surface, contain crocodiles. Somewhere in the depths a crocodile is sleeping off a good meal—or is waiting for the flesh of its victim, which it has dragged down to an underwater hole, to begin to decompose, because despite its sharp teeth the crocodile finds chewing and swallowing difficult. It therefore prefers soft food, and even then consuming it is so strenuous a business that its eyes stand out of its head, and the proverbial 'crocodile tears' flow freely.

Parts of the Shingwedzi Reserve have always been particularly dry. The name itself is an old expression used by Bantu hunters which might be translated as 'Water in sight', referring to the widely dispersed water-holes and to the river of the same name. In winter this river becomes a mere series of unconnected pools, rendered dangerous by the presence of lurking crocodiles, but providing at least a meagre supply of water all the year round.

Before the summer rains refill the river and the water-holes scattered about the veld, animals of all kinds assemble along the banks of the Shingwedzi. For example all 18 varieties of antelope living on the South African plains make their way to this source of indispensable moisture. The noble eland antelope, the shy and graceful little duiker, the waterbuck with its wiry grey coat, the elegant little reedbuck with its unusual whistling cries, the powerful oryx, the gemsbock, and a host of other fascinating animals. . . .

So as to bring order to this wonderland and to protect the animals, the Colonel had a new game rangers' post built on the bank of the Shingwedzi.

With a mere ten native assistants at his disposal, this isolated game protection official had so vast an area of bush and veld to cover that he obviously could not keep a close check on the whole territory. At that time there were no roads, only the roughest of tracks, and the northernmost part of the Reserve had always had a bad reputation as the hideout of numerous shady characters. 'Rogues' corner' this district bordering on the Pafuri River was generally called—a reference to the various smugglers and ivory hunters who based themselves there.

Professional big-game hunters, too, regarded this territory as theirs by right. Every winter hunting parties arrived there from the veld settlements in donkey-drawn tilt-carts with strong iron wheels. They penetrated far into the bush, and there pitched their camps. They succeeded in turning the northern district into a barren wilderness. The majority of the animals were killed for their skins and horns; the rest fled to far-away territories.

In the early days of the National Park it was quite impossible to safeguard the whole of this vast district. The two Reserves had very little income—hardly enough to support their existence. It was quite out of the question to purge 'Rogues' corner' of all the undesirable characters in the area.

For years the very idea of a game reserve was in danger, hanging by a mere thread. Big-game hunters constantly pressed for the territory to be opened up for their use again, while land-hungry farmers regularly put forward claims to be allowed to develop it as agricultural land.

However, the enthusiasts for the game reserve project did not relax their efforts—and the most zealous of them was Colonel Stevenson-Hamilton. In 1916 champions of the opposing views regarding the continued functioning of the Reserve clashed so violently that a government commission was appointed to investigate the dispute.

Fortunately the commission did not only uphold the idea of wild-life protection, but even recommended that the Reserve should be transformed into a vast national park. Those favouring the unrestricted hunting of animals were loud in their disapproval of the decision—while those supporting the conservation of wild life applauded it. Those who loved the old Africa had won a resounding victory, and the area was gradually transformed into a true national park.

Additional supervisory staff were engaged in order to deal effectively with poachers, and a new game rangers' post was constructed in the 'Rogues' corner' of evil repute. Two others were set up at the bridge over the Crocodile River and near Malalane.

At these stations the first game inspectors, the 'old guard' of the Game Reserve, lived their isolated but fascinating lives. They traversed the bush, and cared for the animals under their protection, dwelling in tiny islands of civilization amid the kingdom of the animals. They grew melons, Avocado pears and bananas in gardens; the green shoots of pomegranate bushes climbed along the verandas of the broad, cool houses built in the traditional veld style, each one of them seemingly filled with the atmosphere of wild game and of Africa, with memories of adventures involving lions. . . .

At that time few people—apart from poachers—visited the Reserve. Occasionally treasure-seekers may have gone into the wilds in search of the legendary Kruger millions. They were disappointed.

The real riches of the bush veld were its unique, magical atmosphere, and the beauty of its animal life. Colonel Stevenson-Hamilton had long had it in mind to make the area accessible to visitors. After all, the costs of the undertaking were being borne by the whole community, and so long as the general public received nothing of comparable value in return there was always the danger that the opponents of the national park idea might yet gain the upper hand, so that the territory would be opened up for land development and exploitation in other ways.

Thus it came about that the Sabi and Shingwedzi Reserves were transformed into the great Kruger National Park. The National Park Bill was finally passed by parliament in May 1926—without a single dissident voice being raised.

The Park then began to take shape, under a supervisory council of prominent personalities. Its area was increased, the great expanse of pastureland between the Sabi and Olifants Rivers, together with the mining district which had so long divided the two sections of the Reserve, being incorporated into the Park territory.

New supervisory camps were erected (Satara, Rabelais, and the former seat of the old chieftain Tshokwane), and the Park began to achieve real unity under the name which Colonel Stevenson-Hamilton had chosen so wisely for it: Kruger National Park.

Roads were laid out—not asphalted, but with perfectly serviceable surfaces of stones well suited to the surroundings. Tourist camps were constructed, and the game rangers prepared to receive, protect and study that most demanding and incalculable of all living creatures—the tourist.

Needless to say, the public soon took the Park to its heart. In 1927 the first three cars ventured into the animals' kingdom. The next year saw the number rise to 180, in 1929 it was 850, in 1950 more than 16,000 cars entered the gates of the Park, and in 1960 it was visited by 140,000 people.

During the first few years a great deal of freedom was allowed to visitors. However, although the animals showed a remarkable degree of patience and tolerance, the liberties that were taken with them soon assumed alarming proportions. In one famous instance a picnic party was photographed sitting in groups among some rocks. When the photograph was developed a lion could be seen clearly, watching the picnickers from the bush about ten yards away, almost looking as if it were licking its lips in anticipation. . . .

It was therefore decreed that visitors were to remain in their cars. The animals had soon discovered that cars were neither edible nor dangerous. Since the people in the cars obviously meant them no harm, the animals quickly lost all their fear, and became accustomed to watching the stream of visitors passing by, fascinated by the sight of this motorized cavalcade. Whole families of lion took to staying near and even on the roads so as to watch the parade of human beings. . . .

Two other restrictive regulations also proved to be unavoidable. Driving by night was forbidden, owing to the fact that headlights dazzled the animals, with the result that many were run over. Speed limits also had to be imposed, to avoid raising too much dust and to safeguard both cars and animals. Although the elephant, in common with the other animals, had proved themselves extremely courteous, the very idea of a collision between a furious bull elephant and a speeding car was enough to cause grave concern to the Park authorities.

Over the years those in charge of the Park have learned a good deal about human nature. On the other hand many of the visitors know very little indeed about the Park when they arrive there. Some visit it expecting to see a Hollywood-style parade of animals passing in front of them the whole time. They drive along at the highest permitted speed, their eyes glued to the road. Even a lion standing a couple of yards from the roadside could easily be overlooked in those circumstances.

Anyone who wants to obtain the greatest pleasure from a visit to the National Park must adapt himself to the surroundings. The visitor should forget the hectic tempo of modern life, and accept the old truth that nothing is so good as to get up early and experience dawn on the veld—a panorama of life, light and colour, which unfolds itself before one's eyes as the plains lazily stretch themselves in anticipation of the warm peace of midday. Then millions of birds sing a great hymn of relief in chorus—for another night is past, a night full of shadows and illuminated by pairs of eyes eager for prey. . . .

Africa's Game Protection Areas – Seen Through American Eyes

BY

VICTOR H. CAHALANE

National Park Service, Washington

THE number of wild animals living in their natural state in Africa exceeds that of any other continent. I spent six months touring South Africa, the Congo, Portuguese East Africa and Kenya, studying animal life and especially the problems of the game protection areas—always having in mind a comparison with North America. While details naturally differ, there exist many parallels.

Africa is a vast continent, with an area some 30 per cent greater than North America. Moreover it is, as regards animal and plant life, older. It has been habitable by animals for a far longer period of time than have the lands which are now Canada and the U.S.A. Without debating the question of whether this fact has had a definite bearing on the sub-division of the various species, it can be said that Africa possesses two and a half times as many kinds of birds as America, and many times the number of mammals. As regards the total numbers of large animals, too, those in many individual areas of Africa far exceed the numbers for the whole of America—although the situation was quite different in the North American prairie belt during the eighteenth century. In the game reserves, and in certain parts of the continent where primitive conditions still exist, the animal life of Africa continues to offer a magnificent spectacle even today.

The numbers of animals and species is astonishing. On the first day of my visit to the Kruger National Park I was driven from Punda Maria to the Pafuri River, and then southward to the Shingwedzi camp. During the course of this 11-hour journey, covering some 156 miles, I saw: 17 lechwe antelope; 159 kudu; 426 impala; 1 grysbok; 10 wildebeest or brindled gnu; 54 waterbuck; 22 Nyala antelope; 26 gemsbok; 1 duiker; 1 steenbok; 7 warthog; 24 zebra; 19 elephant; 11 lion; 2 serval cats; several Cape hares; 9 ostrich; 4 large raven; 2 guinea fowl. If I had gone by another route the list would have looked quite different as, for example, the klipspringer and hippopotamus are found only amid certain surroundings, while the giraffe and buffalo remain principally in the southern section of the Park. On the following day we saw along a stretch of some 9 miles a multitude of impala which numbered, at a conservative estimate, more than a thousand.

The Kruger National Park is one of the most famous game reserves, but there are also wonderful spectacles to be seen elsewhere. In the Gorongosa Park in Portuguese East Africa hippopotami were to be seen in dozens, even in groups of fifty or more, along the Urema River, and in the Albert National Park in the Congo some 4,000 hippopotami live along a stretch of 25 miles.

A fundamental difference should be noted before we consider the similarities of the wild-life protection problems encountered in Africa and in America. While the larger carnivorous animals have been practically exterminated in the agricultural and grazing lands of North America, a considerable number of ungulates (hoofed mammals) have managed to survive. Despite severe losses to hunters, the white-tailed elk of the U.S.A. still lives in relatively heavily populated areas. On the other hand the continued existence of most kinds of wild game is incompatible with agricultural development. Many varieties of antelope can apparently live only in such large herds that the breeding of cattle in the same area is out of the question. The buffalo, hippopotamus, rhinoceros and elephant all do considerable damage to the countryside, and are a menace to human settlements, while giraffes cannot exist together with telephone wires and overhead electric cables.

For this reason the Portuguese pursue a policy of wiping out big game in districts where white settlements are planned. In British territories the authorities are less severe in this respect, but the practical result is not very different. That being the case, the creation of game reserves (which, on account of the numbers and habits of the animals, must be very large if they are to be any use) is an absolute necessity if animal life is to survive.

One of our greatest difficulties in America—at least as far as the ungulates are concerned—is the problem of where they can find fodder in winter. Africa has no winter in this sense, but it does have the alternation of dry and rainy seasons.

The animals in Africa therefore find themselves provided with an abundance of food for part of the year; they then disperse over large distances, becoming sleek and fat. When the rainy season ends, however, all plant life loses its moisture, and all water-holes dry up, apart from the deepest ones and those fed by streams. The animals are then compelled to flock to those few, since most of them must slake their thirst at least every day or every other day.

The concentrations of animals which thus occur near sources of water mean that before the end of the dry season there will not be a single leaf or blade of grass left for miles around, and the situation over an even greater area round each water-hole is not much better. In contrast to what is experienced in the

U.S.A., in the northern part of the Yellowstone Park for example, the vegetation in Africa seems to have become accustomed to this wholesale destruction. No sooner have the herds of animals dispersed at the beginning of the rainy season than fresh green shoots begin to spring up all round the water-holes, as though no damage had ever occurred.

In South Africa and the British colonies the game conservation authorities are concerning themselves to an increasing extent with projects directed towards the improvement of water supplies. There are four reasons behind such projects: firstly, grazing areas during the dry season should be extended; secondly, it is hoped to reduce the severe losses of animals which occur during exceptionally dry periods; thirdly, the intention is to enable more animals to survive 'normal' dry periods; and fourthly, new sources of water must be made available for the animals to replace others which they can no longer use owing to the spread of civilization and agriculture. It is often impossible for the herds to travel long distances on account of the increase in the number of human settlements, with the result that they are driven to the water-holes—and therefore the foodstuffs in the vicinity—within the game reserves.

In order to obtain more water, increasing use is being made in the Kruger and Kalahari National Parks of wind pumps, though these have to be protected by strong fences made from old railway lines as a defence against elephants. These animals tend to become annoyed when the water in the tanks fed by the wind pumps becomes exhausted, and if the pump equipment is not adequately protected they will destroy it—iron tower and all. . . .

In the former Belgian Congo the authorities do not attempt to provide additional supplies of water, since they disagree on principle with any interference in natural conditions. Nevertheless the park boundaries are fixed so that existing sources of water are included within the parks.

The problem of the actual and supposed destruction of private property by animals exists in Africa just as it does in America. Although over vast expanses of Africa the larger animals have already been exterminated, in other parts of the continent there is still a great deal of conflict between wild animals and agriculture.

Most kinds of fencing as we know it are useless as protection against the animals of Africa. Zebras and wildebeest, in particular, rush away in a terrified stampede when lions or other dangerous foes have frightened them, and there is no halting their panic-stricken flight. They break through wire fences as though they were made of string. The more massive creatures such as the buffalo, rhinoceros and elephant can only be kept back by highly unusual methods.

For years the small herd of bush elephant protected in the Addo Park in the eastern part of Cape Province caused a great deal of damage and bitterness whenever they broke out of their reserve, overrunning nearby farms and fruit plantations. The first counter-measure put into effect by the authorities was to dump all the orange and grapefruit which were not fit for sale into the elephant reserve, so as to keep the animals from straying while a double electrified wire was erected round their land. This served its purpose for about a year, but then the elephants became accustomed to electric shocks. It was impossible to increase the current in the wires without endangering human lives, so once again the elephants roamed out of their territory, causing havoc on fruit plantations. After that a massive wall of railway lines and steel supports had to be erected, and this has proved effective.

A number of the larger African animals can become dangerous in certain circumstances, but most of these animals will generally avoid man if they see him coming soon enough. The elephant, however, is almost certain to attack if one approaches within 40 or 50 yards of him. Other animals which can inflict fatal wounds on human beings if they are provoked by being approached too closely include the buffalo, rhinoceros, lion and leopard. The otherwise lethargic crocodile is dangerous to any human being venturing into its proximity in the water or on land.

Consequently visitors to African national parks are forbidden to leave their cars—except, of course, in the fenced camps where they can spend the night. Swimming and angling are also prohibited.

Human nature is the same all over the world—whether people come from Chicago or Cape Town. Americans insist on feeding the black bears in Yellowstone Park, and South Africans in the Kruger Park throw food to the large baboons. These baboons are in fact powerful, aggressive animals with an all-embracing appetite and a high level of intelligence, fundamentally more dangerous than the American black bears. Three or four fully-grown baboons are capable of tearing a leopard to pieces. Their inborn ability to climb with great agility enables them to get over all the camp fences, and the Park authorities have to be constantly on the alert to see that visitors do not encourage the baboons with unwise familiarity, since only a certain degree of fear of human beings keeps them at a safe distance.

The preservation of species of animals in danger of dying out is an important problem in Africa, as it is everywhere else. According to Harper (1945) the list of African mammals has been reduced by nine species or sub-species during the past 2,000 years. By comparison America has lost eleven mammals (if we ignore 16 types of grizzly bear, some of which were probably only slight variants).

Several classes of animal in the 'Dark Continent' are now in acute danger of dying out. In South Africa several of the smaller antelope, the white-tailed gnu and the mountain zebra no longer exist in freedom, and only a few live in protected areas. Several other species—the white rhinoceros, the addax, the mountain nyala and several classes of oryx antelope—are restricted both as regards the places where they are still to be found and as regards their total numbers. A comparatively slight change for the worse could probably bring about their extinction.

Biologists and game protection officials in Africa appear to be interested in preserving animal life for its own sake—or, let us say, on account of its beauty. The value of many classes of animal from the hunter's point of view does not influence them at all. The situation is therefore different from that existing in North America. Hunting as a sport seems in general to mean far less in Africa than in America.

The illegal destruction of animal life is a very widespread evil which is extremely difficult to control. The native population, hungry for meat, is steadily increasing in numbers. The game protection officers are highly competent, but they have vast expanses of land to watch.

Various serious complaints of farm and domestic animals are carried by wild animals in Africa. One of the more widely known of these is sleeping-sickness.

In order to check the spread of the tsetse fly great annihilation campaigns have been undertaken against wild animals. In 1942, for example, hunting parties numbering up to 1,500 men all told were given the task of slaughtering all animals larger than wild boar in the Usufolozi Reserve in Zululand (with the exception of the white rhinoceros, which was spared). I have been told that more than 110,000 animals were shot, in an area of 74,120 acres. Only a few of the craftiest and speediest animals were able to escape. It is now hoped that chemical methods at present being adopted in the war against insects will enable the game in infected areas to escape a similar fate in future.

In the Congo mass-slaughter on this scale has always been avoided. Instead an effort has been made to develop local breeds of cattle, which are less profitable than European strains, but at the same time far less prone to catch diseases spread by the tsetse fly.

It is not my intention to discuss the pros and cons of the influence which the existence of beasts of prey exercises on the balance between wild game, farm animals and agriculture in Africa. It should, however, be noted that the existence of carnivora is an important factor in an animal world containing so great a number of herbivorous species. When one remembers the rate at which zebra and antelope, for example, can multiply, it is clear that the removal of the brakes—the meat-eaters—would have very far-reaching effects. Incidentally the activities of the beasts of prey do not constitute the massacre many tourists imagine. Even such powerful members of this class as the lion and leopard often apparently have difficulty in obtaining sufficient food, although they are surrounded by large numbers of potential victims.

The extent to which beasts of prey should be destroyed is a question discussed as heatedly in Africa, at least in the British territories, as it is in America. The former Belgian authorities in the game conservation areas of the Congo avoided interfering in any way with the natural course of animal life, while in the remainder of the country control of wild animals was dependent on economic considerations. The same principle is applied in Portuguese possessions, while in British territories methods vary from place to place.

Although public demands are often made for a reduction in the numbers of certain carnivorous animals—partly for the safeguarding of rare species of game—the weight of opinion in favour of their preservation is clearly stronger and better organized than in America. Moreover visitors to national parks show so overwhelming an interest in seeing (and photographing) the large beasts of prey that other animals such as antelope seem to be practically ignored, even when thousands of them are in the vicinity. When visitors to the Kruger National Park complain 'We've seen nothing again today', that merely means that they have seen no lions. Any steps directed towards a reduction in numbers of the large carnivora would therefore meet with vigorous opposition.

What prospects are there that a sensible animal protection policy will be adopted in Africa? It must be admitted that wild-life conservation in most African territories has been carried out so far in a haphazard manner, on no really firm basis. The Belgians were pioneers in this respect, founding the *Institut ces Parcs Nationaux du Congo Belge*, in which the results of innumerable observations were collected for the information of their park authorities. Very thorough researches were carried out there—far more intensive than any programme of study ever undertaken on behalf of American national parks. The problem has been tackled by means of the investigation of individual cases in the former French West African territories.

The National Park authorities in South Africa, as well as the state governments of Natal and the Transvaal, are now engaging scientists for work in this field. In Kenya the work of game protection still depends largely on the initiative of individual officials, but specialists will doubtless be called in sooner or later. Qualified biologists are at work in Northern and Southern Rhodesia. A great deal of research has still to be undertaken in all these territories.

A number of other important factors stand on the debit side of the balance sheet: the population figures, the living standard, and the need for agricultural and industrial expansion are all constantly increasing. The spread of civilization makes the future of the great African animal world uncertain, to say the least. Nevertheless there are some encouraging signs to be seen. The more widely knowledge of this animal life is disseminated, the greater grows the general public's recognition of its value. Lastly, 'Primitive Africa' is an attraction for tourists, and is therefore an important factor in the economy of African states. Science, too, can come to the aid of the animals—even though it sometimes works destructively on the other side.

In any event the immediate future offers some hope to those who are concerned with the preservation of animal life in Africa.

African National Parks—the Position Today

BY

DR. BERNHARD GRZIMEK

RECENT political changes have made the future prospects of the wild animals of Africa far worse than could have been envisaged even a short time ago. The numbers of African big game, except for those in primeval forests, have probably sunk to less than 20 per cent of what they were before Europeans appeared on the scene during the second half of the last century, although naturally such figures can be estimated only very roughly. Nevertheless there is no danger that any of the best known of the larger animals, such as the leopard, lion, elephant, rhinoceros, hippopotamus, giraffe, etc., will vanish as a species from the face of the earth and so become totally extinct (as happened earlier in this century in the case of the South African quagga and the pure-blooded Burchell's zebra) within the next decade or so, unless something totally unexpected happens. The position in this respect is more serious in Asia.

However, what is now taking place with regard to the wild animals of Africa must give every expert cause for deep concern. True, one optimist has reckoned that game reserves in Africa amount to 5·5 per cent of the entire continent, if the vast wastes of the Sahara are not taken into account. It is difficult to verify this estimate on the basis of the varying figures published from time to time; a colleague of mine arrived at a figure of less than 2 per cent. This is taking no account of the fact that in Africa barren plains, deserts such as the Kalahari, high mountains and similar areas which are of no economic value are often declared to be game reserves, despite the fact that they can contain few wild animals. Furthermore such figures include not only national parks which have been officially decreed as permanent institutions, but also nature reserves, whose area is many times that of the smaller national parks.

In these nature reserves, however, man has every legal advantage over animals, which are only protected as long as the land is not required for agriculture or similar purposes (British Colonial Office, 1953). This percentage estimate also includes numerous 'controlled areas' in which it is often only certain species of animal which are protected at all, and often even these are safeguarded only to a limited extent, together with areas in which protection is afforded to sites of prehistoric finds, exceptional landscapes or vegetation, but not to animals at all.

Numbers of certain well-known animal species have diminished greatly. A few years ago in a publication I myself estimated the total population of the black or pointed-lipped rhinoceros, the world's most common species of rhinoceros, at ten thousand. The I.U.C.N. (International Union for Conservation of Nature), which is supported by most of the world's governments, has now, after consultations with game experts in all parts of Africa, arrived at the figure of thirteen thousand. Thanks to financial support from the American Government Dr. G. A. Petrides of the University of Michigan and Dr. W. G. Swank of the corresponding establishment in Arizona have been able to spend years investigating the situation of wild game in East Africa. The first paragraph of their final report runs as follows: 'East Africa's game resources are rapidly dwindling away. If the present trend continues, the noteworthy herds which still exist in a few places will not survive the next ten to twenty years.' (Wild Life, Nairobi, No. 2, 1960.) In 1959–60 Hopton had to cover some 37,500 miles over all parts of Kenya while making a radiometric survey. He wrote afterwards: 'I have now visited many places again after an interval of forty years, and have taken into account the fact that memory deceives all of us. I spent some weeks among the hills to the west of Magadi, across the Loita plains and in the Mara triangle. It was there that I had my greatest shock. Although there was ample pasture grass, I was overpowered by the fact that after thirty years herds of only hundreds had taken the place of thousands. It is no use deluding ourselves—the situation will continue to deteriorate at an alarming rate in view of the ever-increasing use of land by the inhabitants, legally authorized hunting, and poaching. This is the picture as I see it, but I realize that the problem will probably not be generally recognized in all its gravity.'—Experts of all nationalities examined the world-wide situation regarding wild game at a congress of the I.U.C.N. held at Warsaw in 1960. The conclusion to which they came was that the greatest threat to wild life was in Africa, and that immediate concerted action was required if it was to be countered.

It is necessary to appreciate the nature of the threat hanging over the animal life of Africa.

Even in the 'pre-European' period numbers of wild game in certain areas of Africa had been reduced as the result of hunting by the native population. At that time, however, there were a great many 'holy' places, especially forests and mountains, in which no hunting was permitted—in fact most of these areas were not to be entered by any human beings. These districts in which animals were spared for religious reasons constantly supplied replacement stock to other areas where the game had been wiped out by hunting. Until quite recently many explorers and geologists whose work compelled them to enter such 'taboo' areas paid with their lives for their offence against local laws. Nothing has been observed so scrupulously or has survived so strongly over hundreds and even thousands of years as religious and mystical laws of this kind. The Christian missions and modern developments have destroyed these ancient ideas without replacing them by anything as advantageous to wild animals, and therefore to the nourishment which their meat can provide for the population. The national parks and nature reserves created by governmental decrees are not, like the 'taboo' forests of earlier ages, protected by the native population as a matter of conscience and belief.

I have often pointed out in Siamese daily papers that the wild animals of that East Asiatic land are as valuable a cultural possession of its people as the much admired ancient temples. It is therefore gratifying to record that the Siamese Government has now presented to parliament a nature conservation bill in the introduction to which it is emphasized that the country adheres to the Buddhist faith, and that the protection of life is an important doctrine of Buddhism. The nature protection areas are to be described as 'Buddha-Buja', and their boundaries are to be marked by large notices bearing the words 'Dedicated to the Lord Buddha'. This may well prove a more effective safeguard than the threat of punishment for infringements of the law.

Hunting by Europeans is a serious menace to wild animals in certain parts of Africa, and in others it has a serious psychological effect. Nevertheless it is certainly neither the only nor the greatest danger to animal life. It is true that my son Michael and I have attacked this hunting in our films and publications, but we have done this in accordance with our belief that it would be pointless to fulminate in European books and cinemas against poaching by African natives. They never see the films or books, while such recriminations against the natives for their misdeeds would merely serve to provide an excuse for the 'hunting tourists'. The activities of the poachers must be denounced in Africa itself. Complaints about European big-game hunters before an African audience, or about native poachers when addressing Europeans, always win applause, but they do nothing to improve the situation.

Defenders of modern 'shooting tourists' always emphasize the fact that those visitors to Africa, whose knowledge of hunting may be almost non-existent, operate under strict supervision (after paying a considerable fee which is put to good use), and are only permitted to shoot a small percentage of the wild animals which would have to die in any case, in order to make land available for the creation of new settlements or for the protection of agriculture. This may be true, to some extent, in the excellently administered British colonies and dependencies, especially in East Africa. Unfortunately, however, the Europeans there can obtain hunting licences very cheaply, and often make commercial use of this fact. In many other African colonies and independent states game protection laws are largely ignored. The hunting journal *Game and Dog* (1961 issue, page 276) describes how areas in Portuguese West Africa which had been said in official circles to be the richest in game throughout the colonies were found to have been completely emptied of game by shooting. Eleven professional hunters are constantly at work there, and drive away heavy lorries fully laden with dried meat. 'Hospitality was shown everywhere, an ample supply of porters was provided. The only thing lacking was wild game.'

In the Union of South Africa, as recently transpired from a parliamentary question, the statesman Mr. Erasmus even shot one of the few rhinoceros in a protected area from a helicopter. *Game and Dog* (1960 No. 3, page 82) wrote 'that during the past year more than sixty hunting safaris with altogether 140 hunters had entered the game areas of the Chad Republic. Complaints had since poured in from all sides that hunting in those areas had become far more dangerous on account of the many wild animals which had been hunted but which had escaped with their lives. When sixteen elephants were shot by order of the government in the Goré district eleven of them were found to have received bullet wounds on earlier occasions. An even greater flow of American hunting tourists is pouring into Kenya and Tanganyika, Ruanda and Portuguese East Africa. In Kenya worthwhile trophies are becoming rarer all the time.'

Books about big-game hunters and adventurers in Africa have, I feel, deterred a great many would-be visitors to East and Central Africa. These books have given the general public in Europe and America the idea that a holiday watching elephants and giraffes would involve grave dangers. They imagine it would be necessary to wear high boots for protection against poisonous snakes, that lions and scorpions would threaten them by night, that they would have to undertake perilous journeys on foot, and defend themselves against huge serpents and elephants. The fact that it is possible nowadays to view big game— and to hunt it if so desired—without the slightest danger and in something approaching European standards of comfort is generally concealed by the authors of such books, who are concerned with emphasizing their own energy and courage. The income which British East Africa has recently begun to enjoy from the hunting tourist trade has encouraged other countries of Africa, and to an even greater extent of Asia, to attract hunting visitors, though their activities are not supervised to the same extent as in the British territories. Although reports and complaints about these 'shooting tourists' are on the increase among professional hunters, who are as enthusiastic about game preservation as we are, it remains an undisputed fact that illegal hunting by natives is responsible for the deaths of far more wild animals.

For this very reason, however, the bad example given by European hunting tourists is particularly deplorable from the psychological point of view at the present time when Africans are clamouring for self-government. The British National Park Administration of Kenya complains in its annual report that 'the Africans are all too likely to believe that the wild animals of Kenya are protected only for the benefit of the white man and his rich friends from overseas'.

From time immemorial most of the African tribes have hunted animals with their weapons of limited efficiency, so that man and beast stood on equal terms. The ruthless massacre of the entire animal life in many areas by Europeans and Africans armed with guns during the latter part of the nineteenth century and the early years of the twentieth has meant that a considerable proportion of the population have been robbed, probably for ever, of the meat they need for nourishment, and therefore suffer from a shortage of albumen. The fact that they are no longer allowed to hunt in parts of their own land, the game reserves, is incomprehensible to them. Even our native bearers and the coloured game wardens in the national parks admit freely to us that they went out poaching in their youth, and that their relations would do the same. Modern wire snares and guns enable men to kill pointlessly far more animals than they need for food, purely for the joy of hunting. (This is not, of course, confined to Africans—Kaiser Wilhelm II of Germany was reputed to have killed 44,000 head of game.) Who can make these natives, almost all of whom are illiterate, understand that it is just to punish them for poaching with a year's imprisonment, while Europeans are permitted to hunt?

Recently in an introductory talk given before a showing of our Serengeti film to professional hunters and experts in Nairobi, I reminded them of the development of Europe. In the Middle Ages hunting was a privilege of the aristocracy; they galloped in a cavalcade on horseback after the quarry across the fields of their serfs, while a peasant would have his hand cut off if he slew a wild boar which he found eating his crops. What would have happened to the stags, deer and hares of Europe if, at that time, the peasants had suddenly gained control overnight? This is what is now happening in Africa.

It is undoubtedly better to allow the natives to hunt a proportion of the wild game, not of course in national parks, but in nature reserves and controlled areas as well as in open land. In Kenya experiments have been made along these lines, with encouraging results. Perhaps it will be easier in this way to convince the natives and their political leaders that poaching is wrong; unless this can be done nature conservation is doomed to failure in the long run.

In some parts of Africa tens of thousands of animals are killed by poachers merely for their skins, the meat being wasted. By doing this the poachers are destroying future sources of food for their people. Death by wire traps and other methods of hunting employed by the natives is agonizing for the animals—it is also true to say that many are wounded by Europeans and die a lingering death as a result of their wounds.

The real reason for the disappearance of big game in Africa is the increase of mankind: all other reasons spring from this fundamental fact. At present the population of the world is increasing by some 187,000 human beings every twenty-four hours. The population of Africa, which for centuries remained almost unchanged by comparison with that of other continents, is now beginning to grow very rapidly, and the increase will be even more marked as a result of recent political developments. The land will quite simply be required for new agricultural developments, as grazing land for domestic animals, and for reservoirs. Africa is therefore faced by the same situation which long ago cost the lives of almost all the wild animals of Europe, America and China. Much more serious than hunting itself is the fact that the habitat of wild animals is being destroyed. For example, the tall Watussi tribesmen of Ruanda-Urundi hardly hunt at all, and they certainly never kill a mountain gorilla. However, they keep vast herds of long-horned cattle, not to make use of them but merely out of pride of possession. During recent years they have driven more and more of these cattle, tens of thousands, into the Albert National Park of the former Belgian Congo, although they are forbidden to do this. The cattle have laid waste the comparatively small areas which are the home of the mountain gorilla, reducing the extent of the high-lying bamboo forests so that the great anthropoid apes have less and less space in which to live. The Masai of the Serengeti plains do very little hunting, but their densely packed herds of undernourished cattle destroy all the vegetation, gradually turning the land into a desert. The Masai are constantly cutting down the few bushes and trees in order to build rough fences to keep their cattle together at night during their wanderings. However, those few trees had previously given shade and protection to the few sources of water which flow even during the dry season. One after another has now failed, so in course of time the wild animals, which could supply far more meat per acre for the nourishment of human beings than the domestic cattle which are not native to Africa, are bound to disappear.

With very few exceptions the capture of animals plays only a very minor part in influencing the numbers of the various classes of animals. The African anthropoid apes, gorillas and chimpanzees, which are taken to zoos only as infants, are orphans which survive when whole families are shot 'for the protection of plantations'. It is scarcely possible, or at least a very costly proposition, to capture young animals of these classes without shooting the mothers. After making inquiries everywhere I ascertained that there were altogether 56 gorillas living in zoos in 1954. True, a considerable number of monkeys are also captured for experimental purposes. These are generally rhesus and other small monkeys, great numbers of which live in their native element, but they are frequently transported in such overcrowded containers on board ship and are so poorly provided for that losses of between 20 and 30 per cent are the rule, and are reckoned with in advance by the traders concerned. International regulations are urgently needed, since national laws are hardly a practical proposition owing to the competition between shipping lines. Zoos have scarcely any need to import monkeys of these common classes, as they multiply satisfactorily in captivity. Unfortunately anthropoid apes, too, are sometimes used for experimental purposes. In individual cases careful consideration ought to be given to the possibility of using less rare and highly-developed types of monkey for such purposes.

Wherever man settles the animals are destroyed or driven away. Hardly anyone with a profound knowledge of nature conservation would be so unrealistic as to strive for 'the animals of Africa to be preserved'. In the long run that can only be achieved in a few restricted areas, the national parks. Our primary task is to defend them against the wishes, short-sighted though they may be, of the native population, industrialists, traders and mining concerns.

A national park, unlike many other kinds of nature protection areas, is created by governmental decree, and it can only be done away with or transformed if the legal machinery of the country concerned is set in motion. It is not subject to the arbitrary decisions of a district commissioner or provincial governor. In a national park nature has the upper hand; no human being may settle within its bounds, and no one may interfere with the processes of nature.

In British colonies the point of view was held at one time that 'wild' man is part of nature, and is therefore entitled to a place in a national park. However, the natives cannot be prevented from becoming civilized, from acquiring cars and building metal huts. For this reason the British colonial authorities, like their counterparts in other parts of Africa, came round to the view that native inhabitants have no place in national parks. The question of whether they should be evicted, or whether the section of the national park in which they have settled should lose its national park status is the principal problem in the Serengeti National Park.

Unfortunately the national parks of Africa are not by any means always situated where most of the wild game are to be found, or where the land is most suitable for them. In many cases areas were chosen because no one wanted them, either owing to the fact that they are semi-deserts, or because they are afflicted with sleeping sickness or with the cattle disease—Nagana—which is closely related to it. One example of this is the Murchison Falls Park in Uganda. About the year 1910 the last survivors of an epidemic of sleeping sickness were removed from this once fairly heavily populated area. Thus the wild game remained almost undisturbed for many years, the land lying unwanted. As medical and veterinary science overcame infectious diseases to an ever great extent, the areas of the national parks become all the more sought after as sites for new settlements.

Most national parks are at least partially surrounded by nature reserves in which both natives and Europeans are allowed to settle, but where hunting is either completely forbidden or is restricted. For this reason the fact that the boundaries of the national parks are fixed arbitrarily—not in accordance with the requirements of the animals—has not hitherto proved the drawback it might otherwise have been. The animals are thus enabled to leave the national park at various points. Clearly they do this in large numbers as far as many of the national parks are concerned, although no estimate has yet been made of the numbers. We have definite proofs of considerable movement of stock to and from the Serengeti National Park during recent years. Such migrations are probably of the utmost necessity to many species of animal. During the dry season of the year they have to seek out areas with sappy vegetation and water-holes, or they choose particular places in which their young should be born. In many national parks, therefore, numerous kinds of animal cannot live at all, or only in very small numbers, once the park is surrounded by human settlements. The small Addo National Park in South Africa had for this reason to be surrounded by a fence in order to keep the few elephants there from straying on to nearby farms. It was years before a really 'elephant-proof' fence could be devised and constructed. The cost of fencing off larger national parks would be prohibitive. The Nairobi National Park, which no longer contains any elephants, is partially fenced on the side facing the town. It is now intended, too, to fence large sections of the boundaries of the Kruger National Park and many other parks in Africa. This is partly as a result of demands by veterinary authorities, on the grounds that wild animals spread foot and mouth disease among domestic animals.

All these difficulties, which can only increase in the future, demand scientific research. Hitherto they have been largely neglected, and we lack the most necessary data concerning the life of African big game in its free state. The national park game wardens are all administrative officials or former professional hunters, as is no doubt necessary for the efficient management of such large-scale projects. There is, however, a complete lack of biological researchers and facilities on the spot. Only in the Kruger National Park was there planned, two years ago, a position for a biologist. There is now being built in the Serengeti National Park the 'Michael Grzimek Memorial Laboratory' for the use of resident scientists and their visiting colleagues. The building has been paid for out of contributions by the local population, together with grants from the city of Frankfurt and the West German Government.

It is not at all easy to persuade first-class scientists to accept overseas posts of this kind. Certainly enough biologists can be found willing to spend six months or even three years in Africa while carrying out a research commission. Ambitious young men are, however, seldom willing to settle permanently in the jungle with their families. Even leaving out of account the difficulty of providing schooling for their children, such men generally fear that they would be forgotten at the scientific centres of Europe or America, and would have no future career. In my opinion, therefore, such research posts overseas should be attached to specific European or American universities, so that university professors could control them permanently, send experts there with particular assignments for limited periods, and go there themselves from time to time. It has to be borne in mind that a biologist working in a national park cannot hope to be so versatile that he would never require the assistance of specialists. Furthermore scientists working overseas would retain their places in the academic hierarchy, and would be promoted according to seniority and merit just as though they were working in their own countries.

Most of the new African states are suffering from financial difficulties. It is a considerable drain on the Congo's resources, for example, to support the Albert National Park, with its staff of 400 and its monthly wage bill of £2,800. Light aircraft will have to be employed in the overseas parks. With their help it is easy to check on the numbers of wild animals, and to see where they are massed in different months. The park game wardens, too, could easily be supervised from the air, and they would feel themselves less isolated in the vast expanses of the park territories. A really effective campaign against poachers is impossible without the use of aircraft. If the leading game protection officials travel by air, the park staff can be considerably reduced. The fatal accident to my son Michael has delayed the introduction of aircraft in the African national parks. In the meantime the Serengeti National Park administration have purchased a machine of their own; the director and other officials have learned to fly. This is an example which will certainly be followed all over Africa.

The national parks now contain fewer animals than they would be able to support. The herds of wild game congregate at the few permanent water-holes during the dry season. There are only as many thousand animals as are able to find pasture within some 12 miles of the water-holes during the dry months, and in the rainy season these herds spread out over the whole vast area of the park, once the new green has sprung up everywhere. If it is possible, by means of building small reservoirs, wells with pumps and pipes, etc., to create additional permanent water-supply points, it will be possible to increase the numbers of wild game many times over. A well with wind pump costs about £3,500.

Possibly, however, we are worrying about national parks which will soon disappear in any case. Far more important than to conduct research in them at the moment is to do whatever lies within our power to ensure their very existence in the future. Sooner or later in most parts of Africa the Africans themselves will be in control. So far they have tended to be antagonistic towards national parks and similar institutions. What can we do, nevertheless, on behalf of the parks?

During recent years I have attempted to make it clear to Africans and Europeans that the magnificent wild animals of Africa are a valuable national asset which they ought to care for—for the sake of their own children and mankind as a whole—just as the European nations now cherish such cultural treasures of their lands as the Acropolis, the Louvre, and St. Peter's in Rome. Such self-evident ideas appeared to be so unwelcome even to cultured Europeans that they even attempted to suppress them by means of censorship. We cannot, therefore, expect to be able, in the short time which remains to us, to convince Africans of their truth—above all in view of the bad example which we gave them in former years, and to some extent still give them. Nevertheless this propaganda has some chance of success, for each 'barbaric' race rising to higher things is anxious to avoid appearing too uncultured. It will copy the older, tired civilizations, just as our ancestors imitated the Greeks and Romans. At all events, the Frankfurt Zoological Society has printed coloured posters with text in Swahili which are to be displayed in every village of Tanganyika. The wording says that the whole world envies Tanganyika its wild animals, or points out how much money is brought into the country on account of the lion and rhinoceros. The first mobile cinema unit, costing some £7,000, has already gone into service, showing in the villages documentary films concerning the national parks. We need four or five such units. We are beginning to run competitions in the schools for the best essays dealing with national parks, and to invite politicians, tribal chiefs and school parties to visit the parks. Unfortunately this campaign to educate the Africans about their own heritage has only been begun very late in the day. We Europeans have wasted innumerable opportunities in this respect.

What is the quickest and most effective way to make elephants, lions and giraffes, that is to say national parks, appear worth saving in the eyes of the new coloured politicians?

When I gave a showing of our Serengeti film in the presence of Sir Richard Turnbull, governor of Tanganyika, and his ministers at Dar-es-Salaam, I was afterwards introduced to the members of the government. The Minister of Education smilingly put out his hands as though to defend himself, saying that he had nothing to do with national parks, one of his colleagues being responsible for them. Thereupon I told him how a seventy-year-old man had spoken to me in a street in Arusha the day before. He whispered in my ear, as though ashamed of the fact, that he had lived in Tanganyika for fifty years, but that he had never seen a lion. Ninety per cent of all children in Tanganyika, black, white and brown, never get to know the principal animals of their land, the elephant, lion, rhinoceros, gnu and hippopotamus. The white children sometimes see them in zoos during holidays spent with their parents in Europe. On the other hand 90 per cent of children in Europe have seen the big game of Africa, because of the popularity of European zoos. 'And yet you say, Mr. Minister, that the national parks in Tanganyika are not of educational importance?' This is not to say that more zoos ought to be founded in Africa itself—far from it. It is in national parks that young people can make contact with the natural life of their homeland, and can see what it looked like in the days before it had a large human population.

Africans are hungry for knowledge. Owing to the fact that I mix so frequently with ordinary village folk I know that it is more important to them that their children should have a better education and should make progress than to know who governs them in the capital city. Hitherto the national parks have been visited almost exclusively by Europeans.

Another important possibility is the use of wild game. We Europeans, both farmers and agricultural officials, have brought to Africa more or less the same methods of farming as those to which we were accustomed in our native lands. This has meant that vast expanses of the plains have gradually been transformed into desert wastes. Wild animals have grazed there for thousands of years without destroying the vegetation; fat zebra and gnu roam in unbelievably barren-looking, dry areas, while lion and hyena are free from infectious diseases. By contrast the cows owned by both Europeans and Africans are thin and weedy-looking, and wherever they have taken the place of wild animals during recent years the desert has encroached further and further into what was once pastureland. Nature conservation biologists have confirmed, in the Serengeti National Park as elsewhere in Africa, the fairly self-evident fact that the yield per acre is greater if a proportion of the wild animals native to the area are slain for food than if they are replaced by cattle, sheep or goats. In districts bordering on the Tsavo National Park in Kenya the native population, led by Jan Parker, regularly kill a planned number of elephant, dry the meat, and supply it to the markets along the coast. In Uganda hunting and the growth of human settlements nearby have driven so many elephants into the Murchison Falls National Park that the hungry beasts have stripped the bark off all the trees over an area of many square miles, with the result that in time the trees die. At least 1,200 of these elephants will have to be shot, just as in recent years the surplus hippopotami have been disposed of in the Queen Elizabeth Park (Uganda). In national parks such slaughter occasionally becomes a regrettable necessity, but in other areas wild game can contribute very substantially to the feeding of the population.

However, will we be able to convince the young African governments that the doctrine we are now preaching to them is the right one?

The best way to convince them is to bring foreign tourists to the parks in greater numbers as quickly as possible. I first discussed plans for achieving this with the African Prime Minister of Tanganyika, Dr. Julius Nyerere, in the winter of 1960. I put it to him that no one now living in Africa, whether African or European, appreciates fully the extent to which the outlook of the people of Europe and America has changed during the past few years. Never before in the history of mankind have such a large proportion of the human race lived in cities and towns, having no contact with wild animals—or even with domestic livestock apart from dogs and cats. The fact that the contact with nature and its creatures which seemed absolutely a matter of course to the grandparents of the present generation has almost completely ceased to exist has increased the partiality of countless people to animals in a remarkable way. This fact is reflected in the constantly increasing number of visitors to zoos, and the many which have recently been founded, as well as the way newspapers will often devote more space to items concerning the protection of animals than to reports of accidents in which many people have lost their lives.

In our parents' days only the well-to-do could afford to travel to the Riviera; they would never have been able to believe that today millions of ordinary people, including many from the working classes, spend their holidays in the South of France, in Spain and Italy. Progress in aviation will soon enable Europeans to fly to Tanganyika in five or even three hours instead of eleven as at present. However, apart from Mount Kilimanjaro the country is not sufficiently attractive to compete with Switzerland, the Yellowstone Park or the Himalayas. What the city dwellers, hungry for nature and wild life, will seek and admire are elephants, lions, giraffes and zebras in their natural surroundings—provided that the new African politicians succeed in preserving these animals through the turmoil of the years ahead.

I was not certain whether or not I had convinced Dr. Nyerere, because I have noticed that politicians will generally agree readily enough with everyone, but often act in a totally different manner later. I was therefore delighted when the German Consul in Nairobi told me that during a tour of the United States soon after our meeting Dr. Nyerere had frequently emphasized the importance to his country of its wild animals. A little while later the London *Daily Telegraph* carried an article by a lady journalist who had spoken to him. According to her Dr. Nyerere had said: 'I personally am not very interested in animals. I do not want to spend my holidays watching crocodiles. Nevertheless I am entirely in favour of their survival. I believe that after diamonds and sisal wild animals will provide Tanganyika with its greatest source of income. Thousands of Americans and Europeans have the strange urge to see these animals, and we must ensure that they are able to do so.'

Who knows, though, whether other African political leaders share this opinion, and whether they will be able to get their way even if the flow of tourists is not at first as great as we hope it will be? In order to do what I can to increase the number of tourists I have several times during the winter and spring of 1960–61 made it known over the German television network that it is possible to fly to Serengeti and spend three weeks there for about £200. As a result so many inquiries flooded all the travel bureaux that special tours, which had not previously existed, were arranged at reduced prices. The first of these parties flew to Tanganyika about the beginning of 1961, with the support of the Frankfurt Zoological Society, which was founded in 1858. This first special flight was the precursor of many.

The European colonial administrators were generally of the opinion that when fixing the bounds of national parks they were obliged to respect the wishes of the native population in the area, however ill-informed and, in the long run, self-destructive those wishes were. They believed that a future African Government would make many decisions even more unfavourable to the well-being of the animals. I am not altogether in agreement with them on this point, and the first signs to come out of newly independent territories seem to bear out my opinion. A native government, which badly needs revenue for a young and under-developed land, will presumably decide in favour of the tourist trade and against a few half-starved head of cattle which serve no economic purpose. In this connection it is particularly interesting to find out what has become of the national parks in the African states which have recently achieved independence. The answer seems to be that in cases where the colonial power ran and protected such parks well they have been retained and looked after, but that where little value was placed on them in the past they have come to grief under the new régime.

The Garamba Park was under the control of the National Park Administration of the former Belgian Congo, which was a model to all such organizations in the world under the direction of Dr. Victor van Straelen. It lies in the northern territory of the Congo, bordering on the Sudan. The Belgian administrators were constantly complaining of thefts by poachers from across the unguarded frontier. In the last few years, according to information given by Dr. van Staelen, the poaching had ceased; in the meantime the Sudan had gained its independence. I had heard rumours that the new Sudanese Government had armed their game wardens and that these men had then begun to take a firm line with poachers, not hesitating to shoot at them. Mr. Medani—the coloured head of the Forest and National Park Administration in the Sudan, who recently visited me for a few days in Frankfurt—did not agree that such drastic measures had been adopted. It seems clear, though, that discipline in the Sudanese national parks is now being vigorously enforced.

In the Albert National Park of the former Belgian Congo, which joins on to the Queen Elizabeth National Park of Uganda, the African game wardens continued to perform their duties after the Congo gained its independence, even after their Belgian superiors left. The Belgian scientist, Dr. Verschuren, who stayed at his post, was at once entrusted by the new native governor with the task of advising the newly appointed, entirely inexperienced, Congolese director of the Park. Even when, during the political upheavals and fighting which have since disrupted the land, the area of the Park came under the control of the rival government at Stanleyville, the staff continued their work as before. The fact that in the Congo—unlike British colonial territories—native assistants had not long since been trained so as to be able to take over the administration of the national parks greatly hampers their further development. Efforts are now being made in Tanganyika and Kenya to ensure that the necessary preparation will be complete by the time a change-over may have to be made.

Naturally the initially favourable situation may change overnight, such is the political confusion in many parts of Africa today. Nevertheless it is clear that the splendid wild animals of Africa can certainly be saved, in at least a few places, for the benefit of future generations of mankind, provided that the challenge is accepted vigorously during this period of transition.

Galápagos, the Islands of Tame Animals

BY

DR. IRENÄUS EIBL VON EIBESFELDT

SOME 650 miles to the west of Ecuador a group of volcanic islands thrust their grey lava mountains and cliffs above the Pacific Ocean, an archipelago whose weather-beaten shores are inhabited by the strangest creatures on earth. They were to inspire one of the most revolutionary concepts in the realm of natural science, as they gave Darwin the idea behind his evolutionary thesis which he formulated in his *Origin of Species*. The spot where the Galápagos Islands now lie was once covered by the immense Pacific Ocean, until one day the earth's crust burst asunder, and glowing matter poured up from the interior of our planet. Lava and scoriae piled up on the ocean bed until finally erupting volcanoes appeared above the surface of the seething water. Today the many islands and islets amount to some 3,000 square miles of land, and the highest volcanoes rise to about 4,800 ft. above sea-level. Their sides are pierced and furrowed by recent outbreaks of lava, while numerous small craters are scattered along the coasts. As the slopes cooled down living things were able to establish themselves there. Cacti and other hardy vegetation appeared on the sun-drenched lower-lying slopes, while evergreen woods grew on the damp upper reaches. The seeds of the forebears of those plants and trees, like the ancestors of the animal life now to be found there, came from the far-off mainland of South America, carried by the waves or on the wings of the wind. It is quite understandable that only a few, particularly hardy species were able to survive. Thus we find that some classes of plants and animals which abound in South America are entirely absent. For example there are no liliaceous flowers and no coniferous trees. Nor are there any amphibians, while only one type of land snake and two land mammals (a bat and the Galápagos rat) are native to the islands. Many of the land birds of South America, such as the parrot, are unknown there.

Every creature which reached the Galápagos alive had to adapt itself to conditions totally unlike those to be found elsewhere, with the result that a vast experiment in evolution took place there, producing over the ages remarkable forms of creature which are to be found nowhere else on earth. For example 77 of the 89 types of bird which nest in the archipelago are restricted to these islands. Only here can one see flightless cormorants, the dragon-like marine iguanas which sun themselves in hundreds on the lava rocks, or the giant 'Galápagos' tortoises after which the Spaniards named the islands. Only here, too, is there to be found the astonishing co-existence of tropical and antarctic animals: fur-seals and penguins bask peacefully in the equatorial sun alongside tropical marine iguanas. The cold Humboldt Current, which flows round the islands from the south, brought the creatures of the Antarctic to these tropical islands, where they, too, adapted themselves to the changed conditions, with the result that new varieties, unique to the Galápagos Islands, emerged.

What most surprises visitors to the islands, however, is the extraordinary tameness of the Galápagos animals. If you land between basking iguanas and sea-lions they hardly trouble to move aside. If you remain quiet they will even come up to you inquisitively, and you must be careful lest a mischievous sea-lion steals any article it can get hold of. After a short time you find yourself surrounded by tame animals. Interested thrushes are all around, and a Galápagos buzzard alights on the camping site, so near that you can touch it with your hand, and even feed it with meat by hand. This astonishing tameness of many Galápagos animals is explained by the fact that there is not a single carnivorous animal living on dry land anywhere in the archipelago. In this respect the islands are a miniature paradise, or rather they were until the time when man, the most dangerous of all living creatures, first set foot on those lonely shores.

The earliest visitors landed there most unwillingly. In 1535, as Bishop Tomás de Berlanga was sailing from Panama to Peru, his ship was becalmed in this area. Fresh water was running low, and all the party were delighted to sight land. Great was their disappointment, however, at finding nothing but cacti and stones. 'It looked as though God had caused it to rain stones!' Berlanga lamented. At length he discovered that the sap of the cacti could be extracted and drunk, and this saved the lives of himself and his crew. Bishop Berlanga was the first man to write of the many giant tortoises, so large that a man could easily ride on the back of one of them. Nevertheless he was glad when at last a wind sprang up and he was able to leave the islands. For the time being the islands were of no significance to man. They were difficult to reach, as various ocean currents carried sailing ships in unexpected directions, so that many believed the islands to move about in the sea, with the result that they were sometimes described as the accursed islands, 'Islas Encantadas', and their grim appearance was well suited to this name. Not until the late seventeenth century, when English buccaneers were raiding the west coasts of South and Central America, did they become important. In the quiet bays they divided their spoils and prepared for fresh piratical expeditions. In the interior of Charles Island pirate caves, fitted out as living quarters, can still be seen, and in James Bay on James Island one comes across broken provision jars everywhere. It was famed buccaneers such as Lionel Wafer, John Cook, Basil Ringrose,

William Dampier (a strange combination of scientist, writer and pirate) and Ambrose Cowley who gave the individual islands their English names, mainly those of great national figures. The mariners learned to appreciate the tasty meat of the giant tortoises, and began the slaughter which was continued by whalers in the nineteenth century. Whole shiploads of these creatures were taken away, until finally the tortoises became so rare that it was not considered worthwhile to catch them. The arrival of permanent settlers at the end of the nineteenth century made the situation even worse. Domestic animals such as dogs, cats, pigs and goats were introduced, went wild, and became a plague to the native Galápagos animals, which were not prepared to defend themselves against such foes. Today there are settlements on Chatham, Charles, South Albemarle and Indefatigable. The situation confronting the native animals became more and more menacing, with the result that the government of Ecuador made a number of laws declaring that various species were to be protected throughout the islands.

In the year 1954, twenty years after those laws were made, I visited the islands as a member of the Xarifa Expedition led by Dr. Hans Hass. I was deeply impressed by the many opportunities offered here to the natural scientist, but at the same time I was horrified at the damage being done by man in this unique territory. In the settlements, despite the law forbidding their molestation, we were offered penguins, young tortoises, tortoise shells, and skins of the extremely rare fur-seals. On the seashore we were constantly finding slain sea-lions—in many cases the killer had not even taken the trouble to remove the skin despite its value. As soon as I had returned to Europe I reported what I had seen to the International Union for Conservation of Nature and Natural Resources in Brussels, stating my conviction that effective protection was only feasible if someone was on the spot to see that the law was observed. A biological station should also be set up as a nature conservation centre. The International Union for Conservation of Nature and the Ecuadorian Government both expressed themselves interested in this idea, and support was also obtained from UNESCO. In 1957, on behalf of the organizations mentioned, I toured the whole archipelago for the second time. I found that it was fortunately not too late to take protective measures. There were still untouched islands on which everything remained as it had been before the coming of man, and satisfactory numbers of each of the characteristic Galápagos animals still existed in remote places. We discovered colonies of the Galápagos fur-seal (*Arctocephalus galapagoensis*) which had been considered almost extinct. On Narborough and Barrington we found considerable numbers of the land iguana (*Conolophus subcristatus*). There are even giant tortoises surviving in a few places, and I shall never forget my first encounter with these primeval creatures.

Just before dawn we left Academy Bay on the south coast of Indefatigable Island with two Ecuadorian guides, and struck inland along a narrow, stony path. Soon after sunrise it became unbearably hot in the cactus belt along the coast, through which we had to pass. A heat haze shimmered between the fig and candelabra cactuses, each taller than a man but giving no more shade than the dry vegetation on either side of the path. Nevertheless the little red-throated lava lizards which sped nimbly across the path and the dark cactus finches seemed to enjoy the heat.

The small, unprepossessing finches interested me especially, as it was these birds which convinced Darwin that different species derived from a common original form. He had collected a considerable number of finches, and when he compared the different classes he was struck by their resemblance both in plumage and structure, a resemblance which could hardly be the result of mere chance. Darwin had already doubted the correctness of the theory, generally held in his day, that species were unalterable, from the time when he discovered that each of the larger Galápagos Islands was inhabited by its own variety of tortoise, clearly distinguished from that of any other island. Then, when he saw so clearly before him the variations of a basic type of finch he became finally convinced that these creatures were not all independent and unalterable but all sprang from a common original form. Clearly the ancestors of the Galápagos finches reached the islands long before any other songbirds. We do not know whether the earliest finches lived on seeds or on insects, but whatever they fed on they must have multiplied until a point was reached at which the amount of food available began to limit any further increase. From then on natural selection began to favour variations of the original finch able to nourish themselves in other ways, so that over a period of thousands of years there emerged clearly differentiated members of the finch family. Some are seed-eaters, some biters of grain kernels, some insect-eaters and one even adopts the methods of the woodpecker. He lacks the woodpecker's long tongue, so in order to get insects out of the holes he has enlarged he makes use of a remarkable piece of artistry. Once he has made his hole in the bark of a tree he picks up a cactus prickle or wood splinter, and holding this lengthwise in his beak he pokes about in the hole with it until the insect flies out. He then drops the 'tool' and seizes his prey. An extraordinary instance of the use of a piece of equipment by a bird! The various kinds of finch are distinguished from one another primarily by their beaks: in some the beak is powerful enough to bite tough grain kernels, in others it is thin and suited to catching insects, while others have beaks like parrots. Their different methods of feeding are reflected clearly in the shape of their beaks.

The question whether a species can become divided into different forms without at least temporary geographical isolation is still a matter for dispute among scientists. It is important for the separation of different varieties that the heritage of such varieties should be divided in accordance with particular needs. Many authors consider at least temporary geographical isolation to be necessary. Others, however, point out instances in which such development can take place without geographical isolation, but in which a new variety has the advantage of being able to eat food of a kind not eaten by the original bird.

Scientists call such a case a 'niche': the new variety has a niche of its own in the area it shares with other related classes of bird in which it has no competition from members of the species from which it has developed.

We rested in the shade of a cordia bush, brightly adorned with its yellow blossom, and watched the finches—only for a short time, though, as we had to make our way further inland. At 300 ft. above sea-level the vegetation began to change. The cacti became rarer and smaller, while bushes were larger, soon giving place to genuine trees. Finally we came to damp, luxuriant woodland. Scalesia trees, with straight, slender trunks, their crown and branches very high above the ground, dominated the scene. Here and there were great red-trunked pisonia trees. The ground was covered with fern and mosses, with long trails of beard-moss hanging from the trees and bushes—an astonishing contrast to the barren coastal zone!

Climbing higher, we came at length, some 2,400 ft. above sea-level, to the almost treeless, mist-enshrouded highest point on our route. We changed direction, and after a time began to descend again. Late in the evening we came to open meadows with isolated clumps of trees and bushes, and the sun-bleached shell of an old giant tortoise showed us that we had reached our destination. We pushed on for another hour into the domain of the giant tortoises, but for a time found only the shells of tortoises slaughtered by the settlers. Disappointed and deeply concerned, we camped for the night in our tents.

The desire to explore further got us out of our sleeping-bags early next morning. After a hastily eaten breakfast we spread out in all directions. Just behind our camp site we came upon fresh tracks which led us to a pond. Bathing in it was a giant tortoise of truly astonishing dimensions, only its head and the top of its shell protruding from the water. The dark eyes gazed at us attentively, but there was no other indication that the creature was alive.

One of our Ecuadorian guides waded into the pond and drove the tortoise to the bank by tapping gently on the back of its shell with a stone. Puffing and blowing, the tortoise left its bath, and we were able to measure it. The circumference round the middle of its body was about 8 ft., and it was so heavy that four of us together were unable to lift it. It was a male. That day we found a number of other tortoises, and watched them eating fresh grass. After they had finished a meal they would doze under a bush and allow finches to peck fragments of food or insects from the corners of their mouths.

We found not only live tortoises but also numerous shells bearing the marks of hatchet blows. The settlers evidently sought them out even in this remote part of the island for the sake of the tortoise fat. We found no young specimens, but our guide told us that the tortoises laid their eggs in the dry coastal region, if possible in the most inaccessible places. I visited the area a few weeks later. Here, too, to my sorrow, I found signs everywhere of the ravages of man: shells and bones of giant tortoises were scattered around on the ground. Nevertheless we found some splendid full-sized specimens, and, what pleased us even more, five youngsters about a year old. This find proved that the species is still able to breed successfully, and that effective nature protection measures could yet save it from becoming extinct. One necessary step would be to take action against the wild swine abounding in the area, which destroy great numbers of young tortoises. On other islands, too, tortoises have survived down to the present day, but in many cases their numbers are so small that there is little hope of saving certain of the varieties. A great deal can, however, still be done. The general picture is as follows: On Barrington and Charles the tortoises are undoubtedly extinct. Small numbers still exist on Hood, Chatham, Duncan, Abingdon, and possibly also on Jervis. Tortoises are still to be found on James, but their number is difficult to estimate; they may be more numerous in the inaccessible eastern end of the island. On Albemarle and Indefatigable fair numbers are living and breeding, although they are menaced by domestic animals and men. The most westerly island Narborough also possesses its own variety of tortoise, but only a single specimen has been found. As this island is seldom visited, and no domestic animals have run wild there, prospects for the survival of the sub-species are good.

Narborough Island is one of the most interesting islands in the archipelago from the zoological point of view, since it has been left almost untouched by human beings. Anyone who lands on its black lava shores feels as though he had been taken back thousands of years to the reptile age. Hundreds of dark marine iguanas (*Amblyrhynchus cristatus*) about 3 ft. long sun themselves close together on the rocks. Their appearance reminds one of small dragons. The short-snouted, round head is armoured by means of cone-shaped scales, and the back is surmounted by a long serrated dorsal ridge which continues, though becoming progressively lower, along the creature's extensive, rudder-like tail. The low-lying body is carried on powerful clawed legs. The colouring is black with dark red spots on the sides, the centre of the back and the dorsal ridge having a greenish tint. The coloration and size of the iguanas vary from island to island. Some are small and almost completely black (Tower Island), while some are almost entirely bright in colour, such as the *venustissimus* variety on Hood. The marine iguana is the only member of the iguana family to find its food in the sea. At ebbtide these creatures leave the shores where they have been sunning themselves and eat seaweed left behind on the lower shores by the retreating water. They never require fresh water, having a special gland in front of their eyes which removes the salt from the sea water they imbibe. This gland runs to the nasal cavity, and as soon as salt water is taken in it releases a salt-dispelling fluid far more concentrated than the salt in the sea water. Turtles and various marine birds have similar anti-salt glands. Marine iguanas sometimes remain under water for a time. Near Narborough I saw some eating seaweed six to ten feet below the surface among the coral fishes.

When these iguana lie basking in the sun little ground finches (*Geospiza uliginosa*) and red crabs are often to be seen perched on them and clambering about on their backs. Both are undoubtedly seeking ticks in the folds of the iguanas' skin, and for this reason are tolerated.

During the breeding season each male chooses a patch of ground which he shares with several females, and which he defends against any intruder. If another male approaches, the master of this patch opens his mouth, nods his head, and squirts thin streams of water out of his nostrils. His dorsal comb fully erect, he faces his opponent, standing with his legs extended to their full height. If the rival does not make off the result is a duel, which is fought according to strict rules. The opponents do not bite each other. They lower their heads and advance towards each other, each trying to push the other away with his armoured head. This lasts for some time, until one is forced into a crevice or is pushed over on to his back, whereupon he quits the battle-field. There is another way in which the fight may end: if one of the combatants realizes that he is not a match for his opponent he can surrender, crouching down before the other in an attitude of submission. His foe then ceases hostilities, remaining in a threatening position until the vanquished rival quits the area. Such a battle is therefore fought exactly like a knightly joust governed by the laws of chivalry, the stronger always winning but never wounding the weaker. This fact is of value as regards the survival of the species, as the weaker beast is often not so much inferior as younger, needing further time to mature fully. If they bit one another many of these fights would have fatal consequences, since the marine iguana is equipped with rows of sharp three-cusped teeth. Other vertebrates can be observed engaging in similar 'chivalrous' combats. Thus many poisonous snakes pit their strength against each other, wrestling in accordance with a definite system of rules. When fighting thus against a member of their own species they never make use of their envenomed teeth. In the interior of Narborough there lives a creature related to the marine iguana, the land iguana (*Conolophus subcristatus*). This large yellow or yellowy-brown lizard lives alone or in pairs in self-dug burrows in the earth, and eats cacti and other vegetation of dry areas. Throw a cactus fig to these creatures, and they will at once hurry to the spot and allow themselves to be fed like animals in a zoo! One even took cactus fruits from my hand. If captured, however, they will defend themselves ferociously, and can cause serious wounds with their sharp teeth. Land iguanas were once common on James, Indefatigable, Albemarle, Seymour, Barrington and Narborough. Today, however, they appear to exist in any considerable numbers only on the last two islands named. They have become rare on the other islands, and may already have become extinct on James and Seymour.

On the shores of Narborough Island are to be found two of the most unusual birds of the Galápagos Islands, the flightless cormorant (*Nannopterum harrisi*) and the Galápagos penguin (*Spheniscus mendiculus*). Both live only here and on the coast of Albemarle facing Narborough. The flightless cormorant is the world's largest cormorant, and at the same time the only member of this bird family which has lost its ability to fly. Its wings are still feathered as if for flight, but are short and stunted. This bird demonstrates the fact that the ability to fly can be lost without any grave drawback, provided that no foes are present. Comparable examples are the dodo of Mauritius and the great auk of the northern isles. Both of these have long been extinct, though, and the flightless cormorant is one of the last impressive examples of this strange phenomenon. I have spent many hours by the nests of these remarkable birds. Their nests, which are crude and artless, are built on the bare rock, of seaweed, little twigs and stones. Both adult birds concern themselves with their young, and while one goes fishing the other sits in the nest, protecting the fledglings from the heat of the sun with outstretched wings. I was delighted by the ceremony with which one partner takes over from the other the task of guarding the nest. Whichever partner is returning to the nest gives the other a tuft of seaweed or a star-fish, a courteous gesture which is never forgotten. By bringing some nesting material in this way the homecoming bird demonstrates its friendly intentions. Similar greeting ceremonial is also the rule among a number of other creatures.

The penguins, sea-lions and fur-seals form the 'antarctic' group among the Galápagos animals. As already mentioned, they came to this area with the Humboldt Current, and here underwent gradual changes producing varieties of the original species as known in antarctic waters. I made friends especially with the playful sea-lion (*Zalophus wollebaeci*). Fortunately these creatures are still to be found in most parts of the archipelago, although they are hunted and often wantonly slain by fishermen. Each male possesses a small harem, which he watches over jealously. The stretch of coastline frequented by the sea-lions is divided among these males, each of which is constantly on patrol, swimming close to the shore up and down like a sentry on guard, emphasizing his claim to the stretch of water and calling out loudly the while—no doubt the gist of his message is 'Here I am, and no one else has any right to be here'. If, however, another male ventures into his territory the result is a violent battle, and nearly all the bulls bear the scars of such encounters. Normally, however, each respects the zones of his neighbours. They often meet at the boundaries between their territories. There they raise themselves up before each other and bellow loudly. However, this is merely a demonstration; fights in such circumstances are rare, as each has what he needs. Fights occur when one has as yet no harem, and attempts to make off with the wives of another.

The bulls are not only jealous pashas but also devoted fathers of their families. If they notice that a youngster has carelessly swum out into deep water they will head it off at once and drive it back to the shallows. This fact is of great importance for the preservation of the species, since the waters around the Galápagos abound with sharks, to which any young sea-lion straying too far out to sea can easily fall a victim. The bulls also protect their large families against human beings. They will even follow one on land; it is not their normal element, but I have actually had to run away from an enraged bull sea-lion. They are especially unpleasant if encountered in the water, and while we were diving we had to keep an eye on these agile, pugnacious creatures. By contrast the females and their young are tame and trusting. If you sit on the shore they like to come investigating, and unless you are careful they may easily make off with some part of the diving equipment, and play with it in the surf. If pieces of wood or other debris are thrown to them they will send them up in the air and catch them with amazing dexterity, as though circus-trained.

The females are conscientious mothers, but they are concerned only with the welfare of their own offspring. If another youngster approaches too near it is at once chased away. Mother and children always recognize each other, not only by means of smell but also from their voices. I spent many evenings among colonies of sea-lions, watching the children searching for their mothers. They would make for each female they saw, sniff for a few moments, then go away if it was not their mother. Once I saw a youngster seek vainly through the whole colony, and finally sink down in utter despair on a rock at some distance from the others. In its dejection it began to bleat like a lamb. Its high, tearful Baah, baah could be heard all over the sea-lion colony. Then suddenly from the surf there came an answering, consoling call on a deeper note, Buuuur! Galvanized into life, the youngster left its rock and made its way quickly in the direction from which the answering call had come. It continued to bleat, and its mother to reply, so that a regular duet ensued. I was often able to verify later the fact that the mothers can pick out the voices of their young unerringly from the mass of sound on all sides. They hardly ever make a mistake, and the children, too, recognize their mothers' voices. It is only the very young that become confused.

The other class of seal native to the islands, the Galápagos fur-seal (*Arctocephalus galapagoensis*), is already very rare. These seals were once to be found in every part of the archipelago, but they have always been hunted for their valuable fur, and specimens are now to be found only around the most northerly islands of the group. The fur-seals, like the sea-lions, belong to the group of eared seals, characterized, among other features, by the remnants of auricular organs. By contrast to that of the sea-lion, their coat has a thick 'under-felt'. We found examples on James and Tower. They are even tamer than the sea-lions, and the males show hardly any aggressive inclinations, so that it is possible to move about freely among them. Unfortunately they are still hunted by tunny fishers.

On our journeys among the islands we visited Tower, at the northern end of the archipelago, with its abundance of bird life. This low, sun-baked island does not look exactly inviting from the distance. However, as we got closer we began to appreciate its particular charm, because dozens of birds were soon circling our boat: dark grey lava gulls and lovely swallow-tailed gulls with their red-ringed eyes, frigate birds and numerous boobies, which live up to their name by their loss of much of their booty of fish to the frigate birds; as our boat approached the island boobies landed unceremoniously on the upper-parts and railings. As we entered Darwin Bay we could see that from every bush within sight the red throat-pouches of frigate birds were glowing like rare orchid blossoms. We had arrived during the mating season, when the male birds were making the greatest possible display of their fine colours, squabbling with each other and competing for the favours of the white-breasted females. If one approached, each male would spread its wings, rock its body to and fro in a curious manner, and give vent to its mating cry, a dreadful-sounding 'kyu yu yu yuhuhuhu'. A few males were hatching eggs in crudely constructed brushwood nests in the bushes. The red throat-pouches, so large and magnificent in the courting male, had shrunk to a mere fold of skin in these already married specimens. The frigate bird is a splendid flier with a wingspan of more than 6 ft. The pinions and flight muscles account for 45 per cent of the bird's weight, and accordingly it is a remarkable aeronaut, able to circle in the air for hours. Frigate birds live on fish, those of the Galápagos Islands often seizing it from boobies. They keep a careful watch on the coastline, and if they see that a booby has caught a fish they will dive on it from all sides and harry it until it drops the fish. The frigate birds thus make life far from easy for the poor boobies.

At the time of our visit the boobies, too, were mating. The red-footed boobies, like the frigate birds, were nesting in bushes, while the blue-footed boobies laid their eggs on the ground. The fact that they are accustomed to different nesting conditions is demonstrated by the behaviour of fledglings of the two varieties, which cannot otherwise be distinguished. If you take a young bird of the red-footed variety out of its nest it will try to climb up your arm, while the young of the blue-footed booby stay where they are, cowering anxiously in your hand.

One of the most magnificent of the Galápagos birds is the Galápagos albatross, which breeds only on the southerly island Hood. There I was able to watch their courting games, probably among the most remarkable ceremonies in the whole range of animal life. The pair first move round each other, with measured steps as though dancing, each resting its head alternately on its left and right shoulder, in time with its footsteps. Then they stop, facing each other, and rub their beaks together with rapid movements, the beaks coming together with a sharp tap. Suddenly they raise their heads, open their beaks threateningly, then snap the upper and lower sections together loudly. Then they revert to beak-rubbing, or one (sometimes both) lifts its beak skyward and calls out, in a mournful-sounding voice, 'goh'. They sometimes indulge in another session of beak-snapping, as do storks, but keeping their necks stretched out in front of them. The snapping always ends with the bird suddenly jerking its head upward, so that it points high into the sky, but with the beak pointing towards the partner. While shooting its head up the albatross lets out a cry. If only one claps with its beak the other touches its shoulder at regular intervals with its beak, and remains in this position until the partner leaves off clapping, then it shoots its head up, at the same time clapping the two halves of its beak loudly together once. As a concluding gesture the birds will often bow to each other, point down towards the ground with the beaks, and call 'go go go'. After that they generally settle themselves on the ground. Thus the albatrosses have performed a series of strange antics, whose meaning is not in all cases clear.

Their movements while sparring with their beaks closely resemble the 'begging' action of young albatrosses, and is perhaps formalized begging. The action of pointing the beak in the air is probably a demonstration of peaceful intentions, since the beak—the bird's weapon—is thereby directed away from the other. This gesture is comparable to the greeting of storks, which also indicate friendship by pointing their weapons away, in which position they would clearly be unable to attack.

Storks lay their necks on their backs as they clap with their beaks. The silver heron, on the other hand, greets one of its own kind with its neck pointing out stiffly in front of it, its beak turned away. The principle is the same. The bowing of the albatrosses may be a symbolic gesture suggesting a nesting place; after several such bows the birds will sit down and begin courteously preening each other's feathers.

The more we came to learn about the Galápagos Islands, the more intimately linked did we become with their animal life and their strangely impressive terrain. Many of the islands are really a paradise in miniature. However, there is no doubt that even those parts of the archipelago which have so far remained untouched by man will be utterly spoilt in the near future, unless a permanently staffed nature protection station is set up. In the southern part of Indefatigable Island we found a highly suitable site for such a station, and proposed its foundation to the Ecuadorian Government and the International Union for Conservation of Nature. Both favoured the proposal, and entrusted an international commission with the realization of the project. A foundation has been set up by the International Union for Conservation of Nature, and we confidently hope that the necessary funds will be forthcoming for the construction and running of the station, since what is involved is the saving of unique beauties of nature.

In the commentary to his film 'Serengeti shall not die' the Frankfurt zoologist Bernhard Grzimek has emphasized the fact that the surviving remnants of African animal life are a cultural possession of mankind as a whole, in the same way that our cathedrals and ancient monuments are. It is a symptom of our time that an official body in Wiesbaden, concerned with the evaluation of films, saw fit to object to that idea, as they considered it improper to compare the saving of herds of zebra with the preservation of, say, the Acropolis, or St. Peter's in Rome. In other words many of our fellow human beings do not hesitate to claim that works of men's hands should have precedence over God's creatures. This blindness to true values is certainly symptomatic of our time, but we believe that the majority of civilized men and women have a sense of their responsibility towards the other living creatures of the world. Nature protection is one of our most urgent cultural responsibilities, for that which is now being destroyed in a few years took millions of years to develop, and can therefore never be replaced.

The illustrations corresponding to this chapter are the copyright of Dr. Irenäus Eiblvon Eibesfeldt. Some have previously appeared in his book *Galapagos* (MacGibbon & Kee, London, Doubleday, New York).

'Dangerous' Animals in American National Parks

BY

FRED M. PACKARD,

Administrative Secretary of the National Parks Association, Washington

IT was once said that 'The Americans love their national parks so much they're killing them'—and there is perhaps a grain of truth in that remark. The result of the fact that millions of people descend upon the natural treasures which the parks have been created to preserve sometimes borders on the catastrophic. There are fine camping places in the national parks, but they have now been used by so many people for so many years that the feet of the countless visitors, constantly trampling down the grass, have already destroyed all surface vegetation in many areas. Most visitors arrive by car, and although the roads are generally excellent, thoughtless people will occasionally drive across open ground, leaving ugly marks behind them. Others ignore the rule which forbids the picking of flowers and plants, with the result that the numbers of certain types of cactus and similar plants in several desert parks have suffered severely. A really serious problem arises from the fact that some visitors simply will not accept the fact that the animals in our national parks are *wild*, and that it is therefore necessary to exercise caution when approaching them.

There are few really dangerous animals in North America. True, we have a number of poisonous snakes, but they generally keep out of the way of human beings, and only bite when they are touched or otherwise alarmed at very close quarters. The puma, or mountain lion, is harmless to man, and is seldom to be seen. His chief prey is the red deer.

I once spent a night at about the altitude of the timber line on Long's Peak, in the Rocky Mountains National Park, Colorado. When I awoke in the morning I found the tracks of a large puma near the spot where my head had lain: one of these big cats had come along, sniffed around—and gone on its way.

During the two years I spent studying animals in that park it occasionally happened that I could watch a puma among the rocks above me, seeing how it followed the route I was taking—as inquisitive as any cat. . . . It is seldom that one catches sight of a wolf, for they are few—but they are remarkable animals, symbols of life in the wilds to a greater extent than almost any other creature.

One might almost say that their appearance radiates dignity; they are wise, and possess an extraordinary sense of justice. They are neither evil-minded nor naturally aggressive, having a finely developed sense of working and playing together in groups.

The visitor to a national park seldom sees the animals mentioned so far, but there are others which are more frequently to be met with, and it can be an advantage to know something of their characteristics. The buffalo is peevish, and entirely unpredictable. Buffalo generally ignore people, but they have been known to charge without any evident reason, and the only way to save oneself in such a situation is to reach and climb a tree as quickly as possible. . . . One March day I was travelling through Yellowstone Park with Dr. Adolph Murie, one of the foremost zoologists of the National Park Service, using snow shoes. Suddenly we saw seven bison bulls standing in front of us on a piece of land we had intended to cross. Although it meant making a detour of three miles—doubly difficult with the snow shoes on our feet—Adolph insisted that we should always keep close to trees, in order to remain out of harm's way. As we skirted round the group in this way the bison slowly changed direction so that their heads were always facing us, glaring at us mistrustfully the whole time.

Throughout the greater part of the year the wapiti, the large American red deer, is a completely harmless creature which will flee from man. In the autumn, however, when the mating season begins, the males become warlike; their battle cries re-echo through the forests, and they engage in furious duels, often to the death. Visitors to national parks can watch these fights in perfect safety from their cars—witnessing one is an exciting experience. However, it sometimes happens that a thoughtless tourist, intent on getting a good photograph, leaves his car and approaches too close to the scene of action. In the heat of battle the wapiti naturally regards such an approach as a challenge to fight. His powerful antlers can cause serious, even mortal wounds.

We have two classes of bear in the United States: the little black bear and the rare, enormous grizzly. The black bear, in its natural state, is shy and harmless, fleeing from the proximity of human beings. Once it has overcome its natural reserve, however, it becomes a clown, an actor desiring nothing so much as to attract attention to itself. It has long been traditional to photograph the bears in Yellowstone Park, and some of them have become so accustomed to cars that they pose for photographs by the roadside! If only the visitors would always remember that what they see before them are not tame domestic animals, there would never be any accidents. Unfortunately, though, the antics of the bears are so amusing that the temptation to feed them often becomes irresistible. The car windows are lowered, or the doors are opened, and someone reaches out a hand containing a piece of chocolate or bacon. So far no one has lost his life in this way, but many people have suffered serious scratches, and others have even been maimed for life. The park authorities have now made it illegal to feed bears, with penalties for infringements of this law, and it is hoped that this measure will gradually remove the seriousness of the problem.

When a grizzly appears on the scene the black bears make themselves scarce, since the grizzly is not very companionable, and easily loses its temper. If sufficient respect is shown to the grizzly it will not harm anyone—but its wrath is fearful. It is one of the most powerful of living creatures, and has been known to demolish cars because they contained something edible which attracted it. Until fifteen years ago visitors to Yellowstone used to be shown an unusual spectacle; holes in the ground near the hotels were filled with kitchen refuse. Brown bears and even grizzlies enjoyed raking about there for food. The park keepers, who knew a great deal about the grizzly's character, shuddered every day when they saw these huge beasts mixing with crowds of spectators around the food holes. An end was made of the spectacle, partly because of the danger involved, and partly, too, because it was regarded as buffoonery, something unworthy and flatly contradictory to the spirit of the national park movement—for only when the bears are already half tame can such an exhibition be possible. However, the majority of the grizzlies live in remote parts of the park, where visitors seldom see and disturb them.

Although there are, therefore, some sources of danger to the careless visitor, it is true to say that it is possible for anyone who values wild life in its natural state, and complies with its laws, to travel through the American national parks without a thought of any especial danger. He who approaches wild animals with some understanding for their way of life will be allowed to go among them. They will regard him with calm reserve, but without antagonism. Such acceptance into the community of wild creatures living in freedom is the most precious reward which nature has to offer man.

South America, the Land of Maned Wolves and Ant-eaters

BY

DR. HANS KRIEG

IT isn't easy to write a few pages concerning the oases of the animal world which exist in South America. Which of the many should I pick out? Patagonia with its condors and guanacos? The Gran Chaco, in which nomadic Indians eke out a bare existence? The grandiose forests of the southern Andes, through whose undergrowth of tangled fuchsia and bamboo thickets there glides the pudu, the world's smallest deer? Or the heights above the timber line, where the secretive huemul, the Andes antelope the size of a chamois, is more often to be seen than when down in the wooded valleys? Or shall I write of the eared-seals which live in thousands along remote stretches of the coast, celebrating their weddings and bearing their young, but falling in great numbers every year at the hands of the hunters? True stories could be told of all these, stories of compelling interest opening up aspects of wild life which are unknown and hardly accessible to the modern traveller.

Not so very long ago almost the whole of South America was an immense sanctuary for animal life in its free state. A few coastal strips developed by Europeans and the old colonial centres dating from the times of Spanish conquests, with surrounding territories of limited extent, did little to alter the situation. However, when I think of the changes which have taken place during the few decades of my own lifetime I cannot help feeling—despite my respect for the ability of man—a sense of anxiety: is there not a danger that here and there progress, moving as rapidly as it has during recent years, will destroy things of value which careful consideration and determination might well have saved? I am afraid that many people scoff at such an idea. I raised this point when talking to highly educated and respected South American friends and professional colleagues. Few of them fully grasped my meaning. Most saw the destruction of nature as a necessary factor which has to be reckoned with, and did not agree that these riches must not be squandered, for both cultural and economic reasons. 'What do you want?' they would reply amiably. 'We've still got more than enough wilderness left—vast expanses of it. We want to put them to use for the good of mankind, burn down forests, dig for oil, and tap all the country's national resources as quickly and as thoroughly as possible. What do your landscapes and animals matter in comparison?'

Not all of them are so short-sighted, though. More and more are gradually adding their voices to those who refute the allegation of woolly-headed romanticism and sentimentality levelled against those of us who strive to preserve nature. We are not opposed to economic development, but attempt to bring nature and its beauties into harmony with modern progress, which no reasonable person would wish to sabotage.

In some of the South American states it is recognized as a fact that in time areas as large as possible will have to be transformed into nature conservation parks or national parks in order to protect them from inroads which change the face of the landscape, with its plant and animal life, all too drastically. It is clear that no areas should be chosen for this purpose which will be needed during the foreseeable future for the country's economic development, but it is equally clear that these parks must offer scenic attractions, for they should not only exist but should give as many people as possible, people whose normal surroundings are the deadening wastes of a modern city, a healing glimpse of a far healthier, far more natural form of life. For many years I have known the famous lake Nahuel Huapi in the south of Argentina, whose surrounding district as far as the Chilean frontier is indescribably beautiful. There lies the most famous national park in Argentina. When I was there for the first time no rail connection yet existed with the outside world. Today Bariloche, the lake and its surroundings, are on every tongue. Beside the lake there stands a fashionable hotel, and there are ski-ing huts on the nearby mountains. Even if someone like myself, who does not wholeheartedly agree with such a setting for finding one's way back to nature, flees there from the metropolis of Buenos Aires for a few weeks, he will get some idea of how good it is that nature should not be entirely forgotten—reviled and rejected Mother Nature in whose realm we can be so gay and so healthy. Admittedly the animal world makes no very strong impression there, not only because flirtations and sports push it into the background, but also because, owing to factors in natural history known to experts in the subject, the wild life of the area is not rich in large, imposing animals. Further to the north European deer and also wild swine have been introduced. They have multiplied satisfactorily, and a vigorous foreign tourist industry has attracted hunters from all over the world. I have nothing against this, although as a zoologist I ought to reject such tricks with the fauna of an area. However, the idea of introducing still more kinds of animal—bears, Alpine goats and wild cattle—raises certain problems, even if these animals were really to find (at the start) suitable living conditions. I am reminded of the suggestion that polar bears, which are endangered in their Arctic habitat by hunters, should be saved by transporting numbers of them to the Antarctic. What would the trusting penguins think of that? No one knows what the result of such interference with the balance of nature would be.

I much prefer another idea, and present it for consideration: How would it be if a few of the African animal species which are seriously threatened in their homeland were to be offered sanctuary in suitable areas of the northern, warm part of Argentinian Patagonia? Sufficient land is available, the only drawback being the fact that it is very dry, so much so that sheep cannot graze there. I am not thinking about elephant or rhinoceros, which would undoubtedly suffer from hunger and thirst there, nor of giraffe, buffalo or lion. Would it not be delightful, though, if a few herds of the splendid Grévy zebra or—in so far as the ground is suitable—the mountain zebra, which are becoming ever rarer in Africa, could gallop freely over the land? They would not be there to be hunted, and I personally would be content if they remained half tame, but I consider it quite possible that these animals, which have an astonishing ability to obtain sufficient nourishment from barren land, would flourish and multiply in Patagonia, and that one day some of their descendants might be taken back to an Africa no longer riven by political crises and there set at liberty.

As in Argentina, which now has to its credit national parks and preservation reserves totalling more than 11,500 square miles, the movement towards creating large protected areas in which nature and its world of big game should find refuge has begun to gain ground in other South American countries, in Venezuela for example. However, even leaving out of account the fact that most plans of that nature concern areas in which big game is thinly spread out and the danger from civilization is not yet acute, it must be realized that all nature protection remains mere empty theory unless it is strictly enforced. This is a problem of the greatest importance in other areas beside South America. Certainly excellent laws exist in several South American states for nature protection, hunting and—in cases where they exist—game conservation areas and parks. However, the seat of government is far away, and where there is no plaintiff there is no judge.

The majority of the population, largely of mixed Iberian-Indian stock, are no more ready to accept the idea of nature conservation than that of the protection of animals or chivalry in hunting. They are still at the stage of taking and using ruthlessly for their own purposes any wild creature. Unfortunately the Christian Church, with its teaching that only human beings have souls, tends to encourage the idea of these people that the animal world is theirs to do as they like with it. Even the surviving members of the original Indian races living in the wilds often suffer on account of this concept of the absolute superiority of modern man. Without thorough education and, if necessary, severe punishments no progress can be made. The first condition is, naturally, that the authorities themselves should have a genuine desire for such progress, springing from the fact that they recognize it as a self-evident necessity in civilized life.

In places where Indians still live their free, nomadic life as hunters, it would be senseless and unjust to attempt to stop them obtaining their livelihood from nature as in the past by such measures as imposing strictly limited 'hunting seasons' like the European game seasons. They would not understand the laws, and would evade them without difficulty. However, those tough, unsentimental huntsmen are not wanton destroyers. Only the ancient form of hunting by means of fire, the effects of which I have often seen on the plains, and whose danger to the land and its vegetation means nothing to the primitive tribesmen, should be stamped out wherever the law can be enforced.

While I write all this, a little sad, a little angry and pessimistic despite (or because of) what I owe to countries and people to whom I am indebted for the happiest years of my life, it becomes clear to me that I, as a European, really have no right to claim the prerogative of instructing others. For our own house is not wholly in order by any means, and the countries of the New World have two advantages which we in Europe lack: space and youth. May they make good use of both before it is too late!

IF I WERE TO BE ASKED . . .

The rivers are still rich in fish, many times richer than those of tired old Europe, which are being polluted to an ever-increasing extent by the waste from factories and by drains. The bird-life of South America, too, is still more diverse than that of any other part of the world. There is no lack of reptiles, amphibia and insects of every conceivable size. As for mammals, numbers of the larger forms have certainly declined, but although the land is now largely inhabited by the descendants of cattle, horses and sheep brought from Europe, it should not be forgotten that the classes of mammal still living freely in South America are, from the points of view of natural history and ecology, among the most interesting in the world.

The ungulates, for example, ranging from that weighty cousin of the horse the tapir to the tiny pudu, or the carnivora ranging from the powerful jaguar to the little hurón, have relations outside South America; the opossums, the marsupial rats have overseas connections too, as the (present-day) home of most pouched animals is Australasia. However, there also exist in South America a number of highly unusual mammals which, on the basis of scientifically proved relationships, are classed together under the general name 'Xenarthra'. These creatures make the biologist's heart beat quicker, and also that of the natural historian concerned with the fauna of ancient Egypt: these are the ant-eaters, the sloths and the armadillos, modest survivors of animal families represented in South America during former periods of the world's history by many other species, some of them of enormous size. They are far more ancient, more genuinely South American than the ungulates and carnivora, whose ancestors probably came here from the north at a relatively late period in zoological history.

If I were to be asked (which is very unlikely) where and in accordance with what considerations I think reserves ought to be created, I would begin by commending all that has already been done or planned, even in cases where in the final analysis it is no more than a rest and recreation area for human beings; such an area generally possesses imposing or beautiful landscapes with water, highlands and woods, whether or not it contains any especially impressive animals.

However, over and above such projects I would say to my South American friends: 'First and foremost protect the *animal life* of your countries by the creation of large, well-guarded reserves in which hunting is either forbidden altogether or, under strict supervision, is directed solely towards preserving a healthy balance in nature. Collaborate with neighbouring countries where areas adjacent to national frontiers are concerned, and consider whether, in the case of large-scale and therefore costly plans, it would not be worth while asking for the sponsorship of the International Union for Conservation of Nature and Natural Resources.'

I would recommend that such protection areas should be established in sparsely populated districts, but where the landscapes and therefore the varieties of animals to be found there are rich and varied. It would also be a good thing to choose areas which are not too difficult of access, or which can be made accessible, because everyone who has a mind to should be given the opportunity to visit these oases of the animal world. How to achieve that without unduly disturbing the animals? North Americans, Britons and Canadians experienced in solving this problem will gladly give you advice.

Anyone who makes the most enjoyable river trip up the Rio Paraná and the Rio Paraguay reaches, after a visit to the old colonial town of Asunción, a friendly and splendidly appointed land in the far north-eastern part of Paraguay which I remember almost as a vast national park. To the north, approaching Brazil, it is bounded by the Rio Apa and the Apa Mountains. Woods, watercourses, swamps and savannas contain a fascinating animal world ranging from the tapir to the solemn black roaring-ape and the swift-moving capucin, birds ranging from the great araras and the craw-stork to the tiniest colibri, reptiles ranging from the cayman alligator to the world's largest deadly snake the anaconda, down to a profusion of brightly-coloured lizards and lovely butterflies, while there are abundant fish in the rivers. The jaguar and puma prowl through the reeds and undergrowth—yet none of these creatures will harm man provided that he behaves with consideration.

Somewhat further to the north, on the right bank of the Paraguay River, there is unfolded on Bolivian territory another sub-tropical area: the Chiquitos highlands. I have ridden for months in this district. Formerly regarded as one of the remotest corners of the earth, it is now easily and quickly reached by air. Almost all the typical fauna of the sub-continent can be found there, even sloths. Possibly richer still, more tropical in character is the animal life abounding to the north-west of the delightful Bolivian town of Santa Cruz de la Sierra (in the direction of the Rio Beni). What profusion, what abundant riches both of vegetation and animals!

From Sao Paulo in Brazil a railway runs to the upper reaches of the Paraná; even there, far from its mouth, it is a noble stream. In the corner between this river and the Brazilian–Paraguayan frontier, that is to say in the southern part of the Brazilian state of Mato Grosso, there lies a wondrous land devoid of human habitation. That, too, is an oasis of the animals of South America of which I am especially fond. Nowhere else have I seen so many tapirs and anacondas as by the little Ivinheima River, nowhere else so many giant otters and—especially precious as they are rapidly disappearing everywhere that men come and slaughter them without rhyme or reason—nowhere else so many of the splendid, unjustly persecuted maned wolves or of the placid, trusting great anteaters. To kill these creatures is nothing but crass stupidity. A little way downstream are the famous 'Sete Quedas', the impressive waterfalls and rapids of the Paraná. Continuing downstream the traveller comes to the triangle of land where Brazil, Argentina and Paraguay meet, and to one of the natural wonders of the world, the Iguaçú Falls where the Argentinians, demonstrating wise foresight, have already created a protection area of 212 square miles.

Naturally you will have to spend a certain amount of money, but such plans as I have in mind will only cost a fraction of what any hectic city would demand from you during the same period—and you will be the richer by a true experience.

I have here written only of countries in which I have spent months and years. It would certainly be easy, too, to find vast areas in the more northerly part of the sub-continent about which one might sing a similar song. A good deal has already been done there in the service of nature conservation—I have in mind the Rancho Grande in Venezuela.

We in Europe know how difficult it is to create oases for nature and its free-living animals in areas already used as the scene of human activities. We can look with more than a little envy across the Atlantic to vast areas where careful planning can yet preserve values whose wanton destruction would be a blot on the reputation of any modern state. Civilization without a counterweight to balance it is dangerous—a fact of which educated people ought to be aware.

Madagascar, the Living Museum

BY

LUDWIG KOCH-ISENBURG

THERE is scarcely another part of the world which can compare with Madagascar, the fourth largest of all islands, in importance as a field for biological study. This island, although geologically connected with the African mainland, possesses its own world of animals, vegetation and human beings which has very little in common with that of Africa. It is generally unwise to talk in terms of long-lost continents and prehistoric land bridges, but in the case of Madagascar there can scarcely be any other explanation for the natural phenomena to be found there. What we have in Madagascar, preserved by chance right down the ages to the present day, can be described simply and correctly as a fragment of the world as it existed in the tertiary period, a land in which almost everything is lacking which biologists describe as a 'modern' animal species, but in which many things survive which have long since disappeared everywhere else in the world, swept away by the progressive development of countless centuries.

This country, whose area is as great as that of France, Holland and Belgium combined, shows far more signs of its independence than any other island lying in fairly close proximity to a continental land mass, and bearing witness clearly to its structural relationship with that continent. The extraordinarily rich abundance of hoofed animals (ungulates) native to Africa is wholly absent in Madagascar. The only recently extinct Madagascan hippopotamus and the river pig (*Potamocherus*) which still exists are so clearly African in their origins that there can be no question whatever how they came to be in Magadascar: members of both these species of aquatic animal undoubtedly swam the Mozambique Channel at some not-too-long distant period of history.

Madagascar has no proboscidian animals, no true cats, apes, members of the dog family (jackals, wolves, foxes), no mice, and none of the poisonous snakes so typical of Asia and Africa.

The classes of birds still known in Madagascar and island groups to the north and east (including Mauritius, the other Mascarene Islands and the Seychelles) number more than 300, divided into 59 families. More than a third of these are endemic, that is to say that they are found only here. The fabulous giant ostrich known as the Aepyornis lived in Madagascar, probably until the beginning of the seventeenth century. Dodos, huge flightless birds of the pigeon family larger than turkeys, were common on the Mascarene islands in 1497, as Vasco da Gama reported. The last of these creatures died during the seventeenth century.

On account of its seemingly prehistoric world of animals, combined as they are with a certain number of more recently evolved species, Madagascar still poses problems for the biologist. The presence of lemurs may well be explained by the theory that until the tertiary period a land bridge existed between Madagascar and the nearest point on the coast of Africa some 250 miles away. These creatures are of African-Asiatic origin, and their more 'modern' cousins the apes were probably prevented from reaching Madagascar by inroads of the sea which destroyed the land link with Africa. As various creatures found in Madagascar, notably several of the porcupine family, are known to Asia but not to the African mainland, the implication is that there was also a land bridge joining Madagascar to southern Asia. Why, then, did the huge monitors and pythons of the Old World not find their way to Madagascar? They are undoubtedly species of great antiquity, probably existing before mammals appeared on the scene. The fact that venomous snakes such as adders and vipers are not to be found in Madagascar is comparable to the absence of monkeys and cats—they are 'younger' animal forms. No explanation has yet been given to account for the presence in Madagascar of iguana lizards and boas, as these are creatures which are otherwise restricted to the New World. Their appearance in Madagascar is paralleled by that of the ravenala or traveller's tree, the proud banana tree which is a national emblem of the country; it has no close relations in the whole of the Old World, but two in South America. Why it was that the iguanas and boas of the New World 'came over', whereas the American adders did not, may be explained by the fact that the latter are of more recent origins.

The most characteristic animals of Madagascar are the lemurs, or 'Madagascar cats'. They are so typical a part of this ancient island that the Madagascan world has been described as 'Lemuria'. It is true that the lemuroid family are also represented in southern Asia (by the loris, nycticebus and tarsius) and in Africa (by the galagos or bushbaby)—in fact during the warm tertiary period they even lived in Europe (*Plesiadapis*, *Adapis*). However, lemurs living today outside Madagascar are all small animals hardly the size of a cat, and it is only as nocturnal creatures that they are able to survive in competition with members of the more 'modern' ape family. In Madagascar, on the other hand, they have remained from the earliest times the only native primates, and various different species have flourished. There were even at one time giant varieties as large as chimpanzees, but these became extinct during the quaternary period. Today there still live on the island some 22 species of lemur with about 30 local variants belonging to 10 clearly differentiated classes. They range in size from the mouse lemur (*Microcebus*), which is the size of a rat, to the indris, which grows to a height of about 3 ft. It should be mentioned, however, that numbers of all classes of lemur have greatly diminished in recent years, the decrease being most marked in the case of the larger members of the family.

Literally, before the eyes of the nineteenth and twentieth centuries, the landscapes of this great island—the hot, damp forests of the east coast, the lighter woods of the west, the wilderness of thorn bushes in the south and above all the high-lying woods of the interior—have changed their appearance and character in an alarming manner. The dreadful wasting away of woodlands, which was kept largely in check during the period of enlightened French administration, but which has gone on apace since the country became independent, is a result of the natives' excessive veneration of cattle. At the dawn of history Madagascar was a land of forests. Today hardly a fifteenth part of the former rich forest areas remains wooded. The fauna of the island is to an overwhelming degree that of woodlands, and its fate is sealed with the disappearance of its natural habitat.

The forebears of the 18 or so tribes making up the native population of the island probably arrived there about the year A.D. 1000 from the Polynesian and Melanesian islands. As there is no early documentary evidence to go by, we can learn of their colonization of the island only from word of mouth traditions surviving in the reigning family of the foremost tribe, the Merina. However, there must have been a far earlier influx of human settlers, as some tribes retain characteristics seemingly going back to the Stone Age.

The near-veneration of hump-backed cattle, which borders on religious awe, and which exists, strangely enough, in all the tribes native to the island, was responsible for the destruction of the great forests of the central plateau, since cattle need grazing land. Fires raged in the forests all through the dry season. The five million 'modern' Malagasy inhabitants of the country own some 35 million head of zebu cattle. The herds have no stalls; they literally eat the land bare, and destroy all afforestation projects. Thus the greater part of the island has been turned into a waste land, the mountains in the interior having been denuded of vegetation, and the south transformed into a desert. Even the civilized inhabitants of the capital city are far from appreciating the relationship between woodlands, water, and the fertility of the soil.

At one time finely flowing rivers carried water to the south and west from the thickly wooded central plateau all the year round. Today, at the time of the violent tropical rains they rush unhindered down the valleys, carrying immense quantities of fertile soil into the sea. The huge ostriches of the south were the first creatures to fall victim to the ruination of the forests. Their pastures dried up, the terrain which had supported them becoming a barren desert.

The 'rainy' area along the east coast was more fortunately placed in this respect. The damp monsoons arriving from the Indian Ocean reached the high mountain ranges, and their waters were poured down on to the girdle of forests which covered the eastern coastal strip extending down the whole length of the island from north to south. This chain of woods, which had its equal nowhere else on earth, and which was known as the 'Madagascan Sylva', was destroyed by the natives, aided and abetted by white settlers. The Europeans felled such trees as would yield valuable wood, and the gaps thus torn in the forests allowed fires to complete the work of destruction. From the seaport of Tamatave down to Fort Dauphin in the south only isolated fragments of the old Sylva still survive. However, a splendid pattern of connected primeval forests still exists to the north of the Bay of Antogil. This area receives a considerable volume of rain—some 21 ft. per annum. Considerable parts of it are so swampy that they are inaccessible to man, and it is solely to this fact that it owes its survival.

The vast expanse of thorn woods in the south, the 'Androy Woods', suffered incurable wounds when large areas were cleared to make way for sisal plantations. The various classes of trees with their thorns and large spikes present a strange spectacle which is to be seen nowhere else on earth. In these woods live the last few surviving specimens of the most beautiful of all species of tortoise, and also harmless dumeril boas, which take on all the colours of the rainbow. Little spiny tenrecs no larger than goose eggs, a particular form of the mouse lemur (*Microcebus*), the cat-sized and catlike ring-tailed lemur (*catta*) with its pointed face which looks as though it has been painted and its long tail with black and white rings, together with smaller forms of creeping animals, and the fossa (*Cryptoprocta ferox*), as large as a badger and the most powerful beast of prey on the island, all live in the dry areas. However, the loveliest creatures the thorn woods have to offer are the fleeced makis (*Propithecus avahis*). These lemur, which measure almost 2 ft. in a sitting position, exist in many local varieties, some of them also being found in damp wooded districts. Those native to the thorn woods have pure white, fleece-like coats on their backs, with strongly contrasting black bellies and heads. I have seen groups of as many as 8 or 10 animals of the *Propithecus verreauxi* and *Propithecus diadema* classes making great leaps of up to 30 ft. on to the slender, terribly prickly trunks of thorn trees without injuring their hands. I found that the inner surface of the hands and feet of captured specimens were as though made of hard black indiarubber, a sign of their life in a world of thorns. An unusual feature of the fleeced maki is the fact that its colouring is the opposite to what would be expected: white back and coal-black belly. Almost all mammals have darker backs than bellies. The opposite colouring occurs only in so-called 'asylum' animals, creatures without natural enemies in their normal habitat. Beasts of prey adept at climbing, like large birds of prey, are entirely absent from the fauna of Madagascar.

A cousin of the makis, the indris, now exists in only one form. This member of the lemur family nearly 3 ft. high possesses an almost unnoticeable rudimentary tail, and is still to be found in a few damp wooded areas. The 'Avahis' fleeced maki seems to be even more of a rarity.

On the other hand my observations indicate that the aye-aye (so named in imitation of its cry) or Daubentonia, a fingered animal, may be more numerous than at first appears to be the case. It is not limited to any particular type of woodland, living at scattered points in bamboo thickets, in the damp forests of the east, and in the dry woods of the west. Anyone who keeps his eyes skinned can see here and there in remote corners of the woods this creature's large, covered nests of twigs in the treetops, which are overgrown with liana creepers. The animals themselves are never to be seen during the daytime. Only at dusk will they leave their nests in search of food; they live on insects, fruit, and probably young shoots. It has been noticed that a captive specimen will knock on dead branches to find the whereabout of maggots (*Coleopteren*) which have bored their way into the wood, and which it then extracts from their holes with its withered-looking finger. The appearance of the aye-aye, with its large night-sighted eyes, its almost bare, flat ears and its thick, furry tail, has something fantastic about it. The slender body the size of a cat is covered by long, shaggy hair of various dark shades. The fact that the teeth project somewhat out of its mouth caused the first observers to class this unusual animal among rodents. It is now known for a fact, though, that it belongs among the primates, a true lemur even though it does not greatly resemble other members of the family at first sight. Fortunately the natives regard the aye-aye with a kind of superstitious awe, and leave it in peace.

Members of the lemuroid family are not rapid breeders, a mother giving birth to only one offspring each year; it is born with hair and sight like a monkey. Authorities on the subject have stated that in the case of true lemurs at least, the life-span of the adult animal is remarkably short, and that a female seldom produces more than four or five children in her whole life. If that is correct it is a good example of the way in which the characteristics of a species of animal can be dependent on the fact that its forbears have long lived in an asylum free from natural enemies. Such classes of animal can survive despite a low rate of reproduction and a very limited life-span, without the continued existence of the species being endangered. Nature is never unnecessarily extravagant.

The similarity between the Madagascan fauna and that of Ethiopia, to which it has long been considered to be related, is particularly striking as regards bird life. The East African guinea fowl (*Numida meleagris*) is also found in Madagascar, together with a sub-species (*Numida m. mitrata*), distinguished by its red crown. The game birds are represented by the Madagascan quail (*Coturnix communis*), the francolins by the Madagascan partridge (*Margaroperdix*), and flying poultry by the *Eremialector personatus*. The South African masked dove (*Oenas capensis*) is also to be found in the dry regions of the island. The violet turtle dove (*Streptopelia madagascarienis*) is, however, limited to the island. Nectar-eating birds of the southern areas of the Old World are represented in

Madagascar by the *Cynniris souimanga*. There also exist on the island kingfishers, bee-eaters, night-swallows, etc. A very rare bird is the black vasa parrot (*Corocopsis*) of Madagascar, which is related to the grey parrots of West Africa. Apart from its three principal forms the only parrot found in the island is the beautiful green *Agapornis cana*, the size of a sparrow, so that Madagascar is not at all rich in parrots by comparison with other tropical lands.

Many of the country's animals live only in particular areas of limited size, these areas being divided by territories in which these particular species are not to be found. In many cases those existing in certain areas possess distinguishing features which give them the status of local varieties.

The fauna of this island has given biologists a deep insight into the history of animal evolution. Madagascar is a vast open-air museum in which treasures of animal and plant life have survived down to the present day. Friends of wild life the world over should strive, in close collaboration with the Madagascan authorities, to save what can still be saved, for irreplaceable treasures are in grave danger of being utterly destroyed before our eyes.

The National Parks of the Philippines

BY

DR. WALTER LORCH
Manila

THE temperature at Manila Airport is approaching 80 in the shade as we leave for our aerial tour of the national parks of the Philippines. The cogon grass which grows everywhere to the height of a man harbours cobras, which are responsible for most of the deaths from snake bites which take place on the seven thousand islands making up the Republic of the Philippines.

Flying low in a south-easterly direction we catch sight, on the bank of the largest expanse of inland water in the country, the Laguna de Bay (which has an area of 344 square miles) of the three peaks forming the Banahao–San Cristobal group of volcanoes. Between the National Park of 43 square miles surrounding these peaks and the extinct volcano Makiling further to the west, whose administration was transferred in 1960 from the National Parks and Wildlife Office to the State University, there lie a number of circular crater lakes of various colours, amid coconut palm woods. In the less accessible woods of the Makiling and Banahao areas troops of monkeys (*Macaca philippinensis*) swarm about the upper reaches of the trees, which are overgrown with liana and rattan, while dark brown deer (*Cervus marianus*) go to drink from the mountain streams which are fed by volcanic and frequently radio-active springs.

Between the Laguna and the Pacific coast numerous waterways cut through layers of volcanic rock often hundreds of feet high, careering in rapids past masses of stone lying where volcanic eruptions have flung them, on their way to the Laguna. One of the most beautiful of these recent incisions into the earth's surface was set apart in 1939 as the Pagsanjan Ravine National Park. Like national parks already mentioned, this one is easily reached from the city of Manila with its two million inhabitants. There are excellent roads, and single-day excursions to the Park can be made by car or by one of the cheap native buses. The driver of the swaying 'banca' will proudly point out to his passengers the wild monkeys in the woods of the ravine, and the waterfall which plunges down from a cleft in the rocks. In the tubelike holes created by former outbreaks of volcanic gas there live thousands of the endemic species of bat *Chaerephon luzonis*.

Two great wooded areas of southern Luzon not only serve as national parks, on account of their wonderfully beautiful high-lying woods—they are also sanctuaries of wild animal life. These are the Quezon National Park and the Bicol National Park, both of which were founded in 1934. The new overland road to Bicolandia leads through them. While driving along this road one can sometimes see the blue-green blossoms of a rare form of orchid gleaming in the shadows of the forest, or one meets a collector who offers an orchid in full bloom which he has just found, for a small sum of money. Among the 940 or so different kinds of orchid found in the Philippines an incredibly large number, some 84 per cent, are endemic, that is to say found nowhere else on earth. Sometimes a deep gorge or a lonely mountain peak encircled by primeval forests is the only place where a particular class of orchid is to be found.

Before we land for a short stay in Pili, to the south of the university town of Naga, we see to the right the broad ribbon of the Bicol River on whose banks there are the stalactite caves and cataracts of the small Libmanan National Park; unfortunately the park is accessible only by means of boats and riverside paths. To the left the extinct volcano Isarog thrusts its head into the piled-up cloud banks which almost always hang over the islands. The national park which surrounds it is a little over 35 square miles in area; it contains wonderful gorges and waterfalls, also serving as a wild game reserve.

Incomparably more beautiful than any of the volcanoes already mentioned is the remarkably regular, slender tower of the still active Mayon, which rises to a height of 7,990 ft. above the gay little town of Legaspi on the Gulf of Albay. We now land at its airfield, pausing briefly to take a few colour films of the lower slopes of this volcano, which form a national park some 21 square miles in area, covered with fruit groves. As Legaspi possesses several good hotels we spend the night there, and on the following morning we hire a car to drive to the high-lying lodging house below the summit of the Mayon volcano, from which white smoke still emerges, sometimes accompanied by subterranean rumbling, and the blackened ruins of the church of Cagsawa. It has recently been proposed that these ruins, with their surroundings, should be decreed to constitute a national park. They are an impressive proof of the destructive power of one of this volcano's most violent eruptions; it took place in 1814, more than 1,200 human lives and several villages falling victim to its fury. The Tiwi Hot Springs National Park, only 116 acres in extent, is distinguished by its sulphur and mud springs; it can be reached easily from Legaspi. Unfortunately the far more important terraces of sinter and the unfathomably deep geysers of Naglabong no longer belong to this nearby national park.

We proceed further southwards by another PAL plane, passing over the Sorsogon Peninsula on which is situated the Bulusan Volcano National Park, with an area of 14 square miles. The fronds of tall tree ferns meet high above the woodland road leading to the crater lake, like the vaulting of some great cathedral. Anyone interested in investigating, collecting or photographing rare plants, insects and other forms of wild life found only in the Philippines should on no account fail to include in his itinerary this national park, which is visited every year by some 50,000 trippers, but by comparatively few serious naturalists.

We have now left the largest of the Philippine islands, Luzon, behind us. While the plane circles prior to making a halt at Tacloban, the capital of Leyte, we see the little coastal town of Basey on the opposite shore of the San Pedro Bay. Near the town is the mouth of the Sohoton River, up which one must travel by boat in order to visit the unusual natural stone bridge and the caves, human habitations during prehistoric times, of the Sohoton Natural Bridge National Park. On the way upstream the traveller hears the chorus of voices of the rare *Buceros hydrocorax* birds, which live in small groups in the *Dipterocarp* woods. It is permissible to shoot them for only one month in every other year, but despite this almost complete protection their numbers are diminishing on account of the ever-increasing clearance of forest land in the island world.

We go westwards from Tacloban. On Leyte itself there are three small national parks to which access is difficult; they are laid out round hot medicinal springs. The Camotes Islands are separated from the deep blue of the Pacific by a bright green coral shelf; the slate-grey Lanao Lake on the main island teems with crocodile, and the area has been proposed as a national park. Soon afterwards we reach the oldest town of the Philippines: Cebu City. A good walker, who is able to negotiate considerable differences of altitude at tropical temperatures, can visit the national parks Sudlon and Central-Cebu from here. Before flying back by the direct route from Cebu to Manila we pay a visit, by luxurious Viscount airliner, to Davao, in the extreme south of the island group, which has grown with American-style rapidity, and is now the second largest city of the republic.

The summit of Mount Apo is visible from Davao only in the early morning—after that it always becomes shrouded in clouds. With its height of 9,700 ft. this extinct volcano is the highest mountain in the Philippines, and its National Park of 297 square miles is the largest of the country's 39 national parks; with their total of 952 square miles they occupy more than ·8 per cent of the entire land area of the republic, which amounts to about 115,000 square miles. Unfortunately nearly ten thousand acres of the national park land have recently been freed for agricultural use, as a means of gaining the votes of the refugees from fire-devastated areas. This is all the more regrettable in view of the fact that the Apo National Park contains a number of animal species which have so far been found only here, such as the moon rat (*Podogymnura truei*), a small creature living principally on termites and other insects. On account of its unpleasant smell reminiscent of garlic it is shunned by most beasts of prey. Wild water buffalo or cimarón (*Bubalus moellendorffi*) cool themselves in the swamps of the national park, but those creatures are being driven ever deeper into the primeval forests on the mountain slopes by fires lit to clear woodland for agriculture. The dog-faced flying lemurs (*Cynocephalus volans*) which appear at night, the slow loris (*Nycticebus coucang*), flying squirrels (*Petinomys sp.*) and horse-shoe bats (*Rhinolophus inops*) live on fruit, leaves or insects, and seldom descend to the ground. The palm civet cat (*Paradoxurus minax*) and the Malayan civet cat (*Viverra tangalunga*) with their well-developed musk scent glands (producing a substance used for making perfume) are to be found not only in the Apo National Park but also, fortunately, in many other wooded areas of the Philippines. The ape-eating eagle (*Pithecophaga jefferyi*), with the wild crest of feathers on its head, lives by swooping down to seize one from among the troops of monkeys (*Macaca mulatta*) which live in the primeval forests. These monkeys are also caught, especially in Mindanao, by organized groups of hunters, to be sold to exporters who send whole planeloads of them to the U.S.A. for use in scientific experiments. During the financial year 1959–60 83,655 monkeys and 9,034 birds were exported, to a total value of some £100,000. As in certain other national parks, herds of a small deer of the sambar group (known as the 'usa') are to be found here; this creature is easily tamed, and thrives in captivity. On the other hand the wild boar which abound almost everywhere in the national parks of the Philippines are sometimes dangerous. These beasts can weigh over 110 lb., while a deer weighs only 75 to 90 lb.

It is a regrettable fact that the rare animals of the Philippines, which are to be found nowhere else in the world, live for the most part in none of the national parks so far established, merely being inadequately protected by law on sparsely populated islands. Such a creature is the mouse deer or chevrotain (*Tragulus sp.*), a form of deer found on Palawan, which, despite its name, does not belong among the cervidae but to the tragulidae. Others are the Napoleon peacock pheasant or 'bartic' and the 'tabon', numbered among the *megapodiidae*, which covers its eggs with a mound of rotting leaves. The only place in the world where the last few hundred head of the extremely wild, small buffalo 'Timarau' (*Bubalus armee mindorensis*) are still to be found is on the island of Mindoro, before the gates of Manila; they live in dense bamboo jungles and in the swamps bordering on rivers; it is forbidden by law to hunt, kill, wound or capture them.

Turning back from Davao to Cebu, the traveller begins his flight to Manila. Before making a halt at Bacolod the plane flies round the volcano Canlaon, the centrepoint of a national park of 95 square miles, overgrown with damp, luxuriant woods which contain, among other fauna, the civet cat (*Viverra tangalunga*), which is the size of a domestic cat, and the strongly spotted wild cat (*Felix minuta*), as well as the Philippine speckled deer (*Cervus alfredi*), wild boar and the like. Shortly before reaching the centre of Luzon one sees on the left the east coast of Mindoro, whose flat inland sea forms the Lake Naujan National Park (almost 84 square miles in area), which is very rich in water fowl. This national park was established as recently as 1956, and, together with the proclamation of six other national parks during the post-war period (since the Philippines achieved full independence), proves that the development of the national park idea is still a living force there. It is intended that an area of 35 square miles around the Iglit mountain on Mindoro should form a sanctuary for animals and birds rather than a national park proper. The largest animal and bird sanctuary of this kind is the Liguasan Marsh in southern Mindanao, which was given its present status by order of the Forest Administration on the 1st January, 1941. A low-lying district 170 square miles in area, it is particularly rich in wild duck and other water fowl. In the whole of the Philippines there are 47 families of bird, with 148 species and 620 sub-species, among which, astonishing as it may seem, no more than about a dozen of the native forms are ever kept in captivity. Other areas suggested as animal and bird sanctuaries, apart from Iglit, are Magapit in northern Luzon (30 square miles) and Minasawa Island (17 square miles), which belongs to the Polillo group on the Pacific coast.

In order to see the most important national parks of central and northern Luzon we would do best to travel from Manila by car, or to make use of the not always very comfortable but cheap and hair-raisingly swift-running buses, making for the north. The volcano ruin Arayat is visible from many miles away, rising above the absolutely flat lowlands of central Luzon where rice is cultivated over vast areas. The national park, 24 square miles in extent, which was established in 1933, is the most frequently visited among all the national parks of the Philippines apart from Makiling. However, this is primarily a 'recreation area', with its hotel, open-air bath, pergolas, artificial waterfalls, paths and picnic sites, and one seldom sees a student of nature climbing through the bushy woods at the foot of the mountain to the primeval forests of its upper reaches, listening as he does so to the manifold voices of the birds.

By following another overland route northwards from Manila we could view the Biak-na-Bato National Park, which is notable for its furrowed rocks, stalactite caves containing numerous springs, and unusual kinds of bats. While the land route to Biak-na-Bato is always usable at least in the dry season, the national road running across the mountain range from Bongabon to Baler is often rendered unusable by landslides, falls of rock and fallen trees, so that the Aurora Memorial Park, famed for its herds of wild swine and its large colony of wild duck, is frequently inaccessible. It is no less difficult to reach the small national park near Mangatarem in the province of Pangasinan; its centre-point is formed by the warm medicinal springs of Manleluag.

The boundaries of the three districts together making up the 'Mountain Province' meet at the 7,625-ft.-high Data mountain, the plateau-like centre of a national park of $21\frac{1}{2}$ square miles. Its unusual natural life demonstrates clearly the influence of flora and fauna received in earlier ages from continental Asia by way of Formosa. Some 70 per cent of the flowering plants to be found in the highlands of northern Luzon are endemic. Only here can one find the anemone, gentian, violet, lily, willow, maple, and other varieties of plant life from the mountains of Asia. In the national park dense pine woods (*Pinus insularis*) and, at higher altitudes, oak woods and mountain yews (*Taxus wallichiana*) surround a number of mountain lakes. Only a few examples of the Philippine shrew (*Rhynchomys soricoides*), which is not known to exist anywhere else, have so far been captured; their velvety coat is a dull grey. Large members of the rat family, the *Crateromys schadenbergi* and the *Phloeomys pallidus*, have been brought near to extinction by the hunting activities of Igorot natives. Wild boar and civet cats are still common, though. More than 40 different kinds of birds, including 3 falcons, 3 pigeons and a crimson speckled parrot (*Prioniturus flavicans montanus*), are known to exist in the national park territory around Mount Data. Two park wardens and a labourer are in charge of this national park, which was established as long ago as 1936, and in which visitors can stay in a small lodging house with a brick chimney piece.

Apart from its scenery the Tirad Pass National Park, with the 'Bessang Pass National Shrine' cut out of it, is of only historical interest. On the other hand the two national parks in the Cagayan Valley (where crocodile abound), the Callao Cave and Fuyot Spring are of great importance to students of natural science on account of their limestone caves and other rock faults.

During the return flight northward a visit can be made to one of the most unusual of national parks spread out over the calm coral sea. Its name Hundred Islands is no exaggeration; in fact the total number of islands is more like four hundred. It is true that the limestone islands, their shores deeply serrated by the surf, support only a very limited animal and plant world, but the warm, shallow water separating them teems with rare fish, seaweed and other water creatures. The beaches of many small islands in this area consist of millions of coral fragments, bleached by the sun, together with other small debris, while in the shallow water there lie hundreds of black sea-cucumbers, and further out to sea, six to nine feet down, living corals of many bizarre shapes and many colours can be seen and dived for. The fishes and other small creatures flitting about in the water are a delight to the many biologists who every year set up their headquarters at the state-run hotel in Lucap near the only oceanographic museum and institute of the republic, and from there visit many of the islands in the vicinity in outrigger motor-boats. In addition this national park, which is only some 150 miles from Manila, is visited by more than 30,000 trippers every year.

Instead of returning from the Hundred Islands to the Overland Road No. 3 we choose the picturesque road to Zambales and Bataan, which runs for most of its course along the coast of the South China Sea. In the centre of Bataan Province and Peninsula lies the Bataan National Park of 121 square miles, established soon after the war principally to commemorate the battles between American-Filipino and Japanese troops during the Second World War, but also containing many fine examples of volcanic rock formations. Far easier of access is the Roosevelt National Park, established in 1933 and named after the then American Governor-General, Theodore Roosevelt Jr. New afforestation was begun by the Central Forestry Department, and is now being carried on by the National Park Administration itself; like so many other national parks in the Philippines this one also serves as a wild game reserve.

Despite protection laws put into force by the Americans before the war, and the growing influence of the National Parks and Wildlife Office in Manila, the numbers of native and in most cases endemic wild creatures are diminishing at an alarming rate. The enormous increase of the population, which amounts to some 3 per cent annually, the national over-population and the decrease of the average income per head increases the drain on the country's natural resources year by year, one consequence being a grave threat to its native animals, many species of which are now near to extinction. It is therefore all the more desirable that strengthening of the national park administration, together with the planned establishment of further protected areas, should save for as long as possible, at least in these last oases of the animal world, species which are extremely rare, and in many cases found nowhere else on earth.

Nature Protection in Australia

BY

DR. K. IMMELMANN

A COLD, dark June morning on the south coast of Australia. Dense mist hangs between the tall, slender-trunked eucalyptus trees. We make our way onward with difficulty through the thick, wet undergrowth, sinking up to our ankles in mud. There is a dank smell of decay everywhere around us. A peculiar kind of twilight filters through these woods, in which the 3-ft.-high tree ferns with their huge fronds make us feel as though we had been transported back to the dawn of history. Only the monotonous patter of raindrops breaks the solemn silence. There, suddenly we hear, close at hand, a song of utter enchantment. A bird is singing, at first softly then gradually louder and louder, until the song is being given out in a piercing fortissimo. Meanwhile the rain has begun to come down harder, but we ignore it, and stay here for two whole hours in the streaming rain, unable to tear ourselves away from the magic spell created by the masterly singer as it imitates the sounds of the primeval forest, the laughing of the kookaburra and the chattering of parakeets, the song of the European blackbirds which have been introduced into this land, and the mournful cry of the large cockatoo, combining all these impersonations with its own melodies to form a unique symphony. Slowly and cautiously we push on, and can soon make out a grey bird about the size of a pheasant dancing capriciously to and fro on a mound of earth which has been swept clean of all loose particles, with its long, lyre-shaped tail curved forward over its back. It is a lyre-bird, one of the most remarkable of all songbirds, and at the same time one of the world's most accomplished vocalists. It loves the twilight of the thick eucalyptus woods, and never ventures out into open country. However, dense forests are becoming rare in Australia, where the taking over of land on the east coast for agriculture is assuming ever-increasing proportions, so that the living and breeding areas of the lyre-bird have of late been greatly reduced. However, close to the great city of Melbourne there lies an extensive wild-life reserve, the Sherbrooke Forest, in which these birds enjoy complete protection, and where they have become so accustomed to the presence of human beings that they allow themselves to be watched and photographed at very close quarters. So this feathered songster, at least, seems assured of a secure future here.

Australia is still the most thinly populated continent. With an area about the same as that of Europe it has only ten million inhabitants, and vast expanses are almost devoid of human beings. Nevertheless even in Australia the creation of large wild-life protection areas and national parks is a matter of the greatest urgency, and in many places it is almost too late already, because the relatively few inhabitants of the world's fifth continent have brought about striking changes to its landscape, its animal and plant life, within a very short space of time. Ploughing up of hitherto virgin soil, overgrazing by sheep and cattle, and accidental or deliberately lit bush fires, which devastate millions of acres annually, have robbed large areas of their natural vegetation, and have made it impossible for countless animals to find anywhere to live. The introduction of European animals into Australia, among which the domestic cat, red fox and rabbit are the best-known examples, has meant that the native animals have had to suffer the attacks of foes superior in cunning, which seize much of the available food. Through these imported animals the European has done grave damage even in areas in which he himself has not settled.

Thus it is by no means astonishing that in the fifth continent, as in the other four, wild-life protection is a very present problem, and that many species of animal can be saved from extinction only by vigorous protection measures and the creation of carefully chosen nature reserves. Innumerable small marsupial animals were practically exterminated by beasts of prey brought into the land from overseas. Millions of koala bears fell victim to unscrupulous fur hunters, until only a few hundred were left in the whole of Australia. The marsupial ant-eater of Western Australia has practically died out owing to the fact that its habitat has been destroyed by sheep, while the Tasmanian pouched wolf may now be extinct. Foxes and cats decimate classes of birds which nest on the ground such as the bustard and quail, while senseless, uncontrolled shooting purely for the joy of killing threatens even the monitors, huge lizards which look like dragons of legendary times.

The importance of effective nature protection has long been recognized, but it runs up against difficulties which are peculiar to Australia, since the fifth continent contains no areas set apart and isolated such as swamps, inaccessible jungles or high mountains, natural wild-life sanctuaries which in other parts of the world facilitate conservation. Moreover many kinds of Australian animal undertake extensive but completely unpredictable journeys across country in search of food, and these make the choice of protected areas uncommonly difficult. Finally the ability to adapt themselves to a world around them which has been transformed by the coming of man is less marked in Australian mammals than in those of other continents, and many species could only be saved from extinction by being protected in large reserves where their natural surroundings are preserved. There are also human factors which make effective nature protection remarkably difficult. Nature conservation laws are made by the individual state governments, so one and the same kind of animal may be protected in part of the area in which it lives, while being hunted in another part. Thus although there are many small national parks and reserves, they often serve only to protect particular national monuments, there being a lack of unified planning and co-ordination.

Despite these difficulties with which wild-life conservation in Australia has to contend, it is beginning to register some noteworthy successes. One of the most gratifying results so far is the rehabilitation of the koala bear in the state of Victoria. The koala or marsupial bear is undoubtedly one of the most interesting and most popular of Australian animals. With its soft fur, its round arms and legs, its black snub-nose and big dark eyes it is the prototype of the lovable teddy bear. Unfortunately we in Europe seldom see live koalas, owing to the fact that they are very fastidious in their choice of diet, living almost exclusively on the oily leaves of certain kinds of eucalyptus trees, which we naturally cannot offer them. These little bears are especially popular among Australians; they are strictly protected in every state, and many live in parks and reserves. The fact remains, however, that mankind has a great deal to make up for to these charming creatures. In former years the koala was mercilessly hunted for its soft and valuable fur. In the year 1924 two million koala skins were exported from Australia, and in 1927 in the State of Queensland alone 10,000 licensed koala hunters were at work, between them slaying half a million of the harmless creatures. Even so the koalas did not learn to flee from man; they allowed themselves to be plucked from where they were clinging to the branches of trees, and were then slaughtered in cold blood by the hunters. The number of koalas surviving in the southernmost state, Victoria, when a law was at last put into effect to protect them 35 years ago, was estimated at 500. Certain wooded areas on the coast were set apart as guarded reserves, and koalas were also taken to two islands off the south coast. They multiplied at an astonishingly rapid rate in the reserves, and soon a number had to be captured to avoid over-stocking. Those that had been captured were taken to other places, forming the nucleus of new koala colonies there. Since the introduction of the protection measures more than 7,000 young koalas have been moved from the reserves to fifty other districts, where they have settled down and bred, so that the future of this darling of all Australians is now secure.

However, the koala represents only one example among many. A total of 62 large protected areas have been set apart on the Australian mainland and in Tasmania, although admittedly they amount to only 0·2 per cent of the vast area of the continent. The largest among them is the Mount Kosciusko National Park, founded in 1944, which has an area of some 2,300 square miles, about that of Kent and Surrey combined. It contains splendid Alpine and sub-Alpine eucalyptus woods around the country's highest mountains. Even larger and more impressive than those woods are the forests in the Mount Field National Park of Tasmania, whose eucalyptus trees, some of them more than three hundred feet high, are numbered together with the mammoth firs of California among the world's tallest trees. In these impenetrable forests, which are shrouded in dense mist during the winter months, traces are believed to have been found of the largest beast of prey among the marsupial species, the Tasmanian pouched wolf. For many years there has been no definite proof that this creature still exists, and numerous expeditions which went out to seek it found only tracks and other signs which could not be identified with certainty. The pouched wolf is certainly the most advanced carnivorous marsupial animal, and resembles a small, smooth-haired wolf, although its movements are considerably slower. Like the wolves of the northern hemisphere it hunts by night in small family packs or in pairs, resting in its lair during the day. Only in its chosen surroundings does the pouched wolf differ greatly from its cousin the wolf proper, as it lives only in the thickest and most impenetrable forests, never coming out into the open. However, the forests in south-western Tasmania are so vast, with large tracts still entirely untouched by man, that pouched wolves may well have remained in the depths of the forests until the present day. The far smaller but no less predacious Tasmanian devils live in the Mount Field National Park. There, too, the Australian lyre-bird was introduced, although it was not originally to be found in Tasmania. The attempt is to be made to keep a number of them there, in case the survival of the species on the mainland should become threatened by the increasing use of land for agricultural purposes.

Two further wild-life protection areas lie in the interior of New South Wales and Victoria. The Maquarie swamps are an extensive lagoon system which forms the breeding grounds for millions of water birds, the ibis, heron, spoonbill, black swan and duck, while in the Kulkyne National Park there was created an extensive reserve for the unusual mound birds which are unique among poultry in that they do not hatch out their eggs but cover them with a huge pile of leaves and earth, so that the sun and the warmth of fermentation of vegetable matter cause the eggs to hatch out. In the Australian possessions overseas, too, nature conservation has begun to take on real significance. Thus in the eastern part of New Guinea, which has been administered by Australia since the end of the First World War, the creation of reserves and protection areas is planned in the more heavily populated areas. Finally, the animal life of the Australian-controlled Maquarie Islands, which lie between New Zealand and the Antarctic, has been fully protected since 1932. These islands, which were regularly visited during the breeding season by 200,000 ursine seals, were discovered only in 1810. After ten years of slaughter not a single ursine seal was left alive. Not until long after laws for their protection had come into operation did any ursine seals reappear, and in 1954, after an interval of a hundred and thirty years, the first young seals were brought into the world there. Today many thousands of ursine seals once again live on those islands, and their number is growing every year. Thus there is good reason to hope that in sparsely populated Australia, as in other parts of the world, the idea of nature protection will gain ground to an ever-increasing extent, so that the unique animal life of the continent may be saved for posterity before it is too late.

The Swiss National Park

BY

DR. G. N. ZIMMERLI

Inspector-General of the Swiss National Park

'ONE feels so small in the National Park! It's like having the whole of time before one's eyes—all conceit melts away!'
That was how a student expressed his wholehearted admiration after his first tour on foot through the Swiss National Park. It certainly is a memorable experience, visiting this nature conservation territory, which has an area of some 62 square miles, passing with open eyes and receptive heart through a landscape in which time seems to stand still. Majestic and unsullied mountain forests, meadows and valleys lie in all their pristine freshness, untouched and unaltered by human hand. No sounds of hunting, the baying of hounds or the crash of gunfire, neither berry-pickers nor tree-fellers disturb the tranquillity, or the unbounded freedom of the animals. In accordance with eternal laws, what is too old and decayed falls, and lies where it has fallen, returning gradually to dust and to the womb of mother earth. Above the spot there springs up, wild and untamed, whatever will grow and blossom there. The animals of this wilderness have many a hard fight in their struggle for existence, but they are truly free. Thus they live and die, the creatures of the Swiss National Park.

At the beginning of the present century, when the idea of a national park first came to fruition in Switzerland, the initial problem was to find a suitable area in which to establish it. The commission entrusted with the task of choosing a site decided upon the Lower Engadin, which, with its splendid mountains and valleys and the enchantment of its secluded position, appeared eminently suitable. There was soon unanimous enthusiasm for the project of creating in the Val S-charl and Fuorn district an 'incomparable natural park, dominated by the silver pyramid of the Piz Plavna'.

As the idea grew to the stage at which action had to be taken, wild-life enthusiasts contributed voluntarily towards the establishment and upkeep of the park. Gradually, however, it became increasingly necessary to provide a solid financial basis for the enterprise. In 1909, therefore, there was founded the

'Swiss Association for Nature Protection', whose aim was to supply the necessary monetary support for the National Park. After a time, too, it became possible to obtain an annual financial grant from the State, and further assistance from the Swiss Confederation. A National Park Commission appointed on a national level took on the administration of the park. The Swiss Natural Science Association became responsible for the planning and organization of scientific studies within the park. Numerous specialists were engaged to investigate and record details of such of the park's contents as came within their field of study at the time of its foundation.

These investigations formed the basis for the further course of scientific research into the constant development of the abundant fauna and flora of the National Park itself, and the outgoing and incoming of animals to and from neighbouring districts, some areas of which are highly interesting from the point of view of natural science.

From the outset the National Park Commission accepted as its principal task the creation of an extensive reserve in which every living creature of the district would be safe from human interference. A genuine piece of primeval nature, as free as possible from the influence of civilization, should be made available for the people of the country to see, and for researchers to study in detail. The overriding reason why the Lower Engadin was selected as the site for the national park, apart from the high altitude there of the timber and snow lines (forests 7,190 ft., snow 9,810 ft.), the almost complete absence of human settlements, together with its rich vegetation and diverse animal population, was the fact that the possibility existed there of making the protected area so large that completely natural conditions of life could be encouraged, and would in time flourish. Nature alone was to hold the balance between its various forces. Today, apart from a few guard huts and a laboratory for the investigation of scientific finds *in situ*, there are no human habitations within the bounds of the National Park. True, a motor road runs through it—the road through the Ofen Pass, which was in existence long before the founding of the park—but there are no other roads for traffic in the whole protected area, which is more fortunate in this respect than most of the world's other national parks. Numerous public footpaths traverse the park, opening up the greater part of it to visitors, but it is strictly forbidden for anyone to leave the paths, so that—in accordance with the aims of the national park movement—visitors will not interfere with the animals.

As this park is entirely unfenced it is often more difficult to watch animals than the visitor would imagine, since they have complete freedom of movement. Thus, for example, the red deer generally leave the area during the autumn, moving away to lower-lying, warmer zones, and return to their old haunts in the spring. There can be no suggestion that the animals are becoming tame, although they are naturally more settled here than in places where pursuit by hunters and beasts of prey has sharpened their sense of danger. Here, for instance, marmots can sometimes be seen romping gaily and entertainingly close to the path, quite unperturbed by people passing nearby. In general, however, animals will keep their distance from human beings, ready to flee if attacked, just as they do in parts of the world where they are hunted.

Strict regulations are in force to protect the game reserve. Among the activities forbidden here are the following: to camp, to light a fire or drop any burning material on the ground, to leave paper bags, empty tins or other litter lying about, to attack, capture or kill any animals, or to disturb them by making loud noises, to take or damage nests, eggs or young, to dig up, cut down or pluck plants of any kind, to chop wood from trees, to allow privately owned cattle to graze in the park, to bring dogs, firearms, traps, botanical jars, plant presses, etc. into it, and to take photographs for commercial purposes without permission.

While no animals may be shot in the park, it is also forbidden to feed them. Apart from the fact that it would scarcely be possible to provide equal supplies of foodstuffs for all animals in the remoter areas of the park, access to which is extremely difficult, the very fact of supplying food would be contrary to the basic principle of national parks, which is that the animal world should be left entirely alone to fend for itself according to the primitive laws of nature. In consequence some animals may fall victim to the fury of the elements during hard winters, but the survivors are bound to be particularly strong and healthy. This application of the law of the survival of the fittest also means that the danger of infectious diseases is diminished, since animals capable of withstanding the rigours of the weather necessarily possess more resistance to illness than others, and are less likely to contract diseases.

In conclusion there follows a short summary of facts concerning certain of the best-known classes of animals:

About a century ago the last wolf was shot in Praspöl, and the last lynx was shot in the Val Uina in 1872. The last great bearded vulture was seen in the Engadin in 1888, and the last bear was killed in the Val S-charl in 1904. Animals at present living in the National Park include the red and roe deer, chamois, ibex, marmot, mountain cock and moor hen, white grouse, golden eagle, raven, fox, badger, pine marten, and weasel.

As the ibex is definitely known to have existed in the Engadin during former centuries, although it completely disappeared from this region over the years, it was not a case of interference with the natural order when the park authorities re-introduced animals of this class into the National Park. They soon made themselves thoroughly at home, and their numbers increased steadily. Today there are some 200 of them living contentedly in the park. The chamois and the ibex get on very well together. At salt licks the chamois allows the more powerful ibex to take precedence, but on pastureland herds of these two classes of animal graze near one another, if not actually intermingling.

Beasts of prey have been unable seriously to reduce the herds—in fact they have generally increased in size during the past 40 years, as the following table shows:

	Red deer	Roe deer	Chamois	Ibex
1918	10	60	1,000	—
1920	20	90	1,100	7
1930	130	150	1,170	14
1940	440	120	1,260	100
1950	660	80	1,200	180
1954	600	40	1,300	200
1958	750	80	1,500	270

Red deer had disappeared from the Engadin during the last century, but they settled there afresh, and their numbers increased rapidly thanks to the prohibition on hunting in the National Park. Roe deer first appeared in the Engadin towards the end of the nineteenth century, and have held their own despite slaughter by beasts of prey, and the severe winter conditions in the mountains.

Researchers, inspired by their deep love of nature and the urge to labour in its service, are only now approaching the completion of their task of producing a complete survey of the wild-life resources of the National Park, because so detailed a study of the largest groups of animals spread over an area of 62 square miles of largely trackless country can hardly be accomplished in a lifetime. Nevertheless the Swiss National Park is the most thoroughly explored district in the Alps, and it is there that research into changes in natural conditions can best be carried on. May this Park remain untouched by all future storms as an altar of the highest learning!

The Example of America

BY

DR. O. KRAUS

IT is a remarkable fact that the United States of America, regarded by many people as the land of the most advanced technical progress, unbounded commercial possibilities, and the greatest degree of personal freedom, saw the birth of the now world-wide idea of national parks.

As long ago as 1872, at a time when the struggle between the red Indian tribes and the white pioneers was still raging, the world's first great nature protection area, the National Park by the Yellowstone River in the Rocky Mountains, was founded. It is extremely rich in wild animal life. Eight years previously, as a prelude to this project, the Yosemite Valley, a magnificent gorge of the Sierra Nevada, was decreed by an act of the State of California to be a protected area.

Almost a century has elapsed since then. Admirable work has been done in the meantime: the United States now possess 29 national parks and 83 national monuments. Not only the finest landscapes, but also the most representative examples of American wild life, including animals and plants, were placed under protection: mountain landscapes, forests, coastal strips, erosion ravines, deserts, swamps and moors, extinct and active volcanoes, mighty caverns, and other places of note. They cover a total area of some 30,900 square miles—larger than the whole of Scotland. No one who has had an opportunity to visit the Yellowstone Park, the Grand Canyon of Colorado, the Yosemite Valley, the National Park of the Everglades in Florida or one of the desert parks can fail to appreciate the effect which nature, and the determination of man to protect and retain it, exercise on the visitor. It is truly an unforgettable experience, above all in the opportunity it affords, of seeing animals in their natural surroundings.

All national parks and monuments are owned by the American Government, and therefore by the American people. The management of these vast areas is in the hands of a state organization, the National Park Service, which employs not only a considerable staff of administrative experts and officials, but also scientific workers in all branches. Their work emphasizes the constantly growing awareness that these protected areas are something more than places for public recreation; they are, at the same time, the scene of scientific research, extremely important to the renewal and growth of animal life in its free state, vital points of contact in the inter-related complex of nature. The ecological value of these nature reserves is becoming recognized to an ever greater degree.

The U.S. Government spends some $40,000,000 a year on its National Park Service—a sum which is no doubt unparalleled elsewhere. This American effort is in fact a brilliant piece of far-sighted thinking, and a cultural achievement of the highest order. Hundreds of national parks in all parts of the world testify to the power of their idea now that it has become reality.

Why was it that the United States was ahead of all other nations in the field of large-scale conservation of nature? The reasons are to be found not only in the wild and often breath-taking beauty of the protected areas, but above all in the way the whole idea developed historically. The dominant factor was that the American continent was discovered only comparatively recently, and was opened up very rapidly to civilization. Thus there was no slow organic development over a period of many centuries as occurred in Europe; modern life and communications were quickly extended to areas which in most other respects remain virgin territory. No wonder, therefore, that the damage done to the landscape and to wild life by this rapid growth of civilization was far more conspicuous in America than in most parts of Europe. In consequence, the movement for nature conservation gained force there with far more speed and decision than it did, long afterwards, in the Old World. Fortunately this occurred at a time when vast areas of unspoilt country were still in existence in the United States, especially in the West.

The extent to which this idea has struck a chord in the American character is demonstrated by the response with which it has met: during the year 1954, for example, 48 million Americans visited the country's protected areas—that is to say almost every third American went there once in the year!

The present task is to consolidate, defend, and wherever possible extend this mighty undertaking with all resolution, for there, as throughout the world, the last oases of free, unfettered nature are being threatened by the demands of industrial expansion. This is a real danger even in America, despite frequent assurances that the nation's resources are sufficient to allow the reserves of water power, timber and minerals which exist in many of the national parks to remain untapped, and although, so far, no cable railways have been erected in protected mountain areas. The strong reaction of the National Park Service, and of public opinion in general, against the increasing number of attempts to encroach upon protected areas represents something more than a conflict between groups of opposing interests: it is a struggle between the protecting forces of culture, and the excessive demands of commercial economy. It is generally accepted today that the destruction of such treasuries of nature in its free state would not only rob us of their beauty, it would take from us part of the meaning of life, making an inroad into our own freedom. If it is not possible to preserve inviolate those chosen areas which the Americans themselves have set apart as temples not made by human hands, mankind will show itself unfit to be entrusted by God with this earth and all its wonders.

The Last of the European Bison

BY

DR. ERNA MOHR

WHEREVER wild animals of the bovine race are to be found they have always been regarded as higher game of the noblest kind. Originally two species lived in Europe. One of these, the aurochs, is known to have survived in western Germany until the twelfth century, and until later than that in eastern Europe. The date when this breed became extinct is generally given as 1627, in which year the last pure-blooded aurochs, an old cow, died in the Jaktorowka Forest 35 miles to the south-west of Warsaw. Among varieties living today the Andalusian bull bred for the popular sport of bull-fighting bears most resemblance to the ancient aurochs.

A totally different beast is the European bison, the largest and most imposing of the bovine family native to Europe. After the aurochs became extinct its name was frequently and incorrectly applied to the European bison, and this led to widespread confusion.

The European bison is closely related to its American counterpart, the 'Indian buffalo' of wild-west stories, but in fact a bison rather than a buffalo. All extant forms of bison may derive originally from the *Bison sivalensis*, named after fossilized remains found in the Siwalik Hills of Nepal. From that part of the world these beasts found their way across the Himalayas, which were a less formidable barrier than they are today. Some went east, and crossed the land bridge which then connected Asia with America, where they eventually took on different biological and morphological forms. The steppe bison which remained in the Old World, and of which we find cave drawings made by men of the Stone Age, died out during the post-glacial period, and the two forms of the European forest bison emerged, dwelling in mountainous and low-lying areas respectively.

The mountain bison is found in the Caucasus and hilly areas nearby. The bison of the plains, during its heyday, spread from France throughout the whole of Germany, Austria, Hungary, Poland, and into the Balkans.

There is not a single bison in Lithuania today, nor was there even during the nineteenth century. The only locality where the bison lived during the last century was the virgin forest of Bialowiez to the south-east of the town of Bialystok, lying deep in Polish territory, far removed from the Lithuanian border (82 miles) and also from the nearest point where the population is to any considerable extent Lithuanian (about 70 miles). Bialowiez has nothing whatever to do with Lithuania, whether from the political, ethnographical or linguistic standpoint. It is therefore quite incorrect to refer to the European lowland bison as the 'Lithuanian bison'.

It is known exactly how many of these bison lived in the Puszcza Bialowieska between 1832 and 1922. Between 1845 and 1862 the number exceeded 1,000, between 1850 and 1860 even rising above 1,500, the highest point being reached in 1857 when there were 1,898 of the animals. Within a few years the numbers had fallen, on account of epidemics and as a consequence of unrest in Poland, to some 500 head, with a lowest figure of 380 in the year 1889. In general the territory, large and well-suited to the requirements of these beasts though it is, seems to have been heavily over-stocked—not only with bison but also with other protected livestock. The number of bison the forest is capable of supporting appears to be about 500. When the numbers were greater it became necessary to provide additional food for the bisons, as was done from 1899 onward. Until 1915 the herd remained some 700 strong. The First World War and its aftermath brought about the end of the bisons living freely in the forest of Bialowiez. However, in game reserves and zoos in many parts of the world there remained families of European bison, or at least individual specimens, of very different characteristics, available for breeding purposes. Systematic use was and is still being made of these in the work of reviving the species and ensuring its continued existence.

The weight of an adult bull bison is about 1,870 lb. With an overall length of 11 ft. he is at least 5 ft. high at the hindquarters and about 6 ft. high at the withers—the line of his back slopes steeply downwards from the shoulders. This is due to the long spinal processes of the species. In the bison the hump is part of the bone structure; it is not based on fat as in the zebu and camel.

All breeds of European bison in existence within the past century derive directly or indirectly from the herd in the Puszcza Bialowieska. Many breeders received their original animals direct from that forest, including those of Ascania Nova, Budapest, Schönbrunn and Pless. In other cases a detour was made via Gatschina, a number of European bison including most of those in England having been bred from animals there, and others in continental zoos from stock at Stellingen. The most important colony descended from Bialowiez animals is that at Pless in Upper Silesia, founded in 1865 and preserved since then as a pure-blooded pedigree herd. Despite numerous gifts of animals to zoos for stud purposes, and the authorized shooting of others by distinguished personages, the herd numbered 64 at the outbreak of the First World War in 1914. By 1918, despite war losses, the number had risen to 74. However, the disorder brought about by the Polish uprising, and the period of control by the Inter-

Allied Commission prior to the plebiscite, brought about a rapid reduction in numbers of bison, until finally all that were left were two bulls and a 19-year-old cow. When conditions had returned to normal this elderly female bore several more calves, becoming the matriarch of a flourishing herd in Pless.

After the last free bison in the Puszcza Bialowieska had been shot by a poacher on the 9th February, 1921, the Polish Government decided to act on a national level to create a new home for bison. A forest area of 140 acres was enclosed to form the Zubr Reserve. It lies about midway between Bialowiez and Hajnówka, only a short distance from the main road. During the following years thousands of animal lovers found their way there from all parts of the world. A short account of one such visit follows:

An expert guide leads us into the enclosure—not an animal to be heard or seen! We climb to a raised position—still nothing! Now, however, the old game warden goes deeper into the bison territory; he calls, calls, waits, calls again, and blows his horn. Then activity is to be seen on all sides. Great greyish-brown forms emerge from between the trees, and it is not long before four young cows with the young bull known as Puhacz (= the owl) are standing close to the fence. Not far away there appears the leading bull Borusse, with a train of eight followers. This new Bialowiez herd was founded in 1929. The Polish Ministry of Agriculture, acting through a German animal dealer, purchased the bull Borusse, born in Boizenburg, four cows from Sweden, one bull from Sweden and one from Copenhagen. Unfortunately later research brought to light the fact that only Borusse and two of the cows were pure-blooded European bison. The other two cows and the two Scandinavian bulls were cross-breeds with traces of the American bison and of the grey Ukrainian steppe cattle in their ancestry. Consequently the Poles established a new park at Smardzewice, near Spala, to which they sent the cross-breed bison cows and their offspring, together with a pure-blooded European bison bull, so that the strain could be purified over a period.

Each individual animal is a personality with its own inclinations and habits. The least friendly when we visited Bialowiez was the ten-year-old cow Biserta; she was constantly putting in an appearance just when she was least welcome during photographic sessions, and had to be watched with as much vigilance as all the other animals put together. Her younger sister Biscaya was far more friendly, and completely ignored us provided that we didn't come too close to her calf. She even allowed us to get fairly near the youngster; she stood in the 'attack' position, but did not in fact charge so long as we stayed still. Like most bulls, Borusse is not altogether trustworthy in his dealings with human beings, but on this occasion he was perfectly friendly and approachable. In the previous year he had indicated very clearly the speed at which we were to climb over the protective fence. In general he is very well disposed towards calves, and plays with any that have the courage to disport themselves in his vicinity, although he is the mighty father of the herd. We also saw him good-humouredly jostling the eighteen-month-old Puk, and pushing little Puma aside when she got in his way. Only a few bison bulls get on so well with the younger generation.

The animals have plenty of room to move about; 140 acres are enclosed, and unless one happens to come face to face with Biserta, or approach too close to a cow with calves, it is possible to walk a long way inside the protective fence in perfect safety under the guidance of the game warden—if one is among the lucky few who have official reasons for seeing these splendid beasts at close quarters. Needless to say, not every visitor is allowed to enter the enclosure.

Our journey from the Zubr Reserve in the friendly October sunshine led us to the forest reserve in its lovely autumnal garb. There is no longer a plague of flies in the area at this time of year, although until August these unwelcome visitors can spoil much of the enjoyment of a stay in the depths of the forest. In this woodland reserve no shot is ever heard, no tree felled. Whatever is struck down by a storm lies where it has fallen. On narrow side-paths one has to climb and jump again and again. Only the motor road is kept clear. Trees two hundred years old are no rarity here—many are older. Some trees, partially hollow, have been used by bees as a home and honey store. The peasants knew of these trees, and collected the honey at the appropriate time of year. However, they were not the only enthusiasts for honey: bears were also very fond of it, climbing the trees to help themselves. To prevent this the peasants fastened freely swinging boards over the holes, and these hindered the bears in their marauding activities. Boards of this kind or the hooks from which they were once suspended are still to be seen on some trees—but there are no longer any bears in the forest. We saw a wolf run across the road, though; the wild boar, red and roe deer, lynx and wild cat also live there in freedom.

As long ago as the thirties of this century the Poles attempted to re-introduce bears into this forest. A secure cage was built, with its bars spaced far enough apart for young bears to squeeze between them, but too close together for the mothers to be able to get out. It was hoped that the children would always return to their mothers, making their permanent home in the enclosure. The scheme came to grief, however, owing to the fact that bears and the peasantry could not get on together—the young bears went too near a village and were killed by the inhabitants.

Greater success attended the efforts to re-establish the herd of bison. After the cross-bred beasts had been removed only pure-blooded European bison remained at Bialowiez. They multiplied at a gratifying rate. A new park was established, near Nipolomice, and when that, too, proved a successful breeding ground a few young bison bulls were set at liberty in the Bialowiez forest. It was at once found that they were able to fend for themselves throughout the winter. They were then joined by young bison cows, which gave birth to calves and reared them, so that a small herd now lives there in freedom, some 50 to 60 head in 1961. The creation of pedigree records is certainly made difficult owing to the fact that while it is known which cow has calved, whether her offspring are male or female, and their dates of birth, it cannot be ascertained which bull has sired them. This is, however, of no vital importance owing to the fact that only pure-blooded bison with Caucasian blood in their veins were released in the forest, so that there can be no doubt about the racial purity of the calves born there.

The same holds good in the Soviet sector of the forest. Since the end of the Second World War the frontier between Poland and the U.S.S.R. has run through the forest. In the White Russian part of it, too, bison were allowed to roam freely, and their numbers are increasing at a satisfactory rate. As well as at Bialowiez the U.S.S.R. has a large herd of bison at Serpukhov near Moscow. At many other places breeding pairs and isolated animals are available for the purpose of experimental rearing. The Poles avoid cross-breeding, and have sizeable herds—in addition to those at Bialowiez—at Pless, Niepolomice and Smardzewice, and there are pairs or single animals in several zoos. By their system of de-centralizing the breeding areas the Poles have largely avoided the danger of infectious diseases interfering with pedigree breeding, and they have been able to deliver many pure-bred animals to European and American zoos.

As a result of the war almost all the bison in Germany were wiped out, notably those in East Prussia, on the Darss, in Waren, Boizenburg, Wilhelmstal and Berlin. Only at Springe and Munich-Hellabrunn did acknowledged thoroughbred herds survive, much reduced in size by the chaos at the end of the war. The picture has since changed. Animals from Hellabrunn are now in West and East Berlin, in Rostock, Neumünster, Duisberg, Eulbach and Hardehausen, while thoroughbred European bison from Springe have gone to Hardehausen and Amlishagen. Both establishments have also exported animals, even to America. On the other hand a number of Polish bison have been introduced into Germany.

The breeding of bison in Sweden has gone ahead well. It began originally in the 'Stockholm Zoo' at Skansen, but numbers increased so much that the space available there became insufficient. Then Consul General Axel Johnson came to the rescue, laying out part of his estate at Langsjön near Ängelsberg in the county of Västmanland as a bison park, in order to accommodate the overflow from Skansen. The beasts remained the property of Skansen, and therefore of the Nordic Museum in Stockholm, having been 'boarded out' in Västmanland since 1924.

Both herds grew apace. In 1929 Skansen supplied a number of animals by way of Stellingen to Poland, forming the basis of the new State herd at Bialowiez. The whole herd at Langsjön became the property of Consul General Johnson in 1938, and a new chapter in its history was opened. The herd was moved from Langsjön to a new area near Avesta in Süddalarne. There, after early setbacks had been overcome, breeding proceeded satisfactorily. In order to enlarge the herd and to broaden the basis on which breeding could be carried on, further surplus animals were purchased from Skansen, and two from the stud at Amsterdam. In 1950 the Stockholm Zoo moved all but two breeding pairs away from

Skansen. One of these pairs remained at Skansen, the other went to Julita. All the remaining animals were taken to Avesta, where there is ample space for the bison park to be enlarged.

The formerly important bison herd of the Duke of Bedford at Woburn Abbey in England has always consisted of animals brought over from the continent rather than pedigree stock reared there. Unfortunately a mixed-breed bull was introduced into the Woburn herd in 1924, so that the whole herd gradually lost its racial purity. Not until 1950 were pure-blooded bison bulls received at Woburn: even then, as there were no longer any pure-blooded cows, only eliminative breeding could serve to restore the purity of the stock in the huge Woburn Park. The London Zoo has since received a thoroughbred pair from Poland.

The successful breeding of bison in Amsterdam has been hampered by lack of space, only some zoo enclosures being available, so that surplus animals have had to be sold. The same is true of the Copenhagen strain—no large-scale bison park is available. A 'branch establishment' has now, however, been founded at Aalborg. The zoological gardens of Rotterdam, Antwerp, Schönbrunn, Prague and Budapest made a good start at the rearing of bison, and exchange of animals have enabled breeding to commence in other places. Even Finland, China and South Africa now possess European bison, and specimens are to be found in no fewer than six zoos in North America.

The closing phases of the Second World War, with the utter chaos at the time of the collapse of Germany and immediately afterwards, struck severe blows at the rearing of bison, but less crippling than those caused by the First World War—and less than we feared. Some 35 animals survived the First World War, about 100 the Second and its aftermath. Thanks to a gratifying infusion of youthful vigour into the stock, births have outnumbered deaths through old age, accidents and sickness. Even after a severe outbreak of foot and mouth disease which killed off some 40 animals in two herds we had about 170 pure-blooded European bison in 1954. By the end of 1956 the number had risen to 282, and now, in 1962, we can reckon with a world population of five to six hundred European bison. The majority of these are in Poland, the U.S.S.R. and Sweden. Smaller numbers are to be found in almost all European countries and at six places in the U.S.A., with a pair in Pretoria and one, so far, solitary specimen in Peking.

Nature Protection Parks in the Soviet Union

BY

DR. EDUARD PAUL TRATZ

A STATE whose economy is based on the greatest possible use of its natural resources necessarily runs the risk of exhausting the sources of its wealth. Therefore the principle of employing that wealth must be subordinated to careful planning. Russia, the world's largest state, has based its economic autarchy on the recognition of this fact. On the occasion of the first congress for the protection and development of the natural resources of the U.S.S.R. in 1933 the following significant statement of policy was made: 'Nature protection is an organic part of the structure and economy of the state!'

Nature protection measures in Russia have a past history going back for two centuries. As early as the seventeenth century Tsar Alexei Mikhailovich first created a protected area for the beaver in Kunzovo near Moscow. Later the trapping of the valuable sable and of the falcon was restricted. In 1703 several extensive wooded areas were placed under protection in order to save the trees there, especially those whose diameter exceeded 20 inches, from irresponsible felling. This regulation applied particularly to oaks, elms, larches and pines. During the course of the centuries which followed many laws were promulgated with a view to protecting nature in its original state. Their climax was reached with a highly effective directive, dated 20th September, 1933, which set up a special committee for nature protection areas and their administration to assist the President of the Supreme Soviet. It should be mentioned in this connection that the measures which become law are strictly enforced, and that offences against them are punished severely, the punishment including a fine for the making good of damage caused. Thanks to this fact it is true to say not only that many areas retain their original characteristics to the present day, but also that many classes of animal which appeared to be near to extinction several decades ago again flourish in considerable numbers. Among these are the elk and the saiga antelope. The extent of the danger to the elk is indicated by the fact that as long ago as the 22nd April, 1714, Peter the Great forbade elk hunting in the Government of St. Petersburg. In 1773 a law was made protecting this animal in all parts of the country. Nevertheless numbers of this large member of the deer family diminished to an ever greater extent, frequent political upheavals and the chaos of war playing their part in bringing the elk to the verge of complete annihilation. That was the situation until 1945. Since then the elk has been wholly protected throughout European Russia. The result is that numbers have increased to such an extent that elks not only abound in semi-steppe areas but even, during their nocturnal journeyings, visit the suburbs of Moscow and Leningrad. On one such occasion in 1954 an elk was so startled by a lorry that it fled into a courtyard, where it was captured and taken to the Moscow Zoo.

About twenty years ago the saiga antelope, that strange creature of the steppes with a trunk-like, distended nose, which roamed across almost the whole of Europe during the Ice Age, was listed among the animals which were dying out. Only a very small number still existed on the Kalmykovo steppes. The protective measures introduced on their behalf in the meantime have resulted in the fact that their numbers have multiplied until there are now some 500,000 of these animals on the steppes to the west of the Volga and about a million and a half on the other side of the river. As they had increased beyond the desired level 70,000 had to be shot in 1954. These examples will show clearly that if protective measures are enforced in time many a species of animal endangered by the ravages of man is again able to multiply rapidly.

Specimens of classes of animal which had become rare were also moved to new areas suited to their needs, so that they would have a better chance to flourish and increase in numbers. Among these animals are the sable, the mink, the marten, the beaver, and the Arctic fox.

Thus, for example, numerous beavers were captured in the Voronezh nature protection area and taken to various parts of the U.S.S.R., where they were released. At the present moment more than 10,000 beavers from that area are living in other parts of Russia. Beavers were also taken to other districts from the Herezinsky nature protection area of White Russia.

According to the lastest figures (1961) there are 81 nature protection areas in the U.S.S.R. 26 of these are in the Russian Soviet Federal Republic, 14 in Georgia, 7 in the Ukraine, 5 in Azerbaijan, 5 in Latvia, 5 in Tadzhikistan, 4 in Estonia, 3 in Kazakhstan, 3 in Armenia, 3 in Turkmenistan, 2 in White Russia, 2 in Kirgizia, 1 each in Lithuania and Uzbekistan.

Altogether the area of the state nature protection areas amounts to some 21,230 square miles.

The areas of the individual nature protection areas vary between a few hundred acres and many hundreds of square miles. The nature protection area of the steppes 'Mikhailov New Land' extends over more than 3,475 square miles.

The majority of the nature protection areas of western Russia are situated in the European part of the Caucasus.

The various protected areas of the U.S.S.R. are in very different types of country, including arctic tundras, wooded tundras, east-European taiga, mixed east-European woods, primeval forests of Amur and Ussuri, European wooded plains, desert and semi-desert zones, mountainous districts in Europe and Asia.

The choice and dimensions of protected areas are fixed in accordance with a number of considerations, and in most cases they serve as vast open-air laboratories for biological investigations. For this reason many of them contain scientific research institutions.

Animal Life in the Arctic

BY

ALWIN PEDERSEN
Holte (Denmark)

IN the year 1604, at a time when no one had a clear idea of what the world was like north of the Arctic Circle, the trading ship *Speed* made a voyage from England to the Kola Peninsula. It had been entrusted with the task of opening up a trade route with Russia. The ship, which was in the service of the newly-established Muscovy Company, was commanded by Stephen Bennet.

The journey to Kola passed off without noteworthy incidents. On the return voyage, however, Bennet discovered a small island in the vast polar sea, now known as Bear Island, and he decided to examine it. He therefore landed on it with a few of his men. When they reached the north coast of the island they found themselves confronting a vast number, probably nearly a thousand, of ungainly sea creatures lying asleep in a dense mass. The animals were completely unfamiliar to them. At the same time they found in the sand under their feet shining ivory teeth the length of a man's forearm, and they saw that similar teeth protruded from the mouth of each sleeping colossus. Since ivory was then valued very highly, they determined to enrich themselves by seizing as much as they could of this precious commodity. They used up all their powder and shot on the animals nearest to them, and when the shooting was over fifteen of the great beasts lay dead on the beach. The men cut their heads off and took them aboard the ship as a proof of their adventurous experience.

Bennet's chance discovery of the great walrus colonies of the little island in the polar sea was to be the beginning of the long-drawn-out campaign of extermination against the animal riches of the far north which once seemed inexhaustible—but at the same time the beginning of really practical polar exploration. The walrus colony on Bear Island was soon exterminated, whereupon the hunters concentrated instead on Spitzbergen, which had recently been discovered. There, too, the tireless seafarers came upon one walrus colony after another, some larger than others. Often several thousand animals were found concentrated in a single small bay, so that the water seemed to be boiling. Whole islands appeared to be covered with the sleeping, utterly fearless creatures. In addition another valuable discovery was made there, that of the great northern or Greenland whales, vast numbers of which lived in the Greenland Sea and Barents Sea around Spitzbergen. This discovery put all other activities in northern waters, even walrus hunting, in the shade, and led men to adopt the extremely lucrative career of whaling from that time onward.

At about the same period Russian fur trappers and ivory collectors were pushing eastwards along the north coast of Asia in their quest for mammoth tusk ivory and the precious sable furs, until they learned from natives in the extreme north-eastern tip of Siberia about the existence of vast numbers of ivory and fur-bearing animals with which they were not yet familiar. Although the warlike natives often proved an almost insuperable obstacle, the determined hunters finally reached their destination, the west coast of Alaska, and the rich animal life of the Bering Sea was at their feet. There they saw for the first time —in addition to the fur-seal and a strange, almost antediluvian creature the Steller's sea-cow—the sea otter or Kamchatka beaver, the most valuable of all fur animals. The skins of these creatures and of the sable became the golden fleece of that age, not only inspiring fur trappers to undertake most dangerous missions but also tempting men in high positions to give up the comforts of civilized life and venture out to the wilds of Siberia and the Far East, in the hope of making a fortune there trapping and dealing in furs. In North America, too, the trek of profit-greedy white men towards the icy wastes of the north had begun at about the same time. The French fur trappers known as 'Coureurs de bois' who took so prominent a part in the first exploration of Canada pursued the most valuable fur animal known to them, the Canadian beaver, as far as the timber line. They then pushed on to the Arctic coast of North America, where they were the first to catch sight of the vast herds of reindeer dwelling on the North American tundra, and a hitherto unknown beast, the musk-ox. Fur trapping was highly profitable in this vast wilderness sparsely inhabited by Indians and Eskimoes; it soon led to the founding of the still extant Hudson's Bay Company.

Whalers, scientific and national expeditions penetrated to the most northerly areas of the earth. They found there a highly specialized animal world, including small reindeer or caribou of the far north and a race of heavily-clad musk-oxen accustomed to the icy climate and the long night, but inhabiting the silent wastes far from the world of man only in fairly small numbers.

Almost as soon as these last discoveries had been made the consequences of man's ruthless pursuit of the animals began to be felt in the Arctic.

Even before that the Steller's sea-cow had succumbed to its hunters, after travellers in northern regions had found that its meat, rich in vitamins, protected them from scurvy, the dreaded disease which afflicted seafarers in those days. It was followed by the Greenland whale, which is now also believed to have been completely exterminated. The walrus became extinct in many areas, including Spitzbergen, and only greatly reduced colonies survived elsewhere. In some places, particularly on the west coasts of land masses and island groups which become ice-free earlier than the rest of the territories and are therefore more easily accessible, the hunting of these animals ceased to be worth while. Furthermore the natives protested against the massacre of the land animals and seals, the basis of their existence. This fact has been of deep significance, and has been largely responsible for the ever-increasing volume of demands that animal life should be protected.

The first necessity was to protect or to increase the numbers of such animals as were vital to the lives of the local population. The breeding of reindeer, too, was of great importance. From the earliest times they had existed in the tundras of northern Europe and Asia; now they were introduced into the 'barren grounds' (the treeless plains of North America) and Alaska, making it possible to preserve the still extant herds of wild reindeer in such numbers as were required in the various areas. In territories such as Greenland where fresh reindeer breeding with newly introduced stock was impracticable strict limits were placed on reindeer hunting, and in Spitzbergen it was forbidden altogether.

It was more difficult to devise measures to protect the walrus, and this problem still remains unsolved. This creature has always been of life-giving importance to the polar Eskimoes, the most northerly inhabitants of the earth, and so it remains today. Clearly, then, these Eskimoes still have the right to hunt the walrus to be found in the waters between North America and northern Greenland, and in the eastern part of the North American Arctic Archipelago. No recent information is available concerning the protection of walruses on the Asiatic side of the Bering Strait, but presumably there, too, similar conditions exist to those just mentioned. Another refuge of this creature is the sea channel around Wrangel Island. Of the other two small colonies still existing in the Arctic that on the north-east coast of Greenland is fully protected by law; the second, on the east coast of Novaya Zemlya, may well enjoy similar safeguards, as the necessity for a total prohibition on hunting them was emphasized in Russia many years ago.

The musk-ox, the member of the bovine family native to the most northerly lands of the earth, is completely protected wherever it is still to be found on the Arctic islands to the north of Canada and in the northernmost parts of the American continent proper. The laws protecting this species are binding on the Eskimoes as well as on Europeans. However, limited hunting of the musk-ox is still permitted in Greenland. Several small protection areas for the sea otter, which had been brought to the verge of complete annihilation, have been established in the Aleutians; fortunately numbers have again increased somewhat of late. Protective safeguards were also vitally necessary for the fur-seals of the islands in the Bering Sea, in order to save them from extermination. Highly effective preservation measures were put into force both in the American and Asiatic islands of the group. A limited amount of hunting, under strict control, is still permitted.

The Arctic animal which has been most extensively hunted for its fur during recent times is the Arctic fox. Owing to its extensive distribution over vast areas in the polar region it has, however, been able to survive the effects of widespread hunting, although its cousin the blue fox, whose fur is even more valuable, has been wiped out in many areas. An attempt has been made to save this species by establishing large blue fox farms in many places, especially on islands in the Bering Strait. During recent years, however, the demand for fox furs has greatly diminished, so that in most places the trapping of foxes is now carried out only by the natives.

Although the polar bear has become a rarity in almost every part of the vast area in which he is at home, he still knows no master—he is king of the frozen wastes. If the idea of appointing short or long closed seasons (when the hunting of polar bears is forbidden) is to be of any practical value it will have to be put into force in all the northern lands which these animals visit during their constant wanderings, including international territories.

Seals and whales are in roughly the same position. In the European sector of the Arctic, in particular, the hunting of both seals and whales is carried out principally in international waters. There is, however, one factor which militates in these creatures' favour: hunting operations are always reduced or entirely suspended once the catches become insufficient to cover the by no means small costs of mounting the operations. Whaling and seal-hunting organizations are therefore always interested in keeping the numbers of the animals with which they are concerned high enough to make their continued hunting worth while. This factor applies especially to the saddlebacked and hooded seals, although unfortunately it provides no guarantee that they will not eventually become extinct. Only the more common curly-haired Phoca, which is to be found along almost all Arctic coasts, and to some extent the bewhiskered Phocidae may be successfully protected in particular territories, but they are so important to the livelihood of the inhabitants of those coastal regions that some replacement for them will first have to be supplied if hunting them is ever to be prohibited.

Among the birds the eider ducks, the white grouse and geese enjoy effective protection during the breeding season, or even protection all the year round, in certain areas. Geese in particular require safeguarding when they are moulting, because during that period they lose their ability to fly, and can easily be slaughtered even without the use of firearms, while the colonies of eider duck are disrupted owing to the constant demand for the soft down with which the female lines the nest, so that their nests are seized and destroyed in vast numbers.

There are as yet no national parks in the Arctic. For the time being closed seasons, areas in which one species or another is protected, and total prohibition of hunting in small islands particularly rich in wild life go some way towards fulfilling the functions of national parks. The national park idea in all its fulness is most nearly approached in the North American Arctic Archipelago. Admittedly only the musk-ox is completely protected there, but so stringent are the regulations which govern admittance to this vast territory, and so great are the difficulties to be overcome there, that hunting for profit hardly comes into consideration. Only the few native inhabitants engage in hunting, to supply their own needs. In all probability the abundant animal life which once animated the vast expanses of the far north has gone never to return, and many problems remain to be solved if even such animal population as still remains is to survive. Nevertheless, thanks to the recognition of the fact that it is of vital importance to human existence in those bleak northern lands, the animal world of the Arctic should now have a brighter future ahead of it.

From Hunter to Guardian

BY

DR. ARTHUR LINDGENS

THE history of the chase goes back nearly as far as that of mankind. Prehistoric man must have had a hard life in his struggle against the world of animals around him. Provided with no natural weapons, no claws or sharp teeth, he was at an immense disadvantage when in combat with carnivorous beasts of those times such as the cave lion and cave bear. He had to fight them, because he needed their caves for shelter, he needed their skins as protection against the weather, and he needed the game which the beast of prey slew as food for himself. Terrible battles to the death must have taken place in those days at the dawn of history. However, over a period of thousands of years man's intelligence enabled him to achieve mastery over the world of nature. He succeeded in trapping animals in pits and luring them over cliff edges. Gradually he invented weapons—stone axes and throwing spears—and instead of having to defend himself against wild animals he became the hunter, obtaining his food and clothing from them.

While the conditions under which prehistoric man hunted can only be a matter of speculation, we have far more information concerning this subject in later periods. Only the strongest men engaged in hunting; tribal leaders used the chase to demonstrate their courage and skill to their subjects. The prowess of great kings in the hunting field was celebrated far beyond the bounds of their realms. Above all the name of Nimrod is still remembered today. He was the founder of the Babylonian Empire and the builder of the Tower of Babylon, as well as being the prototype of all great hunters.

The lands in which the ancient Babylonians and Assyrians lived were rich in wild animals, especially lions and elephants. Kings fought against lions on foot, and great was the resulting slaughter. Tiglatpileser I, who flourished about the year 1050 B.C., is reputed to have dispatched a thousand lions with his own hand. Some of these beasts were in districts where wild life abounded in its natural state, but others were from zoological parks and gardens, where they were kept by members of the nobility. The weapons used in fighting them were throwing spears, lances, swords and clubs. Hunting scenes are represented on many ancient reliefs.

With the Persians, too, hunting was encouraged as a means of training for war. Great ceremonial hunts took place, with all the despotic splendour of oriental rulers in those days. Areas which were once rich in animal life have long since ceased to be so, partly because of the spread of civilization, partly because immense tracts of land became dried up, and are now arid desert.

The Egyptians were another race of keen hunters, their prey being big game, and, in particular, creatures of the water. Large animals, principally lions, were slain from hunting chariots and with long arrows. Numerous pictorial representations of hunting at that period have come down to us.

Many ancient races, such as the Greeks and later the Germanic tribes, rated hunting very highly. The goddesses of the chase, Diana and Artemis, were greatly revered, and countless temples were dedicated to them. Hunting was the young man's training in courage, manliness, agility, skill in the handling of weapons and in outwitting an opponent. The hunting dog became the huntsman's inseparable companion. After the large beasts of prey had been virtually exterminated, boar hunting became the 'manliest' sport of the Middle Ages. It cannot be said that hunting in those days had much of the spirit of 'sportsmanship' about it, or even that any such conception was then current at all. What generally took place was in fact mass-slaughter, a magnificent spectacle presented by men of high authority to impress their subjects or visiting nobles. Hunting was a monopoly of the privileged classes. Over the centuries, however, revolutions and other upheavals brought about a change, and hunting gradually became an activity for all classes, a sport often indulged in for recreation.

As hunting became more widespread, the manner in which it was carried out grew to be more humane, and the idea of chivalry towards dumb creatures was born. Nevertheless hunting degenerated again and again into horrifying extermination campaigns directed against the animal world. What frightful mass-murder took place on the mid-west prairies of the United States during the period when bison were being slaughtered wholesale! As recently as a century ago some 60 million of these buffalo lived on the American plains. In the course of a senseless massacre, which was not necessary, either to obtain food or hides, on anything like the vast proportions to which it grew, these herds were almost entirely wiped out—all but a few thousand bison.

During the violent changes, wars and revolutions of the past decades, the herds of European bison, too, have been exterminated, with the exception of a few survivors here and there. Finally mankind—by now possessing modern weapons capable of wiping out the animal world altogether—called a halt to this savage, senseless killing. The demand that wild animals should be preserved in freedom gradually increased in volume. At last governments and enthusiastic animal lovers devoted their energies to the rescue of the animal world. An early pioneer in this sphere was the Boer President Kruger, who in 1884 founded what has since become the magnificent Kruger National Park in the Transvaal.

His splendid example was followed by other governments. National parks and game reserves began to be established in many parts of the world. I need mention only Yellowstone Park in the U.S.A., Jasper and Banff in Canada, and the many great parks in Tanganyika, Kenya, Uganda and the Congo, among the most famous of which are Tsavo Park, Kilimanjaro, the Ngoro-Ngoro Crater, the Serengeti Plains, the Queen Elizabeth Park, the Albert National Park and many, many others. In Europe national parks were created with the result that the chamois was saved from extinction. Private individuals founded nature protection parks as long ago as the turn of the present century. The most important of these was probably Ascania Nova, a paradise for animals established by the Falz-Fein family in the Taurien district of Russia, to the north of the Crimea.

Hunting has become subject to ever stricter, clearer rules and regulations during the past few decades, especially as regards the use of firearms, which in many places were no longer allowed indiscriminately to all and sundry. In other districts guns were prohibited altogether, so that the sound of shooting has become unknown there. Man thus made himself the guardian and friend of the animal kingdom. In fact so much has been done on behalf of animals that in many parts of Africa today the numbers of beasts of prey have increased to the point where police and professional hunters have on occasion to shoot lions and elephants, in order to protect the native population, their herds and agricultural land. While there was formerly no restriction on the shooting of beasts of prey, each huntsman's general licence now allows him to shoot only *one* lion per year.

The question arises whether this development, whose aim is the ever-increasing protection of wild life, will mean that the joy of the chase is lost to us for ever? Will the movement for the conservation of the world of nature ever become so widespread that hunting will be forbidden altogether? Perhaps a huntsman who feels himself no less bound by the idea of nature protection than by that of the hunt may be allowed to express his opinion on this point.

A great many people find that the chase through woods and across open country, which is so exhilarating a part of the joy of hunting, provides them with recreation in the fullest sense, summoning up new strength which helps them to meet the challenge of modern life. This industrial age, and the ceaseless bustle of present-day existence, make relaxation amid nature in the open air all the more important—even necessary. How many prominent people have found recreation and the source of new creative energy in hunting! How much strength derives from the recollection of happy hours in the hunting field! How many friendships, even with members of other races, have been made among huntsmen!

Reflections such as these lead to the hope, in fact the certainty, that hunting will remain to us for all time as something essential—not only to men but also to the retention of vigorous energy in animals. Even if the areas in which guns are allowed to be used should be further reduced, the ideals of hunting, in the humane forms in which the sport is cultivated in civilized lands today, will ever remain valid and of value.

A great many hunters whose early experience was with the gun have since learned to appreciate the pleasure which can be derived from the latest form of hunting—with a camera. This sport is no less fascinating and exciting than stalking with a gun. The author of this article, brought up to the traditional view of hunting, has now learned to value this modern form of the sport as one of the most positive achievements of recent times—incidentally an achievement which, it will surely be agreed, is demonstrated by some of the photographs reproduced in this book. . . .

A great deal more could be written about the welcome change, almost unnoticed but nevertheless inevitable, which the conception of the 'hunter' has undergone, so that today, as everyone in possession of the facts knows, he is likely to carry out far more duties concerned with the *protection* of animals than with *hunting* them in the old sense of the word. It therefore appears not unreasonable to hope that the points of view of the hunter and of the protector of wild life, still regarded a few decades ago as flatly contradictory, may be brought even closer together in future than they are at present. . . .

This is a matter of the utmost importance today, when the preservation of animal life in almost every part of the world can only be made possible by the co-operation of the hunter.

In the countries with a high level of civilization, whether heavily or sparsely populated, protective measures are absolutely vital if any substantial numbers of wild animals are to survive. Since the areas available to them in such countries are very limited in extent, and are often located in districts of coniferous forests which offer little nourishment to vegetarian species, fodder has to be supplied by those concerned with animal conservation. For this purpose crops of suitable feeding-stuffs are sown in woodland clearings and forest glades, while plants are grown beside paths and at such places as disused gravel pits and refuse dumps. Carefully planned supplementary feeding of wild game is of prime importance during the bleakest period of the winter. Artificial salt licks promote the healthy growth of livestock.

The fight against poachers is also extremely important.

The prevention and cure of sickness in wild animals often involves considerable expenditure of time and money. Epidemics, such as the scab which afflicted the chamois of the Bavarian Alps a few years ago, can bring a species to the brink of extinction over wide areas. Modern methods of farming create serious problems. Every year thousands of eggs and newly-born animals are destroyed by farm machines, are maimed by the blades of harvesting equipment, or suffer through artificial fertilizers. Hunting associations have already spent large sums of money in attempts to develop and put into force suitable methods of combating these dangers, and the huntsman contributes greatly to the healthy growth of the wild game population by disposing of crippled, sick and weak specimens. This is a service formerly carried out by the large beasts of prey. In many places if huntsmen are not permitted to take their place the result is the over-stocking of open land and forests, with a consequent grave shortage of food and increased danger of epidemics among livestock. Selective shooting can also regulate the numerical balance between the sexes, and the healthy growth of the stock, with the elimination of aged or otherwise surplus animals.

Thus in highly civilized countries hunting, the care and preservation of wild life have become indivisibly linked, and we are convinced that in the hitherto less fully developed lands, too, the same road is the only one leading to the same goal—the survival of healthy wild life, represented by as many species as possible, in the distant future.

Part Four

THE WORLD'S NATIONAL PARKS AND OTHER
IMPORTANT NATURE PROTECTION AREAS

Some of the World's National Parks and other Important Nature Protection Areas

(As new national parks are frequently established and existing ones change their nature, this list cannot be regarded as exhaustive or up-to-date. In planning visits to national parks or reserves, reference should be made to the latest publications of the International Union for Conservation of Nature).

The date given in brackets after the name of a park or protected area is that of its foundation. In cases where two dates appear the first is that of the earliest conservation measures put in force in the area, often affording only partial protection (e.g. game or forest reserve), the second being that of the year when the area was enlarged or raised to its present status.

The following abbreviations have been employed:

NP=National Park, NM=National Monument (only in the U.S.A.), GR=Game Reserve, NC=Nature Conservation Territory, NR=National Reserve, Sa=Sanctuary. N=north, E=east, S=south, W=west; n=to the north (of), nw=to the north-west (of), etc.

The text generally contains details concerning the size, approximate position (administrative district) and communications with the protected area, accommodation facilities, best period for visits, and a short note on the natural characteristics of the district.

The most important species of animals to be found in the area are generally listed. Since this book is intended for the ordinary reader, the technical names of animals are added only in the cases of particularly rare or little-known species.

The maps are not intended to, and cannot, replace an atlas. They show only places mentioned in the text as being particularly important to anyone visiting the protected areas. The names of countries which have no important conservation areas have been omitted. A circle signifies a national park, a square any other protected district. The differentiation is important, since in accordance with international agreements a national park is open to the general public without restriction (although in practice this is true only in some 90% of all cases), whereas restrictions of various kinds often exist as regards protected areas of other kinds. Naturally there are also other differences which cannot be discussed here.

The protection areas are numbered in geographical order. The same number which each area bears on the map is always given *before* its name in the text.

Africa

Tunisia

1 Bou Hedma Sa (1936) 50 sq. miles.

District of Djebel Bou Hedma—Qued Cherchera—Bled Talha in S of Tunisia, half-way between Gafsa and the Mediterranean. A good road runs through the area. 300–2,700-ft.-high plateau with remains of acacia woods. Dorcas gazelle, maned sheep. Native settlements nearby—extensive poaching. Sa in great danger.

Morocco

Administration of the NP: Forestry Department.

2 Tazeka NP (1950) 2½ sq. miles.

13 miles from Taza. The higher reaches of the 6,530-ft.-high mountain Ibel Tazekka in the central Atlas range. Woods, including cedar.

3 Toubkal NP (1942) 138 sq. miles.

37 miles s of Marrakesh. Part of the upper Atlas range with mountains above 11,550 ft. (Toubkal 13,750 ft.). Wooded bush. Mouflon, mountain gazelle. Accessible by car. Only mountain paths in the park. Although forbidden, nomads graze their sheep in the NP.

Senegal Republic

Administration: Service Eaux et Forêts, Dakar.

4 Niokolo Koba NP (1954) 1,930 sq. miles.

District of Tambacounda, in S, on the frontier of the Guinea Republic. Entrance: road and railway to Tambacounda, airport at Simenti (DC 3). Accommodation: Hotel Simenti (34 beds), camp in Niokolo (14 persons). Visiting period: 25th Dec.–1st May. Elephant, hippopotamus, Cape buffalo, Derby eland, roan antelope, waterbuck, reedbuck.

Mali Republic

Administration: Direction des Eaux et Forêts, Secrétariat d'Etat à l'Agriculture et Eaux et Forêts, Bamako.

5 Boucle du Baoulé NP with GR Badinko and Fina (1950) 2,700 sq. miles.

Boundary approx. 62 miles nw of Bamako. Motor road from Bamako runs through the Sa. Accommodation: 2 camps (Baoulé, 12 persons) on the E boundary, Madina camp (4 persons) on the W boundary. Best visiting period Jan.–April. Bush and wooded savannas, gallery forests. Var. antelope, reedbuck, waterbuck, warthog; rarer: Derby eland, giraffe, Cape buffalo, lion.

Upper Volta, Niger and Dahomey

Administration: Ministère des Eaux et Forêts, Directeur du Service Forestier, Ouagadougou, Rép. de la Haute-Volta, B.P.4.

6 Bontioli GR (1957) 49 sq. miles.
   W Volta. Airport: Bobo-Dioulasso, road from there through Diébougou (94 miles). Accommodation: Bobo-Dioulasso, simple camp in Diébougou. Best visiting period: Feb.–April. Animals as in the W-du-Niger NP.

7 Singou GR (1955) 744 sq. miles, and Arly GR (1954) 293 sq. miles.
   Both in E Volta. These two GR are adjacent. Airport: Ouagadougou. Accommodation: camp in Arly. Road connections: Ouagadougou–Fada–N'Gourma–Pama–Arly: 272 miles. Animals as in the W-du-Niger NP.

8 W-du-Niger NP (1952, 1953) 6,534 sq. miles, of which 1,350 sq. miles are in the Volta Republic, 1,274 in the Niger Republic and 3,910 in Dahomey.
   In the E of the country. Airport: Ouagadougou (Volta) or Niamey (Niger). Accommodation: camps in Diapaga (Volta) and in Tapoa (Niger). Road links: Niamey–Tapoa 96 miles. Niamey–Boton–Diapaga 120 miles. Ouagadougou–Fada–N'Gourma–Kantchari–Diapaga 281 miles. 172-mile-long road from Diapaga in the NP. Best visiting period: Feb.–April. Elephant, hippopotamus, Cape buffalo, various antelope, waterbuck, reedbuck, blue duiker, yellow-backed duiker, warthog, baboon, lion, cheetah.

Republic of Guinea

9 Nimba Mountains NC (1944) 50 sq. miles.
   Near the frontiers with Liberia and the Ivory Coast Republic. Nimba mountain chain (up to 5,800 ft. high) with forests up to 1,660 ft., grassland above that. The most westerly point at which the legendary toad Nectophrynoides vivipara is to be found. Visits can only be made with the permission of the Director of the Institut National de Recherches et de Documentation de la République de Guinée, which administers the area and the biological research station situated within it.

Ivory Coast Republic

Administration: Ministère de l'Agriculture et da la Cooperation, Service des Eaux et Forêts, Abidjan.

10 Bouna GR (1953) 3,475 sq. miles.
   In the NE, Comoé Valley. Road connections: Abidjan–Ferkessédougou. Camps Ouango-Fitni for 40 persons, Bouna, Kakpin. 250 miles of roads in the GR.

Ghana

The protected areas are administered by the Forestry Department of the Ministry of Food and Agriculture.

11 Mole River GR (1958). 900 sq. miles.
NW Ghana. Wooded savannas. As yet no accommodation on the spot. Visitors guided by game wardens.

12 Onuem Bepo GR, 13 sq. miles.
N Ghana. Forest.

13 Aboma GR, 3 sq. miles.
S to mid Ghana. Wooded savannas.

14 Bomfum GR, 7 sq. miles.
S to mid Ghana. Wooded savannas.

15 Owabi Waterworks GR, 5 sq. miles.
Near Owabi Reservoir. Secondary forest.

16 Bia-Shelterbelt GR, 7 sq. miles.
SW Ghana. Forest.

17 Kommenda Native Authority GR, 8 sq. miles.
SW Ghana. Wooded bushland, coastal jungle.

Chad Republic

Administration: Ministère du Tourisme et des Eaux et Forêts, Dep. Eaux, Forêts, Chasses, Fort-Lamy, B.P. 447.

19 Abou-Telfane part-GR, 425 sq. miles.
Near Mongo (312 miles from Fort-Lamy, regular air connections). Mountain massif rising out of a sparsely wooded plain. In the inner mountain valleys: greater kudu (numerous). Best visiting period: Dec.–June.

20 Siniaka-Minia GR (1960) 1,748 sq. miles.
25 miles from Melfi (1 flight weekly), 188 miles from Fort-Archambault. No facilities as yet exist for the reception of visitors, but they are to be provided during 1962. Abundant animal life: elephant, black rhinoceros, giraffe, Cape buffalo, various antelope, waterbuck, greater kudu (in the mountains), warthog, lion, leopard, baboon, numerous species of birds, including pelican, marabou, geese, ducks near water-holes; there are also crocodile, monitor and python.

21 Zakouma GR (full protection), 926 sq. miles.
38 miles from Am-Timan, where there are landing facilities for DC 3—at present 1 flight weekly through Broussard. Various routes link Zakouma with Fort-Lamy (500 miles) and Fort-Archambault (188 miles). Camp in GR, guides. Roads and observation posts in GR. Visiting period Dec.–May. Exceptional opportunities for watching wild animals. Very large herds at the permanent water-holes. Light woods, wooded savannas, inundation areas. Elephant, black rhinoceros, giraffe, Cape buffalo, lechwe, roan antelope, waterbuck, warthog, ostrich, lion, leopard.

22 Manda GR (full protection), 418 sq. miles.

Very close to Fort-Archambault. Best visiting period Dec.–June. Plain with light woods and savannas on the Chari River. Elephant, various antelope, giraffe, warthog, lion, leopard. Animal watching difficult; the game are shy on account of the numerous villages.

Cameroon Republic

Administration: Ministère de l'Economie Nationale, Direction des Eaux et Forêts, Yaoundé, B.P. 194.

18 Waza NP (1932, 1961), 656 sq. miles.

In the N of the country, between the 11th and 12th degrees north. Routes in: from Fort Lamy, 88 miles (Feb.–June), from Maroua via Mora, 81 miles (end of Oct.–end of June). Landing strip of 1,800 yards for DC 4. Accommodation: Camp Waza (40 persons), 250 miles of roads in NP. Best visiting period: Nov.–end of June. Grassland and bush savanna. Elephant (200), giraffe (2,000), some 40,000 antelope of various kinds, ostrich (300), lion (100), cheetah (100), numerous water birds.

23 Benoué GR (1932) 695 sq. miles.

Between the 8th and 9th degrees north. Contains source of the Bénue. Accessible only on the W from the road Ngaoundéré–Garoua. Accommodation: Campement du Buffle noir (8 persons), Campement du Bel Elan (8 persons), Campement du Capitaine (16 persons). 84 miles of roads. Best visiting period Jan.–June. Wooded and bush savannas. Elephant, black rhinoceros, hippopotamus, Cape buffalo, Derby eland and other large antelope, lion, leopard.

24 Boubandjidah GR (1947) 1,080 sq. miles.

Between the 8th and 9th degrees north. Only accessible in the S from Tcholliré–Touboro road. Accommodation: Campement du Rhinoceros (4 persons). No roads within GR. Visiting period Jan.–June. Elephant, black rhinoceros (200), hippopotamus, Cape buffalo, antelope, lion, leopard.

25 Faro GR (1947) 1,274 sq. miles.

Between the 8th and 9th degrees north. Accessible in the S from the Poli–Mana road. Accommodation: Campement des Hippopotames (4 persons). Visiting period: Jan.–June. Elephant, hippopotamus, black rhinoceros, Cape buffalo, antelope, lion, leopard.

Central African Republic

Administration: Direction du Service des Eaux, Forêts et Chasses de la République Centrafricaine, B.P. 830, Bangui. In the places mentioned below as possessing accommodation facilities there are available bungalows with sanitary arrangements: simple camps exist on the edges of NP and GR areas.

26 Miaméré-Miadiki GR (1940) 965 sq. miles.

Sub-prefecture N'Délé. Airport: N'Délé, 32-mile-road from there. Accommodation:

N'Délé. Best visiting period Jan.–June. Elephant, giraffe, Derby eland and other large antelope. Lion, leopard.

27 Koukourou-Bamingui GR (1940) 580 sq. miles.
   Sub-prefecture N'Délé. Airport: Fort-Crampel or N'Délé, in each case 78 miles by road. Accommodation: Fort-Crampel or N'Délé. Best visiting period Jan.–June. Elephant, black rhinoceros, Cape buffalo, Derby eland and other large antelope. Lion, leopard.

28 Bamingui-Bangoran NP (1916, 1940) 3,865 sq. miles.
   Sub-prefecture N'Délé. Airport: N'Délé, 48-mile-road from there. Accommodation: N'Délé. Best visiting period Jan.–June. Elephant, black rhinoceros, Cape buffalo, giraffe, Derby eland and other large antelope.

29 Vassako-Bolo NC (1916, 1940) 580 sq. miles.
   In the sub-prefecture N'Délé, 32-mile-road from there. Accommodation: N'Délé. Best visiting period: Jan.–June. Elephant, black rhinoceros, Cape buffalo, Derby eland and other large antelope. Lion, leopard.

30 Gribingui-Bamingui GR (1934, 1940) 1,930 sq. miles.
   Sub-prefecture Fort-Crampel. Airport: Fort-Crampel, 62-mile-road from there. Accommodation: Fort-Crampel. Best visiting period Jan.–June. Elephant, black rhinoceros, giraffe, Cape buffalo, Derby eland and other large antelope. Lion, leopard.

31 Aouk-Aoukalé GR (1922, 1960) 1,232 sq. miles.
   Sub-prefecture Birao. Airport: Birao, 78-mile-road from there. Accommodation: Birao. Best visiting period Jan.–May. Elephant, giraffe, Cape buffalo, larger species of antelope.

32 Saint-Floris NP (1933, 1960) 390 sq. miles.
   Sub-prefecture Birao. Airport: Gordil or Birao, 112-mile-road from there. Accommodation: Dongolo in the NP. Best visiting period Jan.–May. Elephant, giraffe, Cape buffalo, various antelope, lion, ostrich. Very abundant bird life. Crocodile.

33 Ouandjia-Vakaga GR (1925, 1960) 3,725 sq. miles.
   Sub-prefecture Birao. Airport: Gordil or Birao, 78-mile-road from there. Accommodation: Birao. Best visiting period Jan.–May. Elephant, giraffe, Cape buffalo, Derby eland and other large antelope, ostrich, lion.

34 Yata-N'Gaya GR (1960) 1,968 sq. miles.
   Sub-prefecture Birao. Airport: Birao, 62-mile-road from there. Accommodation: Birao. Best visiting period Jan.–May. Elephant, giraffe, Cape buffalo, various large antelope, lion, leopard.

35 André Felix NP (1960) 656 sq. miles.
   Sub-prefecture Birao. Airport: Birao, 62-mile-road from there. Accommodation: Birao. Best visiting period Jan.–May. Elephant, giraffe, Cape buffalo, various antelope, lion, leopard.

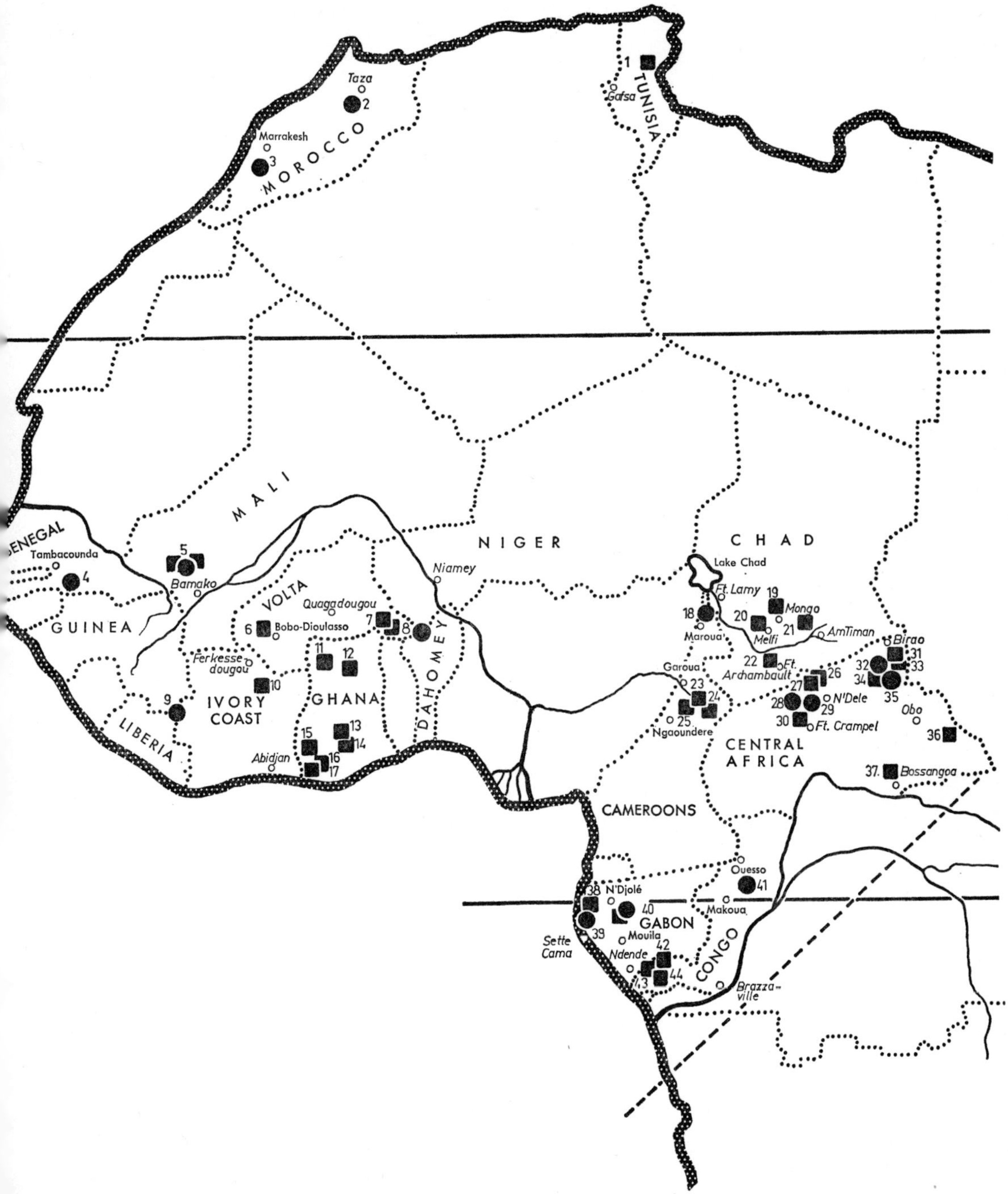
TUNISIA
Gafsa
1
Taza
2
Marrakesh
3
MOROCCO
MALI
ENEGAL
Tambacounda
4
GUINEA
5
Bamako
VOLTA
Quagadougou
6
Bobo-Dioulasso
7
8
Ferkessedougou
9
10
IVORY COAST
LIBERIA
11
12
GHANA
13
14
15
16
17
Abidjan
DAHOMEY
NIGER
Niamey
CHAD
Lake Chad
Ft. Lamy
18
19
Mongo
20
21
Melfi
Maroua
AmTiman
Birao
31
32
33
34
35
22
Ft. Archambault
26
27
N'Dele
28
29
30
Ft. Crampel
Garoua
23
24
25
Ngaoundere
Obo
36
CENTRAL AFRICA
37.
Bossangoa
CAMEROONS
Ouesso
41
38
N'Djolé
40
Makoua
GABON
39
Sette Cama
Mouila
Ndende
42
43
44
CONGO
Brazzaville

36 Zemango GR (1925, 1940) 3,668 sq. miles.

Sub-prefecture Obo. Airport: Obo. Best visiting period Jan.–July. Elephant, giraffe, Cape buffalo, Derby eland and various other large antelope. Lion, leopard.

37 Nana-Barya GR (1935) 850 sq. miles.

Sub-prefecture Bossangoa. Airport: Bossangoa, 94-mile-road from there. Accommodation: Bossangoa. Best visiting period Jan.–July. Elephant, black rhinoceros, Cape buffalo, Derby eland and other large antelope. Lion, leopard.

Gabon Republic

Administration: Direction des Eaux et Forêts, Section Pisciculture, Chasse Pêche, Libreville.

38 Petit Banbam GR (1956) 174 sq. miles.

Some 19 miles from the Atlantic coast at 0° 3′ south and 9° 3′ east, in an almost uninhabited region. Low hills, wooded in the W, savannas in the E. Elephant, antelope, sitatunga, Cape buffalo (numerous), leopard, gorilla, chimpanzee. Accessible by light aircraft from Libreville (30 mins.).

39 Petit Loango NP (1956) 193 sq. miles.

On the Atlantic coast between 2° south and 9° 3′ east. Accessible by boat from Sette Cama. Woods, savannas, lagoons. Elephant, hippopotamus, Cape buffalo, sitatunga, various monkeys and water birds.

40 Okanda NP and Ofoué GR (1946) 174 sq. miles.

In the central plain of Gabon, s of Ogooué between N'Djolé and Booué, 0° 3′ south and 11° 3′ east. Woods, savannas on the boundary. Elephant, Cape buffalo, gorilla, chimpanzee. Difficult of access.

42 Nyanga Nord GR (1956) 70 sq. miles.

19 miles se of Mont Fouari GR. Situated half on territory of the Republic of the Congo (Brazzaville). Reached by the Dolisie–Mouila road. Mountainous, wooded territory. Animals as in the Mt. Fouari GR.

43 Mont-Fouari GR.

A fifth of its area is in Gabon, the rest in the Republic of the Congo. Road from Ndéndé (Gabon). See Republic of the Congo.

Republic of the Congo (Brazzaville)

Administration: Service des Eaux et des Forêts de la Rep. du Congo, Pointe-Noire, B.P. 143.

41 Odzala NP 1940) 425 sq. miles.

Between 0° 35′ and 1° 05′ north and 14° 40′ and 15° 05′ east. About 88 miles sw of Ouesso. Airport: Makoua (route Brazzaville–Makoua–Ouesso–Bangoui), 70-mile-road from there to the NP. Visits only with full safari equipment. Best visiting period 15th

June–15th Aug. Secondary forests, savannas. Elephant, hippopotamus (numerous), Cape buffalo, various small antelope, gorilla.

44 Mont-Fouari GR (1956) 695 sq. miles.

Surrounded by 166 sq. miles of partially protected land, between 3° south and 11° 3' east. 125 miles from Dolisie (on the road to Mouila, Gabon). Camp with 3 bungalows (12 persons). Savannas, Mount Fouari, which is wooded. Elephant, Cape buffalo, waterbuck, reedbuck and antelope.

Ethiopia

45 Managasha NP (1958) 12 sq. miles.

In the hills w of Addis Ababa. Administered by the Forestry and Hunting Department of the Ministry of Agriculture. Primarily game protection area.

Congo Republic (Leopoldville)

46 Garamba NP (1938) 1,900 sq. miles.

In the NE, on the Sudan border. Air connection. Stanleyville–Bunia. Vast grassy and wooded savannas, somewhat hilly, broken up by shallow valleys. Elephant, hippopotamus, square-lipped hippopotamus (some 1,000 head, 1959!), giraffe, Cape buffalo. May be visited only with special permission.

52 Albert NP (1929) 3,124 sq. miles.

In the E of the country, bordering on Uganda. Reached via Stanleyville as far as Goma airport, then bus to Rwindi Camp. Or Bunia airport in the N. Or via Entebbe–Kasese airport (Uganda). Accommodation: Rwindi Camp in the S, Ishango-Kasindi Camp in the N.

The NP extends from Lake Kivu and the Virunga volcanoes in the S across the plains w of Lake Edward as far as the glacier-capped Ruwenzori Mountains in the N. Vegetation of extreme diversity. Altitudes between 2,300 and 16,600 ft. Elephant, hippopotamus, Cape buffalo, various antelope, gorilla, lion.

58 Kagera NP (1934) 970 sq. miles.

NE of Usumbura, on the border of Ruanda. Approached via Stanleyville to Goma airport, road from there to Gabiro. Tourist hotel in Gabiro. Hilly landscape, broken up by swampy plains near the winding Kagera River. Numerous species of antelope, zebra.

78 Upemba NP (1939) 4,528 sq. miles.

In the centre of Katanga, some 190 miles n of Elisabethville. Airport: Elisabethville. Landscape full of contrasts, with the high Kibara Mountains, the Kamolondo trough with large lakes and broad plains. Elephant, Cape buffalo, zebra, antelope, numerous water birds. May be visited only with special permission.

Uganda

Administration of the NP: Trustees of the National Parks of Uganda, Entebbe. Information: East Africa Tourist Travel Association, P.O. Box 2013, Nairobi, Kenya.

45
Addis Ababa

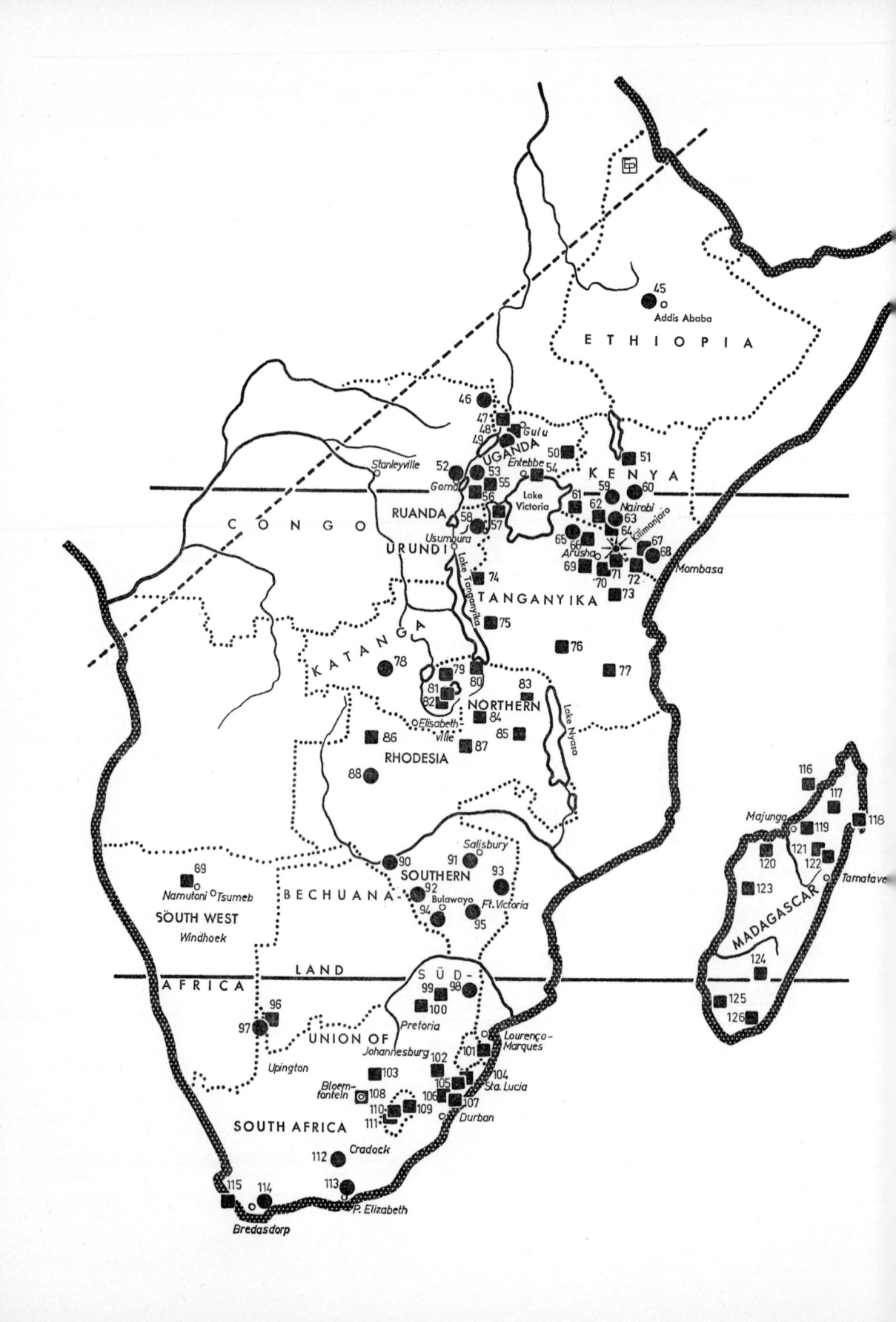

ETHIOPIA

46
47
48 Gulu
49
UGANDA 50
Stanleyville 52 53 Entebbe 54 51
55 KENYA
56 59 60
Goma 58 57 Lake 61 Nairobi
RUANDA Victoria 62
URUNDI 63 Kilimanjaro
Usumbura 64 65 66 67
Arusha 68 Mombasa
69 71 72
CONGO 74 70 73
TANGANYIKA
75
76
KATANGA 78 77
79
81 80 83
82 84
Elisabeth- NORTHERN
ville 85
86 87
RHODESIA Lake Nyasa
88
116
117
Majunga 119 118
Salisbury 120 121
90 91 122 Tamatave
SOUTHERN 123
89 92 93
Namutoni Tsumeb Bulawayo Ft.Victoria MADAGASCAR
SOUTH WEST 94 95
Windhoek BECHUANA- 124
96 SÜD- LAND 125
99 98 126
97 100
UNION OF Pretoria
Johannesburg 102 101 Lourenço-
Upington 103 Marques
Bloem- 104
fontein 108 105 Sta. Lucia
110 106 107
109 Durban
SOUTH AFRICA 111
112 Cradock
115 114 113
Bredasdorp P. Elizabeth

Administration of the GR: Game and Fisheries Department, Ministry of Natural Resources, Entebbe.
The natives have certain hunting concessions in the GR.

47 Square-lipped or 'white' rhinoceros reserve, west bank of the Nile, 250 sq. miles.

48 Aswa Lohin GR (1959) 39 sq. miles.
In NW Uganda, bordering on the Murchison NP. Dry wooded savannas. Elephant, Cape buffalo, hartebeest and smaller forms of antelope.

49 Murchison Waterfalls NP (1952) 1,505 sq. miles.
NW Uganda, on the NE bank of Lake Albert. Approached via Entebbe to Gulu airport. Accommodation: Paraa Safari Lodge. Grass plains. The park contains the famous M. Falls of the Victoria-Nile. Large numbers of hippopotami and crocodile in the river. Elephant, black rhinoceros, Cape buffalo, giraffe, several species of antelope, lion, leopard. Extensive poaching.
Elephant protection area near Acholi, 1,352 sq. miles.
Bugungu hippopotamus and elephant protection area, 183 sq. miles.

50 Debastian GR (1958) 772 sq. miles.
28 miles w of the frontier with Kenya. Considerable herds of various big game, Cape buffalo, lion, leopard. To prevent excessive grazing a limited number of hunting licences are issued. The natives have grazing rights in the GR.

53 Queen Elizabeth NP (1952) 772 sq. miles.
250 miles w of Kampala. Access: from Entebbe to Kasese by air, then by road connections. Accommodation: Mweya Safari Lodge (bungalows). The NP includes the Kazinga Channel, which connects Lake Edward with Lake George. It adjoins the Albert NP in the Congo. Tropical jungle, old volcanic terrain, swamps, grassy plains. Elephant, hippopotamus, Cape buffalo, various species of antelope, lion, leopard; water fowl. Extensive poaching.

54 Entebbe game and bird sanctuary, by Lake Victoria, 194 sq. miles.

55 Toro GR (1946) 202 sq. miles.
In SW Uganda. Savannas and swamps. Elephant, hippopotamus, buffalo, lion, leopard.

56 Kigezi GR (1952) 200 sq. miles.
In SW Uganda. Grassy plains and wet tropical forests. The GR serves as a buffer zone between the Queen Elizabeth NP and the densely populated areas to the s.
Kigezi gorilla sanctuary, SW Uganda, 17 sq. miles.

Kenya

The protected areas in Kenya are administered by the 'Trustees of the Royal National Parks of Kenya', P.O. Box 2076, Nairobi. Information concerning wild animals is also given by the East African Wild Life Society, P.O. Box 20 110, Nairobi. The authorities in charge of the protected areas are often unable, owing to current shortages of money and staff, to give satisfactory protection to the districts in their care. There is room for considerable improvement, too, in the accommodation available for visitors. The complete preservation of the animal world and its natural habitat is the principal intention of the national parks, which are under the jurisdiction of the park authorities. With the exception of the Nairobi NP the parks contain no human settlements apart from the accommodation of the park staff. 'National Reserves' (NR) are a combination of woodland and wild game preservation areas, in which hunting is forbidden. However, the natives, as owners or long-standing users of the land, have many rights which frequently run counter to the demands of complete protection of animal life.

51 Marsabit NR (1948) 10,615 sq. miles.

In N Kenya, 125–250 miles n of Nairobi. Two roads from Nairobi. Accommodation: Uaso Nyiro Lodge on the river of the same name, and Marsabit Forest Lodge. Semi-desert with thorn bushes, crossed by the Matthews and Ndotos Mountains. In the extreme NE the desert gives place to the volcanic Marsabit Mountains. Altitude of the NR 1,980–8,000 ft. Part of the E bank of Lake Rudolf belongs to the reserve. Abundant big game, including giraffe, black rhinoceros, Grévy zebra, Cape buffalo, kudu, ostrich. Natives tribes have grazing rights. Continual struggle for the best pastureland.

59 Aberdare NP (1950) 228 sq. miles.

SW Kenya. High mountain area with dense woods, bamboo thickets, moors. Elephant (numerous), black rhinoceros, Cape buffalo, bushbuck, bongo. The parkland is surrounded by numerous settlements. A main road crosses the Aberdare Mountains in a N-S direction by a pass at 11,550 ft. Branch roads lead off from this main road.

60 Mount Kenya NP 228 sq. miles.

Area around Mt. Kenya (17,100 ft.), which lies on the equator. Many mountain lakes, glaciers, moraines, high-lying moors. Many rare kinds of mountain plant, numerous species of birds and small animals. No big game. The boundary of the park is at an altitude of nearly 11,000 ft. Accessible only on foot or on horseback.

61 Mara NR (1950) 252 sq. miles.

On the SW frontier of Kenya. One of the most impressive jungle landscapes in Africa. Broad, open grassy plains, bordered on the W by a ridge of hills, furrowed by many rivers. Large numbers of numerous species of big game. Masai territory; constant competition between their herds of cattle and the wild animals. Tsetse area! Accessible only by a genuine safari.

62 Ngong NR (1950) 464 sq. miles.

A road crosses the Ngong Mountains. No accommodation for visitors. Adjoins the Nairobi NP, whose herds of animals wander constantly to and fro between the park and the reserve. Grassy plains with acacia woods, the Ngong Mountains to the W. Altitude 4,950–7,930 ft. Part of the NR is in the Great Rift Valley, sinking to 2,500 ft.

63 Nairobi NP (1946) 44 sq. miles.

Situated only 6 miles from the city of Nairobi. Closed April, May, 1st Nov. until 15th Dec., every night. No night-time accommodation in park, but hotels of all kinds in Nairobi (airport). Guides. Illustrated handbook (106,787 visitors during 1958). Largely grassy plains and wooded savannas (acacia), more densely wooded in W, deep river valleys in E. High ground rising to between 5,300 and 6,650 ft. Nine Somali families live in the park. Giraffe, zebra, impala, gnu, hartebeest, Grant and Thomson gazelle, black rhinoceros, lion.

64 Amboseli NR (1948) 87 sq. miles.

S of Nairobi, on the border with Tanganyika. Two roads from Nairobi airport to the NR. Accommodation for 40 persons in Ol Tukai Lodge. Near Kilimanjaro, the highest mountain in Africa (19,340 ft.). Altitude of the NR 3,980 ft. The extremely dry country (volcanic ash) is broken up by a few swamps and springs, where herds of wild animals assemble. Acacia woods. Many species of large African animals. The land belongs to the Masai.

67 West-Chyulu NR (1948) 145 sq. miles.

Closed to visitors at present. S Kenya, bordered on the W by Tsavo NP. The westerly Chyulu Mountains are of comparatively recent volcanic origin. Particularly impressive landscape. No surface water, but heavy falls during the rainy season. Numbers of wild animals not particularly large.

68 Tsavo NP (1948) 7,720 sq. miles.

In SE Kenya, nw of Mombasa. Main road from Mombasa. Some 500 miles of roads in park. Accommodation in park: Kitani Lodge, Aruba Lodge. Park closed: April, May, November, December. Considerable losses through poaching. Semi-arid bush with two main rivers. Altitude 1,980–6,950 ft., in the W sector a volcanic area with the famous Mzima Springs. Many kinds of euphorbia, acacia trees. Largest numbers of wild animals in Kenya, especially elephant, black rhinoceros, hippopotamus, Cape buffalo, many kinds of antelope, lion.

Tanganyika

Administration of the NP: Trustees of Tanganyika National Parks, Dar-es-Salaam. Information for tourists: East Africa Tourist Travel Association, P.O. Box 2013, Nairobi, Kenya.

65 Serengeti NP (1940, 1959), 4,825 sq. miles.

N Tanganyika. Accessible by car or plane from Nairobi. Accommodation: Seronera Safari Lodge and Ngorongoro Safari Lodge. Savannas with acacia woods, bush. Rocky high ground, altitude 3,640–7,250 ft. Largest herds of wild animals still existing anywhere in Africa. According to the calculations of Dr. B. Grzimek and his son Michael Grzimek they total some 370,000 head. Elephant, giraffe, roan, oryx beisa, eland, topi, Thomson gazelle, impala, gnu, waterbuck, hartebeest, black rhinoceros, Cape buffalo, zebra, ostrich, lion, leopard, cheetah. The Grzimeks ascertained that at least a large part of the herds leave the park territory for lengthy periods during their annual wanderings, and are then hunted. There is also poaching in the park itself. For further information concerning this unique territory and its problems see the book by Dr. Grzimek, *Serengeti Shall Not Die*, Hamish Hamilton, London, 1960.

66 Ngorongoro Crater (1959) 2,510 sq. miles.

NE Tanganyika, adjoining the Serengeti NP. Access and accommodation: see Serengeti NP. Guides and vehicles available. High-lying floor of a vast crater, which rises to some 10,000 ft. above the surrounding countryside. Varied terrain: dry grassland, thorn bush, rain woods on the crater slopes, bamboo thicket, moors. Large animals on the crater floor as in Serengeti NP. In the higher-lying parts elephant, mountain reedbuck, black rhinoceros, leopard, numerous species of mountain birds. The Masai have grazing rights in the plains.

69 Lake Manyara NP (1961) 374 sq. miles.

Can be reached by car. Hotel (built 1961). Area between the western wall of the Great Rift Valley (5,950 ft.) and Lake Manyara (2,980 ft.), half of which lies within the NP. Three streams feeding the lake flow through the NP. Swamps, gallery forests, acacia woods, grass and salt plains, soda flats near the lakeside. Elephant, hippopotamus, black rhinoceros, Cape buffalo (often in large herds), zebra, oryx, Thomson and Grant gazelle, impala, waterbuck, Bohor's reedbuck, white-bearded gnu, lion, leopard. Thousands of water and swamp birds of many kinds, large numbers of pelicans and flamingos.

Game Reserves (GR)

The Tanganyikan game reserves, in which hunting is prohibited, are administered by the Game Department, Ministry of Natural Resources, Dar-es-Salaam. A permit is required to visit most of the reserves. Adequate experience, equipment and guide are necessary. No accommodation for tourists.

57 Nyamirembe GR (1959) 452 sq. miles.

On the W shore of Lake Victoria. Can be reached by car. Densely wooded hills, with rocky escarpments rising to 3,650 and even 5,000 ft. Sable antelope, reedbuck, Sharpe's steenbok, hartebeest, hippopotamus, crocodile, many kinds of water fowl. Tsetse area! Uninhabited.

70 Mount Meru GR (1951, a protected area even under German rule) 100 sq. miles.

32 miles w of Kilimanjaro. A motor road, footpaths. Higher reaches of Mt. Meru from 5,450 ft. to its summit (15,050 ft.). Rain forest, bamboo, heathland, craters. Elephant, black rhinoceros, Cape buffalo, colobus monkey, bushbuck, mountain birds.

71 Kilimanjaro GR (1951, a protected area even under German rule) 733 sq. miles.

NE Tanganyika. Can be reached by car. Five shelter huts for mountaineers. The GR covers the upper reaches of Kilimanjaro, from 5,950 ft. to the summit (19,340 ft.). Rain forests, moors, tundra, permanent snow and ice. Elephant, black rhinoceros, Cape buffalo, eland, Abbott's duiker, colobus monkey, leopard, many species of birds.

72 Mkomazi GR (1951) 1,352 sq. miles.

In NE Tanganyika. Adjoins, on N, the Tsavo NP in Kenya. Can be reached by car. Lodging house. Very dry area 600–5,450 ft. above sea-level, with isolated mountains rising about 2,000 ft., broad plains. Thorn bush with semi-desert vegetation. Elephant, black rhinoceros, Cape buffalo, oryx, lesser kudu, gazelle, lion, leopard.

73 Tarangire GR (1957) 540 sq. miles.

In NE Tanganyika. Thorn bush. Elephant, black rhinoceros, black-tailed gnu, impala, waterbuck, oryx, Coke's hartebeest, eland, lesser kudu, zebra, ecological research station.

74 Gombe Stream GR (1945) 69 sq. miles.

On the shore of Lake Tanganyika s of the border with Ruanda-Urundi. Reached by motorboat, mountain paths. Narrow strip of steep, wooded mountain land, rising to between 2,300 and 4,960 ft. above the lake. Gallery woods by the numerous rivers. Chimpanzee, red colobus monkey, Cape buffalo, waterbuck, leopard.

75 Katavi Plain GR (1951) 733 sq. miles.

In SW Tanganyika, 38 miles e of Lake Tanganyika. Reached by car. Woodland, thorn bush, grassy plains, lakes. Large herds of Cape buffalo, elephant, hippopotamus, reedbuck, eland, roan antelope, topi, lion, leopard. The International Red Locust Control Service has two permanent camps in the area.

76 Rungwa River GR (1951) 7,720 sq. miles.

In the S of central Tanganyika. Wooded hills with some rocky peaks. Swampy valleys. Elephant, sable and roan antelope, greater kudu, Cape buffalo. There is a road leading to a village in the heart of the GR, beside the River Rungwa. Tsetse area!

77 Selous GR (1951, a protected area even under German rule) 11,585 sq. miles.

In the S of central Tanganyika. Area in which the three source streams of the River Rufiji unite. Grassy plains, woods, waterside thickets. Elephant (numerous), hippopotamus (numerous), Cape buffalo, Nyasa black-tailed gnu, Lichtenstein's hartebeest, sable antelope, greater kudu, eland, lion, leopard.

Northern Rhodesia

88 Kafue NP (1950) 8,610 sq. miles.

In the S of Northern Rhodesia. The park staff (52 persons) come under the Department for Hunting and Fishing. Accessible by road or air. Over 500 miles of roads in the park. Accommodation and service available. Especial facilities for foreign scientists. Introductory talks for visitors in Ngoma Camp. Park open mid-June—beginning of November. In the N part woodland, broken up by large expanses of grass, Kalahari Plains in the S. The River Kafue flows through the park for 100 miles. All but 200 of the natives have been moved away. Especially rich in antelope, including sable, eland, roan antelope, wildebeest, gnu, kudu, impala, lechwe (200), bushbuck, reedbuck, puku, waterbuck, duiker, klipspringer, sitatunga, elephant, hippopotamus, black rhinoceros. Cape buffalo, warthog, zebra, lion, leopard.

Game Reserves (GR)

The game reserves come under the Department for Hunting and Fishing. The aim of the authorities in these reserves is the protection of all animals, the prevention of poaching, illegal wood-cutting and bush fires.

79 Mweru Marsh GR (1942) 1,210 sq. miles.

N Northern Rhodesia, near the Congo border. The E boundary follows a ridge of hills, at whose foot lie two lakes. To the W of Lake Mweru Wantipa there extends swampland, with rushes and papyrus, merging slowly into the dry grassland in the W. The plain is surrounded by sparse woods. Elephant (1,160 head, 1960), Cape buffalo, hippopotamus, zebra, wildebeest, roan, sable and eland antelope, reedbuck, bushbuck, marsh antelope, grysbok, sitatunga, duiker (two species), wild boar, black rhinoceros (few), lion, leopard. Extensive poaching. The dry grassy plains w of the swamp area are a principal breeding ground of the red locust.

80 Sumbu GR (1942) 818 sq. miles.

On the S coast of Lake Tanganyika. Reached most easily by boat from the lake. Limited accommodation. The ground rises steeply from the rocky shore to a bush-covered chain of hills. Two small grassy plains in the interior. Elephant, hippopotamus, Cape buffalo, eland, roan, sable and marsh antelope, wildebeest, bushbuck, blue duiker, klipspringer, grysbok, warthog, zebra, lion, leopard, hyena. Extensive poaching.

81 Lusenga Plain GR (1942) 340 sq. miles.

NE Northern Rhodesia. On the left bank of the River Kalungwishi: an area of woods and savannas. Elephant, Cape buffalo, roan, eland, sable antelope, wildebeest, waterbuck, reedbuck, klipspringer, duiker (3 varieties), warthog, zebra.

82 Isangano GR (1957) 325 sq. miles.

On the E edge of the Bangweulu inundation area. Woodland in the N and E sectors, grassy plains in the S. Several permanent rivers. Black lechwe antelope, roan antelope, eland, gnu, duiker, oribi, elephant, Cape buffalo, warthog, lion. Extensive ravages by poachers.

83 Luangwa Valley GR (1942). S section, 3,205 sq. miles, on both banks of the River Luangwa; N section, 1,792 sq. miles, on the W bank.

In the NE of Northern Rhodesia. Can be reached by car. 200 miles of roads in the reserve. Several camps for visitors. Open 15th June–30th Oct. (Closed during the rainy period). Flat valley floor on the W bank, bordered on the W by the Muchinga hills, on the E of the river hilly land. Acacia woods. The swiftly-running river often alters its course. The old channels are devoid of water during the dry season, but when the rains come the whole valley is flooded to a distance of several miles from the river. Elephant (some 2,800 head), waterbuck, sitatunga, roan antelope, eland, kudu, bushbuck, impala, Cape buffalo, Thorniecroft's giraffe (200–250), zebra, hippopotamus, lion, leopard, wildebeest and duiker on the lower reaches of the mountains. Rare: sable antelope, reedbuck, oribi, cheetah. Black rhinoceros (300 in 1958!). During the dry season large numbers of animals, in search of water, wander outside the reserve, and are hunted.

84 Lavushi Manda GR (1941) 580 sq. miles.

In the SE of the Bangweulu swamps. Sparse woods, with low, generally bare hills in the E. The River Lukulu runs through the GR, dividing it in two. Elephant, Cape buffalo, wildebeest, roan, sable antelope, waterbuck, marsh antelope, reedbuck, bushbuck, duiker, grysbok, warthog, lion, leopard. Serious poaching and bush fires.

85 Lukusuzi GR (1942) 1,050 sq. miles.

NE Northern Rhodesia, at the entrance to the Luangwa Valley. Wooded. Primarily an elephant sanctuary. In addition good stocks of all other wild animals native to the country, including black rhinoceros and gnu. The elephants pass to and fro in considerable numbers between this GR and the Luangwa Valley GR, as well as the game reserve lying beyond the border in Nyasaland. Extensive poaching. Serious losses caused to the herds of wild animals through anti-tsetse measures, and the re-entry of native settlers.

86 Lunga GR (1951) 650 sq. miles.

SW Northern Rhodesia, between the Rivers Kabompo and W-Lunga. Woods in the N and S. Two small grassy plains. Elephant, hippopotamus, Cape buffalo, eland, roan, sable and lechwe, gnu, waterbuck, reedbuck, impala, klipspringer, sitatunga, various kinds of duiker, bushbuck, zebra, warthog, wild boar, lion, leopard, cheetah. Facilities for visitors if they give prior notice of their visit.

87 Kasanka GR (1941) 151 sq. miles.

To the s of the Bangweulu swamps. The heart of the GR is a vast swamp of papyrus and reeds which stretches from the point where the Rivers Musola and Kasanka join, along the latter to the River Mlembo. On the banks of the numerous rivers flowing towards the swamp area there are large expanses of grass, and woods on higher ground. Sitatunga in the swamps! Elephant, gnu, eland, reedbuck, marsh antelope, waterbuck, sable and roan antelope, several kinds of duiker, Sharpe's grysbok, warthog, zebra, hippopotamus, Cape buffalo, lion, leopard. Not for general visiting, but provision is made for individuals who are especially interested and give prior notice of their arrival.

Southern Rhodesia

The park authorities come under the control of the Secretary of State for the Interior.

90 Victoria Falls NP (1931, 1952) 204 sq. miles.

NW Southern Rhodesia. Road, rail and air connections. Camping. Accommodation and service. Near the Victoria Falls on the Zambezi, 7 miles above Livingstone. The 5,620-ft.-wide river plunges down 365 ft. into a gorge which is only 100 ft. wide, running at right-angles to the previous course of the river. The NP extends 38 miles upstream along the S bank of the Zambezi. Jungle along the river bank gives place to damp forest, which owes its extraordinary density to the spray it receives constantly from the falls. Elephant, kudu, sable antelope, roan antelope, eland, bushbuck, waterbuck, reedbuck, duiker, Cape buffalo, hippopotamus, warthog, crocodile. More than 220 kinds of birds. Electric cat-fish (Malapterurus electricus) in the river.

91 Robert McIlwaine NP (1952) 60 sq. miles.

19 miles sw of Salisbury. Near Lake McIlwaine (9 sq. miles, rich in fish). Hilly bush savannas. Ancient pictures on rocks. Sable antelope, kudu, waterbuck, gnu, reedbuck, duiker, grysbok, wild boar, warthog, baboon, long-tailed monkey, leopard, crocodile. More than 250 species of birds. Arboretum containing trees of over 200 named species.

92 Wankie NP (1928, 1949) 5,058 sq. miles.

Nw of Bulawayo. Can be reached by bus and car. Accommodation and service. Observation platforms at the Nyamandhlovu Cauldron. Park opens June–Nov. Wooded district, and large stretches of the Kalahari plains. More than 50 species of wild animal and many different birds.

93 Rhodes Inyanga NP (1950) 131 sq. miles.

On the E border of Southern Rhodesia. Accessible by bus or car. Accommodation and service for visitors in the park. Mountains up to 9,250 ft. in the E and centre of the park, plains in the W and SW. Several rivers with lovely waterfalls. Most of the hills are grass-covered. Small evergreen woods. Tree ferns. Mount Inyanga (9,380 ft.) the highest peak in Southern Rhodesia. Kudu, waterbuck, reedbuck, grey duiker, wild boar, hyena, striped jackal, banded mongoose, aardwolf, baboon, leopard. Numerous kinds of bird.

94 Matopos NP (1953) 383 sq. miles.

31 miles s of Bulawayo. Accessible by bus or car. Accommodation and service in the park. Parts of the granite Matopos Mountains, wooded in places, large flat wooded savannas. Caves containing rock pictures dating from the middle Stone Age. Orchids. Five large and many smaller lakes. Giraffe, eland, gnu, sable antelope, impala, kudu, klipspringer, giant shrew, baboon, leopard. Numerous kinds of bird.

95 Mushandike NP (1954) 51 sq. miles.

19 miles from Fort Victoria, from where it can be reached by road. Accommodation and service. Near Mushandike reservoir. Densely wooded hills. Sable antelope, kudu waterbuck, reedbuck, duiker, grysbok, klipspringer, leopard.

South West Africa

89 Etosha Pan NC 26,000 sq. miles (more than half the area of England!).

In the N of the country. Approach: from Windhoek via Tsumeb airport. 400 miles of roads in the protected area. Two camps, one of which (Namutoni) was formerly a German fort. Vast level bush savannas surrounding the salt pan (1,390 sq. miles) itself. Enormous herds of springbok, black-tailed gnu and zebra. Large numbers of elephants. Thousands of flamingos. Smaller herds of oryx. Lions.

Bechuanaland

96 GR area in the SW of the country (Kgalagadi district), bordering on the Gemsbok NP in the Union of South Africa. Wooded savannas, semi-desert. Game wardens will act as guides.

Union of South Africa

The five NPs under the control of the Union Government are administered by the National Parks Board of the Union of South Africa, P.O. Box 787, Pretoria.

97 Kalahari Gemsbok NP (1931) 3,585 sq. miles.

In the NW of Cape Province, 206 miles n of Upington. Kalahari semi-desert. Large dunes of red sand, maximum annual rainfall only about 5 inches! Acacias, thorn bush. A small family of genuine bushmen live in the park. Gemsbok (several thousand head), springbok (1,000–1,500), gnu, hartebeest, eland, ostrich, lion, serval, caracal, brown and spotted hyena. Honey badger, wild boar, etc. Numerous kinds of bird, including the secretary bird. Access: Johannesburg–Kimberley–Upington (airport). Accommodation: bungalow camp 'Twee Rivieren' at the entrance to the park from South Africa, Mata-Mata at the entrance from SW Africa. Make reservations in good time through:

The Warden of the Kalahari Gemsbok NP, P.O. Askham via Upington. Park open all the year round, December and January extremely hot! The NP is adjoined by a protected area of 425 sq. miles in the Bechuanaland Protectorate.

98 Kruger NP (1892, 1936) 7,908 sq. miles.

In NE Transvaal, on the border with Mozambique. Bounded in the S and N by the Crocodile and Levubu Rivers, in the E by the Lebombo Mountains. This vast protected area covers about a fiftieth part of the total territory of the Union of South Africa. Approach: Johannesburg–Lourenço Marques (Mozambique). Rail links from all ports and towns of South Africa via Johannesburg–Pretoria to Nelspruit. Hire cars from there. There are, however, no cars to be hired at the stations along the railway line Crocodile Bridge–Skukuza, which runs through the park. Excellent road connections. Accommodation: 14 camps with bungalows of various sizes, tents, some restaurants and shops. Camping places: Malelane (S entrance), (150 persons), Crocodile River Bridge (72 persons), Pretoriuskop (oldest camp in the NP, very well equipped), Lower Sable (250 persons), Skukuza (rail terminus, administrative centre), Nwanedzi, Orpen, Satara (250 persons), Olifants River, The Gorge, Letaba (400 persons), Malopene, Shingwidzi (250 persons), Punda Maria (120 persons). Good road web in the park. Open: 15th May–15th Oct. From the 15th Oct.–15th May only the area around Pretoriuskop and Skukuza is accessible. Accommodation to be reserved in good time through: The Director, National Parks Board, P.O. Box 787, Pretoria. Telegram address: Natpark, Pretoria. Magnificent illustrated handbook *Our National Parks*, obtainable from there. See the chapter of this book, 'The animals' kingdom: Kruger National Park', by T. V. Bulpin. According to the latest statistics the park contains about 100 species of mammals, 390 of birds, 77 of reptiles and 30 of amphibians.

112 Mountain Zebra NP (1937).

Cape Province, near Cradock. A mountainous district. For the preservation and breeding of the last Cape mountain zebras (now about 25 head). Also eland, blesbok, white-tailed gnu, mountain reedbuck, klipspringer, bush duiker, baboon, ostrich. NP closed to visitors.

113 Addo Elephant NP (1931) 26 sq. miles.

In the extreme S of Cape Province, between the Suur Mountains and the valley of Sonday River, 40 miles n of Port Elizabeth. Impenetrable thorn bush. 29 of the almost exterminated Addo elephants (Loxodonta a. africana) in a fenced cage of 10 sq. miles. 11 species of antelope, Cape buffalo. Visitors can watch the elephants by night from a special platform. Access: Harbour and airport at Port Elizabeth, road from there. Accommodation: good hotel a few miles from the park. Refreshments supplied in the park. See illustrated guidebook, *The Addo Elephants*, obtainable from the park administration in Pretoria (see above).

114 Bontebok NP (1959) 10 sq. miles.

In the extreme S of Cape Province. Rocky plateau, which sinks slowly to a sandy plain. Herd of 150 bontebok, a beautiful species of antelope which is now extinct apart from these and a few other specimens living on farms. Duiker, grysbok, grey reedbuck. Nearest town Bredasdorp. By rail or road from there. As yet no accommodation for visitors.

Provincial Sanctuaries

Cape Province

115 Cape of Good Hope NC (1939) 26 sq. miles.

At the southernmost tip of the Cape Peninsula. Savanna with rock fragments. Numerous kinds of animal.

Natal

Administration: The Natal Parks, Game and Fish Preservation Board.

101 Ndumu GR (1924, 1947) 38 sq. miles.

Thorn bush savannas, fig woods beside large lake. Hippopotamus, large number of crocodile. No accommodation available.

102 Mkuzi GR (1912) 96 sq. miles.

Thorn bush savannas, Fig woods. Black rhinoceros, impala. Accommodation.

104 St. Lucia GR and Park (1897, 1939) 184 sq. miles.

Lake St. Lucia and its surroundings. Three or four large herds of hippopotamus, many kinds of water fowl. Guided tours. Hutted accommodation.

105 Hluhluwe GR (1951) 88 sq. miles.

In Zululand, 188 miles n of Durban (airport), near St. Lucia. Almost all classes of animal native to Zululand, including square-lipped rhinoceros, black rhinoceros, kudu, impala, waterbuck, gnu, zebra, Cape buffalo. Camp huts in the park.

106 Umfolozi GR (1897) 112 sq. miles.

To the n of Durban (airport) near St. Lucia, approaching Mozambique. Undulating thorn bush savannas. Most important sanctuary for the square-lipped rhinoceros, 700 head! Also black rhinoceros. Guides. Accommodation: hotels in St. Lucia. Camp huts in Charter's Creek.

107 Richards Bay GR (1935) 3 sq. miles of water.

Lagoon. Mangrove thicket. Numerous water fowl.

109 Giant's Castle GR (1903, 1952) 92 sq. miles.

Grassy steppes on the higher reaches of the Drakensberg Mountains, including some peaks such as Giant's Castle (10,780 ft.). Numerous highland antelope, including eland, mountain reedbuck, leopard. Native guides are available.

110 Loteni NC (1953) 8 sq. miles.

High grassy slopes on the Drakensberg Mountains. Eland, mountain reedbuck, oribi, etc. Hutted accommodation.

111 Rugged Glen NC (1950) 3 sq. miles.

Grassy mountain slopes with small evergreen woods. Typical highland animal and plant life. White-tailed gnu (!).

Orange Free State

103 Willem Pretorius GR (1956) 203 sq. miles.

Bush savannas, wooded slopes of the Doorn Mountains. Allemanskraal reservoir. Blesbok, springbok, black-tailed gnu, hartebeest, eland, impala, zebra. Accommodation and service.

108 Franklyn GR (1928) ¾ sq. mile.

On the outskirts of Bloemfontein. Hill with bush savanna. Blesbok, springbok, eland, duiker, grysbok, zebra.

Transvaal

Administration: Nature Conservation Section of the Provincial Government.

99 Barberspan NC (1954) 13 sq. miles.

Bird sanctuary with research station on Lake Barberspan. Thousands of birds, including flamingo, pelican, winter home of migratory birds. Private quarters.

100 S. A. Lombard NC (1949) 14 sq. miles.

Blesbok, springbok, impala, wildebeest, grey duiker, Cape buffalo. Wild life research station.

Madagascar

The nature protection laws put into force by the French colonial administration on the 31st December, 1927, specified 10 protection areas, situated in the five climatic zones of the island. An extension of the laws in 1939 added an eleventh protection area.

116 Lokobé Sa 4 sq. miles.

On the island of Noss-Bé in the NW. Damp forest. Lemur macaco.

117 Tsaratanana Sa 229 sq. miles.

Contains the highest mountain on the island (9,515 ft.). Woods extensively damaged by fire. Lemur macaco, Galidia sp. and Cryptoprocta sp., green tree frogs, Acrantophis (giant snake).

118 Cape Masoala Sa 82 sq. miles.

Wooded mountains below 1,660 ft. Animal life as in Betampona Sa. In addition the lemurs Propithecus verreauxi coronatus and P. diadema candidus.

119 Ankarafantsika Sa 260 sq. miles.

On the NW coast, in the hinterland of Majunga. Woods whose foliage falls during the dry season, partly ravaged by fire. Coquerel's lemur (Propithecus verreauxi coquereli), glossy ibis.

120 Namoroka Sa 23 sq. miles.

Mountainous area with many caves. Decken's lemur (Propithecus verreauxi deckeni).

121 Zahamena Sa 256 sq. miles.

E of Lake Alaotra. Almost inaccessible, scarcely explored area with mist-enshrouded woods at 5,950 ft.

122 Betampona Sa 6 sq. miles.

Between Tamatave and the Bay of Antogil in the E. Low mountain chains with primeval forest. Indris, Lemur variegatus, Phaner furcifer, aye-aye, Hapalemur griseus.

123 Antsingy Sa 320 sq. miles.

A chalky area with innumerable caves and ravines. Decken's lemur. Strange Madagascan chameleon: Leandria perarmata, earth-dwelling. Blind troglodytic fish.

124 Andringitra Sa 116 sq. miles.

Mountain massif on the S plateau. Propithecus diadema holomelas, Lemur variegatus, L. mongoz and L. catta.

125 Tsimanampetsotsa Sa 68 sq. miles.

In the extreme S, along the salt lake of the same name. Semi-desert with dry bush, thorn woods, Chalk caves, in which are blind troglodytic fish Typhleotris madagascariensis. Numerous water birds, including flamingo. Tortoises: Testudo radiata and Pyxis arachnoides. Lemurs: Propithecus verreauxi, lepimur and catta.

126 Andohahela Sa 116 sq. miles.

Massif of the same name in the extreme SE. Interesting vegetation with elements of the damp E coast and of the semi-deserts in the S. Abundance of heather on the peaks. Eupleres goudoti.

In all 951,000 acres of Madagascan soil are under nature protection. This area could suffice for the preservation of the country's natural treasures. However, supervision is lacking. The lack of roads and usable paths, the absence of accommodation make effective guarding of the sanctuaries virtually impossible. On paper all appears to be well, but even in the days of the French administration robbery, fire-raising and illegal hunting could be kept sufficiently in check only on the densely populated central plateau. Above all the annual 'Tavy' of the natives, the burning of the woods, has a devastating effect almost everywhere. The colonial administration did not dare to punish whole villages as an example. Whether the new, native government will do so remains questionable. It is useless to talk to the natives, whose view of life is that of the Stone Age, coloured by superstition, about nature protection. To them the land is there to provide pasture for herds of zebu, and wild animals represent so much meat—unless they come under a tribal taboo, a 'fady'.

North America

Canada

Administration of the NPs: National Park Service, Ministry of Northern Affairs and National Resources, Ottawa.

4 Wood Buffalo NP (1922) 17,370 sq. miles.

Between Lake Athabasca and the Great Slave Lake in N of Alberta and the North West Territories. Can be reached in summer by river steamer from the terminus of the Waterways railway. Air link with Fort Smith. No accommodation facilities in the park. Vast GR with extensive forests and expanses of grass. Originally founded to preserve the last surviving herds of forest bison (Bison bison athabascae). In 1947 some 6,700 prairie bison (Bison bison bison) were taken to the area from the former Buffalo NP near Wainwright, and they have now largely inter-bred with the forest bison. Total stock 12–14,000 head (1960).

5 Jasper NP (1907) 4,170 sq. miles.

On the E side of the Canadian Rocky Mountains, on the border between Alberta and British Columbia. In the park is the town of Jasper, accessible by road and rail. Hotels. Camping. 625 miles of footpaths and bridle paths. Several ranges of high mountains divided by deep valleys. Highest peak Mount Columbia, 12,300 ft. Numerous glaciers, including Columbia Ice Field, 132 sq. miles! Coniferous forests. Abundant animal life.

7 Mount Revelstoke NP (1914) 100 sq. miles.

In the Selkirk Mountains, British Columbia. Accessible by main road or rail. Accommodation in the park or in the nearby town Revelstoke. High mountain plateau (6,000 ft.) with meadows and small lakes. Reindeer, white-tailed deer, grizzly, black bear. Flourishing bird life.

8 Glacier NP (1886) 521 sq. miles.

In the Selkirk Mountains of British Columbia, at present only accessible by rail via Calgary. From 1962 the Trans-Canada Motorway will run through the NP. Camping only, no hotels or accommodation houses. Glacier NP is bordered on the N by the Hamber Provincial Park, and is thus connected with the Jasper, Banff and Yoho NP. High mountain area with glaciers, lakes, dense coniferous forests, tundra. Snow goat, elk, wapiti, reindeer, white-tailed deer, grizzly, black bear. Many kinds of birds.

9 Yoho NP (1920) 500 sq. miles.

On the W slopes of the Rocky Mountains, British Columbia. Bordered on the E by Banff NP, on the S by Kootenay NP. Road connections. Park settlement Radium Hot Springs. Hotels, camping, road network, 250 miles of footpaths and bridle paths. Splendid high mountain landscape with a great many lakes, charming streams and waterfalls (the Takakkaw Falls have a drop of 2,000 ft.). Rich plant and animal life.

10 Elk Island NP (1913) 75 sq. miles.

Central Alberta, 44 miles e of Edmonton. Motorway, railway, camping. Hilly area with ash/poplar woods, numerous small lakes. Park fenced in. 700 prairie bison, 200 elk, 350 wapiti, white-tailed deer.

11 Banff NP (1887) 2,560 sq. miles.

On the E slopes of the Canadian Rocky Mountains (Livingstone Chain), along the border between the provinces of Alberta and British Columbia. Parts of the park border on Jasper NP and Yoho NP. Can be reached by road or rail: Calgary. Air link: Winnipeg–Edmonton and Calgary. Two settlements in the park: Banff (pop. 3,000) and Lake Louise (pop. 50). Numerous good hotels and camping places (more than a million visitors annually). Over 688 miles of bridle paths and footpaths. Parts of the park are famed winter sports centres (mountain railway, ski lifts, etc.). Two museums (Geology, plant and animal life, Indian culture). Open all the year round. High mountain area (up to nearly 12,000 ft.), numerous large glaciers, lakes, thermal springs, primeval forest. Snow goat, bighorn sheep, wapiti, elk, white-tailed deer, grizzly, black bear, puma; eagle.

12 Kootenay NP (1920) 540 sq. miles.

On the W slopes of the Rocky Mountains in the border area between Alberta and British Columbia. Main road Banff–Windermere runs through the park. Excellent accommodation. Impressive mountain scenery. Hot mineral springs. Abundant plant and animal life.

13 Prince Albert NP (1927) 1,505 sq. miles.

In central Saskatchewan. Can be reached by main road. Accommodation in park (Marlboro Hotel, Flamingo and Southsider Motels). Thousands of large and small lakes and streams amid coniferous and leafy woods. On an important migratory route for birds (water fowl)!

14 Waterton Lakes NP (1895) 205 sq. miles.

SW Alberta, on the U.S. frontier. Accommodation in park. Camping. N continuation of Glacier NP in the U.S.A. Wild area of high peaks with dense coniferous forests, rich plant and animal life.

18 Riding Mountain NP (1929) 1,160 sq. miles.

In western Manitoba. On main road. Camping. Accommodation in Wasagaming in the park. Wooded mountain area about 1,000 ft. high rises unexpectedly from the surrounding plains. A much-visited holiday area.

27 Cape Breton NP (1936) 367 sq. miles.

In the N of Cape Breton Island, which lies to the N of Nova Scotia, between the Atlantic and the Gulf of St. Lawrence. Rugged coastal mountains with coniferous forests. Fishing villages on the park boundaries. The Cabot Trail main road runs through the NP for more than 60 miles. Camping. 25 miles of footpaths. Open all the year round.

28 Prince Edward Island NP (1936) 7 sq. miles.

25-mile-long coastal strip on the N shore of the island of the same name in the Gulf of St. Lawrence. Accessible by road. Camping. Numerous small fur animals and birds.

29 Fundy NP (1948) 77 sq. miles.

New Brunswick, N bank of Fundy Bay. Accessible by road. Camping. Thickly wooded coastal mountains rising to 1,000 ft. Elk, white-tailed deer, black bear, numerous kinds of birds.

31 Point Pelee NP (1918) 6 sq. miles.

Peninsula in Lake Erie, Ontario, s of Detroit. Main road. Camping. 50 miles of bathing beach. Densely wooded in S, N area covered by ponds and swamps, used in spring and autumn by thousands of migratory birds as place of rest.

Provincial Parks

The following parks are virtually large game reserves.

Ontario

Administration: Parks Division, Province of Ontario, Department of Lands and Forests, Toronto.

ALASKA
1 Fairbanks
Anchorage
2
3
4 Ft. Smith
CANADA
5 Edmonton
6
7
8
9 Banff
10
11 Calgary
12 Windermere
13
14
15
16
17
18
19
20
21
22
23
24
25
26
27
28
29
30
31 Detroit
Port Angeles 32
Seattle
Tacoma
33
West Glacier 34
35
Gardiner
Red Lodge
36
37
Grant's Pass
Medford
Klamath Falls
Redding
40
Red Bluff
38 Wyoming
41 Salt Lake City
39 Buffalo Gap
Hot Springs
42 Denver
Marysvale
44
Durango 45
46 Ellsworth
47
43 Fresno
48
Visalia
Cedar City
49
50
54
53
USA
51 Cave City
Knoxville
52 Asheville
Phoenix
55
56 Tucson
Carlsbad 57
El Paso
Alpine 58
MEXICO
59 Miami
60 Monterey
61 S. Luis Potosi
62
Guzmán
63
Mexico
64
65
66
Vera Cruz
67 Puebla
68
69
77
71
74
76
72
75
GUATEMALA
70
73

19 Quetico P (1913) 1,838 sq. miles.

20 Oberer Lake P 533 sq. miles.

30 Algonquin P (1893) 2,708 sq. miles.
Hotels, camping.

Quebec

Administration: Parks Div., Department of Lands and Forests, Quebec.

23 Laurentides P (1895) 3,570 sq. miles.
Numerous lakes and streams. Elk, wolf, etc.

26 Gaspesian P (1937) 1,315 sq. miles.
On the Gaspé Peninsula, s of the St. Lawrence River, including the Shickshock Mountains with the 4,160-ft.-high Mt. Jacques Cartier. Principally reindeer Sa.

25 La Verendrye P (1939) 4,692 sq. miles.
Numerous lakes and streams. Accommodation.

Fish and game sanctuaries

Administration: Department of Game and Fisheries.

21 Mistassini Fish and GR (1953) 5,140 sq. miles.

22 Chibougamau Fish and GR (1946) 3,360 sq. miles.
80-mile-long stretch along both sides of the Montreal–Abitibi main road. Numerous lakes and streams. Abundant animal life.

24 Kipawa Lake Fish and GR (1950) 988 sq. miles.

Saskatchewan

6 Lac La Rouge P (1939) 1,126 sq. miles.
Area of lakes with spruce and poplar woods. Accommodation.

15 Cypress Hills P (1932) 17 sq. miles.
Pronghorn, wapiti and other game. Summer accommodation and motor camp.

16 Duck Mountain P (1932) 80 sq. miles.
Woods, lakes. Elk, wapiti.

17 Moose Mountain P (1932) 152 sq. miles.
Area of lakes with poplar and birch woods. Abundant animal life.

United States of America

In 1959 the U.S.A. possessed 29 national parks with a total area of some 20,845 sq. miles. 20 of these parks each have an area of more than 150 sq. miles.

In addition there were in 1959 83 so-called national monuments. This description is given to protected areas which are of especial prehistoric, historical or scientific importance. These 'monuments' are all smaller in area than national parks, but together they cover some 14,090 sq. miles—nearly twice the size of Wales. Some of these national monuments are also of great importance as regards the survival of particular species of animals.

Finally there were in the U.S.A. in 1960 280 game and bird sanctuaries with a total area of more than 44,000 sq. miles. They are not administered by the National Park Service but by the U.S. Fish and Wildlife Service, which comes under the Federal Government. In these sanctuaries either all or at least certain classes of animal are fully protected.

Nearly all national parks in the U.S.A. contain hotels, hutted accommodation, splendidly equipped camping sites, restaurants, public roads and transport, etc. The excellent road maps, which are to be had everywhere, show all parks and national monuments, so that the visitor travelling by car can choose whatever approach route appears to him to be most advantageous. Guidebooks, often very comprehensive, are published for the individual parks. These contain all worthwhile information, and copies are sent out by the administration of each park on request. The appropriate address is therefore always given as part of the data concerning the parks which follows.

Among the many classes of animals to be seen in the various parks only those of especial importance are listed here.

National Parks of the U.S.A.

1 Mount McKinley NP (1917) 3,030 sq. miles.

Alaska. Park administration: McKinley NP, Alaska. Rail links from Seward and Fairbanks direct to the park. Air link to the park. Open 10th June–15th September. Part of the Alaska Range, including the highest mountain in North America, the glacier-covered Mount McKinley (20,300 ft.). Other principal peaks: Mount Foracer (18,690 ft.), Mount Hunter (15,790 ft.). Numerous glaciers, including the 38-mile-long Muldrow Glacier. White pine woods on the higher mountain slopes, mixed woods of birch, poplar and willow in the valleys. Broad tundra expanses. Especially important Sa for the animal life of the north: 34 species of mammals and 112 of birds (80 of them breeding in the park). Reindeer (some 25,000 head), elk, white bighorn sheep (Dall), grizzly bear, wolf, wolverine, red lynx, snow owl.

32 Olympic NP (1938) 1,322 sq. miles.

Olympic Peninsula, NW State of Washington. Administration: Port Angeles, Washington. Transport from Edmonds, Washington and Victoria, British Columbia, to Port Angeles. Open all the year round. Mountainous district surrounding Mount Olympus, 8,260 ft. The W side of the mountain massif, falling towards the Pacific, has very heavy rainfall—on the coast some 145 inches, on the upper reaches about 260 inches per annum. On the other hand the E side of the massif is very dry. Great contrasts in vegetation: in the W great rain forests with abundant ferns, mosses, lichens. Numerous glaciers, wild mountain streams, lakes. Roosevelt elk (6,000 head), black-tailed deer, snow hare, beaver, mountain beaver, puma, black bear.

33 Mount Rainier NP (1899) 378 sq. miles.

State of Washington. Administration: Longmire, Washington. Railway stations: Tacoma, Seattle, Yakima. Best visiting period June–Sept. Part of the Cascade Range.

The principal peak in the park is Mount Rainier, 14,500 ft., a volcano which was last active in 1870, and which is covered by a vast blanket of ice consisting of 25 linked glaciers. Mountains and valleys in the vicinity covered with dense forests of Hemlock firs, Douglas firs, red cedar and white pine. 130 species of birds and 50 mammals, including snow goat, wapiti, black-tailed deer, snow hare, grey marmot, beaver, mountain beaver, black bear, coyote.

34 Glacier NP (1910) 1,582 sq. miles.

N Montana. Administration: West Glacier, Montana. Railway stations: West Glacier, East Glacier. Best visiting period: 15th June–15th Sept. During this period hotels and other accommodation are open in the park. The Waterton Lakes NP is adjacent, across the Canadian border. Splendid Rocky Mountain scenery with deep gorges, glaciers, lakes, primeval coniferous forests. Large stocks of game, including snow goat, brown bighorn sheep, elk, wapiti, mule deer, white-tailed deer, grizzly bear, black bear, fish marten, wolverine, red lynx, beaver.

35 Isle Royale NP (1940) 210 sq. miles.

The largest island in Lake Superior, Michigan. Administration: Houghton, Michigan. Reached by motorboat. Dense, mixed forest covers the island. Elk, coyote, snow hare, beaver, 200 kinds of birds.

36 Yellowstone NP (1872) 3,418 sq. miles.

NW Wyoming, Montana, Idaho. Administration: Yellowstone Park, Wyoming. Railway stations: Gardiner, Red Lodge, Montana; West Yellowstone, Idaho; Cody, Gallatin Gateway, Wyoming. Open: 20th June–12th Sept. Provided that the roads are free of snow restricted accommodation facilities also exist from the 15th May onward and until the 15th September. High-lying territory in the Rockies of spectacular beauty, volcanic in origin. Some 10,000 hot springs, about 3,000 geysers (the world's greatest geyser area)—some throw water up to 50 ft., water about 90° c. Numerous waterfalls (height up to 330 ft.) and lakes, including Lake Yellowstone, 140 sq. miles. Especially rich in wild life, including bison, elk, pronghorn, bighorn sheep, wapiti (several thousand), mule deer, grizzly bear, black bear. More than 200 kinds of birds, including white pelican, whooping swan.

37 Crater Lake NP (1902) 250 sq. miles.

S Oregon. Administration: Medford, Oregon. Airport: Medford; railway stations: Klamath Falls, Grant's Pass. Park open all the year round, May–Sept. recommended. The centrepoint of the park is a deep blue lake, some 20 sq. miles in area, in the crater of the extinct volcano Mazama. The lake has a circumference of 19 miles, and it is surrounded by wonderfully coloured rock walls 500 to 2,000 ft. high. The remainder of the park territory is mountainous, with coniferous forests. Abundant animal life, including black bear, black-tailed deer, beaver, golden eagle, osprey,

38 Grand Teton NP (1929, enlarged 1950) 482 sq. miles.

NW Wyoming. Administration: Moose, Wyoming. Airport: Jackson. Rail connections as to Yellowstone Park. Open 15th June–15th Sept. Mountain massif standing alone, with imposing high peaks, glaciers, lakes, moraines. Abundant wild life, in particular wapiti, elk, mule deer, bighorn sheep, beaver, grizzly bear, black bear, whooping swan.

39 Wind Cave NP (1903) 44 sq. miles.

S Dakota. Administration: Hot Springs, South Dakota. Railway stations: Hot Springs, Buffalo Gap, Pringle. Open all the year round. Immense limestone caverns in the Black Hills, only 10 miles so far explored. Park surface: prairie, Bison, pronghorn, wapiti, white-tailed deer, prairie dog, typical prairie birds.

40 Lassen Volcanic NP (1916) 124 sq. miles.

NE California. Administration: Mineral, California. Railway stations: Red Bluff, Redding. Open: summer, exact period dependent on the weather. Part of the Cascade Range. Surrounds the only still active volcano in the U.S.A., the 10,500-ft.-high Lassen Peak. Numerous cones of extinct volcanoes. Lakes, coniferous forests. Black-tailed and mule deer.

41 Zion NP (1919) 224 sq. miles.

S Utah. Administration: Springdale, Utah. Railway stations: Cedar City, Marysvale. Open all the year round. High plateau, scored by canyons more than 4,300 ft. deep and many miles long. The steep walls of the gorges demonstrate surprisingly bizarre rock formations in various colours. More than 150 species of birds. Mammals include bighorn sheep and puma.

42 Rocky Mountain NP (1915) 404 sq. miles.

Colorado. Administration: Estes Park, Colorado. Railway stations: Denver, Greeley, Granby. Open all the year round. A particularly magnificent part of the Rocky Mountains with 65 peaks over 10,000 ft., many with great glaciers, numerous lakes, vast virgin forests, extensive mountain pastures. Wapiti, mule deer, brown bighorn sheep, beaver (particularly numerous), great marmot, various kinds of squirrel, black bear, coyote, fish marten. Great numbers of birds.

43 Yosemite NP (1890) 1,186 sq. miles.

California. Administration: Yosemite National Park, California. Open all the year round, recommended June–Sept. The heart of the park, which lies in the Sierra Nevada, is the Yosemite Valley, formed by the Merced River running through it; it is up to a mile wide, with granite cliffs rising to 4,300 ft. Great waterfalls plunge down from the side walls, including the famous Yosemite Fall with a drop of some 2,250 ft. Giant sequoia trees in the woods. 200 species of birds and 78 of mammals, including mule deer, black bear.

44 Bryce Canyon NP (1928) 57 sq. miles.

S Utah. Administration: Springdale, Utah. Airport: Salt Lake City. Nearest stations: Cedar City, Marysvale. Park open all the year round, accommodation available 10th May–1st Nov. A vast, amphitheatre-shaped box eroded from a plateau by rain, frost and flowing water, leaving innumerable mighty stone pillars which glow yellow and orange. It is unique in the whole world. The remaining park territory consists of hills covered with coniferous forests. Puma, mule deer, numerous forms of lizard. Abundant bird life.

45 Mesa Verde NP (1906) 80 sq. miles.

SW Colorado. Administration: Mesa Verde NP, Colorado. Stations: Grand Junction, Montrose, Durango (Colorado), Gallup (New Mexico). Open: 15th May–15th Oct.

Large plateau, which rises some 2,300 ft. above the plain, furrowed by ravines, covered by dense coniferous forests. Remarkably well-preserved cliff dwellings of pre-history and the Pueblo India civilization. Mule deer, black bear, coyote. Bighorn sheep and wild turkey reintroduced into the area.

46 Acadia NP (1919) 42 sq. miles.

Maine. Administration: Bar Harbor. Station: Ellsworth. Park open all the year round, hotels only in summer. On Mount Desert and au Haut islands and Point Schoodic. Northerly offshoots of the Appalachians. Mixed woods on glacial mountains. Atlantic coast. Lakes and sea bays. Numerous kinds of water fowl. Beaver.

47 Shenandoah NP (1935) 302 sq. miles.

Virginia. Administration: Luray, Virginia. Open all the year round. Accommodation: 1st April–1st Nov. A section of the Blue Ridge, forming part of the Appalachian mountain system. Medium-sized mountains with mixed woods. White-tailed deer, numerous smaller mammals, abundant bird life.

48 Sequoia and King's Canyon NP (1890 and 1940 respectively), together 1,310 sq. miles.

California. Administration: Sequoia NP, Three Rivers, California. Stations: Fresno, Visalia. Open all the year round. The parks are joined. Magnificent high mountain scenery of the southern Sierra Nevada, formerly glacial, with fine valleys, numerous lakes. Large virgin stocks of giant sequoia trees, the largest trees on earth, accompanied by white pine, other pines, Douglas firs, Californian cedars. Bighorn sheep, mule deer, grey marmot, mountain beaver.

50 Grand Canyon NP (1919) 1,004 sq. miles.

N Arizona. Administration: Grand Canyon, Arizona. Station: Cedar City, Utah. Open all the year round, best visiting period 1st June–30th Sept. The heart of the park is a 89-mile-long stretch of the canyon which the Colorado River has carved out of the rock plateau. The canyon is 188 miles long in all, nearly a mile deep(!) and, towards the top, as much as 9 miles wide. Unique rock crags and pinnacles, subsidiary canyons, which glow red and yellow. On the floor of the canyon desert conditions exist, while on the higher levels, between 6,500 and 8,600 ft., there are coniferous woods. The flora and fauna are similarly differentiated. 60 species of mammal (including pronghorn, bighorn sheep, mule deer, puma, prairie wolf), 180 kinds of birds, 25 of reptiles.

51 Mammoth Cave NP (1941) 78 sq. miles.

SW Kentucky. Administration: Mammoth Cave, Kentucky. Station: Cave City. Open all the year round. Vast system of limestone caves, 150 miles explored, down to a depth of 400 ft. Stalagmites, stalactites, subterranean rivers, waterfalls, lakes. Numerous bats, blind troglodytic fish, eyeless crabs. Park above ground: wooded hills. Very rich in birds (170 species).

52 Great Smoky Mountains NP (1940) 720 sq. miles.

W North Carolina and E Tennessee. Administration: Catlinburg, Tennessee. Stations: Knoxville, Asheville. Open all the year round. Includes some of the highest points (up to about 6,600 ft.) in the eastern Appalachians. Last remnants of forests containing 130 species of trees, and particularly beautiful rhododendrons and azaleas. Since the district has enjoyed protection its wild life has increased, including white-tailed deer, black bear, wild cat.

57 Carlsbad Caverns NP (1930) 68 sq. miles.

SE New Mexico. Administration: Carlsbad, New Mexico. Airport: Carlsbad. Nearest stations: Carlsbad, El Paso. Accommodation: in White's City and Carlsbad, not in the park. Open all the year round. Largest and most remarkable labyrinth of limestone caves in the world. The explored section is 24 miles long, depth down to 1,485 ft.! Inhabited in summer by millions of bats (11 kinds). Surface: semi-desert with typical flora and fauna.

58 Big Bend NP (1944) 1,118 sq. miles.

Texas, on the Mexican border. Administration: Big Bend NP, Texas. Stations: Alpine and Marathon. Open all the year round, best visiting period May (cactus blooms!). Wild mountainous country with deep ravines; vast deserts with typical cactus and jucca vegetation. Typical desert fauna. In addition: pronghorn, mule deer, white-tailed deer, puma, black bear, beaver, peccary. Many classes of bird.

59 Everglades NP (1947) 2,300 sq. miles.

S Florida. Administration: Homestead, Florida. Airport and station: Miami. No accommodation in the park—overnight stay in Miami or Homestead. Park open all the year round. Viewed most conveniently by boat. Vast swampy area, tropical climate, with palms, cypress trees, wilderness of reeds, mangrove woods on the coast, containing numerous waterways. Famed for its abundant bird life, especially of many kinds of swamp and water birds, including red spoonbill, white ibis, wood ibis, 10 kinds of heron. Many species of snake: American crocodile, pike alligator. Among the mammals: puma, black bear, white-tailed deer, opossum, American manatee (sea-cow).

'National Monuments' (NM) which are of considerable significance for the preservation of wild animals.

2 Katmai NM (1918) 4,165 sq. miles.

S Alaska. Administration: Mount McKinley NP, Alaska. Open June–Sept., daily air service from Anchorage via the military airfield Naknek to Brooks River Camp or Coville Lake Camp within the NM. Steamer from Seattle, State of Washington, to Anchorage. Station: Anchorage. Remarkably wild mountain area with active volcanoes. Sub-arctic coniferous forests. Elk, reindeer, silver fox, wolf, wolverine, fish marten, mink, fish otter, lynx, beaver, Alaska bear.

3 Glacier Bay NM (1925) 3,590 sq. miles.

S Alaska. Administration: Sitka NM, Sitka, Alaska. Information concerning possibilities of flying to Gustarus, and charter motorboats: Alaska Visitors Ass., Juneau, Alaska. Glacier-covered mountain ranges, with many bays and inlets. Coastal area with many islands. Especially at the time of bird migration many thousands of ducks, geese and other water birds of many kinds. Sea bears. On the mainland: black-tailed deer, snow goat, beaver, wolverine, mink, wolf, black bear, grizzly bear, Alaska (Kodiak) bear. Salmon spawn in the rivers.

49 Colorado NM (1911) 28 sq. miles.

Administration: Fruita, Colorado. Open all the year round. Deep, sheer-walled canyons of red sandstone. Semi-desert. Bison, wapiti, mule deer.

53 Channel Islands NM (1938) California, Islands of Santa Barbara and Anacapa, 1½ sq. miles.

Sea-lion, numerous sea birds. Nearest towns on the coast: Hueneme, San Pedro. Administered by the Sequoia NP. No official boat service.

54 Joshua Tree NM (1936) 862 sq. miles.

California. Administration: Twenty-nine Palms, California. Station: Indio. Desert and semi-desert with numbers of Joshua trees—giant juccas. Typical desert fauna, including desert bighorn sheep, coyote.

55 Organ Pipe Cactus NM (1937) 512 sq. miles.

SW Arizona. Administration: Ajo, Arizona. Stations: Phoenix, Tucson. Open all the year round. Typical desert and semi-desert with corresponding flora and fauna. Tree-high organ pipe cactus. Desert bighorn sheep, pronghorn, white-tailed deer, mule deer, peccary, interesting birds and invertebrates.

56 Saguaro NM (1933) 98 sq. miles.

Arizona. Administration: Tucson, Arizona. Station: Tucson. Open all the year round, best visiting period April–May (cactus blooms). Semi-desert with woods of candelabrum cactus trees up to 50 ft. high. Most interesting desert flora and fauna. (Desert mule deer, coyote, peccary and black bear).

Mexico

According to the latest details available Mexico possesses 45 NPs. Only those have been chosen for inclusion here whose size and terrain appear to make them important for the preservation of the animal world. Unfortunately little precise information has been forthcoming.

60 Cumbres de Monterrey NP (1939) 952 sq. miles.

Nuero Leon. A mountainous area of the Sierra Madre Oriental with dense coniferous woods.

61 El Cogorron NP (1936) 96 sq. miles.

San Luis Potosi. Numerous springs, mountain streams, ravines, Aerolito reservoir.

62 Los Mármoles NP (1936) 91 sq. miles.

Hidalgo. San Vicente Canyon and Mount Tengando.

63 Nevado de Colima NP (1936) 88 sq. miles.

Guzmán City and Cauauhtémoc. Active volcano. Sub-tropical woods on the lower levels, evergreen coniferous and oak woods on the higher.

64 Nevado de Toluca NP (1936) 260 sq. miles.

Zinacantepec. Volcanic mountains of the same name, up to 1,510 ft., with lovely crater lakes.

65 Iztaccihuatl-Popocatepetl NP (1935) 99 sq. miles.
Puebla, Morelos, Mexico. Surroundings of the two extinct volcanoes of the same names, over 16,500 ft. high.

66 Cofre de Perote NP (1937) 45 sq. miles.
Vera Cruz. Around the 14,150-ft.-high mountain of the same name, whose slopes are covered with coniferous woods.

67 La Malinche NP (1938) 152 sq. miles.
Tlaxcala, Puebla. Mountain area with coniferous woods.

68 Canon del Rio Blanco NP (1938) 215 sq. miles.
Vera Cruz. Area containing the source of the Rio Blanco, temperate forests.

69 Pico de Orizaba NP (1936) 76 sq. miles.
Puebla, Vera Cruz. Highest mountain in Mexico (18,830 ft.).

Guatemala

The national parks of Guatemala have been created principally with a view to protecting the landscape—from excessive tree-cutting, erosion of the soil, over-grazing—and to guard facilities for the supply of fresh water. In some cases the boundaries are not yet specified. In many there are only small animals, principally squirrels and other rodents of various kinds, together with small carnivorous animals. In these cases no specific names are given in the details which follow.

70 Atitlan NP (1955)
Sololá Province. Road connections. Accommodation and service. Lake of Atitlan, active volcanoes, dense tropical forests. Several villages by the lakeside. Atitlan diver (Podilymbus gigas), endemic.

71 Cerro del Baúl NP (1955)
Quezaltenango Province. Accessible by air or by car. Mountain area, volcanic in origin, up to 7,950 ft. high, wooded.

72 Santa Rosalia NP 15 sq. miles.
Zacapa Province. Accessible by railway or car. Mixed woods. White-tailed deer.

73 El Pino NP 2 sq. miles.
Guatemala Province. Accessible by car. Mountainous area up to 6,200 ft. Cypress woods.

74 Laguna el Pino NP (1955).
Santa Rosa Province. Accessible by car. Flat countryside with cypress woods.

75 Los Aposentos NP (1955).
Chimaltenango Province. Accessible by car. Mountainous area with many springs, wooded with Montezuma firs. Source of the Rio Guacalante.

76 Rio Dulce NP (1955).
Covers the area around Lake Izabal and the Rio Dulce from its mouth in the Atlantic

to the ruins of San Felipe Fort. Accessible by plane, railway, motorboat. Recommended: Boat trip up the Rio Dulce. Tropical jungle with numerous ferns, orchids. Savannas. Dow's tapir, roaring ape, white-tailed deer, jaguar.

77 Tikal NP (1955)

Area of El Petén in N Guatemala. Accessible by plane or on horseback. Mountainous area with tropical forest. Dow's tapir, white-tailed deer, racoon, spectacled bear, jaguar, puma, ocelot.

South America

Venezuela

Administration of the national parks: Ministry of Agriculture, Caracas.

1 Henry Pittier NP (Rancho Grande NP) (1957) 348 sq. miles.

In the coastal cordillera on the Caribbean Sea. Tropical rain jungle with rich animal world, especially numerous birds, including many colibris. Footpaths, camping sites in preparation. Accommodation: Maracay, roads from there.

2 Guatope NP (1958) 348 sq. miles.

Mountainous district, whose woods have been partially destoyed by former clearance by fire. Founded principally to safeguard the water supply of Caracas.

3 Sierra Nevada de Merida NP (1952) 618 sq. miles.

In the Venezuelan Andes, near the border with Colombia. High mountain area with the Pico Bolivar (16,350 ft.), many glacier lakes. Mountain railway.

British Guiana

4 Kaieteur NP (1930) 45 sq. miles.

Accessible by steamer, small boat or plane from Georgetown. Accommodation for 30 people. Wooded banks of the Rivers Potaro, Mure and Elinku. Kaieteur waterfall 735 ft. high.

Brazil

5 Paulo Alfonso NP (1948) 66 sq. miles.

Area of the famous waterfalls of the Paulo Alfonso River into the Sao Francisco River. Road link with Maceió.

6 Sooretama Sa 58 sq. miles.

In Espirito Santo State. Tropical flora and fauna.

7 Rio Doce Sa (1944) 116 sq. miles.

In Minas Gerais State. Principally lagoons with typical flora and fauna.

9 Iguaçu NP (1939) 792 sq. miles.

On Iguaçu River, bordering on the Argentinian province of the same name. Dense virgin forests with many species of animals. Difficult of access. Best approached by plane from Sao Paulo or Rio de Janeiro.

Maracay
Caracas
1
2
VENEZUELA
3
Georgetown
4
BRIT. GUIANA
17
LAPAGOS Is.
cuador)
BRAZIL
5
Maceió
6
7
Rio de Janeiro
São Paulo
8
9
10
CHILE
ARGENTINA
Buenos Aires
11
12
Bariloche
13
Comodoro Rivadavia
14
15
Santa Cruz
16

Argentina

The administration of the Argentinian NPs is not yet satisfactory. Visits by tourists are almost completely haphazard. The introduction of European and Asiatic animals (e.g. red, axis and fallow deer, wild pig, hare, pheasant) has proved extremely dangerous to the native vegetation and animals. See the chapter by Dr. Hans Krieg in this book!

8 Finca del Rey NP 139 sq. miles.

In the N, on the Bolivian frontier. Almost sub-tropical vegetation. Great ant-eater, tamandua, tapir, jaguar, numerous species of birds.

10 Iguaçu NP 212 sq. miles.

Area of the famous waterfalls 6 miles above the mouth of the river of the same name into the Parana. Misiones Province, on the Brazilian frontier. Another protected area on the Brazilian side. Road and boat connections. Accommodation building by the falls.

11 Lanin NP 2,162 sq. miles.

In the SW of Neuquén Province n of Nahuel NP. Cordillera area around the 12,465-ft.-high volcano Lanin, 25 glacier lakes. Araucaria woods.

12 Nahuel Huapi NP (1934) 3,030 sq. miles.

Within this territory, much of which has lost its original character owing to its extensive use as a tourist resort, there are six 'strict reserves' with a total area of some 230 sq. miles. In the cordilleras, Neuquén Province. Road and rail links between Buenos Aires and Bariloche (hotels), in park. Territory around Lake Nahuel Huapi, 208 sq. miles. High mountain district with numerous other lakes. Beech (Nothofagus) woods. Puma, condor.

13 Los Alceres NP 1,930 sq. miles.

In the cordilleras, Chubut Province. Road to José de San Martin. Large mountain forests, lakes. Huemul (Andes deer).

14 Perito Francisco P. Moreno NP 598 sq. miles.

In the S cordilleras, Santa Cruz Province. Road Comodoro Rivadavia–Perito Morena. Glacier mountains Tres Hermanos, Penitentes, Hermoso, and high plains. Guanaco, huemul, mountain cat (Oreailurus colocolo), Darwin's nandu ostrich (Pterocnemia pennata), black-necked swan.

15 Los Glaciares NP 2,586 sq. miles.

In the Andes on either side of the 50th degree south. Santa Cruz Province. Road links from Santa Cruz to Lago Argentino and Lago Viedma. Glacier area between Piz Fitz Roy (11,230 ft.) and Piz Paine (8,125 ft.), with the two lakes Argentina and Viedma, each about 50 miles long. Beech woods. Huemul, pudu, guanaco, Darwin's nandu, condor.

Chile

Chile possesses a considerable number of nominal NPs. However, their supervision leaves so much to be desired that in many cases it would be misleading to describe them as protected areas at all. Many of these areas are primarily woodland reserves, intended to prevent further erosion of the soil or to conserve the water in the source districts of important rivers. These, too, are often severely damaged by illegal grazing and theft of timber. Possibly the nearest thing to a fully protected area is the island region extending down to Cape Horn (16); the protection afforded there is advantageous to the local fauna, principally sea birds.

Ecuador

17 Galápagos Islands
See the chapter by Dr. Eibl von Eibesfeldt!

Asia

India

The administration of the NPs and GRs is in the hands of the forestry authorities of the individual states, not the central government. A forestry official is responsible for each Sa, his address always being given here. It is advisable to write to these officials in good time before visiting the NP or GR, asking for further details, reservation of accommodation, etc. The book *India's Wild Life Sanctuaries* (1961) by E. P. Gee is warmly recommended.

1 Dachigam Sa.

In Kashmir, 12 miles from Srinagar on a good road. First-class hotels in and around Srinagar, also houseboats. Accommodation building in Sa. Best visiting period April–Oct. Splendid mountain scenery, with peaks up to 13,000 ft. Special Sa for the hangul (Kashmir deer). Also musk deer, collared bear and brown bear, wild boar, numerous species of birds. In order to see the hangul deer one must visit the district during the winter months, from Nov. onward, as the deer then come down from the high mountains. Administration: The Game Warden, Jammu and Kashmir State, Sringagar, Kashmir.

2 Corbett NP (1935) 125 sq. miles.

156 miles ne of Delhi. Accessible by road or by rail (termini Ramnagar and Haldwani). From Ramnagar 32 miles to Dhikala, where the main accommodation building for the park is situated. Protection huts in Sultan, Sarapduli, Boxar, Peterpani, Gaujpani, Jamunagwar. Eight observation towers in the P. Jeep, riding elephants. Best visiting period: March–April, also Feb. and May. Park closed 1st June–31st Oct. Foothills of the Himalayas, mountain streams, forests. Principal sanctuary for the tiger. Also leopard, hyena, Himalayan bear, jackal. Wild elephant, sambar, axis and muntjak deer, hog deer, crocodile. Administration: The Chief Wild Life Warden, U.P., Wazir Hasan Road, Lucknow, Uttar Pradesh.

3 Keoladeo-Ghana Sa 11 sq. miles.

100 miles s of Delhi, 32 miles w of Agra, road and rail links. Station: Bharatpur, 1 mile from there (taxi). Accommodation: Shanti Kutir Hotel in Sa. Boats. Best Sa in India for water fowl! Main breeding period: July, August (until Oct.). Birds include

Indian stork, ibis, spoonbill, heron (3 varieties), sarus crane. Information: The Div. Forest Officer, Bharatpur, Rajasthan.

4 Shivpuri NP 62 sq. miles.

On the main Agra to Bombay road, 72 miles s of Gwalior, narrow-gauge railway from Gwalior. Bungalow and guest house of the Public Works Div. in Shivpuri. Reservations through: The Executive Engineer, P. W. Div., Shivpuri M. P. Small hotel in the town. Over 60 miles of roads in the park. Many observation towers. Open all the year round. Leafy woods, expanses of grass, lakes. Serow, nilgau antelope, sambar and axis deer, wild hog, bear, hyena, tiger (particularly good opportunities for photographing), leopard. Abundant bird life. Information: Conservator of Forests, Shivpuri, Madhya Pradesh.

5 Chandraprabha Sa 31 sq. miles.

In the Vindhayan Mountains, 44 miles from Vanarasi. Good road from there. Well equipped accommodation building, observation towers and riding elephants in the Sa. Open all the year round, best visiting period Dec.–April. Intended to become second Sa for the Asiatic lion, three specimens introduced in 1957. Serow, nilgau antelope, sambar and axis deer, wild hog, leopard, bear. Numerous kinds of birds. Information: The Chief Wild Life Warden, U.P., Wazir Hasan Road, Lucknow, Uttar Pradesh, or: The Divisional Forest Officer, Vanarasi Forest Div., Ramnagar P.O. Uttar Pradesh.

6 Hazaribagh NP 75 sq. miles.

On the main road between Patna and Ranchi in Bihar, 10 miles from the town of Hazaribagh. Road links with Barhi, Bagodar and Ranchi. Nearest airport Patna, 125 miles away (bus, taxi). Nearest station Koderma, 20 miles (bus). Accommodation buildings in Rajderwa and Harhad. Ten observation towers. Open all the year round, best visiting period Dec.–May. Wooded, hilly country. Most native wild animals are present, but still in rather small numbers at present. Administration: The Div. Forest Officer, Hazaribagh Div. Bihar.

7 Jaldapara GR (1941) 37 sq. miles.

To the S of the railway line linking Bengal and Assam with the rest of India. Nearest station: Hashimara, 1 mile from there. Road link with Cooch Behar. Air service (2 or 3 times a week) Calcutta–Hashimara (airport 3 miles from the GR). Bungalow in Barodabri. Riding elephants. Best visiting period: Nov.–April. Sa for the Indian rhinoceros (50–60 head), sambar and hog deer, muntjak, wild pig, wild elephant, tiger (rare). Administration: The Div. Forest Officer, Cooch Behar Div., Cooch Behar P.O., West-Bengal.

8 Manas GR 105 sq. miles.

In the extreme NW of the N Kamrup district of Assam, near the border of Bhutan. Road connection with Gauhati (94 miles), road in the GR usable from Oct. until May. Accommodation in Motharguri (2 rooms), no service, camping site. Riding elephants. Best visiting period: 15th Oct.–April. At the foot of the Himalayas, where the Manas River breaks through to the plain by way of a splendid ravine. Numerous species of animal and bird. Administration: The Conservator of Forests, Western Circle, Shillong, Assam.

9 Kaziranga GR (1926) 166 sq. miles.

Swamp district on the S bank of the Brahmaputra. The accommodation building lies near milestone 135 along the main road from Gauhati airport. Jorhat airport is 60 miles to the E. Can be reached in a few hours by plane from Calcutta. Road links with Gauhati and Jorhat. Overnight accommodation and service in Kaziranga Guest House, accommodation (without service) in the guard houses Baguri and Arimora. No motor roads in the Sa. Riding elephants. Two observation towers. Best visiting period Nov.–April. Indian rhinoceros (at least 250), gaur, sambar and hog deer, wild pig, wild elephant. Numerous kinds of birds. Administration: The Div. Forest Officer, Sibsagar Div., Jorhat P.O., Assam.

10 Gir Forest.

In the former Principality of Junagadh, nw of Bombay. 38 miles from Junagadh via Mendarda. Road and rail connections from Bombay with Sasan in the Sa. Three flights per week from Bombay to Keshod, which is 38 miles from Sasan. Accommodation building in Sasan. Jeeps. Best visiting period Jan.–May. Last specimens of the Asiatic lion (Panthera leo persica), 290 head (1955), serrow, nilgau antelope and four-horned antelope, sambar and axis deer, wild pig (principal prey of the lions). Administration: The Conservator of Forests, Junagadh Circle, Junagadh, Bombay State.

11 Kanha NP 97 sq. miles.

In the central Indian highlands, 34 miles sw of the district capital Mandla. Road links with Jabalpur (38 miles) in the N and with Balaghat in the S. Train from Mandla or Jabalpur, nearest station Chiraidongri, 28 miles from Kanha. Accommodation buildings in Kanha and Kisli. Network of unmetalled roads in the park. Best visiting period: April–June. Park closed mid July–mid Nov. Riding elephants. Parklike scenery. One of the best-stocked animal sanctuaries in India! Barasinga, axis and sambar deer, muntjak, gaur, tiger, leopard, bear, hyena. 90 species of birds. Administration: The Div. Forest Officer, West Mandla Div., Mandla, Madhya Pradesh.

12 Ranganthittoo Sa 166 sq. miles (water and islands).

Islands in Cauvery River. 1 mile from Srirangapatna, 9 miles from Mysore. Road connections, ferry. Hotels in Mysore. Accessible all the year round. Best visiting period: June–Aug. Large breeding colonies of many kinds of birds, including Indian stork, heron, ibis, cormorant. Administration: The Div. Forest Officer, Mysore Div., Mysore.

13 Vedanthangal Sa 74 acres.

Chingleput district, 53 miles s of Madras. Road. Train to Karungluzhi. Hotels in Madras. Boat available. Best visiting period: Dec.–Jan. Reservoir with large colonies of storks, spoonbills, various herons, ibis, cormorant. Information: Chief Conservator of Forests, Madras 14.

14 Bandipur Sa (1941) 310 sq. miles.

In Mysore, on the main road between the town of Mysore and Ootacamund, about 50 miles from each of these towns. Nearest airport Bangalore. Rail and road connections from there to Mysore (bus, taxi). The Sa borders on the Mudumalai Sa in Madras. Animals move about between these two areas at various seasons of the year. Accommodation and service: three guard huts, a motel (being built). Observation towers, guides, riding elephants. 80 miles of good roads in the outer protected area. Best visiting period: April–June. Open all the year round. Light woods. Gaur, wild elephant, sambar, muntjak, wild pig, Hulman monkey (Langur), bonnet macaque, bear, tiger. Administration: The Div. Forest Officer, Mysore City, Mysore.

15 Mudumalai GR (1940, 1956) 114 sq. miles.

On the main road Mysore–Ootacamund, two guard huts (accommodation and service) 40 miles from the latter. 6 observation towers, 44 miles of unmetalled roads in the GR. Best visiting period: March–June. Hilly, densely wooded area at the foot of the Nilgiri Mountains. Wild elephant, gaur, sambar, axis deer, muntjak, four-horned antelope, wild pig, langur, bonnet macaque, tiger, leopard, bear.

16 Periyar Sa 262 sq. miles.

In Kerala, on the border with Madras. Main road Cochin–Madurai. Nearest stations: Kottayam (75 miles) and Madurai (88 miles). Airports: Cochin, Madurai. Road connections (bus) from all these places. First-class hotel, Aranya Nivas, in Thekkady in the Sa, bungalow in Edapalayam, two accommodation houses in the interior. Open all the year round. Motorboats. District around Lake Periyar (10 sq. miles), wooded mountains. Wild elephant (numerous), gaur, sambar, muntjak, bear, tiger, leopard. Many kinds of birds. Information: The Game Warden, Peermade, Kerala.

Ceylon

The national parks and protected areas of Ceylon come under the Ministry of Trade and Commerce, Colombo. Inquiries concerning travel routes, etc., should be addressed to the Dept. for the Administration of National Parks of that Ministry.

17 Wilpattu NP (1938) 252 sq. miles.

Visits allowed only by motor vehicle (220 miles of Jeep paths). Overnight accommodation for 12 people. Principally sandy expanses with some rocky eminences and 40 lakes. Sambar deer, leopard, many species of birds.

18 Senanayake Samudra Sa 35 sq. miles.

Water and swamp birds.

19 Gal Oya NP (1954) 98 sq. miles.

Area surrounding the Gal Oya reservoir. Wooded savannas and mountain chains. Valley of River Gal Oya. Only footpaths. Restaurant by the reservoir, two small bungalows for visitors. Visitors are always accompanied by a game warden guide.

20 Amparai Sa 148 sq. miles.

Large numbers of water and swamp birds of many kinds. Extensive herds of elephant.

21 Ruhuna NP (1938, 1954) 92 sq. miles.

Bush savanna with rocky eminences and water-holes. Visits permitted only in motor vehicles. (32 miles of jeep paths). Park bungalows for 16 people.

Apart from the national parks Ceylon also possesses four so-called 'strict nature protection districts' with a total area of 234 sq. miles, and 22 game reserves totalling 315 sq. miles.

KASH-
MIR
Srinagar

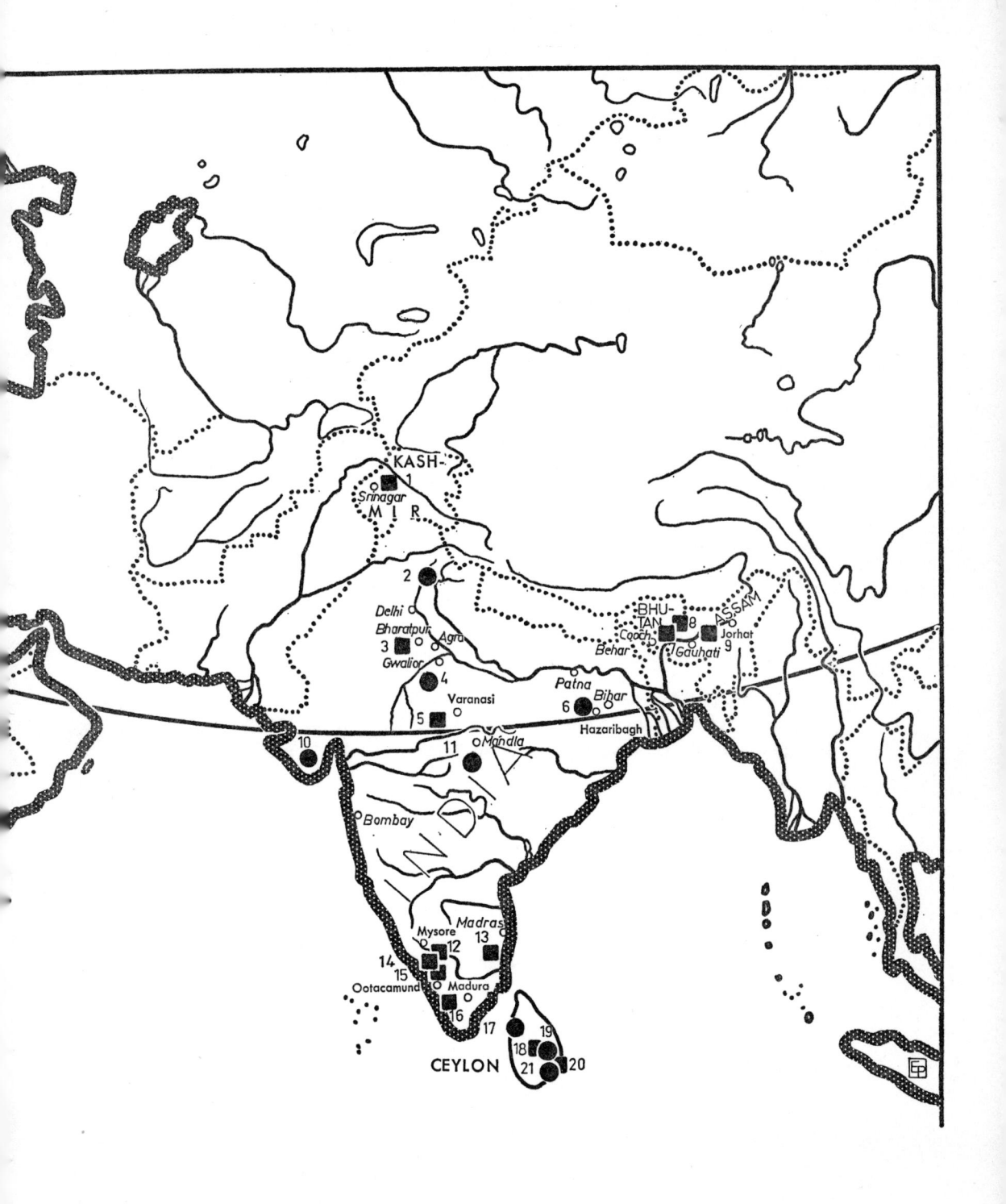

Delhi
Bharatpur Agra
Gwalior
Varanasi
Patna
Hazaribagh
Bihar
Cooch
Behar
BHU-
TAN
Gauhati
ASSAM
Jorhat

Mandla

Bombay

Mysore Madras
Ootacamund Madura

CEYLON

221

Japan

Administration and information: Nature Conservation Society of Japan, c/o Ministry of Welfare, 1-2 chome, Kasumigareki, Chiyodaku, Tokyo.

1 Akan NP (1934) 338 sq. miles.

NE Hokkaido. Nearest stations: Kushiro, Kawayn, Teshikaga. Mountain range with five active volcanoes, hot springs, mud gushers, lakes, coniferous forest. Alpine roses, azaleas. Brown bear, sika deer, marten, fish otter, snow hare.

2 Daisetsuzan NP (1934) 896 sq. miles.

In central Hokkaido. Nearest station: Kamikawa. Volcanic area including the highest peak on the island, the 7,745-ft.-high Asahi, virgin coniferous forests, hot springs. Brown bear, marten, snow hare.

3 Shikotsu-Tôya NP (1949) 382 sq. miles.

SW Hokkaido. Nearest stations: Kutchan, Oshamanbe. Volcanic mountains, hot springs, crater lakes. Brown bear, snow hare.

4 Towada-Hachimantai NP (1936, 1956) 321 sq. miles.

In the N of the main island. Stations: Amori, Morioka. Mountain landscape with the Towada crater lake, hot springs, tundra. Collared bear, serow (Capricornis crispus), marten.

5 Bandai Asahi NP (1950) 792 sq. miles.

Northern part of the main island. Stations: Tsuruoka, Fukushima. Volcanic mountains with the Gassan volcano, on its lower slopes beech, oak and maple woods, on the upper reaches hemlock, spruce-fir and tree of life. Alpine flora above the timber line. Collared bear, pink-faced macaque, serow.

6 Nikko NP (1934, 1950) 543 sq. miles.

N of Tokyo. Stations: Numata, Nikko. Good hotel in the NP. Volcanic mountains, lakes, hot springs. Collared bear, pink-faced macaque, sika deer, serow, marten.

7 Jôshinetsu-kogen NP (1949, 1956) 730 sq. miles.

In the centre of the main island. Stations: Nagano, Karmizawa. Good hotel in the NP. 1,000–1,650 ft. high plateaux, above which rise many volcanoes. Hot springs. Collared bear, sika deer, serow, marten.

8 Chichibu-Tama NP (1950) 470 sq. miles.

N of Tokyo. Stations: Kobuchizana. Tachikawa. Mountains with dense forests. Some 20 peaks above 6,600 ft. Collared bear, pink-faced macaque, sika, serow, wild pig, marten.

9 Chubu-Sangaku NP (1934) 655 sq. miles.

In the centre of the main island. Stations: Matsumoto, Omachi. Good hotels in the NP. 'Japanese Alps' area, with many deep ravines and crater lakes. Hot springs. Collared bear, pink-faced macaque, serow, wild pig.

10 Fuji-Hakone-Izu NP (1936, 1950) 367 sq. miles.

W and S (Izu) of Tokyo. Stations: Odawara, Joshida, Atami, Ito, Mishima. Good hotels in the NP. Neighbourhood of the volcano Fujiyama (12,400 ft., emblem of Japan) and coastal stretch (Izu). Pink-faced macaque, sika deer, wild pig, marten.

11 Joshino-Kumano NP (1936, 1950) 214 sq. miles.
S coast of the main island. Stations: Joshino, Shingu. Good hotels in the NP. Coastal range. Collared bear, serow.

12 Setonai-kai NP (1934, 1956) 254 sq. miles.
Mainly comprises the sea lane between the main island Honshu and the island Shikoku with its coastal strips, peninsulas, innumerable islands. Black pine. Many fishing villages on the shores. The world's only 'sea park'. Stations: Kobe, Beppu. Hotels in the NP.

13 Kirishima NP (1934) 83 sq. miles.
In the S of the island Kyushu. Stations: Kirishimajongu, Kurino. Hotels in the NP. Volcanic mountains. Sika deer, wild pig.

Burma

The game reserves here listed are under the control of the forestry authorities. Further information concerning travel and accommodation should be obtained from the forestry office in each of the nearest large towns mentioned in connection with the GRs.

14 Pidaung GR 278 sq. miles.
Near Myitkyina. Station: Myitkyina. Elephant, gaur, banteng, sambar deer, muntjak, tiger, leopard, Malayan bear, various pheasants.

15 Kyatthin GR 105 sq. miles.
Near Shwebo. Station: Shwebo, n of Mandalay. Thamin deer.

16 Shwe-u-daung GR 807 sq. miles.
E Kata. Station: Kata. Sumatran rhinoceros, elephant, gaur, banteng, serow, sambar deer, muntjak, tiger, leopard, Malayan bear.

17 Maymyo GR 49 sq. miles.
Near Mandalay. Road and rail to Maymyo. Muntjak, many kinds of birds.

18 Shwezet-taw GR 213 sq. miles.
Near Minbu, on the Irrawaddy. Rangoon–Mandalay road to Magwe. Gaur, sambar deer, thamin deer, muntjak.

19 Kahilu GR 62 sq. miles.
Near Thaton, road and railway Rangoon–Moulmein. Sumatran rhinoceros, serow, sambar deer, muntjak.

24 Mulayit GR 54 sq. miles.
Near Taunggyi. End of a branch line which runs E from the main line Rangoon–Mandalay. Muntjak, wild pig, tiger, leopard.

25 Moscos Islands GR 20 sq. miles.
Off the coast of Tenasserim. Train: Rangoon–Moulmein–Ye, road from there to Tavoy. Sambar deer, muntjak, wild pig.

Thailand

Administration: Royal Forest Department, Bangkok.

20 Doi Inthanon NP (1959) 51 sq. miles.
 In N Thailand, Iomtong district. Includes the highest mountain in Thailand (8,550 ft.).

21 Erawan Waterfall NP (1959) 782 sq. miles.
 Kanyanaburi Province, Muang and Panom Tuan districts. Mountainous area with numerous streams and waterfalls, and abundant animal life.

22 Tung Slang Luang NP (1959) 425 sq. miles.
 Phitsanulok Province, Wang Tong district. Road connections. Mountainous area, great waterfalls. Elephant, gaur.

23 Pukadeung NP (1947) 134 sq. miles.
 45 miles se of Loey Province. 4,460 ft. high plateau with coniferous forests and particularly abundant bird life. Villages of Sritan 2 miles from the foot of the mountains. Mountain paths. Overnight accommodation for 10 people in the park headquarters.

26 Khao Yai NP (1959) 800 sq. miles.
 Nakhon Ratchasima and Prachinburi Province, near Nakorna-Yok, Suraburi. Several mountain ranges, source area of large rivers. Great waterfalls. Large numbers of animals. Road to the summit of the Khao Yai.

South Viet Nam

Administration: Direction National des Eaux et Forêts, Service du Protection de la Nature, 295, Ben Chuong-Duong, Saigon.

27 Trang-Bom NP (1958) 1½ sq. miles.
 On national road No. 1, 32 miles from Saigon and 12 miles from Bien-Hoa. Road and rail connections. Accommodation: Saigon. Best visiting period: Dec.–May. Wooded. Malayan bear, tiger, leopard, wild pig, macaque. Many kinds of birds.

Malaya

28 King George V NP (1938) 1,683 sq. miles.
 N of Kuala Lipis, in the states of Pahang, Trengganu and Kelantan. Mountainous area around the 7,185-ft.-high Tahan. Elephant, Sumatran rhinoceros (Didermocerus sumatrensis, very few specimens), gaur, tapir, sambar deer, Malayan bear, tiger, leopard. Open all the year round, Nov.–Jan. not recommended. Park administration in Kuala Tahan. Accessible by boat from Jerantut Ferry, 12 miles s of Kuala Tembeling, which can be reached by rail or road. Modern rest house and bungalows in the NP. Guides.

Philippines

Administration: Parks and Wildlife Office, Binondo, Manila. Visiting periods: the

NPs of the Philippines can be visited practically all the year round. However, as this is a tropical area the months of Dec.–Feb. as the comparatively coolest are the most suitable for visits by Europeans. During the typhoon period (June–Nov.) there is heavy rainfall, but the sun comes out for several hours almost every day. The names of places following the area of each NP in the following list are those of the communities and provinces in whose territory the NP in question lies.

29 Tirad Pass NP (1938) 24 sq. miles.

Angaki, Concepcion, Sigay and Suyo, Cervantes (Ilocos Sur) in N Luzon, 216 miles n of Manila. The S of the NP is on the Tagudin–Suyo road, the N on the Concepcion–Angaki road, both suitable for cars and having bus routes. Accommodation and service in the SW of the NP at San Fernando (airport, harbour, terminus of the railway to N Luzon). Historically important NP; rough mountain area rising to 4,650 ft., covered with Benguet pine and other timber. Sambar deer (Cervus marianus), Philippine warthog (Sus verrucosus), monkeys, numerous species of birds.

30 Callao Cave NP (1935) $\frac{3}{4}$ sq. mile.

Penablanca (Cagayan). 312 miles n of Manila in N. Luzon. 9 miles from the town of Tuguegarao (Isabela), from there along the provincial road to the village of Buyo near Iguig (Cagayan). Neither accommodation nor service in the NP. Point of departure is Tuguegarao. Limestone ridge with numerous caves (bats), scored by ravines with walls 200–340 ft. high. The Molave forest contains sambar deer, warthog, pigeon, wild poultry, etc.

31 Hundred Islands NP (1940) 8 sq. miles.

Alaminos (Pangasinan) in central Luzon, 156 miles n of Manila and 32 miles w of Dagupan City. Train to Dagupan City, by bus or car to Lucap on the Gulf of Lingayen, from there by motorboat or outrigger boats to the various islands. Accommodation and service in the state rest house in Lucap, where there are also an oceanographic institute and fishery school, with museum. Hundreds of islands, with innumerable caves, in the coral sea, with white sandy beaches and unique marine life. Indian pigmy goose, swallow, Philippine bulbul, dove, and various unusual birds.

32 Mount Data NP (1936) $21\frac{1}{2}$ sq. miles.

On the borders between the sub-provinces of Benguet, Ifugao and Bontoc (Mountain Province in N Luzon), which meet at this point. From Manila by air, train and bus, or car, to the 'summer capital' Baguio City, which offers splendid accommodation and service. From there along the national road No. 11 Baguio–Bontoc by bus or car, on the zigzag road through the NP; footpaths to the points of attraction. 'Vista Lodge' Hotel within the park. Refreshing mountain climate, high rock pinnacles, ravines, waterfalls, numerous springs; world-famous Ifugaos tribes; dense virgin pine woods (Pinus insularis). Sambar deer, warthog, giant rat, civet cat; wild poultry, dove, snipe, falcon, parrot.

33 Fuyot Spring NP (1938) 3 sq. miles.

Ilagan (Isabela), N Luzon, 258 miles n of Manila. From Ilagan by the Cagayan Valley national road to Marana, then by horseback along paths to the spring. No accommodation or service in the park. Dipterocarp woods, hilly terrain rich in animals, with two caves and wonderful springs. Sambar deer, warthog, monkeys, dove, partridge, etc.

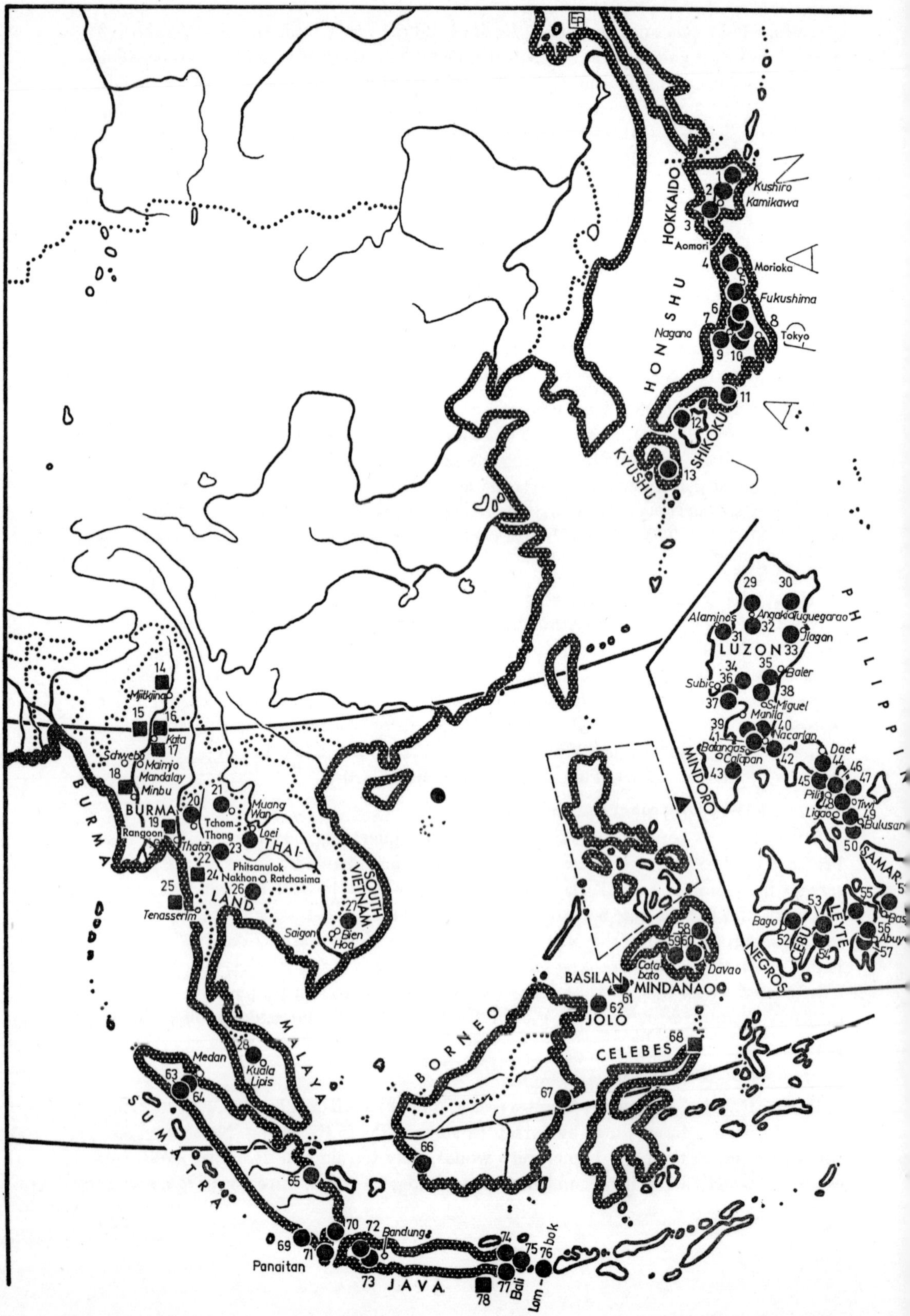

HOKKAIDO
Kushiro
Kamikawa
Aomori
Morioka
Fukushima
Nagano
Tokyo
HONSHU
SHIKOKU
KYUSHU
JAPAN
PHILIPPINES
LUZON
Alaminos
Angaki
Tuguegarao
Ilagan
Baler
Subic
S. Miguel
Manila
Nacarlan
Batangas
Calapan
MINDORO
Daet
Pili
Tiwi
Ligao
Bulusan
SAMAR
Bago
CEBU
LEYTE
NEGROS
Abuyo
BASILAN
MINDANAO
Cotabato
Davao
JOLO
CELEBES
BORNEO
MALAYA
Medan
Kuala Lipis
SUMATRA
Panaitan
Bandung
JAVA
Bali
Lombok
BURMA
Mjitkjina
Kata
Schwebo
Maimjo
Mandalay
Minbu
Rangoon
Thaton
Tenasserim
Tchom Thong
Muang Wan
Loei
THAILAND
Phitsanulok
Nakhon Ratchasima
SOUTH VIETNAM
Saigon
Bien Hoa

34 Mount Arayat NP (1933) 14 sq. miles.

Arayat (Pampanga) in central Luzon. Bus routes between San Fernando and Cabanatuan City on the overland road No. 10 pass near the entrance, which is 56 miles n of Manila. Rest house in the NP itself. Accommodation and service only outside the NP; it can easily be visited on a single-day excursion from Manila. Extinct volcanic ruins amid the broad rice plains of central Luzon. Cogon wild grass with secondary bush wood, changing to forests on the upper third of the mountain. Sambar deer, warthog, wild duck, wild poultry, etc. Game and birdlife reserve.

35 Aurora Memorial P (1937) 9 sq. miles.

Bongabon (Nueva Eciya) and Baler (Quezon): 148 miles n of Manila in central Luzon. A road runs from the provincial capital Cabanatuan City (hotels and restaurants) via Bongabon through the NP to Baler and the Pacific coast. Often unpassable in the mountains. Through the park by paths on foot or on horseback. Accommodation and service only in Cabanatuan City. Well-watered mountain woods (part of the cordillera running along E Luzon), dipterocarp type. Deer, wild pig, Mindoro water buffalo (Bubalus arnee mindorensis), civet cat, monkeys, monitor lizard, python; doves, red jungle fowl, eagle, hawks, partridges, rails, woodpeckers, parrots, owls, etc.

36 Roosevelt NP (1933) $5\frac{1}{2}$ sq. miles.

Hermosa (Bataan), Dinalupihan (Bataan), Subic (Zambales). On the bus route between greater Manila and the towns in Zambales Province; entrance directly on national road No. 3 (for Zambales). Accommodation and service only in the townships of Olongapo (w of the NP) and Dinalupihan (e of the NP). Dipterocarp and molave-type forest with characteristic fauna. Ravines, rocks, hot springs.

37 Bataan NP (1945) 121 sq. miles.

Hermosa, Orani, Samal, Abucay, Balanga, Pilar, Bagac and Morong (all Bataan). 66 miles nw of Manila on the Bataan Peninsula of central Luzon. By motorboat from Manila, across Manila Bay, or by bus round Manila Bay to Balanga and other places from where the park in the interior of the peninsula can be entered. Rest houses and simple hotels in the coast towns on the Bataan Peninsula near the park. Rugged volcanic mountains, wooded, sometimes reaching to Manila Bay. Principally of historical significance, with its military relics of the Second World War, but also a GR: sambar deer, warthog, monkeys, civet cat, lizards, snakes, doves, jungle fowl, parrots, etc.

38 Biak-na-bato NP (1937) 8 sq. miles.

San Miguel (Bulacan), central Luzon, 73 miles n of Manila, near the overland road. From overland road No. 5 either by asphalt road to Sibul Sorings ($1\frac{1}{2}$ miles from the Madlum cave), or by the earlier rough road to Biak-na-bato memorial. Paths in the park territory. Neither accommodation nor service in the park itself, but available in San Miguel (Bulacan). Of primarily historical importance (Filipino war of independence against the Spaniards), but also game and bird sanctuary (doves, red jungle poultry, insect-eating birds, sambar deer, warthog, monkeys, lizards, snakes). Limestone range, much broken up, covered with molave forest; huge stalactite caves, caves with springs and other rock features.

39 Mount Makiling NP (1933) 15 sq. miles.

Los Banos (Laguna) and Santo Tomas (Batangas). College station of the Manila

Railroad Company. An hour's car ride s from Manila. Buses every 15 minutes from greater Manila to Los Banos, from there by jeep into the NP itself. Overnight accommodation in the nearby townships Los Banos, Calamba and San Pablo. Small restaurants in the park itself. Thick, multi-tiered forest; more than 3,000 types of wood vegetation. Hot and cold springs, volcanic mud geysers, wild duck, wild poultry, sambar deer, warthog, tabon (mound nest builder), doves, rails.

40 Pagsanjan Ravine NP (1939) $\frac{1}{2}$ sq. mile.

Cavinti and Lumban (Laguna), only 54 miles se of Manila. Can be reached on day excursion from Manila by good asphalt road (No. 21). Upstream from the rest house to the Caliraya or Pagsanjan waterfall, rapids downstream. A new approach road leads direct to the falls. Accommodation and service in Los Banos, rest house in Pagsanjan. Volcanic canyon, forested (ferns, monkeys, doves); water navigable upstream from the rapids to the waterfall and the deep cauldron below it.

41 Mts. Banahaw-San Cristobal NP (1941) 43 sq. miles.

Lukban, Tayabas, Sariaya, Candelaria and Dolores (all Quezon Province) and Rizal, Naccarlan, Lilio, Majayjay (all Laguna), together with San Pablo City. 88 miles s of Manila, in central Luzon. From San Pablo City and Lucena (both by rail), and accessible from all the townships surrounding the mountain massif by first-class roads. Simple accommodation and service in San Pablo City and Lucena. Volcanic group rising to 7,230 ft., heavy rainfall. Mantle of forest animated by sambar deer, warthogs, red jungle fowl, parrot and many other species of birds.

42 Quezon NP (1934) $3\frac{1}{2}$ sq. miles.

Atimonan, Padre Burgos and Pagbilao (all in Quezon). 113 miles se of Manila, traversed by the asphalted overland roads No. 1 running towards S Luzon. Also accessible by train from Manila (Pagbilao or Padre Burgos stations). Rest house in the NP. Accommodation only in the rest house on the Pacific coast in Atimonan; hotels and restaurants in the provincial capital Lucena, the best starting point. Mountains up to 1,330 ft. high with dense dipterocarp forests. Water conservation area. Monkeys, sambar deer, warthog, giant lizards, parrots, doves, jungle fowl.

43 Naujan Lake NP (1956) 84 sq. miles.

Naujan, Pola and Victoria (Oriental Mindoro) in the E of the island Mindoro, 100 miles by air s of Manila. From Manila by plane or ship (or ferry from Batangas) to Calapan, then by jeep to near the lake, and by motorboat on the lake itself. Simple accommodation in Calapan (Mindoro). The lake, some 230 ft. deep and rich in fish, with two small islands, forms the heart of the NP. Coastal strip with secondary vegetation forming breeding grounds for many rare species of birds. 20 small rivers flow to the sea; hot springs. Crocodile.

44 Bicol NP (1934) 20 sq. miles.

Basud and Daet (Camarines Norte), Lupi and Sipocot (Camarines Sur) in S Luzon. On both sides of overland road No. 1 from Manila to Legaspi City, along the border between the two Camarines, and easily accessible by car or bus from Daet or Naga City (airport and station). Best accommodation in Naga City, more primitive in Daet.

Unusual high-lying forest of dipterocarp type with abundant fauna (sambar deer, warthog, monkeys).

45 Libmanan NP (1934) 49 acres.

Libmanan (Camarines Sur) in SE Luzon. 270 miles se of Manila, 14 miles nw of Naga City (station and airport), with motor vehicles on overland road No. 1 to the nearby township Libmanan. Neither accommodation nor service in or near the NP. Best visited from Naga City. Probably the longest stalactite cave in SE Asia, with subterranean rivers and waterfalls, stalactites and stalagmites, inhabited by innumerable bats. The forest cover, preserved as a water conservation measure, makes this also a game and bird sanctuary.

46 Mount Isarog NP (1935) 38 sq. miles.

Naga, Calabanga, Tinambac, Goa, Tigaon and Pili (all in Camarines Sur), S Luzon or Bicolandia; 280 miles se of Manila. To Naga City by train, plane or overland road No. 1. From Naga by bus or car to the village of Consocep, which lies 8 miles from the Napantaran Summer Resort in the park. Rest house being built. Good accommodation and service in Naga City. Greatly eroded volcanic remains with dipterocarp forest, parts of which are still inhabited by Negritos (who live in tree houses, hunt with bow and arrow). Sambar deer, warthog, monkeys, red jungle fowl, doves, parrots, owls, hawks, endemic birds.

47 Caramoan NP (1938) 116 acres.

Caramoan (Camarines Sur), on a peninsula in S Luzon, 338 miles s of Manila and 57 miles e of Naga City. As far as Naga City by rail or air, then by bus to Partido, from Partido to Caramoan by boat, from Caramoan to Oroc-Osoc by road, then on horseback (or on a local carabao), or on foot to the park, a mile away. Simple accommodation and service in Caramoan only. Greatly faulted limestone range, running to the Pacific coast, with the Paniman and other caves, subterranean river and other features. Monkeys, warthog, wild fowl, parrots, purple fowl, doves, owls, hawks, monitor lizards, etc.

48 Tiwi Hot Springs NP (1954) 124 acres.

Tiwi (Albay), 336 miles s of Manila in S Luzon. Airport, station and harbour at Legaspi, which has excellent hotels. 28 miles from there on first-class overland road to Tiwi. Hotel with canteen in the park. Hot medicinal and mud baths in the surrounding bush, with numerous birds (rails, red jungle fowl, kingfisher, sun bird, owls, swallow, hawk, goat-sucker, pigeons, finches and insect-eating birds).

49 Mayon Volcano NP (1930) 21 sq. miles.

Albay, Camalig, Guinobatan, Libog, Ligao, Malilipot and Tabaco (all in Albay Province), in S Luzon, 342 miles se of Manila. Best starting point is Legaspi City, connected with Manila by overland road and railway, also airport. Buses run round the park; on the asphalt road from the N cars can reach an altitude of up to 5,550 ft. Excellent accommodation and service in hotels in Legaspi City. In the park itself, at 2,810 ft., there is a roomy rest house, from which it is possible to climb to the summit of the volcano. Guides obtainable in Legaspi City and in Tabaco (only 14 miles from the volcano). Volcano perfectly symmetrical in shape, one of the loveliest in the world,

7,990 ft. high. Its lower reaches are almost devoid of timber, much broken up, but dipterocarp forest above. Sambar deer, warthogs, monitor lizards, doves, hawks and various endemic birds.

50 Bulusan Volcano NP (1935) 14 sq. miles.

Casiguran, Barcelona, Bulusan, Irosin and Juban (all in Sorsogon). 394 miles s of Manila, 62 miles from Legaspi (terminus of the railway from Manila to S Luzon, also airport), 28 miles from the provincial capital Sorsogon. An asphalted branch road runs between high tree ferns from the national road No. 1 (from Bulusan) to the park entrance. By ship from Manila to Bulan, then by bus or car to the park, 17 miles away. Small rest houses and bathing establishment on the crater lake in the park. Canteen open day and night. Extinct volcano 5,150 ft. high, with only a few remnants of forest, otherwise plantations. Crater lake within steep walls, underground water outlet. Hot and cold mineral springs. Giant ferns, orchids, palms. Sambar deer, warthog, monkeys, jungle fowl, parrots, doves, hawks, lizards, rare insects. Numerous endemic species of lower animal and plant life.

51 Sohoton Natural Bridge NP (1935) 3 sq. miles.

Basey (Province and island of Samar in the Visayas group). Airport and harbour at Tacloban City (Leyte), opposite Basey, the point of departure for the journey upstream along the Sohoton River by hired motor or rowing boat. Road from Basey through the park under construction. Neither accommodation nor service in the park, but all amenities in the capital of the island Leyte, 6 miles to the w. Natural rock bridge over a river. Formerly inhabited stalactite caves, rapids and waterfalls. Dense dipterocarp forest with sambar deer, warthogs, monkeys, wild fowl, etc.

52 Mount Canlaon NP (1934) 95 sq. miles.

Bago, La Carlota, La Castellana, Murcia, Canlaon and San Carlos (all Negros Occidental) and Vallehermosa (Negros Oriental), 103 miles nw of the university centre Dumaguete City (airport) and 18 miles se of Bacolod City (airport and harbour). Airports in Bacolod City (w of the NP) and Dumaguete City (103 miles se of the NP). Bacolod City and Dumaguete City can also be reached by steamship from Manila. From Dumaguete or Bacolod by bus or car to near the NP. Footpaths lead up to the crater. Accommodation only in Bacolod or Dumaguete City. Extinct volcano with geologically interesting rock formations, waterfalls, hot springs, gorges, dipterocarp forest with characteristic fauna: monkeys, sambar deer, warthogs, jungle fowl, civet cat. The Cogon lowland, 13 sq. miles, is used as pasture; quail abound.

53 Central Cebu NP (1937) 59 sq. miles.

Toledo, Balamban (Cebu) and Cebu City on the island of Cebu in the Visayas group. 350 miles by air se of Manila. Can be reached from Cebu City, the 'southern cross' of the republic and an important harbour. The provincial road Cebu–Balamban passes within a mile of the NP. First-class accommodation and service in Cebu City, not in the NP. A few large patches of forest remain on the otherwise de-forested lime island of Cebu. Ground greatly broken up. Mammals and birds abound (sambar deer, warthog, civet cat, wild fowl).

54 Sudlon NP (1936) 2½ sq. miles.

Cebu City, island and province of Cebu in the Visayas group. 350 miles by air s of

Manila, 4 miles w of Cebu City. Although it is so near to Cebu City, only the provincial road Cebu–Mabulo–Sudlon (for cars) runs near the park. The park itself is then reached on foot, on horseback or on a caraboa. Cebu is the air transport centre of the Visayas, and an important port. Neither accommodation nor service in the park, but all facilities in Cebu. Unusual remnants of dipterocarp-type forests on the island of Cebu, which has been practically denuded of timber in historical times, and has suffered much structural breaking up. Plateau 2,650 ft. above sea-level, with waterfalls and caves. Game and bird sanctuary. Historical mementos of the Filipino uprisings against the Spaniards during the nineteenth century.

55 Tongonan Hot Springs NP (1937) 1 sq. mile.

Ormoc (province and island of Leyte in the Visayas group). 330 miles by air se of Manila. From Ormoc (reached by bus from Tacloban City) to the village of Valencia $7\frac{1}{2}$ miles away, then on horseback or carabao to the spring. Alternatively from Ormoc up the Bao River. Simple accommodation with service in Ormoc. Boiling hot medicinal spring amid a dipterocarp forest, which is broken up by steep-walled ravines.

56 Mahagnao Volcano NP (1937) $2\frac{1}{2}$ sq. miles.

Burauen and La Paz (island and province of Leyte in the Visayas group). 360 miles by air s of Manila. Accessible only by paths from the township of Burauen, which is $7\frac{1}{2}$ miles away. Burauen can be reached from Tacloban (airport and harbour). Accommodation and service only in Tacloban City. Volcanic crater, two lakes, multi-coloured volcanic rock formations, hot medicinal springs. Dipterocarp forest. Wild ducks, hawks, wild fowl, sambar deer; abundant fish.

57 Kuapnit-Balinsasayao NP (1937) $1\frac{1}{2}$ sq. miles.

Baybay and Abuyog (province and island of Leyte in the Visayas group). 375 miles by air s of Manila. Accessible from the provincial road between Baybay and Abuyog. Neither accommodation nor service in the park. Virgin dipterocarp forest. Inhabited by, and named after, two species of birds.

58 Mainit Hot Spring (1958) 5 sq. miles.

Compostela (Davao) on Mindanao, 580 miles by air se of Manila and about 66 miles n of Davao City. From Davao (airport and important harbour) by car or bus northward along national road No. 1. First-class accommodation and service in Davao City. Wooded hills, with sambar deer, warthogs, monkeys, red jungle fowl, doves, owls, goat-suckers, hawks, singing birds, etc. The centre-point is a hot medicinal spring.

59 Liguasan Marsh GR (1940) 170 sq. miles.

Dulawan, Liguasan, Pikit and Pagalungan (all in Cotabato) on Mindanao, 627 miles by air s of Manila. 30 miles along overland road No. 5 from Cotabato City (airport and harbour) to Lambayong and Buluan, or along No. 1 to Pagalungan and M'lang from there with guides into the GR itself. Only very primitive accommodation and service in the nearest townships listed. The only specific GR on the Philippines. One of the best breeding grounds of the republic for water birds. Vast fresh-water swamp with nipa palms, water hyacinths, rushes, etc., harbouring ducks, herons, rails and other water birds, also fish and shellfish; many monkeys, sambar deer, warthogs, etc., on the adjoining land.

60 Mount Apo NP (1936) 297 sq. miles. (Largest NP in the Philippines).

Kidapawan (Cotabato), Guianga and Sta. Cruz (Davao), in the S of the island Mindanao. 600 miles by air se of Manila. By car from Davao City along road No. 1 to Cotabato City as far as Kidapawan, then on footpaths and bridle paths into the park. First-class accommodation and service in Davao City, none in the park itself. Dense dipterocarp forest gives place to mossy woods up to the 9,700-ft.-high summit of the extinct volcano. Hot mineral springs, waterfalls, a lake and precipices. Ape-eating eagle (Pithecophaga jefferyi), endemic Philippine moon rat (Podogymnura truei).

61 Basilan NP (1939) 25 sq. miles.

Lamitan (Basilan City) on Basilan Island, situated w of Mindanao. 550 miles by air s of Manila. A ferry goes to Basilan City, where there are also private airfields. From Lamitan to the village of Obit, from there by a forest road to the park. Neither accommodation nor service in the park itself, but both available in Basilan City and, better, in Zamboanga City. Mountainous area, up to 3,370 ft., covered by luxuriant forest, including pure stocks of almaciga. Rivers, waterfalls, springs with abundant fish. Sambar deer, warthogs, monkeys, parrots, wild fowl, doves.

62 Mount Dajo NP (1938) ¾ sq. mile.

Patikul and Talipan (Sulu) s of Jolo, the capital of the Sulu islands, 580 miles by air s of Manila. Jolo has an airport; it is best to proceed from there by horse or carabao, as the village of Banag, which can be reached by road, is still a mile e of the park boundary. Accommodation and service only in nearby Jolo. Abruptly rising mountain block (sparsely wooded), which has often served as a natural fortress. Herds of hog deer (Cervus porcinus), warthogs and other animals. Swarms of flying dogs.

Indonesia

All the 116 nature sanctuaries and national parks of Indonesia were founded under the Dutch administration. They are at present controlled by the 'Department for the Protection of Nature of the Forest Service'. These areas together total rather less than 8,500 sq. miles. The details which follow are only those of areas important to the preservation of animals. In all cases where no specific reference is made to accommodation facilities in or near the NP, the district town is the best starting place.

63 Gunung Löser NP (1934) 1,608 sq. miles.

N Sumatra. Atyeh district. Starting place for the NP: Kutatjane. Elephant, Sumatran rhinoceros (Didermocerus sumatrensis), sambar, tiger, tapir, orang-utan.

64 S. M. Langkat NP (1938) 824 sq. miles.

E Sumatra, Langtat district. Elephant, serow (Capricornis sumatraensis), sambar, tapir (Tapirus indicus), orang-utan (Pongo pygmaeus), tiger.

65 Berbak NP (1935) 733 sq. miles.

Central Sumatra. Djambi district, woods and swamp. Sumatran rhinoceros, tapir, banteng.

66 Kotawaringin/Sampit NP (1936) 1,352 sq. miles.

SE Kalimantan (SE Borneo), Kotawaringin and Sampit district. Banteng, orang-utan, proboscis monkey (Nasalis larvatus). Many species of birds.

67 S.M. Kutai NP (1936) 1,184 sq. miles.
SE Kalimantan (SE Borneo), Samarinda district. Sumatran rhinoceros, banteng, sambar.

68 Tangkoko-Batuangus NC (1919) 17 sq. miles.
N Sulawesi, Celebes. Manado district. Can be reached from port of Bitung. Anoa buffalo (Bubalus depressicornis), Celebes pig deer (Babyrousa babyrussa), hammer fowl (Megacephalon maleo).

69 Sumatera-Selatan NP (1935) 1,378 sq. miles.
S Sumatra. Bengkulu/Lampung district. Elephant, Sumatran rhinoceros, serow, sambar, tapir, macaque, gibbon.

70 Way Kambas NP (1937) 502 sq. miles.
S Sumatra. Lampung district. Starting point for NP: Telukbetung (small hotels). Elephant, Sumatran rhinoceros.

71 Udjung Kulon-Panaitan NP (1921) 212 sq. miles.
An island and peninsula on the W coast of Java. Pandeglang district. Dense jungle. Udjung Kulon: Javan rhinoceros (Rhinoceros sondaicus), about 40 specimens (1961), tiger, Pulau panaitan: volcanic island: muntjak, kantchil (Tragulus javanicus), banteng (Bibos sondaicus).

72 Tjikepuh NP 39 sq. miles.
W Java. Sukabumi district. Banteng, sambar, tiger, leopard, many species of birds.

73 Penandjung NP (1934) 2 sq. miles.
W Java. Garut district. Banteng, sambar, tiger, leopard, many species of birds.

74 Baluran NP (1937) 96 sq. miles.
E Java. Situbondo district. Rest house in the NP. Banteng, sambar, tiger, leopard.

75 S. M. Bali NP (1941) 77 sq. miles.
NW tip of Bali. Gilimanuk district. Bali cattle (domestic form of the banteng), sambar, tiger, white star (Leucopsar rotschildi).

76 Padar Rintjah NP (1938) 62 sq. miles.
Islands, between Flores and Sumbawa, with protected area for the Komodo monitor (Varanus komodoensis).

77 Banjuwangi-Selatan NP (1939) 240 sq. miles.
E Java. Banjuwangi district. Banteng, sambar, tiger, leopard.

78 Nusa Barun NC (1920) 23 sq. miles.
E Java. Djember district. Timor sambar (Cervus timorensis), giant squirrel (Ratufa bicolor albiceps), bankiva fowl (Gallus gallus bankiva), brown gannet (Sula leucogaster), monitor (Varanus salvator).

Australia
Australia possesses several hundred national parks and nature protection areas. They are administered by various authorities in the individual states.

Cobourg
Peninsula

Northern
Territory

Western

AUSTRALIA   Queens

Australia

South
Australia

Perth
9 5

9
Kangaroo Is.

brook Is.

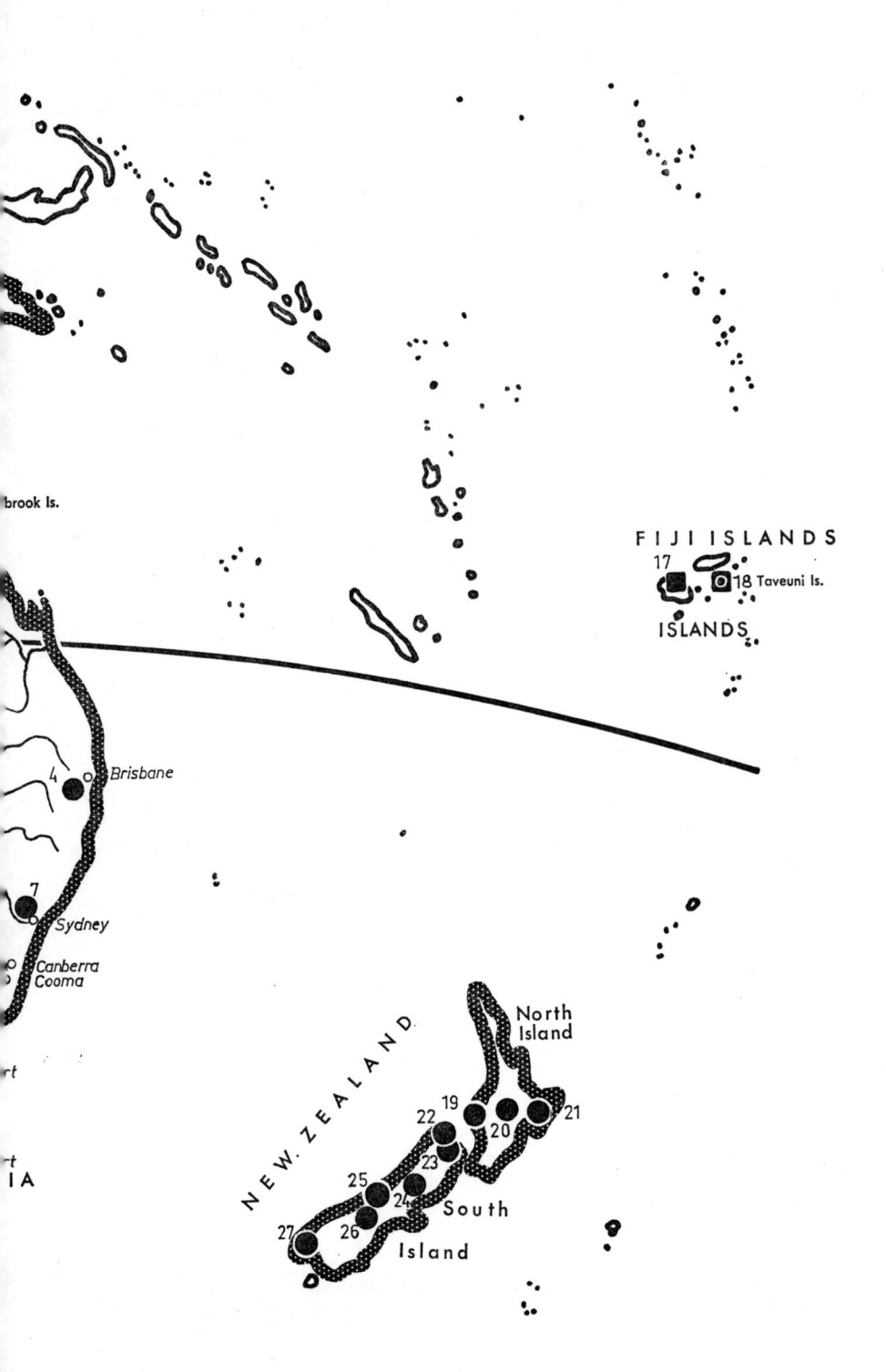

FIJI ISLANDS
17
    18 Taveuni Is.
ISLANDS

4 Brisbane

7
  Sydney
  Canberra
  Cooma

NEW ZEALAND
                North
                Island
        22 19
              20 21
           23
     25
        24 South
     27 26   Island

New South Wales: Minister of Lands, Sydney. There is a separate administration on the spot for each NP.
Victoria: National Parks Authority, under the Prime Minister, Melbourne.
Queensland: Forestry Department, Brisbane.
South Australia: Board of Commissioners of the National Parks and Wildlife Reserves, Adelaide.
Western Australia: Fauna Protection Advisory Committee, Perth, and local authorities.
Tasmania: governing bodies for each NP.
Northern Territory: Northern Territory Reserves Board.

Although in principle the entire animal world is protected in each NP and similar territory, many are primarily recreational areas for the population, and a large number are of mainly botanical importance. Even among those which are of considerable importance for the preservation of the animal world we can deal with only the most significant:

1 Cobourg Peninsula NC (1924) 100 sq. miles.
N of the Van Diemen Gulf, Northern Territory. Peninsula with very jagged coasts, wooded savanna in the interior. Several classes of kangaroo, many species of birds.

2 Hinchinbrook Island NP 150 sq. miles.
Queensland. The large island park, with jagged peaks and characteristic woods.

3 Eungella NP 185 sq. miles.
Queensland. Tropical forests with endemic fauna.

4 Lamington NP (1915) $7\frac{1}{2}$ sq. miles.
S of Brisbane. Station: Lamington/Queensland; harbour and airport: Brisbane. Accommodation: O'Reilly's Guest House in the park. Sub-tropical rain forest (eucalyptus, casuarine) on the slopes of the McPherson Range of E Australia. Small forms of kangaroo, koala, duck-billed platypus, nyla (funereal cockatoo), popinjay.

5 John Forrest NP $7\frac{1}{2}$ sq. miles.
12 miles e of Perth in the Darling Range of W Australia. Airport and harbour: Perth. Accommodation in Perth. Light, dry eucalyptus woods with grassy and cycad undergrowth. Incomparable carpet of flowers in early spring (August–October). Porcupine ant-eater (Tachyglossus aculeatus), banded marsupial ant-eater (Myrmecobius fasciatus), small kangaroos (Wallabia irma).

6 Macquarie Marshes 78 sq. miles. (Boundaries not yet definitely fixed).
New South Wales, 162 miles nw of Sydney. Station and airport: Wellington/NSW. Best visiting period after rain, principally in summer. Extensive swamp and lagoon area near the Macquarie River, flooded following rain. Breeding colonies of ibis, spoonbill, various herons, black swan, ducks and other water and swamp birds.

7 Blue Mountains NP (1959) 240 sq. miles.
New South Wales, 62 miles w of Syney. Road and rail connections with Sydney. Accommodation and service in the park. Footpaths. Mountainous district (sandstone formation) with deep ravines, valleys with open woods, dense rain forests, abundant animal life.

8 Kulkyne NP (1941) 85 sq. miles. (Boundaries not yet definitely fixed).

Extreme NW of Victoria. Accommodation: Ouyen/Victoria. Station and airport: Mildura or Ouyen. Extends for about 32 miles along the largest river in Australia, the Murray River, with water birds (including pelican), and duck-billed platypus. Away from the river low eucalyptus trees. Undergrowth of 'porcupine' or spinifex grass (Triodia). Principal protection area for the mound-bird, which builds a 'hatching oven' for its eggs out of earth and rotting vegetation. Also bustards, emus, grey great kangaroos. Best visiting period after rainfall, especially in summer (Nov.–Jan.).

9 Flinders Chase NC (1919) 2,008 sq. miles.

In the W part of Kangaroo Island, S Australia. Road network on the island. Black-faced kangaroo, wallaby, porcupine ant-eater, koala, black swan, pelican.

10 Wyperfeld NP (1921) 216 sq. miles.

NW Victoria. Road connections. Accommodation huts, sand tracks. Semi-desert, in the E a few small rivers in whose valleys there are clumps of trees. Black-faced kangaroo, emu and many other birds, some of them rare.

11 Mount Kosciusko State Park (1944) 2,318 sq. miles.

New South Wales. Station: Cooma/NSW; Airport: Canberra. Accommodation: Hotel Kosciusko in the park. Best visiting period: July–Sept. (early spring). Largest Australian stocks of Alpine and sub-Alpine eucalyptus trees, with Eucalyptus forests in the valleys. Various kinds of kangaroo, wombat, marsupial badger, duck-billed platypus.

12 Mount Buffalo NP (1898) 42 sq. miles.

NE Victoria. Road connections. Accommodation and service in the park. Granite plateau (up to 6,950 ft. high) with forests, expanses of grass in the valleys. Various kinds of kangaroo, porcupine ant-eater, wombat, many species of bird including lyre-bird.

13 Sherbrooke Forest Reserve 4 sq. miles.

Immediately s of Melbourne. Airport and harbour: Melbourne. Accommodation in Melbourne or Ferntree Gully/Victoria. Best season for visiting during winter (May–July), the mating period of the lyre-bird. In the southernmost part of the East Australian Coastal Range. Hills and valleys covered with dense eucalyptus woods. Yard-high tree fern. Principal attraction is the lyre-bird (Menura novae-hollandiae), whose antics and singing at pairing time can be observed at very close quarters.

14 Wilson's Promontory NP (1905) 158 sq. miles.

S coast of Victoria. Main road connection with Melbourne. Accommodation and service in the park. The NP includes an 82-mile strip of splendid coastline with many bays; inland are mountains, river valleys with fern gorges. Wide variety of fauna, including koala, wombat and emu.

15 Lake St. Clair NP (1922) 502 sq. miles.

Tasmania. Airport: Queenstown; harbour: Devonport. Accommodation: in Derwent Bridge, 38 miles e of Queenstown, or in the chalet 'Waldheim' in the park. Vegetation generally as in the Mount Field National Park, also containing sub-Alpine forests and Alpine pastureland, together with an endemic form of conifer.

16 Mount Field NP (1916) 65 sq. miles.

Tasmania. 50 miles w of Hobart. Harbour and airport: Hobart. Accommodation in New Norfolk. Visits are worthwhile at all periods of the year. Extremely dense eucalyptus forests with beech and tree fern. Possibly harbours the last specimens of the Tasmanian pouched wolf. Also Bennet's kangaroo, Tasmanian devil (Sarcophilus harrisii), marsupial badger. Lyre-bird introduced.

Fiji Islands

The Fiji Islands possess five nature protection areas, which are administered by the Forest Department. Two of these, in particular, are important as sheltering many species of bird, some of them rare.

17 Naqaranibuluti NC (1958) 1 sq. mile.

Within the Nadarivatu-Nadala forest protection area. Mountainous, with steep slopes which are covered with forest. Rare orchids. Only footpaths.

18 Ravilevu NC (1959) 15 sq. miles.

In the SE of the island of Taveuni. Mountainous (up to about 2,300 ft. above sea-level); waterfalls, ravines. Only footpaths.

New Zealand

Administration: National Parks Authority, Ministry of Lands, Wellington.

North Island

19 Egmont NP (1900) 125 sq. miles.

Around Mt. Egmont, the sacred mountain of the Maoris. Sub-tropical forests, sphagnum moors. Kiwi. Road connections. Mountain paths. 14 mountain huts and hotels.

20 Tongariro NP (1894) 250 sq. miles.

Ruapehu mountains, highest peaks on the island with small glaciers, three active volcanoes, forests, grassy plains. Road connections. Marked mountain paths. Mountain huts, guest houses.

21 Urewere NP (1954) 702 sq. miles.

Mountainous country with dense forest, wild mountain streams and great waterfalls. Abundant bird life, including kiwi. Accessible by road or boat. Hotel by Lake Waikarciti.

South Island

22 Abel Tasman NP (1942) 50 sq. miles.

Coastal territory on Tasman Bay, with offshore islands and reefs. Forests, sandy bays. Accessible by road or boat. Camping.

23 Nelson Lakes NP (1956) 216 sq. miles.

Two lakes, surrounded by densely wooded hills. Road connections.

24 Arthur's Pass NP (1929) 370 sq. miles.

Part of the S New Zealand Alps with forests, glaciers, abundant bird life, including grey kiwi, kea (Nestor notabilis). Accessible by train or car.

25 Westland NP (1960) 328 sq. miles.

W side of the New Zealand Alps with forests, glaciers, lakes. Accessible by road. Mountain paths.

26 Mount Cook NP (1953) 268 sq. miles.

Part of the S Alps with 17 peaks over 10,000 ft., many glaciers (Tasman Glacier 20 miles long). Accessible by road or air. Many mountain huts.

27 Fjordland NP (1952) 4,514 sq. miles.

Mountainous coastal strip with many fjords, waterfalls, lakes and rivers. Lower levels wooded. Only habitat of the takahe (Notornis hochstetteri), a flightless rail of which some 100 specimens survive, and of the very rare owl-parrot (Strigops habroptilus). Great numbers of characteristic New Zealand birds. Many seals along the coast. Accessible by car, boat or plane. Two hotels, numerous camping sites.

Europe

Finland

The Finnish nature protection authorities distinguish between 'national parks', areas of especial scenic beauty which are open to all visitors, and 'nature parks', protected areas, some of which may be visited only with special permission, or in which visitors are not permitted to leave the marked footpaths.

Even in the southern part of the country there are many smaller protected areas, but the most extensive, and at the same time most important as regards the preservation of wild animals, are situated in the north. They may be visited only in summer and early autumn.

The terrain is more or less the same in all these areas: Ice-Age glacial formation, numerous lakes, many of which contain islands, large expanses of moor and heathland, birch and pine woods. The animal population is also similar in the various districts. The comparative tameness of the birds is a feature which surprises visitors from other parts of Europe.

Mammals commonly to be seen are: elk, reindeer, Alpine hare, brown bear, wolf, lynx, wolverine, pine marten, otter.

1 Kevo Nature P (1956) 134 sq. miles.

General position: in the most northerly tip of Finland, near Utsjoki, Lapin lääni. Mountainous district with the ravine of the Kevo River. Accessible by car from Utsjoki (12 miles) or Inari (47 miles); hotels and camping sites in both places.

2 Lemmenjoki NP (1956) 148 sq. miles.

General position: in the far north of the country, 150 miles n of Rovaniemi. Wild ravine of the Lemmen River with waterfalls, wider sections resembling lakes. Pine woods. Heath, fjäl. Road ends at Jomppanen; from there by motorboat (ordered through the Finnish Travel Agency in Inari) to the park boundary (about 6 miles). Hutted accommodation near the park.

3 Pallas-Ounastunturi NP (1938) 194 sq. miles.
General position: In the NW tip of Finland, about 125 miles nw of Rovaniemi. Typical fjäl district. Nearest airport: Ivalo (on the route to the Arctic Ocean) (hotels, camping), 48 miles from there. 80 miles from Sodankylä (on the route to the Arctic Ocean), hotels, camping.

5 Maltio Nature P (1956) 58 sq. miles.
General position: Lapin lääni, 12 miles from Savukoski. Typical fjäl country. Nearest airport and station: Rovaniemi (106 miles). Hotels and camping there, also in Savukoski, which can be reached by car.

6 Pyhätunturi NP (1938) 12 sq. miles.
General position: 22 miles n of Kemijärvi. Most southernly mountain massif of Finland (1,790 ft.), very jagged. 'Sacred mountain' of the Laps. Accessible by car from Kemijärvi. Lodging houses, camping.

7 Pisavaara Nature P (1938) 20 sq. miles.
General position: Lapin lääni. Moors and heaths, woods. Nearest airport and station: Rovaniemi (20 miles). Hotels and camping there.

8 Runkaus Nature P (1956) 24 sq. miles.
General position: Lapin lääni. Vast expanse of virgin moorland. Nearest airport and station: Rovaniemi (28 miles). Hotels and camping there.

9 Oulanka NP (1956) 39 sq. miles.
General position: About 53 miles se of Kemijärvi. Wild district along the Oulanka River and its tributaries. Accessible by car from Kemijarvi. Accommodation and camping facilities in Kiutaköngäs.

10 Linnansaari NP (1956) 3 sq. miles (excluding area of water).
General position: 22 miles nw of Savonlinna. Some 20 larger and numerous smaller islands in Lake Haukivesi. Breeding ground for ospreys. Accessible by motorboat from Savonlinna. Camping.

11 Jussaari Nature P (1956) ⅜ sq. mile.
General position: Uudenmann lääni. Rocky islands and cliffs. Bird sanctuary, including razorbill, eider duck, gulls, tern, grey-lag goose. Nearest stations: Tammisaari (12 miles) and Hanko (10 miles); hotels and camping at each.

Sweden

Note: Visits to parks situated n of the Arctic Circle are recommended only between mid-June and mid-September. Information: Svenska Naturskyddsföreningen, Riddargatan 9, Stockholm.

12 Vadvetjakko NP (1920) 9½ sq. miles.

Norrbottens Län. Nearest airport Kiruna, nearest station Vassijaure. Road only to Kiruna. Accommodation facilities: Abisko Turiststation (Hotel). The most northerly NP in Sweden, with far-northern mountain scenery around Mount Vadvetjakko, encompassing large expanses of reindeer pastureland with interesting flora and abundant avifauna. Elk, reindeer, Arctic fox, snow hare, lemming. Raven, buzzard, white grouse.

13 Abisko NP (1909) 19 sq. miles.

Norrbottens Län. Nearest airport Kiruna, nearest station Abisko. Road only to Kiruna. Accommodation facilities: Abisko Turiststation, which is in the park (hotel). Abisko NP is the most thoroughly explored mountain area of Sweden. Working facilities and accommodation are provided free for research scientists who wish to study the area in the Natural Science Station of the Swedish Academy of Science at Abisko. The greater part of the park is within an area of birch woods. Varied flora: rhododendron, Plantera oliganta, trollius, geranium, Poa alpina, dryas. Elk, reindeer, pine marten, otter, ermine, Alpine hare. Abundant bird life.

14 Stora Sjöfallets NP (1909) 534 sq. miles.

Norrbottens Län. Nearest airport Kiruna, nearest station Gällivare. Accommodation facilities: Suorva. Birch and pine woods. The waterfalls have largely been spoilt as scenery by the erection of hydro-electric power stations. Elk, reindeer, pine marten, brown bear, wolverine.

15 Sareks NP (1909) 734 sq. miles.

Norrbottens Län. Nearest airport Kiruna, nearest station Porjus. Accommodation facilities: Aktse. Largest NP in Sweden and in Europe. It is bordered on the N by the Stora Sjörfallets NP. A district of high mountains with glaciers. Abundant fauna and flora. 22 species of mammals, 102 of birds, 1 reptile and 1 amphibian. Mammals include elk, reindeer, bear, Alpine hare, Arctic fox, wolverine, wolf.

17 Muddus NP (1942) 190 sq. miles.

Norbottens Län. Nearest station: Porjus. Accommodation facilities: Porjus, Harspranget, etc. Largest forest in Sweden (spruce, pine), low mountains, picturesque valleys. North of the Arctic Circle. Brown bear.

19 Sonfjället NP (1909) 10 sq. miles.

Härjedalen. Nearest station: Hede. Accommodation facilities.: Hede. Birch and pine woods. Brown bear.

20 Töfsingdalen NP (1930) 5 sq. miles.

In the N of Dalarna Province. Road Falun–Räatvik–Mora–Särna–Sörvattnet. Particularly impressive spruce forest. Wolverine, brown bear.

21 Ängsö NP (1909) ¼ sq. mile.

Stockholms Län. Nearest airport Stockholm, nearest station Norrtälje. Accommodation facilities: Bergshamra. This NP is on an island, and can only be reached by boat. Woodland (coniferous, with patches of leafy trees), pastureland and a small farm. Fauna and flora typical of central Sweden.

22 Gotska Sandöns NP (1909) 1½ sq. miles.

General position: Gotska Sandön island. Accommodation facilities: none in the park, except in the lighthouse and pilot station. The whole NP, apart from a 100–200-yard-wide coastal strip, consists of dunes, which are covered for the most part with coniferous woods. Abundant bird life, including herring gull, hooded gull, tern, eider duck.

Swedish bird sanctuaries

Sweden possesses 71 birds sanctuaries with a total area of 1,930 sq. miles. No visits may be made by the public during the breeding period (1st April–30th June). Especially recommended:

16 Sjaunja district, Norbottens Län.

18 Mittadalen, Jämtlands Län.

23 Kävsjön, Kronobergs Län.

24 Stora Karlsö, Gotlands Län.

25 Ottenby, Kalmar län.

Great Britain

(There are 95 National Nature Reserves—46 in England, 28 in Scotland—totalling 179,704 acres or 280 square miles. The second largest Scottish reserve, Inverpolly, 42 square miles, established in 1961, contains wild cat, red deer and golden eagle.)
Administration: The Nature Conservancy, London Headquarters, 19 Belgrave Square, London, S.W.1.
For Scotland: The Nature Conservancy, Headquarters for Scotland, 12 Hope Terrace, Edinburgh, 9.

26 St. Kilda NC (1957) 3 sq. miles.
 Rock Island in the Atlantic about 62 miles w of the Outer Hebrides. Remarkable breeding area for sea birds: vast colonies of fulmar petrels and puffins. Breeding in 1959: 44,256 pairs of gannets, 7,660 pairs of kittiwakes, 13,850 pairs of guillemots.

27 Ben Eighe NC (1951) 16 sq. miles.
 Ross-shire, Scotland. Mountainous area around Loch Maree. Typical of the NW Scottish Highlands, which have been almost completely deforested by centuries of burning to clear land for agriculture, and over-grazing. Red deer, Alpine hare, wild cat, pine marten, golden eagle, ptarmigan. Nature Conservancy research station. Accommodation: Kinlochewe.

28 Cairngorms NC (1954) 61 sq. miles.
 Inverness-shire and Aberdeenshire. Granite massif, formed by Ice-Age glaciers, rising to about 4,000 ft., with numerous peaks, lakes, high-lying moors, heaths, Scots fir woods. Red deer, roe deer, Alpine hare, golden eagle, ptarmigan, golden plover. Accommodation: Aviemore, Braemar.

29 Rhum NC (1957) 41 sq. miles.
 Inverness-shire. Island of volcanic origins in the Inner Hebrides, with mountains rising to 2,650 ft. Seals, 1,500 head of red deer.

30 Caerlaverock NC (1957) 9½ sq. miles.

Dumfries-shire. Marshy land between the River Nith and the Solway Firth. Breeding ground and winter quarters of numerous species of water and marsh birds, in particular: pink-footed, white-fronted, barnacle and grey-lag geese, shoveler duck, gadwall and pintail ducks, oyster-catchers.

31 Skomer Island NC (1959) 1 sq. mile.

Island w of the Pembroke Peninsula, S Wales. Second largest puffin colony in Great Britain. Guillemot, razorbill, shearwater (tens of thousands), various gulls. Large colony of seals. Only scientific researchers are permitted to visit Skomer, but there are large colonies of the same birds on the nearby uninhabited islands Grassholm and Skokholm. Guided tours leave Pembroke harbour for these islands once or twice a week during summer. Accommodation: Pembroke.

Poland

32 Wolin NP (1960).

General position: district Szczecin, locality Wolin. Park administration in Wolin. Nearest airport: Szczecin. Distance Szczecin–Wolin Pomorski by train 52 miles. Accommodation: guest houses on the Baltic coast. Best visiting period: June–Sept. Highly characteristic sections of the coast, stands of beech, dunes with typical flora; osprey, sea eagle, cormorant, tern.

33 Osiedle Kormoranow Reserve (1956) 50 acres.

General position: district Koszalin, locality Czluchow, Rzecznica forest area. Nearest airport: Gdansk. Station: Przechlewo—distance from Gdansk 106 miles. Largest cormorant colony in Poland (some 150 nests) in an old beech wood by the River Brda.

34 Kudypy Beaver Reserve (1958) 13½ sq. miles (including a total reserve of ¾ sq. mile).

General position: district Olsztyn, locality Olsztyn, Ostroda. Kudypy forest area. Nearest airport: Gdansk. Station: Olsztyn—distance from Gdansk 106 miles. Beaver colony of about 40 in the River Pasleka. Mixed woods and pine woods.

35 Marycha Beaver Reserve (1960) ¾ sq. mile.

General position: district Bialystok, locality Sejny, Wigry forest area. Nearest airport: Warsaw. Station: Suwalki—distance from Warsaw about 220 miles. Beaver colony (36 specimens) in the River Czarna (Marycha). Extensive woods, with pine, birch, alder and aspen trees.

36 Czerwone Bagno Reserve (1957) 8½ sq. miles.

General position: district Bialystok, locality Augustow, Rajgrod forest area. Nearest airport: Warsaw. Station: Grajewo, distance from Warsaw by train 162 miles. Herds of elk live freely in the woods and on moors.

37 Bialowiez NP (1947) 18 sq. miles.

General position: district Bialystok, locality Bielsk Podlaski. Park administration in Bialowiez. Nearest airport: Warsaw. Station: Bialowiez-Palac—distance from Warsaw 171 miles. Accommodation: hut at the park entrance. Best visiting period: May–Sept. Greatest forest in Poland on the Narew River. European bison (some in enclosure, some free), elk, lynx, brown bear, beaver, black stork, owl, heath cock.

38 Kampinos NP (1959) 80 sq. miles. Sanctuary: 71 sq. miles.

General position: district Warsaw, localities: Nowy Dwor, Pruszkow, Sochaczew. Park administration in Kampinos—9 miles from Warsaw. Accommodation: Hotels in Warsaw. Characteristically wooded inland dunes. Reserve for elk, some of which live in freedom.

39 Tatra NP (1938, present dimensions since 1954) 83 sq. miles.

General position: district Krakow, locality Nowy Targ. Park administration in Zakopane. Nearest airport: Krakow. Journey to Zakopane: 66 miles by bus or 92 miles by train. Accommodation: Horels in Zakopane, camping sites on the borders of the park, huts within the park. Best visiting period: June–Sept. Highest mountain massif in Poland, of Alpine character. (Geological structure: crystalline and sedimentary). Highest mountain: Rysy, 8,260 ft. Numerous lakes and caves. Alpine vegetation. Chamois, marmot, brown bear, lynx, golden eagle, owl. The park continues on the far side of the frontier with Czechoslovakia, with another 197 sq. miles of park territory there!

40 Pieniny NP (1932, present dimensions since 1954) $8\frac{1}{2}$ sq. miles.

General position: district Krakow, locality Nowy Targ. Park administration in Kroscienko. Nearest airport: Krakow. Station: Nowy Targ—distance from Krakow 80 miles. Bus station: Kroscienko—distance from Krakow 73 miles. Accommodation: simple guest houses in Szczawnica, Kroscienko and Czorsztyn, villages near the park boundaries. Mountain hut at the entrance to the park near Szczawnica. Best visiting period: May–Sept. Cliff area of great geological interest (highest eminence Trzy Korony, 3,250 ft.), with the picturesque ravine of the River Dunajec. Beech and pine woods. Wild cat, owl.

41 Bieszczady NP (planned) 17 sq. miles.

General position: district Rzeszow, locality Lesko. Nearest airport: Rzeszow. Rail connection: station at Ustrzyki, 180 miles by rail from Krakow and 106 from Rzeszow. Eastern parts of the Carpathians on Polish soil, with remains of beech forest and great expanses of pastureland. Highest peak: Krzemien, 4,415 ft. Largest number of lynx in Poland; brown bear, wild cat, owl, black stork.

German Democratic Republic

Information: Institute for Land Research and Nature Protection, Halle/Saale, Am Neuwerk 4.

42 Die Lewitz NC (1938) 27 sq. miles.

SE Schwerin, Ludwigslust district. Area of meadows and woods watered by the Rivers Elde and Stohr. Important bird sanctuary. Breeding birds: sea eagle, kite, bittern, crane, black stork, swan, various classes of ducks and water fowl, laughing gull, colonies of terns.

43 Müritzhof NC (1949) 24 sq. miles.

East bank of the Muritz, area of Waren and Neustrelitz. Bird sanctuary, Breeding birds: crane, sea eagle, osprey. Largest assembly of cranes in Germany.

44 Steckby Beaver Sa (1955) 4½ sq. miles.
N Aken, Zerbst area. Meadow and dunes with pine wood. Beaver, bird Sa.

German Federal Republic

Information: Nature Protection Office, Government of Upper Bavaria, Munich 22, Maximilianstrasse 39.

45 Ammergebirge NC (1961) 77 sq. miles.
Upper Bavaria. Nearest stations: Oberammergau, Griesen. Accommodation: Linderhof, Graswang, Oberammergau, Griesen. Chamois, red deer, marmot, raven.

46 Karwendel NC (1959) 74 sq. miles.
Continued on Austrian soil. Upper Bavaria. Nearest stations: Lenggries, Krünn, Wallgau, Mittenwald. Accommodation in these towns, also in Fall, Vorderriss and Hinterriss. Huts of various Alpine associations. High Alpine mountain area. Chamois, red deer, marmot, raven.

47 Königssee NC (1960) 80 sq. miles.
Upper Bavaria. Nearest station: Königssee. Accommodation: Berchtesgaden, Königssee, Ramsau (hotels, guest houses, private board), huts of various Alpine associations (Watzmannhaus, Wimbachgrieshütte, Funtenseehaus, Riemannhaus, etc.). Mountain massif of the Watzmann, Steinernes Meer and Hochkalter. Ibex (sometimes moving across into the Austrian Blühnbach Valley), chamois, red deer, marmot, golden eagle, white grouse, raven.

Switzerland

48 Swiss National Park (1909–1913) 62 sq. miles.
Lower Engadin. Nearest stations: Schuls, Zernez, Schanf, Zuoz. Accommodation in these places: hotels, guest houses, private board; park hotels Il Fuorn and Süsom Givé in the park. Protective hut in the Val Cluozza. Other good headquarters are the mountain villages S'charl in the S'charl Valley and Tschierv in the Münster Valley. Best visiting period: June–Sept. Ibex, chamois, red deer, roe deer, marmot, golden eagle, heath cock, black cock, white grouse. See the chapter by Dr. N. Zimmerli, 'The Swiss National Park'.

Italy

49 Gran Paradiso NP (1919) 308 sq. miles.
Aosta district (W Alps). Nearest airport: Turin; nearest station: Aosta. Accommodation: hotels, guest houses and private board in numerous towns and villages of the valleys which surround the park territory: Val di Cogne (Cogne 16 miles from Aosta), Valsavaranche (Degioz 15½ miles from Aosta), Val di Rhemes (Rhemes St. Georges 15 miles from Aosta, Chanavey and Rhemes Notre Dame 22 miles from Aosta). Bus services to Aosta, Val dell'Orco, Val Soana. Three huts of the Italian Alpine Club (without service) in the park itself. The huts used by the park administration may only be used if special permission has been obtained. Best visiting period: June–Sept. Park management: Piazza San Carlo 206/III, Turin. Local supervision: Via Gramsci 3,

Aosta. High mountain massif (Gran Paradiso 13,400 ft.). Ibex (4,000, the largest stock in Europe) chamois (3,000), marmot, Alpine hare, ermine, golden eagle, owl, white grouse.

France

50 Camargue Bird Sanctuary (1928) 52 sq. miles.

Delta at the mouths of the Rhône, S. France. Nearest airport: Marseilles, nearest station: Arles. Accommodation: hotels and guest houses in Arles and Saintes-Maries-de-la-Mer. Advantageous visiting periods: May–June, Sept.–Oct. Abundant bird life, including bee-eater, little egret, night heron, purple heron, avocet, oyster-catcher, curlew, flamingo. See the chapter, 'Experiences in the Camargue', by E. Waldhoer-Haehnle.

Hungary

The nature protection areas are administered by the National Nature Protection Council, which comes under the Ministry of Agriculture. The following are of especial importance as regards the preservation of the animal world:

51 Kisbalaton NC (1951) $5\frac{1}{2}$ sq. miles.

Swampy territory sw of Lake Platten. Bird Sa, species including cormorant, purple, white, grey and squacco herons, spoonbill. During the breeding period only scientific observers are permitted to enter the area: at other times other visitors are received, but only with the written permission of the National Nature Protection Council.

52 Fehértó NC (1939) $1\frac{1}{4}$ sq. miles.

In the S of the country. Swampy ground and salt lakes. Bird Sa, especially for migratory birds. Entrance as to the preceding NC territory.

Austria

Information: Institute for Nature Protection of the Austrian Nature Protection League, Burgring 7, Vienna 1.

97 Karwendel NC (1943, 1947) 278 sq. miles.

Adjacent, on the S, to the NC in Upper Bavaria. See German Federal Republic, No. 46! Terrain, flora and fauna as there. Achenkirch, Eben, Jenbach, Vomp, Terfens, Gnadenwald, Absam, Thaur, Innsbruck, Zirl, Seefeld, Scharnitz. Numerous mountain huts. Tyrol.

98 Venedigergruppe NC (1940).

With Wildgerlostal, Krimmler Achental, Obersulzbachtal, Untersulzbachtal. A magnificent high mountain district. Chamois, marmot, golden eagle. Krimml (waterfalls!). Wald, Neukirchen (Salzburg Province).

99 Grossglockner and Pasterze with Gamsgrube NC (1935) 14 sq. miles.

Heiligenblut (Kärnten). Chamois.

100 Hinterstoder Priel NC 232 sq. miles.

Limestone range with particularly attractive mountain woods (stone pine, larch). Red deer, chamois, golden eagle. Accommodation: Hinterstoder (Upper Austria).

101 Neusiedler Lake and Lakeland, countryside and bird protection area (1940).

Low-lying natron salt lake on the Hungarian border s of Vienna. Rich bird life, including spoonbill, purple, white and grey herons, avocet, great bustard. Accommodation in numerous villages, among which the following are particularly well placed: Illmitz, Apetlon, Podersdorf and Rust. Favourable visiting periods: May or early autumn (bird migration!).

Yugoslavia

A. *People's Republic of Croatia*

54 Risnjak NP (1953) 12 sq. miles.

Rijeka district in the Gorski Kotar area. Nearest airport: Rijeka; nearest station: Delnice, or Lokve (Zagreb–Rijeka line). Accommodation in park in the Alpine House (4,660 ft.). The Risnjak NP lies in the W section of the Dinaric Alps. Limestone and dolomite structure, with many remarkable fault features. The Risnjak (5,050 ft.) forms a barrier, dividing the climate and vegetation of northern, continental Croatia from that of the southern, Mediterranean part of the land. The range is covered with vegetation rich in fossils. Many areas of virgin forest remain. Brown bear, wolf, fox, badger, red deer, roe deer, heath cock. Park administration in Crni Lug.

55 Plitvicka jezera NP (1949) 74 sq. miles.

Gospic district in the Lika area. Nearest airport: Zagreb: nearest station: Vrhovine (Zagreb–Split line). Accommodation: Hotel Plitvice in the park. The Plitvitzer lakes lie in the Lika area between the mountain massifs Mala Kapela and Liska Pljesevica. The greater part of the park is covered by beech and pine woods, spruce woods, with some oak and hop-beech. Brown bear, wolf, fox, badger, pine marten and stone marten. Otter, roe and red deer, heath cock. Park administration in Plitvicki Ljeskovac.

56 Paklenica NP (1949) 14 sq. miles.

Dalmatia. Zadar area. Nearest airport: Split; nearest station: Sibenik (Zagreb–Split line, Sibenik branch line). Accommodation in the hotels of Zadar and in the mountain hut on the Stirovac in the Velebit, near Vaganski. Paklenica lies on the S slopes of Velebit. Characteristic features of this NP are the picturesque ravines Velika Paklenica and Mala Paklenica, and numerous subterranean caves. Woods of beech, black pine, oak, hornbeam. In the Mala Paklenica valley: brown bear. Park administration in Starigrad.

60 Mljet NP (1960) 12 sq. miles.

Dubrovnik area of Dalmatia. Nearest airport: Gruda (near Dubrovnik); nearest station: Dubrovnik. Steamer service: Dubrovnik–Mljet. Accommodation: Hotel Strazicic in the park. Hotels in Dubrovnik. The NP covers the western part of the island of Mljet. Characteristic features of the park: the large and small lakes (Veliko jezero, Malo jezero), probably once bays of the sea. The whole expanse of the park is covered by rich evergreen vegetation with typical, very well preserved woods of Aleppo pine.

On the little island in the large lake there is a thirteenth-century Romanesque church, in the port of Polace the ancient 'Palatium' palace of the third century. Abundant lake fauna. The outer sea bays shelter the extremely rare monk seal.

B. People's Republic of Montenegro

57 Durmitor NP (1952) 124 sq. miles.

Zabljak district. Accommodation: well appointed hotel in the park. The park lies on the edge of broken ground. Fir, beech, white pine, at the upper limit of the forest a broad plantation girdle of pine; large expanses of grassland. Among the 14 lakes the Black Lake (Crno jezero) is the most beautiful and the richest in trout. The park contains the village of Zabljak and other settlements, important summer holiday resorts and winter sports centres. Part of the park is state hunting land.

C. People's Republic of Serbia

59 Fruska gora NP (1961) 85 sq. miles.

Autonomous district of Vojvodina. Nearest station: Novi Sad. Accommodation: several hotels and chalets on the Iriski Venac, Crtanovci, Popovica and Zmajevac, all in the park. Famed for its flora and fauna. Landscapes of great scenic beauty.

D. People's Republic of Bosnia and Herzegovina

58 Hutovo Blato Bird Sa near Capljina (1954) 12 sq. miles.

Mostar district. Nearest station Capljina (Sarajevo–Mostar–Dubrovnik line). Bus from there to the reserve ($4\frac{1}{2}$ miles). Accommodation: hotel in Capljina, another on Karaotok in the reserve. About 270 different kinds of wading birds, including grey heron, little egret, squacco heron, moor hen, grey-lag goose, various ducks, dwarf cormorant.

E. People's Republic of Slovenia

53 Triglavski Narodni Park (1961) $7\frac{3}{4}$ sq. miles.

Kranj area, Bohinj district. Nearest airport Ljubljana, another in summer at Lesce-Bled. Bus routes from both to the park. Nearest station: Bohinjska Bistrica (Ljubljana–Jesenice–Gorica line). Bus from there to the park (35 mins.). Accommodation: three hotels by the Lake of Bohinj; chalet by the lower border of the park at the foot of the Komarca (2,180 ft.); in the park itself the chalet by the 5th Triglav Lake (5,560 ft.) and Alpine hut on the Prehodavci Saddle (about 6,600 ft.); outside the park (90 minutes away) there is the comfortable Komna Alpine Hotel (5,040 ft.). The Triglav National Park extends in gentle curves from S to N from the chalet (2,185 ft.) above the 2,650-ft.-high vertical Komarca wall into the valley of the seven lakes as far as Kanjavec on its N border (8,380 ft.). Its E border is formed by the Stador–Ticarica–Misseljski konec mountain chain, constructed of older trias lime (no strata), pushed forward by more recent Jurassic rock strata. In the valley there are seven glacier lakes and various signs of geological activity. The noblest natural feature is the 200-ft.-high Savica waterfall in the Komarca. In the lower part of the park there are well preserved woods of spruce, beech and larch, with larch on the higher levels up to the timber line, then only some pine plantations and Alpine roses. Chamois, Alpine hare, golden eagle, black cock, raven, owl.

F. People's Republic of Macedonia

61 Galicica NP (1958) 90 sq. miles.

Ohrid district. Summer airfield: Ohrid; station: Bitola. Regular bus service from there to Ohrid. Accommodation: hotels in Ohrid. Several convalescent homes at the foot of the Galicica and by the Ohrid and Prespan Lakes. Galicica is an Alpine mountain massif, and only part of it comes within the NP. Wide varieties of flora and fauna. Brown bear, lynx.

62 Perister NP (1948) 40 sq. miles.

Bitola district. Nearest airport: Bitola. Accommodation: two chalets and a tourist lodging house in the park itself. Lynx, brown bear.

Albania

Administration: Forestry Authority.

63 Lura NP (1956) 12 sq. miles.

25 miles ne of Burreli. Accessible by car, only mountain paths in the park. Deja and Lura Mountains, 3,300–7,420 ft. high. Forest. Many mountain lakes. Bear, lynx.

Greece

64 Olympus NP (1938) 15 sq. miles.

Administration: Forestry Commission in Katerini. Road and railway: Thessaloniki–Katerini. Hotels there. Mount Olympus, on the W coast of the Gulf of Thessaloniki, 9,550 ft. high. Mediterranean vegetation. *Game reserves for the protection of the bezoar goat*. Rocky islands. May be visited only by scientific investigators.

65 Chioura. 66 Antimylos, Dias.

Crete

67 Samarias GR (1953) 3 sq. miles.

District in the White Mountains. Bezoar goat. Accessible by motorboat from nearby villages. Administration: Forestry Administration in Khania.

Turkey

Administration of the NP: General Direction of Forestry, Ministry of Agriculture, Ankara.

68 Manyas Bird Sa (1959) 124 acres.

NE bank of Lake Manyas, Balikesir. By the village of Sigirci near the port of Bandirma

St. Kilda
26
27
28
29
Rhum
30
31
Pembroke
GREAT BRITAIN
12
14
15
16
17
Porjus
18
19
20
S W E D E N
Norrtalje
Stockholm
21
22
23
24
Kalmar
25
Wolin
32
Szczecin
33
Schwerin
Neustrelitz
42
43
Przechlewo
Dessau
44
GERMAN DEMOCR
REPUBLIC
WEST GERMANY
39
FRANCE
45
Mittenwald
46
47
Oberammergau
Königssee
Zernez
97
98
99
100
101
SWITZERLAND
48
HUNG
51
52
53
Ljubljana
Zagreb
Delnice
49
Aosta
Turin
ITALY
50
Arles
Marseilles
Camargue
54
55
56
Sibenik
57
58
Split
Dubrovnik
Mljet
60
ALBANIA
YUGOSLAVIA

Pechora
Komi A. S. S. R. ■ 70

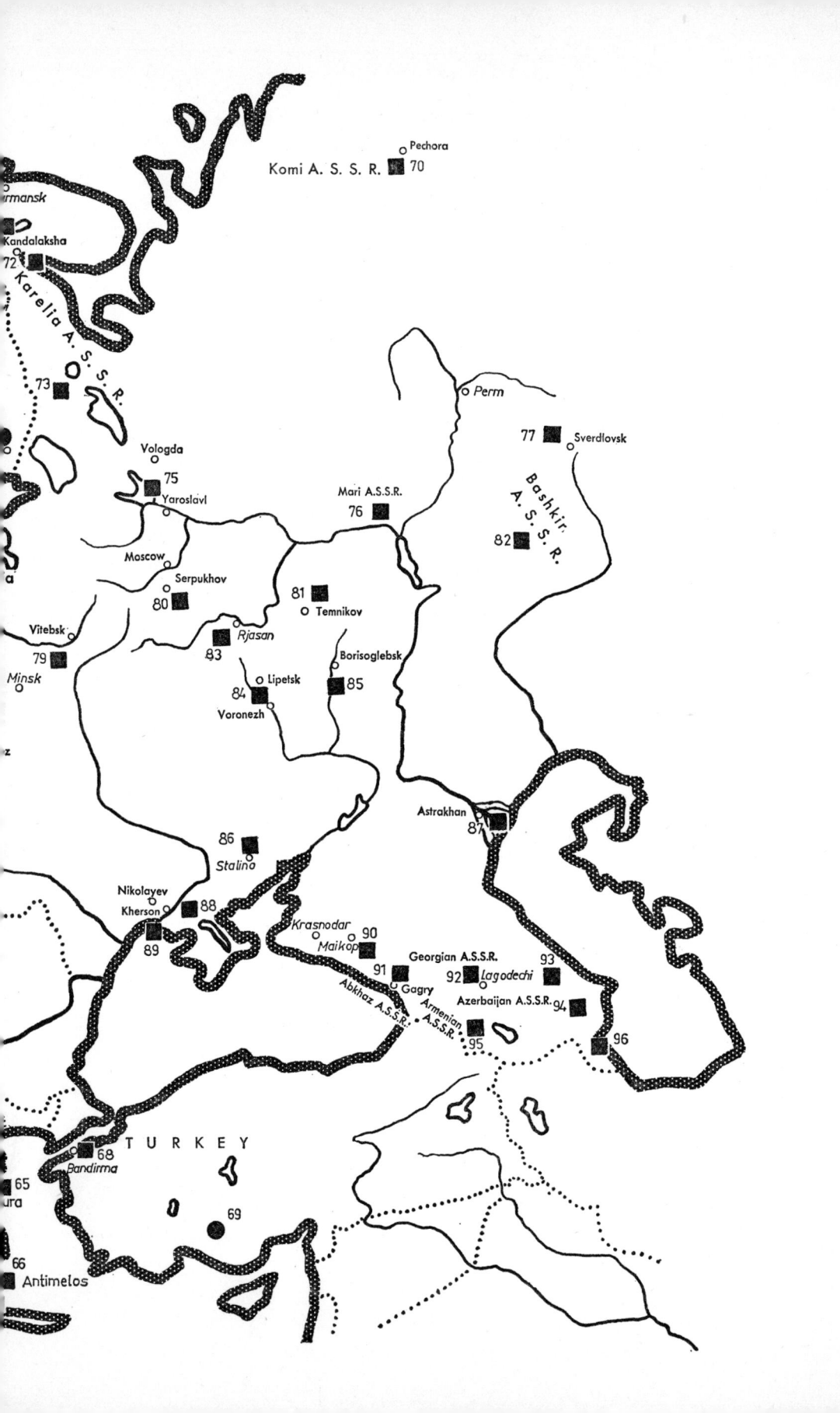

rmansk
Kandalaksha
■ 72
Karelia A. S. S. R.
■ 73

Vologda
■ 75
Yaroslavl

Perm
■ 77 Sverdlovsk

Bashkir A. S. S. R.
■ 82

Mari A.S.S.R.
■ 76

Moscow
Serpukhov
■ 80

■ 81
Temnikov

Vitebsk
■ 79
Minsk

Rjasan
■ 83

Borisoglebsk
Lipetsk
■ 85
■ 84
Voronezh

Astrakhan
■ 87

■ 86
Stalino

Nikolayev
Kherson
■ 88
■ 89

Krasnodar
Maikop ■ 90
■ 91 Gagry
Abkhaz A.S.S.R.
Georgian A.S.S.R.
■ 92 Lagodechi
■ 93
Azerbaijan A.S.S.R. ■ 94
Armenian A.S.S.R.
■ 95
■ 96

TURKEY
■ 68
Bandirma
■ 65
ura
● 69

■ 66
Antimelos

on the S coast of the Sea of Marmara. Several hundred breeding pairs of spoonbills, cormorants, dwarf cormorants, grey, silken, night and rail herons, bittern.

69 Karatepe-Arslantas NP (1958) 16 sq. miles.

In the S of the central part of the country, 37 miles from the Mediterranean, 225 miles from the Syrian border. Oak and pine woods. Roe deer, wild boar, wolf, jackal, eagle. Accommodation: Adana, and a motel in the park. The woods suffer damage by the inhabitants of 6 villages who own land in the park.

Soviet Union

Administration: Academy of Sciences: Biological Section, Nature Protection Commission, Kravchenko Str. 12, Moscow V–331.

1. Russian Soviet Federal Socialist Republic

12 Altai Sa 3,532 sq. miles.

Altai Mountains, autonomous province. Leafy and coniferous woods on the lower levels. Sub-Alpine and Alpine zone. Altai maral (Cervus elaphus sibiricus), elk, musk deer, reindeer, brown bear, snow leopard, sable, grouse, black cock, wood grouse and white grouse (Lagopus mutus and L. lagopus).

13 Barguzin Sa 958 sq. miles.

NE coast of Lake Baikal. Buryaat A.S.S.R. Mountainous area with coniferous forests on the lower levels. Elk, musk deer, brown bear, wolverine, otter, Transbaikal sable; Baikal seal (Phoca hispida sibirica) by the banks of the Ushkan islands, heath cock.

14 Kronotzk Sa 3,725 sq. miles.

Kronotzk Peninsula, Kamchatka. Birch woods. The only active volcanoes in the Soviet Union, thermal springs, geysers; mixed woods. Reindeer, bighorn sheep (Ovis canadensis), brown bear, sable, Steller's sea-lion (Eumetopias jubata), bird islands: Lunda cirrhata, Cepphus grylle. Numerous water birds spend the winter by the warm-water lakes.

15 Sichote-Alin Sa 2,160 sq. miles.

Coastal territory on the Sea of Japan, Tetyukhe district. Mountainous. Yellow flanked deer (Cervus elaphus xanthopigus), goral (Naemorhedus goral), elk, wild boar, tiger, leopard, brown bear (Ursus arctos mandschuricus), sable, yellow-throated marten (Charsa, Martes flavigula).

16 Suputin Sa 61 sq. miles.

Near Ussurysk and Vladivostok. Mixed woods. Yellow-flanked deer, East-Asiatic roe deer (Capreolus capreolus bedfordi), wild boar, sable, heath cock.

17 Sudzin Sa 540 sq. miles.

Coastal mountain range in the vicinity of Nachodka on the Sea of Japan. Sika deer, goral (Naemorhedus goral).

18 Kedrovaya Padyi Sa 58 sq. miles.

Coastal area near Vladivostock. Woods of far-eastern type. Sika deer (Cervus nippon), roe deer, musk deer, wild boar, leopard, brown bear, marten (Martes flavigula), mandarin duck (Aix galericulata).

70 Pechora-Ilytch Sa 2,758 sq. miles.
Proitzk-Pechora district of the Komi A.S.S.R. Coniferous forests. Reindeer, sable, heath cock.

71 Lapland Sa 612 sq. miles.
Area of Lake Imandra, Murmansk Province. Mountain tundra, light pine woods. Reindeer, beaver.

72 Kandalaksha Sa 78 sq. miles.
Murmansk Province. Kharlov, Veshnyak and many other islands in the Kandalaksha Gulf (Barents Sea). On the islands tundra, with fir, pine and birch woods. Numerous bird islands with colonies of razorbill, cormorant, kittiwake, eider duck. Velikiy Island: elk, brown bear, lynx, wolverine.

73 Kivatsh Sa 40 sq. miles.
Kondopozh district, Karelia A.S.S.R. Fir taiga, sphagnum moors. Kivatsh waterfall on the Suna River. Elk, brown bear, sable, moor cock, black cock, wood grouse.

75 Darwin Sa 644 sq. miles.
Vologda and Yaroslavl provinces. District of the Rybnisk reservoir. Fir forests, high-lying moors. Elk, brown bear, lynx, moor cock, black cock, wood grouse, numerous wading and water birds.

76 Mari Sa 114 sq. miles.
Mari A.S.S.R. Mixed woods. Brown bear, otter, heath and moor cocks.

77 Denezhkin Kamenyi Sa 566 sq. miles.
Sverdlovsk and Perm provinces, Ural Mountains. Mountainous area with spruce, pine and fir forests, mountain tundra. Reindeer, brown bear, wolverine, sable, moor cock, black cock, wood grouse.

80 Prioksko-Terrasnyi Sa 18½ sq. miles.
Moscow Province, in the vicinity of Serpukhov. European bison (in enclosure and at liberty).

81 Mordva Sa, Smidovich Sa 116 sq. miles.
Mordvinian A.S.S.R., n of Temnikov. Coniferous and leafy forest. Elk, musk deer (Desmana moschata), beaver, brown bear, otter, heath and moor cocks.

82 Bashkir Sa 310 sq. miles.
Burzyan district, Bashkir A.S.S.R. Fir and birch taiga. Elk, brown bear, burunduk (Eutamias sibiricus), flying squirrel (Pteromys volans), moor cock, black cock, wood grouse.

83 Oka Sa 87 sq. miles.
Ryazan Province. Mixed woods in the area flooded by the River Pra, lakes, swamps. Animals include musk deer (Desmana moschata).

■ 70-96
See
Map of
Europe

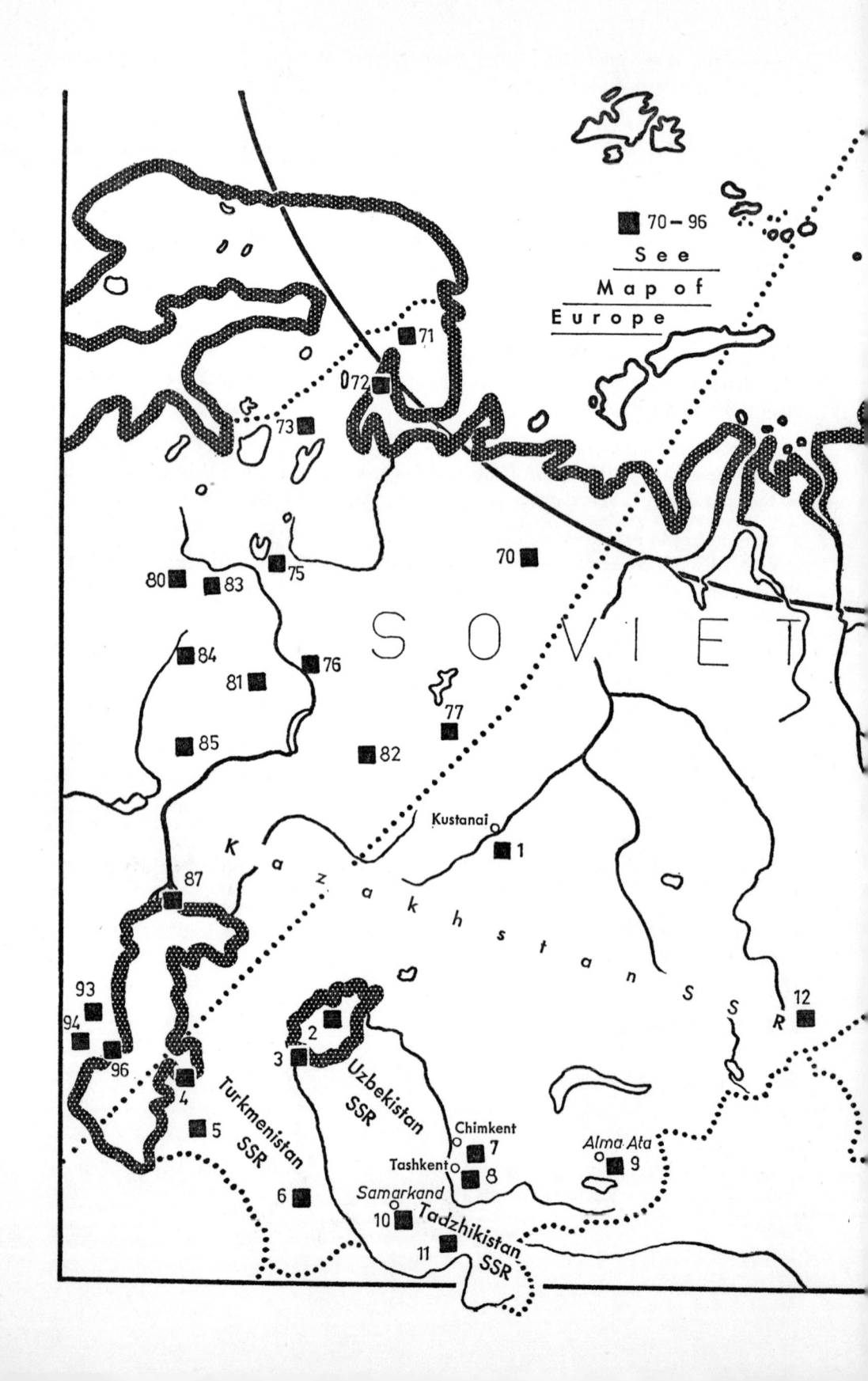

Kamchatka
14

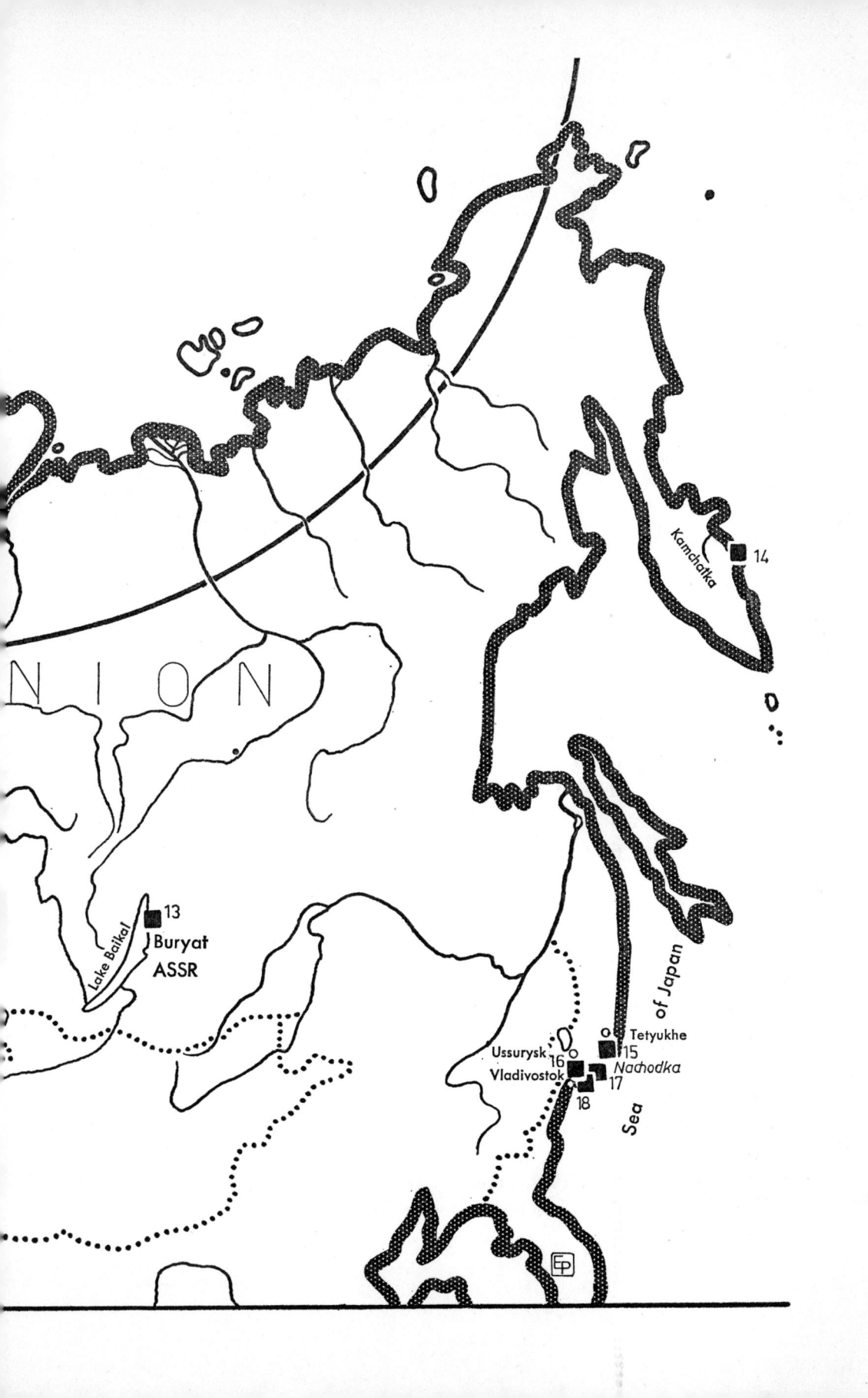

NION

Lake Baikal
■ 13
Buryat
ASSR

Tetyukhe
Ussurysk ○ ■ 15
■ 16 Nachodka
Vladivostok ■ 17
■ 18

Sea of Japan

84 Voronesh Sa 119 sq. miles.

Voronesh and Lipetzk Provinces, on the upper Don. Oak and pine woods. Red deer, beaver (on the Usman River).

85 Khoper Sa 62 sq. miles.

Voronesh province, between the towns of Borissoglebsk and Novo-Khoper. Inundation area of the River Khoper. Woods and meadows. Beaver, Desmana moschata, European bison (small herd in semi-free surroundings).

87 Astrakhan Sa 292 sq. miles.

Volga Delta, Astrakhan Province. Inundation area with meadows and thickets of rushes. Large expanses of Caspian lotus (Nelumbium caspium) and water-nut (Trapa natans). Wild boar, otter; numerous breeding birds, including curled-crested pelican and pink pelican (Pelecanus crispus and P. onocrotalus). Numerous species of water birds at the migratory and moulting seasons.

90 Caucasus Sa 972 sq. miles.

Area of Krasnodar, s of Maikop. Beech and fir forests, Caucasian rhododendron. Sub-Alpine and Alpine meadowland. Severtsov ibex, chamois, red deer, hybrid bison herd in free surroundings.

2. Ukraine

86 Khomutov Sa 4 sq. miles.

Novo-Azovsk district. Steppe, semi-desert, desert, with characteristic vegetation. Long-eared hedgehog (Hemiechinus auritus), tiger polecat (Vormela peregusna).

88 Ascania Nova 2 sq. miles.

Tchaplin district, Kherson Province. Founded by the German Falz-Fein family. Virgin steppe (Festuca sulcata, Stipa) with characteristic fauna: bobak, ground squirrel, bustard. Research station concerned with the introduction of animals from other countries.

89 Black Sea Sa 40 sq. miles.

Tendrovskaya land tongue, Yagorlytzk peninsula. Coastal islands, steppe country inland. (Kherson and Nikolayev Prov.). Numerous steppe and water birds; their winter quarters!

3. White Russia

79 Berezin Sa 260 sq. miles.

Vitebsk and Minsk Prov. Mixed woods. Elk, wild boar, beaver.

4. Uzbekistan S.S.R.

3 Amu-Darya Sa 232 sq. miles.

Kara-Kalpak autonomous S.S.R., delta of the Amu Darya. Swamp woods and steppes. Saiga antelope (Saiga tatarica), gazelle (Gazella subgutturosa), pelicans (Pelecanus crispus and P. onocrotalus), and many other species of water bird.

8 Tchatkal Sa 135 sq. miles.
   Tashkent Province. Wooded mountain area. Siberian ibex (Capra ibex sibirica), marmot, snow leopard (Uncia uncia), brown bear (Ursus arctos leuconyx), porcupine (Hystrix hirsutirostris), bearded vulture (Gypaëtus barbatus).

10 Zaamin-Guralash Sa 30 sq. miles.
   Samarkand Province. Mountain woods. Siberian ibex (Capra ibex sibirica), argali (wild sheep, Ovis ammon polii), brown bear, lynx.

5. Kazakhstan S.S.R.

1 Naurzum Sa 695 sq. miles.
   Semiozerny district, Kustanai Province. Steppes with isolated lakes and woods. Roe deer, wild boar, great and little bustards, moor hen.

2 Barsakelymess Sa 76 sq. miles.
   Barsakelymess Island in the Aral Sea. Kzyl Orda Prov. Gazelle, saiga, kulan (Equus hemionus hemionus, introduced). Numerous water birds, including flamingo.

7 Aksu-Dzhabagly Sa 270 sq. miles.
   S Kazakhstan Prov., se of Chimkent. Mountainous area with the ravine of the River Aksu (12 miles long, 1,300–1,650 ft. broad, 3,400 ft. deep!). Argali (Ovis ammon polii), snow leopard (Uncia uncia), brown bear, great and little bustards.

9 Alma-Ata Sa 494 sq. miles.
   Alma-Ata Province. Mountain area, glaciers. Siberian red deer (Altai-maral, Cervus elaphus sibiricus), Argali (Ovis ammon polii), gazelle (Gazella subgutturosa), brown bear (Ursus arctos leuconyx).

6. Georgian A.S.S.R.

91 Ritzin Sa 61 sq. miles.
   Gagry district of the Abkhaz A.S.S.R. Mountain area. Siberian ibex, chamois.

92 Lagodechi Sq 50 sq. miles.
   Lagodechi Province. High mountain area, with leafy woods consisting of many tree species on the lower reaches. Siberian ibex, chamois, red deer, lynx.

7. Azerbaijan A.S.S.R.

93 Zakataly Sa 280 sq. miles.
   Belokan and Zakataly districts. Mountainous area with leafy woods consisting of many species of trees on the lower reaches, rhododendron on the upper. Ibex, chamois, red deer, wild boar, brown bear, lynx, heath cock and black cock.

94 Turianchay Sa 108 sq. miles.
   Kutkashen, Agdash, Pukhin districts. Light juniper and pistachio woods. Black francolin (Francolinus francolinus).

96 Kyzylagach Sa 360 sq. miles.

Kirov Gulf of the Caspian Sea, with numerous islands. Winter quarters for numerous water and wading birds.

8. Lithuania

78 Zhuvintas Lake Sa 12 sq. miles.

Kapruk district. Area surrounding the lake. Breeding ground of numerous wading and water birds, including wild swan.

9. Estonia

74 Matsalu Sa 135 sq. miles.

Area of flooding from the River Kazari. Breeding and rest ground for many wading and water birds. Largest grey-lag goose colony in the Baltic (100 breeding pairs), nesting places of eider ducks.

10. Tadzhikistan S.S.R.

11 Tigrovaya Balka Sa 159 sq. miles.

Pyandsh district. Swampy area, stone, salt and sand desert. Gazelle, black vulture (Aegypius monachus), snake-eagle (Circaetus gallicus).

11. Armenian A.S.S.R.

95 Garnin Sa 102 sq. miles.

Mountainous area around the Rivers Azat and Veda. Mixed woods, sub-Alpine pastureland. Circular-horned sheep (Ovis musimon ammon), bezoar goat (Capra aegagrus), wild boar, brown bear.

12. Turkmenistan S.S.R.

4 Gassankuli Sa 270 sq. miles.

Coastal area on the Caspian Sea. Winter quarters of numerous water birds. The only breeding ground of the black francolin (Francolinus francolinus) in central Asia.

5 Badchyz Sa 290 sq. miles.

Marysk Province. Hilly steppes, partly salt, vast pistachio woods. Gazelle, kulan (Equus h. hemionus), cheetah.

6 Repetek Sa 95 sq. miles.

Chardzhou Province. Eastern part of the Kara Kums. Gazelle, desert monitor (Varanus griseus).

799
E
Engelhardt
Survival of the free

LEE COUNTY LIBRARY
SANFORD, N.C.